Exploring Unseen Worlds

Frontispiece: William James c. 1894. Photograph by Mrs. Montgomery Sears. (pfMS Am 1092, James family photographs.) Courtesy Houghton Library, Harvard University. Reprinted by permission.

Exploring Unseen Worlds

William James and the Philosophy of Mysticism

G. William Barnard

STATE UNIVERSITY OF NEW YORK PRESS

Published by
State University of New York Press, Albany

© 1997 State University of New York

For information, address State University of New York Press,
State University Plaza, Albany, N.Y., 12246

Production by Marilyn P. Semerad
Marketing by Theresa Abad Swierzowski

Library of Congress Cataloging-in-Publication Data

Barnard, G. William (George William), 1955–
    Exploring unseen worlds : William James and the philosophy of
mysticism / G. William Barnard.
        p.   cm.
    Includes bibliographical references and index.
    ISBN 0-7914-3223-8 (hardcover : alk paper). — ISBN 0-7914-3224-6
(pbk. : alk paper)
    1. James, William, 1842–1910—Contributions in study of mysticism.
2. Mysticism—Comparative studies.   3. Mysticism—Psychology.
I. Title.
BV5083.B29   1997
291.4'22'092—dc20   96-13103
                                                              CIP

10 9 8 7 6 5 4 3 2 1

To Renew ঌ
Partner of the Heart,
Fellow Explorer of Unseen Worlds

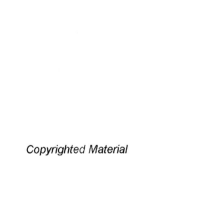

Contents

Chapter Two

Contents

Chapter Three

"Fields within Fields within Fields": Mysticism and a Jamesian Psychology of the Self 147

Chapter Four

Beyond Words, Beyond Morals: The Metaphysical and Ethical Implications of Mysticism 213

Contents

Chapter Five

Telling Truths, Touching Realities: Spiritual Judgments,
Saints, and Pragmatism   273

ix

Preface

> When you speak from the heart you can kindle the fire in the
> hearts of others. Through recognition you actually begin to
> awaken the soul which is asleep. And fire spreads—there is
> nothing more catching than love.
> —Reshad Feild, *The Last Barrier*

I approach, with no little trepidation, the task of giving due credit to
all of those people who offered their support during the years of effort
and joy that it took to create this book. I already know that anything
that I write could never begin to express adequately the gratitude that
I feel towards all of those who encouraged me during this time—but
here goes.

Most of all, I want to thank my wife Sandra—not just for her
editorial skills (even though that alone would be worthy of pages of
praise), but more importantly, for her love, for her belief in me, for her
wisdom, and for her depth. My debt is incalculable.

I also could not have completed this book if not for the immea-
surable support given to me by my parents. Besides putting up with
my moans and groans and assorted gnashings of teeth, they gave me
the precious gift of letting me know that they were genuinely interested in my progress. (Thanks for your "saintly" comments, Dad!)

My karmic obligation to Jeff Kripal is also immense. I must have
performed lifetimes of austerities to merit this friend's close reading
and insightful remarks. His humor and prodding kept me going.

Don Browning also deserves a long round of applause. (I have
particularly vivid memories of our friendly jousting about the limits
of the finite God. Thanks for pointing out those theological land mines
for me, Don.)

Thanks go out as well to David Tracy for his enthusiastic encouragement and to Gary Ebersole for his perceptive observations. Kudos
also to Larry Sullivan for his continued interest in my work, even after
having been lured away to the wilds of Harvard.

I also benefited greatly from the questions and astute recommen-
dations of my colleagues at Southern Methodist University—especially
for their close reading of sections from chapters 2 and 3. The comments and suggestions of the anonymous readers of the initial manu-
script of this work were also deeply appreciated.

Preface

In addition, I want to thank the editorial staff at SUNY Press for their energetic and focused assistance throughout this project. I am also grateful to the American Academy of Religion for their prompt permission to reprint (in chapter 2) portions of an article previously published in the *Journal of the American Academy of Religion*: G. William Barnard, "Explaining the Unexplainable: Wayne Proudfoot's *Religious Experience*," *Journal of the American Academy of Religion*, 60 (Summer 1992): 231–56.

Scores of other colleagues, friends, and family members also contributed to the creation of this book, in ways that they may never fully realize. If not for their love, their encouragement, and their ability to nurture the growth of my spirit, this work could not have been accomplished.

Finally, I would like to acknowledge the spiritual power that (who?) is the true author of this book—at least of those sections that are worthwhile. Opening myself to this power unexpectedly transformed an academic task into something more: an eye-opening, often joyous, exploration of my own unseen worlds.

Chronology

1842   William James born in New York City, 11 January
1844   James family travels to Europe
        Henry James Sr.'s religious crisis
1852–55 Schooling in New York City
1855–58 Schooling in England and France
1858–59 Schooling in Newport, R.I.
1859–60 Schooling in Switzerland and Germany
1860   Studies painting with William Morris Hunt in Newport, R.I.
1861   Enters Lawrence Scientific School, Harvard University
1864   Enters Medical School, Harvard University
1865–66 Research expedition in Brazil with Louis Agassiz
1867–68 Studies in Germany. Attempts to recuperate from ill health
1869   Receives M.D., Harvard University
1869–72 Ill health and depression.
1873–74 Instructor in physiology and anatomy, Harvard University
        Ill health, travels to Italy to recuperate
1875   Teaches first psychology course, Harvard University
        Establishes first laboratory of experimental psychology, Harvard University
1876   Assistant professor of physiology, Harvard University
1878   Marries Alice Howe Gibbons
        "Remarks on Spencer's *Definition of Mind as Correspondence*" published
1879   Begins teaching philosophy, Harvard University
1880   Assistant professor of philosophy, Harvard University
1882   Travels in Europe
        January: Death of Mary Walsh James (mother)
        December: Death of Henry James, Sr. (father)
1884   "What is an Emotion" published
        The Literary Remains of the Late Henry James (edited by William James) published
1885   Professor of philosophy, Harvard University
        Helps found the American branch of the Society for Psychical Research

Chronology

Introduction

> Now I am going to tell you something. I don't know what
> heading it comes under, and whether or not it is relevant here,
> but it must be relevant at some point. It is not anything new,
> but I would like to say it.
> —Chuang Tsu, *Inner Chapters*

The American psychologist and philosopher William James (1842–1910)
is one of the founding fathers of the academic study of mysticism.
Almost every contemporary scholarly text on mysticism acknowledges
James's importance to the field with at least a passing nod to this "Ur-
figure" from the past. Unfortunately, until this point, most studies of
James's work in mysticism have focused almost exclusively on his
classic work, *The Varieties of Religious Experience*. To concentrate on
the *Varieties* in this way is understandable. It is by far the most important source for gaining an understanding of James's views on mysticism. However, a much richer and more detailed grasp of his philosophy and psychology of mysticism emerges when the bare bones of his
explicit discussions on mysticism in the *Varieties* are fleshed out to
include his other, less well-known, investigations of mystical states of
awareness. One of the most important tasks of this book is to gain just
this sort of full-bodied appreciation of James's interest in mysticism.

This book has another task to perform as well. In addition to
describing and analyzing James's theoretical discussions of mysticism,
Exploring Unseen Worlds also makes a concerted effort to point out the
ways in which his epistemology, psychology, metaphysics, ethics, and
theories of truth can offer provocative and powerful contributions to
our contemporary philosophical and psychological understandings of
the nature of mysticism. Throughout this text, I look at James's work as
a whole in order to open up the possibility that this intriguingly persuasive voice from the past may perhaps offer unexpected solutions to
dilemmas that currently bedevil numerous studies of mysticism.

It is my hope that *Exploring Unseen Worlds* sheds new light on
both James and mysticism, and that it does so in a way that is accessible, not just to specialists, but to anyone interested either in James's
ideas or in the comparative study of mysticism. Current works in
philosophy are often either so abstruse that only those initiated into

the arcane world of philosophical rhetoric can hope to understand them or they are so narrowly focused and specialized that they are of interest only to an equally specialized minority of professional philosophers. If James were alive today, I think that it is safe to say that he would be appalled at this turn of events, since he was convinced that a broad range of complex philosophical issues can and should be communicated in a way that is vivid and easily understood.

James often fumed at the dense, almost impenetrable, prose of many of the philosophers of his time. He was bothered by philosophical jargon, not because of any snobbish need on his part for aesthetic purity, but rather, because he strongly felt that philosophers needed to break free from the insular security of the ivy-covered walls of academia in order to address, clearly and simply, some of the most pressing and important questions of life: Who am I? Why am I here? What is the nature of reality? Why is there evil? What actions are good? What is truth? What can I hope for after death? Is there a meaning to life? What, if any, is my connection to God?

Throughout his career James struggled to formulate lucid and convincing responses to these types of questions, and offered his proposals in a format that was accessible to the educated public of his time. (Most of his books were originally given as popular lectures.) Nonetheless, if James were alive today, it is perhaps also safe to say that his attempt to reach out to a broader audience might well be viewed with suspicion by many, if not most, philosophers. In a very real sense, James's unique style of philosophizing presents a dramatic challenge to many of the entrenched, often taken-for-granted, notions of what forms of discourse are acceptable in contemporary academic circles. Charlene Haddock Seigfried, a contemporary Jamesian scholar, aptly notes that James's approach to philosophy is unusual in that it is a "conjunction of science and poetry, of fact and theory, of exact descriptions and flights of fancy, of accurateness and passion."[1] James's language is not that of the logician, who attempts to "elaborate a consistent system and avoid errors of technique," but rather, it is the language of a poet, who strives to "create such a compelling interpretation of life that the reader can appropriate it as her own."[2] James's philosophy not only denotes and specifies; it also connotes, evokes, stirs. James's works serve to remind us that philosophical discourse can impel; it can move us; it can and should possess a transformative thrust.

James was a firm believer that the philosopher's role should not be confined to critical analysis and logical argumentation, or be limited to esoteric exchanges between academics. Gerald Myers, a noted

Introduction

scholar of James's work, points out that "from the beginning
[James] . . . was convinced that the philosopher ought to take his ideas
to market, that the public needs those ideas as values by which to live,
and that the ideas themselves are tested and refined by public response."[3] James was determined to make philosophical inquiry open
and accessible to those who did not live within the cloistered halls of
academia because he believed that genuine philosophical work, in
order to be worthwhile, should be persuasive; it should offer a clear,
reasonable, and workable vision of the self and of reality that could
enable individuals who were previously deadened by nihilistic despair to regain a sense of purpose and meaning in their lives. From
James's pragmatic perspective, a philosophical vision that did not transform lives was certainly not valuable, and it was quite possibly not
even true.

While writing this book, I have tried to remember James's emphasis on the transformative function of philosophy. Therefore, although I spend a great deal of time and care describing and analyzing
James's ideas, I do so not out of some vague reverence for musty relics
from the past, but because I believe that James's philosophical and
psychological insights are vitally important resources for contemporary philosophical reflection. In keeping with this intention of using
James's thought, rather than simply admiring or condemning it from
a safe distance, there are several places interspersed throughout this
text in which I go beyond a simple descriptive analysis of James's
work in order to offer my own constructive "neo-Jamesian" proposals.
I make no claims that these proposals are in any way complete or
systematic. Instead, I see them as schematic outlines that suggest
possibilities for further research. Nonetheless, while I recognize full
well the sketchy, tentative nature of these proposals, I would argue
that it is here, more than anywhere else in the book, that I am truly
being faithful to James's work. James the pragmatist would be pleased,
I am sure, that his ideas are not simply described and analyzed, but
are also applied to some of the most directly pertinent philosophical
questions of today.

I also think that James the psychologist would sympathize with
my inability, within the confines of this work, to do equal justice to
every aspect of his thought. (For instance, sadly, James's fascinating
insights on the will and on habit get short shrift in this book.) As
James goes to great pains to point out in *The Principles of Psychology*,
our moment-to-moment experience of life is itself always rooted in
choices: we perceive a world that is at least partially molded by what
we choose to notice, by what we are hoping and expecting to see. In

the same way, a creation of a work such as *Exploring Unseen Worlds* is also a matter of choices: what to include, what to leave out, what to emphasize, what to ignore. At each step of the way I have brought my own selective interests, philosophical agendas, and personal passions to my reading of James's enormous corpus and the even more voluminous secondary literature on James.

In particular, I see James through the lens of my own interest in comparative mysticism. As such, it is perhaps inevitable that in this book the reader will meet a "mystical" James, a James that might not be as easily recognizable as James the tough-minded pragmatist or James the psychologist. I would like to think, however, that James the pluralist would heartily approve of this new "mystical" rendering of his life and thought, especially if it brings to light aspects of his work that were previously either ignored or overlooked.

My choice to focus on the "mystical" James has, naturally enough, affected the organizational structure of the book itself. I see *Exploring Unseen Worlds* as an opportunity, both to tease out the mystical implications of James's work, and to compare and contrast James's ideas with alternate perspectives drawn from a wide variety of mystical traditions. Hidden in the nooks and crannies of this book are Islamic mystics, Taoist recluses, Kalahari !Kung healers, and Hindu goddesses. They appear in a flash, and then just as suddenly, they are gone, but hopefully their brief manifestation in the pages of this text will serve to illuminate an abstraction, or to clarify a difficult idea, or to reveal the complexity of a philosophical dilemma. It is quite likely that there will be some academic specialists who will object to my willingness to summon the numinous presence of these religious figures without sufficient ritual genuflections towards the guardians of the gates of their particular discipline: the voluminous footnotes, the arcane jargon, the requisite postmodern assumptions, the "thick" descriptions. My hope, however, is that most scholars in the field will pardon my presumption, seeing my forays into their territory less as arrogant attempts to make unsubstantiated claims of expertise and more as relatively restrained, primarily illustrative, endeavors on my part to offer the "mystical" James an opportunity to converse briefly with this wide and colorful variety of spiritual figures.

My choice to focus on the "mystical" James has affected the format of *Exploring Unseen Worlds* in another way as well, since in many ways, this text is simply my sustained attempt to unpack a definition of mysticism that is, I argue, implicit throughout James's work. A careful examination of James's writings reveals that mysticism, for James, is a way of life that is centered around *experiences of*

4

powerful, transformative, personally interpreted, contacts with transnatural realities. This definition draws attention to the way in which James's interest in mysticism fuses four distinct, yet interrelated fields of knowledge: (1) the epistemological; (2) the psychological; (3) the metaphysical; and (4) the normative. What makes any study of James's work so difficult (and so rewarding!) is that these four typically separate areas of study are often deliberately intertwined in James's work: facts and values merge, the self radiates out (or in) to deeper levels of reality, experiences are the "stuff" of the universe, metaphysical claims are normatively justified, and so on. For the sake of clarity, however, I have organized this book as if it were indeed possible to tease apart James's epistemology, psychology, metaphysics, and pragmatism. After an initial chapter spent exploring the mystical dimensions of James's life as well as his overt discussions of mysticism, chapters 2 through 5 focus on the mystical implications of James's epistemology, psychology, metaphysics, and pragmatism— even though this way of organizing the material at times has forced me to make what seems to be almost arbitrary choices as to which chapter certain of James's more holistic concepts belong.

The first chapter of this book is an attempt to establish clearly the depth and breadth of James's interest in mysticism. Not only do I track down the numerous moments in which James, throughout the course of his career, explicitly discusses themes related to mysticism, but I also trace the ways in which James's fascination with mysticism was affected by his other philosophical interests (in particular his interest in what was then called "psychical research"). Chapter 1 is the most explicitly biographical and historical chapter. It is here that I seek to demonstrate how James's interest in mysticism was kindled and sustained by a series of intriguing, if somewhat muted, personal mystical experiences. James was not a mystic, but he did possess a "mystical germ," a seed of openness to mysticism that was, I contend, nurtured and supported by his own sporadic experiences with mystically tinged states of awareness. This chapter also attempts to show the highly ambivalent nature of James's appraisal of mysticism, and draws parallels between James's complex, double-edged understanding of mysticism, and his equally complex, equally ambivalent, relationship with his mystically inclined father, Henry James, Sr.

After the first chapter's initial reconnaissance of James's ruminations on mysticism, chapter 2 places James's understanding of mystical experience within the larger context of his theories of the nature of experience in general. To begin with, I show how, unlike classical empiricists such as John Locke and David Hume, James's epistemology

5

(developed primarily in his massive work, *The Principles of Psychology* and then altered and refined in his *Essays in Radical Empiricism*) makes room for mystical experiences, provided that these experiences, like sensory experiences, can be validated by their interaction with other experiences in life. However, I go on to point out that, for James, mystical experiences do not have a privileged position, in that mystical experiences, like any other experiences, are shaped by each person's language, culture, historical setting, and personal predispositions.

This recognition by James that mystical experiences are molded by a variety of linguistic and cultural factors is strikingly similar to the "constructivist" position articulated by Steven Katz, Wayne Proudfoot, and others, a position that is increasingly dominant in the contemporary philosophy of mysticism. However, unlike the constructivists, a radical empiricist understanding of mysticism also defends the need to recognize the *given-ness* and *otherness* of what the mystic experiences, the dialectical give-and-take between the "experiencer" and "what is experienced." Chapter 2 attempts to show that a radical empiricist perspective on mystical experience highlights the ways in which this "otherness" or "giveness," while crucially affected by the mystic's ingrained interests and cultural assumptions, is also experienced as a power outside of the mystic's control, a power capable of resisting arbitrary interpretations put upon it, a power that is capable of initiating revolutionary changes in the worldview of the mystical experiencer.

In this chapter, I also note that in the context of James's radical empiricism, even the very the notion of a separate "knower" and "known" becomes problematic when viewed through the lens of James's theory of "pure experience." This theory postulates that everything that exists is inherently neither physical nor mental, but rather, is an expression of a more primal nonduality (pure experience) that forms the basis for traditional dualisms, such as subject/object or mental/physical. This notion of pure experience is significant to the study of mysticism not only because it overcomes the often negative assessment of mystical experience as a purely *subjective* event, but also because it overturns the philosophically problematic understanding of mystical experience as an interaction between two ontologically separate "things": the mystic and what the mystic experiences.

Chapter 3 continues to investigate the ways in which James struggles to emphasize both the connections and the separations between "the one experiencing" and "what is experienced." It accomplishes this task primarily by exploring James's attempts to formulate a "field" model of the self. In this model, the self (and reality) is seen as a nexus of constantly changing, interrelated, co-penetrating "fields," fields which possess no absolute beginnings nor endings, yet which manage to maintain a functional distinction between one other. A field model of the self permits James to argue that the self is integrally linked with wider and deeper levels of consciousness, and yet simultaneously allows him to argue that the self maintains its status as an independent agent with free will and moral responsibility.

In chapter 3, I point out that the "full self" for James is, in a sense, the *whole* field—not only the present center of consciousness, but also a margin of vaguely sensed feelings and tendencies. This margin in turn shades off into a subconscious self—a dynamic, complex, yet hidden selfhood which, in its turn, is conjoined with an indefinitely vast multitude of higher (or broader) levels of consciousness. James hypothesizes that these levels of consciousness are what flood into "ordinary" awareness during mystical experiences. In this chapter, I attempt to demonstrate that James views these higher (or broader) levels of consciousness in two ways. From one perspective, these levels of consciousness can be seen as aspects of the self: they are our "wider selves"; they are powerful forces deep within our own being that are willing to aid us in our salvific and self-transformative efforts, if we invite their assistance. However, from another perspective, these "wider selves," these more inclusive consciousnesses, can just as adequately be pictured as existences with purposes and goals of their own, levels of being which have experiences that occur "as it were, over our heads."[4] This "ambidextrous" nature of the field conception of the self allows James to emphasize, at different times, that the transformative effects of mystical experiences are the result of both "natural" *and* "supernatural" causation. For James, the self is thus both what is transformed as well as the "divine" initiator of transformation; it is both the subject and the object of mystical experiences.

Chapter 4 amplifies the work begun in chapter 3, with a more explicitly "theo-metaphysical" focus. Here I attempt to show that, according to James, mystical experiences not only present us with evocative information on the structure of everyday reality, but also provide us with intriguing evidence for the putative existence of a transnatural "unseen world." James argues that the testimonies of mystical experiences, if unsupported by public philosophical discussion, do not authoritatively prove that "unseen worlds" actually exist (and these testimonies certainly cannot be trusted to give reliable and consistent details of the specific nature of these other "realms"). However, James also insists that mystical experiences can and should undermine our taken-for-granted, unexamined, naturalistic conceptions

7

of reality. Moreover, James is willing to claim that mystical experiences can and should provide philosophers with the "raw data" that is necessary to create a convincing, morally fruitful, yet nondogmatic, theo-metaphysical "picture" of the nature of reality as a whole.

In chapter 4, I argue that James's "pluralistic pantheism" is his attempt to create such a theo-metaphysical model. Intrigued by the monistic implications of profound mystical experiences, and yet morally unsatisfied with the monism of his time, James struggled to articulate his alternative: a self-consciously open-ended and yet philosophically defensible position in which we and "God" (in this case meaning the widest possible field of consciousness) can be seen as both separate and connected—a philosophical position in which the further limits of our being can be understood as plunging into a "mother-sea" of consciousness, without a concurrent violation of our integrity and moral freedom as individuals.

The theo-metaphysical focus of chapter 4 is followed by the normative focus of chapter 5. Based on a type of retrospective analysis, where I illustrate how the seeds of James's pragmatism are at work in the *Varieties*, I point out that much of James's discussion of spiritual healing, conversion, and saintliness is an attempt to warrant pragmatically his belief in the reality and goodness of the "unseen world" contacted in mystical experiences. In chapter 5, I seek to demonstrate that the truth-claims that James makes for the reality of these "unseen worlds" are justified not by any alleged correspondence to some predetermined paradigmatic reality, but instead, by the positive transformative effects "on the whole" and "over the long run" which come about as a result of those mystical experiences.

James's pragmatic methodology itself needs to be critically examined, and perhaps the best place to begin this task is with its most detailed instantiation: James's assessment of saintliness. In chapter 5, I contend that is important to realize that saintliness *is* linked to mysticism for James; I argue that even if it is not made explicit, James's assessment of saintliness can be seen as a pragmatic evaluation of the potentially positive value of sustained, deep, transformative contacts with a transnatural reality—that is, I attempt to demonstrate that James's assessment of saintliness is a pragmatically based evaluation of mysticism. In this chapter, I do not contend that James is rhapsodic about all aspects of saintliness; although he does recommend "let us be saints,"[5] the sainthood he advocates is a new, improved version— a nondogmatic, critically aware, tolerant, nonsectarian, non-excessive, modern saint. For James, if sainthood is to be judged positively, it not only has to satisfy the "vital needs" of the saint, but it also has to be in harmony with a wide range of other needs present in the saint's own culture. In addition, and perhaps less obviously, James asserts that it is vitally important to judge the worth of a saint's actions, because if the *behavior* of the saint is found to be good, then this good behavior in turn authorizes the *beliefs* behind that behavior (as long as those beliefs do not also encourage behavior that should be condemned). In other words, for James, the truth of what the saint mystically experiences is warranted by the transformations in the saint's own life and by his or her effects on others, "on the whole" and "over the long run."

Interspersed throughout each chapter, I attempt to point out ways in which James's philosophical understandings can be applicable to contemporary issues in the philosophy of mysticism, and I offer my own tentative suggestions on ways in which James's ideas might be altered or extended to address these issues. My hope is that this book will succeed in drawing attention to the numerous ways in which James's radical empiricism, philosophical anthropology, pluralistic pantheism, and pragmatism both affect and are affected by his understanding of mysticism. I do not intend to prove that James's ideas fully answer all the problems that confront the philosophy of mysticism; indeed, I think that James's position could benefit from a conversation with several different contemporary philosophical alternatives. However, I do believe that a careful study of James's ideas can make a significant and valuable contribution to the study of mysticism. More work certainly needs to be done, but a renewed interest in the philosophical and psychological perspectives offered by William James is certainly a good place to begin any exploration of the unseen worlds that reveal themselves to us in the course of studying the dynamic textures of mystical life.

9

❧ 1 ❧

Establishing Foundations: Ladders and Laughing Gas, Phantoms and Fathers

The series of coincidences that could not be explained, the meetings with these strange people who seemed to be pieces of a jigsaw puzzle; all these things served to show my doubting mind a truth that could not be denied—there are laws governing our existence about which we have no understanding at all. Our lives are ruled by forces which, although invisible and intangible, have power greater than anything that can be seen or experienced in the physical world.

—Reshad Feild, *The Last Barrier*

You must not rest satisfied with the repeated oft-broken echo of that original sound. You must transport yourselves into the interior of a pious soul and seek to understand its inspiration. In the very act, you must understand the production of light and heat in a soul surrendered to the Universe. Otherwise you learn nothing of religion.

—Frederick Schleiermacher, *On Religion*

Expanding the Boundaries of the Mystical

Given the importance of William James to the fields of psychology, philosophy, and religious studies, it is astonishing that there has never been any focused, indepth examination of his decades-long fascination with mysticism. By far the best place to begin this investigation is with *The Varieties of Religious Experience*.[1] The centrality of mysticism in the *Varieties* is evident: several times in the course of this work, James postpones answering important theoretical questions until the chapter on mysticism, which according to James is "the vital chapter from which the other chapters get their light."[2] But James's discussion of mysticism in the *Varieties* is not just limited to this "vital" chapter. Instead, James's fascination with mysticism pervades the entire book. This fascination is, however, easy to miss because it seems, on the face of it, that James's focus is on religious experiences, not mystical experiences per se. However, a closer look at the text reveals that the *religious* experiences that James spends so much time examining in the *Varieties* are also, at least from his perspective, *mystical* experiences.

It is easy to miss this interconnection between "religious experience" and "mystical experience" in James's thought. James himself never overtly comments on the intimate connection between mystical experiences and religious experiences in the *Varieties*, and so it is easy to assume that, for James, mystical experiences are a subset of the broader category of religious experiences in general (which is how mysticism is typically understood today). If mystical experiences were understood in this way by James, then most of the *Varieties* would not, in fact, directly apply to his understanding of mysticism, because James's explicit focus in the *Varieties* is on religious experiences. However, James had a unique conception of what should or should not be designated as "mystical." Unlike the contemporary tendency to limit the term "mystical" to a rather narrow band of unitive states of consciousness, James saw "mystical experiences" as encompassing a broad and fluid spectrum of mental states, ranging from deep poetic insight, déjà vu, ghostly visitations, and psychedelic experiences to the more overtly religious ecstasies and unitive experiences. From James's perspective, while certain mystical experiences are "religious," other mystical experiences are not (at least overtly). Therefore (and here the plot thickens), the category of "mystical experience" for James is actually in some ways *wider* and *more* inclusive than the category of "religious experience"— not the reverse. For instance, James might say that an uprush of creative insight is "mystical," and that sensing a "presence" in a room is "mystical," and that a state of altered consciousness brought on by drugs is also "mystical," but none of these experiences would be seen by James as overtly "religious." Conversely, he would say that very mild and diffuse religious experiences, such as feelings of consolation, protection, or an increased understanding of scripture, *are* religious *if the person attributes these experiences to the influence of a transnatural source*, but they would not necessarily be termed "mystical" by James.

However, these two basically separate categories ("mystical experience" and "religious experience") at times can and do intersect; they do so in the category of "religious mysticism," a highly potent subset of religious experiences in general—the mystical experiences that James claims are at the "root and centre"[3] of religious experience. Therefore, while not all mystical experiences can accurately be called religious, and not all religious experiences can be considered mystical, all *powerful* religious experiences are mystical for James, and these are the types of experiences that fill the pages of the *Varieties*. The "varieties" of religious experiences that James is interested in exploring in the *Varieties* are typically not prosaic, "nonmystical" religious experiences. James, for specific methodological reasons, is primarily interested in investigating those experiences that are vivid, powerful, and extreme—experiences that are clearly "mystical" in James's expanded sense of the term. It is crucially important to recognize this congruence between religious experiences and mystical experiences in the *Varieties*. If this connection is not kept in mind, it is easy to overlook the fact that while James's theories may appear to deal only with *religious* experience, they almost always *also* are applicable to his discussion of *mystical* experience.

But what exactly is it that makes an experience "mystical" for James?[4] In the *Varieties*, James gives us some clues. In the chapter that is specifically focused on mysticism, James states that he limits the term "mystical experiences" to those experiences that have four particular qualities.

The first mark of what characterizes a mystical experience for James is *ineffability*. According to James, people who have mystical experiences find, after returning to an ordinary state of awareness, that it is impossible to express adequately what occurred to them during their mystical experience. They discover that words do not accurately reflect the richness and depth of that experience. Their descriptions are simply not adequate; these descriptions neither correctly represent what was experienced, nor do they allow others to share in any meaningful way what the experiencer personally and directly perceived. James points out that in this way, mystical experiences are more closely aligned to "feelings" than they are to concepts, in that feelings are directly experienced.

It is crucial to point out at this juncture that James is not equating mystical experience and emotion. As we will investigate more fully in chapter 2, "feeling" is a highly nuanced technical term for James, and encompasses much more within its boundaries than just "emotion." Admittedly, however, mystical experiences are at least homologous to emotional states for James, in that there is an immediacy and depth to both types of experiences that has to be personally experienced and which cannot be adequately reflected in words. As James points out, people really only know what love feels like when they have been in love themselves, and in the same way, the depth of mystical experiences are also only truly known to people who themselves have had mystical experiences.

The second mark of a mystical experience for James is its *noetic quality*. Even though James has just noted the similarity of mystical experiences to "states of feeling," he points out that they are *also* often described as "states of knowledge."[5] For James, mystical experiences "are states of insight into depths of truth unplumbed by the discursive intellect. They are illuminations, revelations, full of significance and importance . . . and as a rule they carry with them a curious sense of authority for after-time."[6] James is not being careless when he affirms that mystical experiences can simultaneously be both states of "feeling" and states of "knowledge." This integration of "feeling" and "knowledge" is based on an epistemological distinction that James articulates in his earlier work, *The Principles of Psychology*. In the *Principles*, James discusses the differences between two types of knowing: "knowledge about" and "knowledge by acquaintance." "Knowledge about" is discursive knowledge; it is the publicly accessible, rationally articulated, conceptually mediated knowledge of something. On the other hand, "knowledge by acquaintance" is nondiscursive knowledge; it is the immediately received, intuitively understood, perceptually based "is-ness" of something. Although post facto these two types of knowledge can be reflectively separated from each other, in actuality, they interact in every concrete moment of knowing. "Knowledge by acquaintance" provides the "raw data" that "knowledge about" then refines and elaborates upon with its conceptual, linguistic and cultural categories. "Feelings," for James, are particularly good examples of this synthesis of "knowledge by acquaintance" and "knowledge about"; they are not just emotive, but also are cognitive—they are "states of knowledge." To the extent that mystical experiences are also combinations of these two types of knowledge (a claim that will need to be carefully investigated in chapter 2), they can be understood, without contradiction, as being both "states of feeling" (emotive) *and* "states of knowledge" (cognitive), since feelings themselves are also simultaneously emotive and cognitive.

The final two marks of what characterizes a mystical experience for James are *transiency* and *passivity*. James claims that these two characteristics are less crucial to a proper understanding of the phenomenology of mystical experience than the previous two marks (ineffability and noetic quality). This reluctance to make transiency and passivity universal characteristics of mystical experience was, in retrospect, a wise decision. James's information on non-Christian mystical traditions was extremely limited, and this lacuna negatively affects his discussion of these two characteristics.[7] For instance, in the section which deals with the apparent transiency of mystical experiences, James

14

points out that mystical experiences cannot be sustained for long, an hour or two at best. While this observation might accurately reflect the information James had available at the time (information drawn primarily from Protestant conversion narratives), it certainly does not take into account the numerous narratives by mystics in (for instance) Zen, Sufism, and Hinduism, who claim to have achieved a permanent alteration of consciousness, a plateau of superconscious awareness that the mystic rests in while going about his or her life in the everyday world. Therefore, James's emphasis on the transient nature of mystical experience is, at best, only partially accurate, and at worst (as will become apparent in chapter 5), undermines his understanding of the crucial interrelationship that exists between mysticism and saintliness.

James's discussion on the transiency of mystical experience does, however, contain some helpful (if relatively terse) insights. For instance, after he points out that the vividness of a mystical experience tends to fade in the memory of the mystic after he or she comes back to everyday awareness, James goes on to mention, almost as an aside, that if the mystic has more than one experience, then it is possible that he or she might begin to notice a continuity in the various experiences, and that in some cases the experiences might even seem to develop and become richer and more significant to the mystic.

This very brief mention of mystical experiences as part of an ongoing process is in vivid contrast to James's primary emphasis on those mystical experiences that come unexpectedly, that seem to explode in the person's awareness with little or no warning or preparation. These spontaneous and sporadic mystical experiences, which were a hallmark of the Protestant conversion process in James's time, form the bulk of the narratives of vivid religious experiences in the *Varieties*. There are a few exceptions: James somewhat wistfully mentions that compared to Catholicism with its disciplined practice of meditations designed to unite the soul with God, Protestantism has perhaps left behind something of value. James comments that "it is odd that Protestantism, especially evangelical Protestantism, should seemingly have abandoned everything methodical in this line. Apart from what prayer may lead to, Protestant mystical experience appears to have been almost exclusively sporadic."[8] James also notes that "Hindus, Buddhists, Mohammedans, and Christians all have cultivated [mystical experiences] methodically," and goes on to describe, very briefly, the Hindu "training in mystical insight" or yoga, where the disciple by "diet, posture, breathing, intellectual concentration, and moral discipline" can gain an "experiential union . . . with the divine" by entering into "*samādhi*," a "superconscious state."[9] He even includes a

15

short, if rather obscure, description of different stages of Buddhist *dhyāna* and a surprisingly long passage from the autobiography of Al-Ghazzali, a Persian Islamic mystic and philosopher. But on the whole, James's attention in the *Varieties* is focused primarily on those mystical experiences which appear spontaneously, rather than on those that occur as part of a disciplined spiritual life.

Interestingly, however, for James there ultimately is little difference between mystical experiences that arrive unexpectedly and those that are methodically cultivated. In his discussion of *passivity*, the fourth mark of what constitutes a mystical experience, James points out that:

> Although the oncoming of mystical states may be facilitated by preliminary voluntary operations, as by fixing the attention, or going through certain bodily performances . . . when the characteristic sort of consciousness once has set in, the mystic feels as if his own will were in abeyance, and indeed sometimes as if he were grasped and held by a superior power.[10]

In the age-old discussion about the relative merits of "grace" or "self-effort" (a discussion that has certainly not been limited to Christianity), James, in the final analysis, stresses the priority of grace. For James, the various spiritual disciplines such as meditation, breathing exercises, visualizations, and so forth, simply prepare the way for the onset of a mystical experience that may or may not happen; he emphasizes that a mystical experience cannot be "forced" into consciousness by these various spiritual techniques. According to James, the purpose of these "voluntary operations" is, ironically, to short-circuit the ability of aspiring mystics to perform voluntary actions. Spiritual techniques strip the would-be mystics of their sense of self, and this dissolution of the boundaries that define that self opens up the possibility of an influx of heightened awareness from a transnatural source.

James recognizes that, in many ways, mystical experiences, at least on the surface, seem quite similar to several "psychical" phenomena, such as "alternative personality, . . . prophetic speech, automatic writing, or the mediumistic trance,"[11] in that individuals undergoing both mystical and psychical experiences believe that a "higher" or "deeper" power is initiating and ultimately controlling the process. But he also emphasizes that, unlike psychical phenomena, which often are not be remembered once the subject returns to ordinary consciousness and which may not have any lasting impact on the psychic's everyday life, mystical states of awareness "are never merely interruptive. Some memory of their content always remains, and a profound

16

sense of their importance. They modify the inner life of the subject between the times of their recurrence."[12]

However, it is important not to be deceived by James's apparent theoretical separation between mystical and psychical phenomena. James also repeatedly emphasizes that the differences between mystical and psychical phenomena are often difficult to detect in the actual narratives of the lives of mystics. These two categories ("mystical" and "psychical) are simply not rigidly demarcated for James; for instance, there are many times in his writings that James will use the label "mystical" to refer to phenomena that he more typically would put under the category of "psychical," for example, the sense of a ghostly presence or a medium's clairvoyant knowledge. While this blurring of the boundaries between what is "mystical" and what is "psychical" may, at times, be based on a careless use of terminology by James, it is just as likely that his liberty with the terms "mystical" and "psychical" is rooted in his awareness of how many spiritual experiences are typically a complex fusion of both psychical and mystical components.

An Unseen Definition of Mystical Experience

Even though it may appear that James's detailed discussion of the most common characteristics of mystical experiences (i.e., the four "marks" of ineffability, noetic quality, transiency, and passivity) is a definition of mystical experience, in actuality, this discussion is not so much a definition as it is a phenomenological description of the most widely found qualities in most mystical experiences. However, a close investigation of James's work on mysticism as a whole does reveal an *implicit* definition of mystical experience. Mystical experiences for James (I will claim) are *experiences of powerful, transformative, personally interpreted, contacts with transnatural realities*.

First, every mystical experience, in James's sense of the term, must be *experiential*. That is, mystical experiences are first hand events; they are "seen," "felt," and "intuited" far more than they are "read about," "thought through," or "believed."

Second, mystical experiences, according to James, are also *powerful*. An experience is "mystical" if it is intensely felt, highly charged, and profoundly significant. As was pointed out above, religious experiences are "mystical" only if they have a particular level of potency. Having a nice warm feeling of thankfulness to God or to Amida Buddha does not qualify as a mystical experience. Further, nonreligious

17

experiences must also live up to this specification. For example, being mildly high on drugs or alcohol would not be a mystical experience, according to this definition.

Third, not only are genuine mystical experiences experiential and powerful, they must also, from James's perspective, be *transformative*—they can and should revolutionize a person's (and ideally a community's) life. For instance, James notes that religious conversion experiences are almost always mystical because of their ability to radically transform the way people understand their world and themselves. By the same token, non-religious experiences are "mystical" only if they succeed in significantly altering a person's worldview. For instance, simply noticing a new detail in Picasso's *Guernica* would not qualify as a mystical experience, but having a revelatory insight into the hidden meaning of *Guernica* that catalyzes a radically new way of perceiving the world *would* qualify as a mystical experience.

Finally, mystical experiences for James involve *personally interpreted contacts with transnatural realities*. James is not a reductionist. Even though he does recognize the complex ways in which our bodies, minds, and cultural backgrounds influence the final makeup of every mystical experience, he also insists that mystical experiences are more than simply an amalgam of physiological, psychological, or sociological factors. For James, mystical experiences are important sources of data on the existence of realms of reality or dimensions of consciousness that exceed (even while interpenetrating) our everyday "natural" reality or our typical waking consciousness. The existence of these "unseen worlds" is not dogmatically affirmed by James, and he is certainly no ardent defender of any particular description of the contours of the "landscape" and "scenery" of these worlds or levels of awareness; but he does feel that these experiences are best understood as a dynamic interaction of two factors: a transnatural source (or sources) and a person's interpretative framework (which is structured and generated by his or her subjective interests, as well as various physiological and sociological factors). James claims that the phenomenology of these experiences always indicates an "otherness" within the experience, even if that "otherness" is understood as a deeper level of one's own being.

James's Mystical Germ

James believed in the reality of unseen worlds and was convinced that mystical experiences served a vitally important personal and social function, yet his sympathetic and receptive investigation of mysticism was honed by a keen critical awareness. He did not take the claims of the mystics at face value, and he was a virulent opponent of any sort of dogmatic certainty—whether "mystical" or "scientific." But James did take the accounts of mystical experiences seriously, and he believed that the metaphysical and theological claims made by different mystics provided vivid and suggestive hypotheses about the nature of reality.

Although James was fascinated by mysticism, James himself was not a mystic, that is, he was not someone who had frequent and profound mystical experiences. As he stated in a letter written in 1904 to Prof. James H. Leuba:

> My personal position is simple. I have no living sense of commerce with a God. I envy those who have, for I know that the addition of such a sense would help me greatly. The Divine, for my active life, is limited to impersonal and abstract concepts which, as ideal, interest and determine me, but do so but faintly in comparison with what a feeling of God might effect, if I had one. This, to be sure, is largely a matter of intensity, but a shade of intensity may make one's whole centre of moral energy shift. Now, although I am so devoid of *Gottesbewusstsein* in the directer and stronger sense, yet there is *something in me* which *makes response* when I hear utterances from that quarter made by others. I recognize the deeper voice. Something tells me:—'thither lies truth'—and I am sure it is not old theistic prejudices of infancy. Those in my case were Christian, but I have grown so out of Christianity that entanglement therewith on the part of a mystical utterance has to be abstracted from and overcome, before I can listen. Call this, if you like, my mystical germ. It is a very common germ. It creates the rank and file of believers.[13]

James's "mystical germ" appears to have been nurtured by a few personal experiences that could certainly, in James's sense of the word, be called mystical. One of these experiences occurred in 1898. James was in the Adirondack Mountains, one of his favorite spots in which to escape from the pressures and demands of both domestic and academic life. He had climbed for five hours up New York's highest peak, the 5,344 foot Mt. Marcy; after hearing the sounds of axes in the valley below, he hiked for another hour to Panther Lodge Camp, where he met a group of young female college students. That night on the slopes of Mt. Marcy, sleep eluded him. Writing afterwards in a letter to his wife Alice, he describes the powerful "state of spiritual alertness" that gripped him that night. He goes on to write:

Exploring Unseen Worlds

The influences of Nature, the wholesomeness of the people round me . . . the thought of you and the children, . . . the problem of the Edinburgh lectures [the basis for the *Varieties*], all fermented within me until it became a regular Walpurgis Nacht. I spent a good deal of it in the woods, where the streaming moonlight lit up things in a magical checkered play, and it seemed as if the Gods of all the nature-mythologies were holding an indescribable meeting in my breast with the moral Gods of the inner life. The two kinds of Gods have nothing in common—the Edinburgh lectures made quite a hitch ahead. The intense significance of some sort, of the whole scene, if one could only *tell* the significance; the intense inhuman remoteness of its inner life, and yet the intense *appeal* of it; its everlasting freshness and its immemorial antiquity and decay; its utter Americanism, and every sort of patriotic suggestiveness, and you, and my relation to you part and parcel of it all, and beaten up with it, so that memory and sensation all whirled inexplicably together; it was indeed worth coming for, and worth repeating year by year, if repetition could only procure what in its nature I suppose must be all unplanned for and unexpected. It was one of the happiest lonesome nights of my existence, and I understand now what a poet is. He is a person who can feel the immense complexity of influences that I felt, and make some partial tracks in them for verbal statement. In point of fact, I can't find a single word for all that significance, and don't know what it was significant of, so there it remains, a mere boulder of *impression*. Doubtless in more ways than one, though, things in the Edinburgh lectures will be traceable to it.[14]

James's assessment seems correct; much of his discussion of mysticism in the *Varieties* is indeed implicit in this letter describing his "Walpurgis Nacht" experience. For instance, James insists that the experience could not be adequately described, yet he also maintains that it contained complex, if impossible to articulate, strands of knowledge (i.e., it was ineffable and noetic). The experience also arrived spontaneously, disappeared after a fairly short period of time, and could probably not be reproduced by an act of will (that is, the experience was transient and had within it elements of passivity). In a very real, albeit muted way, the experience held within itself all the four qualities that James considered the most important marks of a genuine mystical experience.

This account of James's "Walpurgis Nacht" experience also aligns with my formulation of the implicit Jamesian definition of mystical experiences—that is, *experiences of powerful, transformative, personally interpreted, contacts with transnatural realities.* For instance, the experience appears to be the result of an inextricably interwoven

20

fusion of subjective and objective components: it was neither the product of just James's own psyche, nor the consequence of an unadulter-
ated revelation of divinity. It also made an intensely vivid impression
on James and provided him with plenty of material for further productive philosophical work on issues that had long haunted him.

Unfortunately, that night had other less positive consequences.
The next morning at six o'clock James and his companions hiked back
up to the top of Mt. Marcy, and then trudged ten and a half grueling
hours back to his shanty in Keene Valley. The return hike was especially strenuous, and ultimately disastrous, because James had chival-
rously insisted on carrying a double load, the guide's pack as well as
his own, so that the guide could in turn carry the young women's
packs. The overexertion of this journey strained his heart, producing
the damage that would ultimately lead to James's death twelve years
later.

James's "Walpurgis Nacht" on the slopes of Mt. Marcy was not
the only moment that he experienced states of consciousness that could
be described as "mystical." Experimenting with the effects of nitrous
oxide, undergoing a variation of a "dark night of the soul," and going
through several other unusual experiences towards the end of his life
(all of which will be described in detail later in this chapter) produced
an extraordinary openness in James to mysticism. It seems then that
James's claim at the beginning of his discussion on mysticism in the
Varieties, that "my own constitution shuts me out from . . . enjoyment
[of mystical states] almost entirely and I can speak of them only at
second hand,"[15] must be understood to mean that since these experiences were quite infrequent and did not produce in James that certainty that is common in most mystical experiences, James did not
consider himself to be, as he put it, a "professional mystic."[16] However, it also seems indisputable that the memory of their occurrence,
combined with what he calls his "mystical germ," were sufficient to
create in James a lively interest in mystical states; they also solidified
within him the personal certainty that our typical awareness in this
day-to-day world is only one of the many levels of consciousness that
the universe truly contains.

However, James was not always so open to mysticism. Although
in the Varieties James chastises those who use the words mysticism
and mystical "as terms of mere reproach, to throw at any opinion
which we regard as vague and vast and sentimental, and without a
base in either facts or logic,"[17] he was often himself guilty of doing just
this in his early writings. As will soon become apparent, James remained profoundly ambivalent about mysticism; on the one hand, his

21

religious intuitions and metaphysical speculations were nourished by the information he gleaned from reading various accounts of mystical experiences; but, on the other hand, the ethicist in James was profoundly disturbed by the moral implications of mystical experiences, especially since James typically linked mysticism with his philosophical *bête noire*, monism.

Climbing the Mystical Ladder

One of James's primary criticisms of the monistic philosophers of his time was that their methodology was overly deductive, that is, they began their philosophical task with certain monistic assumptions about the structure of the universe as a whole and then imposed this assumption of oneness onto their subsequent investigations of the distinctly pluralistic universe of our everyday experience. James as an empiricist wanted to reverse this order. He thought that the first priority of a philosopher should be to gather concrete data on the workings of the universe as we actually experience it. Only after this first step of gathering data is accomplished should the philosopher be willing to make generalizations or to formulate hypotheses on the nature of the universe.

This inductive strategy is stunningly apparent in James's philosophical assessment of mystical experience in the *Varieties*. Example after example of specific mystical experiences crowd the pages of the *Varieties*, and these accounts are given top billing. It is only after these concrete narratives of mystical experiences have had their turn on the stage that James himself goes on to provide a few highly compressed, yet often remarkably insightful observations. This is not to say that the accounts of mystical experiences are presented in a hodgepodge, chaotic fashion. James is certainly willing and able to organize his data, and in this organizational process, James makes no pretense at complete objectivity; he continually emphasizes the creative and vitally important role played by the philosopher's subjective interests, and he recognizes the way in which these interests structure scientific conclusions. But, on the whole, it is apparent that James attempts to be faithful, as far as possible, to the qualities inherent in the mystical experiences themselves and he makes every effort not to impose arbitrarily a set of dogmatically rigid philosophical assumptions on the experiences themselves.

This inductive methodology is particularly evident in James's depiction of the "mystical ladder" in the *Varieties*. James wants to acquaint the reader with a very wide variety of mystical experiences, which, in his opinion, "are best understood when placed within their series, studied in their germ and in their over-ripe decay and compared with their exaggerated and degenerated kindred";[18] he attempts to aid us in this comparative process by creating a "ladder" of mystical experiences.

The lower rungs of this ladder are populated with descriptions of mystical experiences that have no evident religious meaning, while the upper rungs of the ladder contain accounts of mystical experiences that are profoundly and unmistakably religious. Evidently then (although he does not say so explicitly), James determined the position of a particular experience on the mystical ladder by using the criteria of "more religious" or "less religious."[19] It appears, therefore, that even though James did not consider every mystical experience to be inherently religious, he apparently did believe that they were *more* mystical to the degree that they were *more* religious.

James's construction of his mystical ladder is not without its weak points. One of the major difficulties is that he never clearly states the criteria by which he determines the degree of "religiosity" of specific experiences, making it seem at times almost arbitrary whether a certain type of experience is "higher" or "lower" on the mystical ladder. Another area of confusion centers around his determination to rank mystical experiences as "higher" or "lower" on the mystical ladder in the first place. The high/low imagery leads us to think that James is making a normative determination. By using a hierarchical metaphor, it is easy to assume that James is claiming that one particular experience is *better* than another, when in fact, he is only using the degree of religiosity of a mystical experience as a convenient way of giving a tentative order to the mass of mystical narratives that he has collected.

Perhaps the best way to illustrate these various difficulties is by examining the "ladder" itself, starting with its lowest rung.

On this lowest rung, James includes a relatively broad cluster of experiences. It is here that he situates such experiences as new insights into a deeper meaning of a phrase or saying, as well as moments such as when particular words, sights, smells, sounds, poetry, or works of art trigger an elusive, powerfully evocative emotional response within us. As James says, "we are alive or dead to the eternal inner message of the arts according as we have kept or lost this mystical sensibility."[20]

The next step up the ladder is reserved for those experiences commonly known today as "déjà-vu"—those times when a person has the disturbing and puzzling sense that he or she has previously experienced exactly what is occurring at the present moment. Possibly James considers these moments of awareness as "mystical," since they

23

"bring a sense of mystery" and a "feeling of an enlargement of perception"; but even James had to recognize that these moments of déjà-vu
are "intrinsically insignificant."[21] However, (interestingly enough) this
very lack of importance also means that these "dreamy states" are not
particularly alarming either, and therefore James rather curtly dis-
misses the "rather absurdly alarmist view" taken by one researcher
who connects these "'dreamy states'" with epilepsy and insanity.[22]
This dismissal does not mean that James sees no connection between
mysticism and insanity. As will become apparent later in this chapter,
James was convinced that there were many possible correlations between mystical states and different types of mental illness; but James's
common sense and ever-present tolerance simply would not allow
him to authorize the more hard-nosed view of certain psychologists of
his time that déjà vu was an indication of mental illness simply because it altered a person's prosaic level of awareness.

James's next step up the mystical ladder supposedly illustrates
"deeper" mystical states of awareness, but unfortunately, there is very
little indication as to why these states are deeper than what was previously described. For instance, James relates the account of one man
who expresses that, "'I am oppressed now and then with an innate
feeling that everything I see has a meaning, if I could but understand
it. And this feeling of being surrounded with truths which I cannot
grasp, amounts to indescribable awe sometimes'."[23] Although it could
easily be argued that this narration *does* describe a more profound
experience than déjà vu (why déjà vu is on the ladder at all is a
mystery in itself), it is *not* so clear why James decided that this experience was more mystical than receiving insights from works of art or
being powerfully affected by the beauty of nature.

James's next example, however, certainly *does* deserve to be called
"more extreme."[24] Here James offers J. A. Symonds's description of an
invasive trance state. Symonds comments that this trance state "took
possession of my mind and will, lasted what seemed an eternity, and
disappeared in a series of rapid sensations, which resembled the
awakening from anaesthetic influence."[25] Symonds indicates that it is
difficult to describe this state of consciousness, but suggests that as it
progressed he gradually lost touch with his sense of space and time,
which produced, frighteningly, a disappearance of his usual sense of
self as well. Symonds then goes on to note that his ordinary consciousness was progressively replaced by an awareness of "a pure, absolute,
abstract self."[26] The universe for Symonds became formless, and
Symonds felt that he "had followed the last thread of being to the
verge of the abyss."[27] He then gradually returned to his normal aware-

ness, not with the sense of loss so common to many mystics, but instead, with a deep sense of gratitude that he had been able to revert back to his more customary state of awareness. Symonds was also haunted afterwards with an agonizing question: which state of consciousness was real and which was illusory—the trance state revealing that "formless state of denuded, keenly sentient being," or the "surrounding phenomena and habits which veil that inner self and build a self of flesh-and-blood conventionality"?[28] Even more frightening for Symonds was the question, "What would happen if the final stage of the trance were reached?"[29]

This narrative (which could be seen as extremely religious if viewed through the lens of several Eastern traditions) is dismissed by James's comment that it is "suggestive of pathology."[30] However, once more it is not clear why James makes this rather negative assessment, unless it is a rhetorical device used to link this trance experience with the states of consciousness which occupy his next rung up the mystical ladder, states of consciousness that are also often labeled as pathological: the experiences of intoxication brought on by alcohol and anaesthetics.

Laughing Gas Revelations

James was acutely aware during much of his life of the dangers of the abuse of alcohol (one of his younger brothers, Robertson, was a severely troubled alcoholic), but in his discussion of the potential mystical aspects of alcohol and anaesthetics in the *Varieties*, he theorizes that underneath the more obvious, and often unattractive, reasons for getting intoxicated, lies the power of alcohol "to stimulate the mystical faculties of human nature, usually crushed to earth by the cold facts and dry criticisms of the sober hour."[31] For James, people use intoxicants not just to relax or to loosen their inhibitions, but also because these different drugs have the possibility of opening us up to levels of consciousness to which we are normally closed.

James is open to, and even perhaps overly appreciative of, the mystical effects of intoxicants (they are, after all, fairly high on his mystical ladder!) because of his own experiences with nitrous oxide. The mystical potential of this anaesthetic, which is perhaps better known today as the "laughing gas" used by some dentists (in a much more controlled and diluted fashion than in James's day) attracted his attention when he read Benjamin Paul Blood's pamphlet, "The Anaesthetic Revelation and the Gist of Philosophy." According to

25

James, nitrous oxide has a remarkable ability to produce a mystical state of awareness. He writes:

> Depth beyond depth of truth seems revealed to the inhaler. This truth fades out, however, or escapes, at the moment of coming to; and if any words remain over in which it seemed to clothe itself, they prove to be the veriest nonsense. Nevertheless, the sense of a profound meaning having been there persists; and I know more than one person who is persuaded that in the nitrous oxide trance we have a genuine metaphysical revelation.[32]

James goes on to reveal that he had earlier experimented himself with the drug and from that experience he came to one unshakable conclusion:

> It is that our normal waking consciousness . . . is but one special type of consciousness, whilst all about it, parted from it by the filmiest of screens, there lie potential forms of consciousness entirely different. We may go through life without suspecting their existence; but apply the requisite stimulus, and at a touch they are there in all their completeness. . . . No account of the universe in its totality can be final which leaves these other forms of consciousness quite disregarded. How to regard them is the question,—for they are so discontinuous with ordinary consciousness. Yet they may determine attitudes though they cannot furnish formulas, and open a region though they fail to give a map. At any rate, they forbid a premature closing of our accounts with reality.[33]

James had previously detailed his experience with nitrous oxide gas in a chapter of *The Will to Believe* entitled, "On Some Hegelisms." In this chapter, James begins his depiction of his experience with nitrous oxide by encouraging others to perform the same experiment. He is convinced that beneath the superficial differences of each individual's experience under nitrous oxide, a similar depth of revelatory truth will manifest itself. Commenting on his own experience with nitrous oxide, James notes that "as with every other person of whom I have heard, the keynote of the experience is the tremendously exciting sense of an intense metaphysical illumination. Truth lies open to the view in depth beneath depth of almost blinding evidence."[34]

At its peak, James's own nitrous oxide mystical experience was characterized by an "immense emotional sense of *reconciliation*," a new perception in which "the centre and periphery of things seem to come together" and in which "the ego and its objects, the *meum* and the *tuum*, are one."[35] James's first response to this experience was to be utterly convinced that his previous pluralistic philosophical beliefs were incorrect and that monism was, after all, the truer philosophical perspective. This conviction was fueled by the mystical insight he received while in the altered state of awareness catalyzed by nitrous oxide, an insight which led James afterwards to several startling conclusions. For instance, he notes:

> "that every opposition . . . vanishes in a higher unity in which it is based; that all contradictions, so called, are but differences; that all differences are of degree; that all degrees are of a common kind; that unbroken continuity is of the essence of being; and that we are literally in the midst of an infinite, to perceive the existence of which is the utmost we can attain.[36]

James goes on to emphasize the ineffable nature of this experience. As he points out:

> It is impossible to convey an idea of the torrential character of the identification of opposites as it streams through the mind in this experience. I have sheet after sheet of phrases dictated or written during the intoxication, which to the sober reader seem meaningless drivel, but which at the moment of transcribing were fused in the fire of infinite rationality. God and devil, good and evil, life and death, I and thou, sober and drunk, matter and form, black and white, quantity and quality, shiver of ecstasy and shudder of horror . . . and fifty other contrasts figure in these pages in the same monotonous way.[37]

Depending upon one's aesthetic sensibilities, it is possible to conclude that James was perhaps overly harsh in his judgment of what he wrote while intoxicated. The following are a few samples of what he wrote or dictated in his "perfect delirium of theoretic rapture":

> Agreement—disagreement!!
> Emotion—motion!
> Die away from, *from*, die away (without the *from*).
> Reconciliation of opposites; sober, drunk, all the same!
> Good and evil reconciled in a laugh!
> It escapes, it escapes!
> But —
> What escapes, WHAT escapes?
> Emphasis, EMphasis; there must be some emphasis in order
>   for there to be a phasis.
> No verbiage can give it, because the verbiage is *other*.

27

Incoherent, coherent—same.
And it fades! And it's infinite! AND it's infinite!
If it wasn't going, why should you hold on to it?
Don't you see the difference, don't you see the identity?
Constantly opposites united![38]

James's enthusiasm for this monistic insight was, however, soon radically transformed. He mentions that as his experience progressed a startling change occurred:

> the flood of ontological emotion . . . [changed from] the rapture of behold-
> ing a process that was infinite . . . into the sense of a dreadful and ineluc-
> table fate, with whose magnitude every finite effort is incommensurable
> and in the light of which whatever happens is indifferent. This instanta-
> neous revulsion of mood from rapture to horror is, perhaps, the strongest
> emotion I have ever experienced.[39]

These violent mood swings happened repeatedly for James; he finally concludes that "a pessimistic fatalism, depth within depth of impotence and indifference" was the final outcome of this "revelation," and that "*indifferentism* is the true result of every view of the world which makes infinity and continuity to be its essence."[40]

This account of James's experiment with nitrous oxide gives us a glimpse of the strengths of James's character. We see here not only James's courageous receptivity to the unknown and the unconventional (as well as his openness to ideas that could reverse years of personal philosophical work), but also his willingness to share this unorthodox experience with his academic colleagues. Further, James's comments on his nitrous oxide experience are also an immensely fertile source of insights into the roots of James's later, more developed philosophical stance on mysticism. To begin with, this account is a clear demonstration of his methodology: phenomenological reporting first, followed by an intellectual and ethical assessment. We can also see evidence here of James's later stress on the emotional aspects of mystical experience, as well as the characteristics of ineffability, noetic quality, transience, and inner unity that James repeatedly associates with mystical experience in his later philosophy of mysticism. Finally, this account also illustrates the ways in which James's repeated emphasis on the theme of reconciliation in his philosophical work—both the reconciliation between the self and God that is stressed in the *Varieties* as well as the reconciliation between mind and matter that was attempted in his later radical

28

empiricism—is intimately connected with his understanding of mystical experience.

In the *Varieties*, James's fascination with the reconciling aspects of mysticism are emphasized, and his earlier (*The Will to Believe*) reluctance to embrace the monistic insights of his experience has been somewhat muted. He asserts in the *Varieties* that his own experiences "all converge towards a kind of insight to which I cannot help ascribing some metaphysical significance. The keynote of it is invariably a reconciliation. It is as if the opposites of the world, whose contradictoriness and conflict make all our difficulties and troubles, were melted into unity."[41] James recognizes that a belief in the reconciliation of opposites is perhaps logically troubling to some (himself included), but he also maintains that this reconciliation is a reality that is insistent and self-evident, at least for those who have personally experienced this "anaesthetic revelation."[42]

A Pluralistic Mystic

Few people in James's life were more insistent about the importance and self-authenticating quality of the mystical insights received while using anaesthetics than his long-time friend and confidant, Benjamin Paul Blood. Before continuing up the mystical ladder, it is important to spend some time reviewing James's relationship with Blood. As was mentioned above, Blood had first attracted James's notice in 1874 with the publication of his pamphlet, "The Anaesthetic Revelation and the Gist of Philosophy." Many years later, James wrote: "I forgot how it fell into my hands, but it fascinated me so 'weirdly' that I am conscious of its having been one of the stepping-stones of my thinking ever since."[43] Blood and James began an active correspondence with each other in 1887 and continued to exchange letters regularly with each other until James's death in 1910.

Blood lived in Amsterdam, New York, and was, as James put it, a "character"—a small-town landowner (apparently a town favorite) with the time and inclination to dabble in metaphysics, who was, nonetheless (to James's delight), also quite physically developed; in one of his first letters to James, Blood included a picture of himself from his early days when, as he put it in the letter: "I had lifted by a chain on my right shoulder and around my right arm, 1160 lbs."[44] Blood was a prolific writer, yet he rarely attempted to publish any of his ideas in the standard academic forums of that time, preferring, instead, to publish most of his ideas in letters in small local newspapers. This seemingly self-imposed philosophical humility was perhaps not simply a demonstration of Blood's lack of desire for public acknowledgment, but rather may reflect Blood's unwillingness to engage in the stylistic requirements of most conventional philosophical journals. Blood was temperamentally far more suited to compose grandiloquent assertions on the nature of reality than he was to construct a logically supported, cohesive philosophical argument. As James himself told Blood: "For single far-flung and far-flashing words and sentences you're the biggest genius I know; but when it comes to constructing a whole argument or article it seems to be another kettle of fish."[45]

Despite James's friendly criticism of Blood's purple prose, he continued to be intrigued with Blood's mystical insights. In "A Pluralistic Mystic," the last work James saw published before his death, he attempts both to make Blood's thought accessible to a larger philosophical audience and to utilize the authority of Blood's own mystical experiences to support his own philosophical pluralism. James admits that he is impressed by the monistic utterances of many mystics:

> The practically unanimous tradition of 'regular' mysticism has been unquestionably monistic; and inasmuch as it is the characteristic of mystics to speak, not as the scribes, but as men who have 'been there' and seen with their own eyes, I think that this sovereign manner must have made some other pluralistic-minded students hesitate, as I confess that it has often given pause to me. One cannot criticize the vision of a mystic—one can but pass it by, or else accept it as having some amount of evidential weight.[46]

James could not ignore mysticism, but he also would not accept its authority to determine the truth about the nature of reality. Even as late as "A Pluralistic Mystic" James continued to be ambivalent about mystical experience. Although he perceived it as having a number of appealing characteristics (for example, it was empirical; it often had quite valuable social and personal consequences; and it appeared, in one form or another, in almost every culture), he also perceived some less positive aspects of mystical experience (for example, its inaccessibility to public scrutiny, its resistance to philosophical assessment, and its tendency to undergird a dogmatic belief system). To make matters even worse, he realized that mystical experience usually affirmed a monistic understanding of reality, an affirmation that Blood's initial writings did nothing to disconfirm.

James was at first dismayed by the monistic tone of Blood's writing, but he later discovered, much to his pleasure, that Blood's earlier monistic musings were in time superseded by a more defiant, and pluralistically tinged, message. In "A Pluralistic Mystic," James announces with no little satisfaction: "I confess that the existence of this novel brand of mysticism has made my cowering mood depart. I feel now as if my own pluralism were not without the kind of support which mystical corroboration may confer. Monism can no longer claim to be the only beneficiary of whatever right mysticism may possess to lend *prestige*."[47] James recognizes, however, that it is difficult, if not impossible, to disentangle the monistic and pluralistic strands of Blood's thought. He confesses that he is unable to determine whether Blood's overtly pluralistic statements indicate that he has been converted from his previous monism, or whether Blood is simply being inconsistent, or even whether this back and forth movement from monism to pluralism is only a type of "dialectical circling"; nevertheless, James sticks with a pluralistic interpretation of Blood's basic intention and announces: "[Blood's] philosophy, however mystical, is in the last resort not dissimilar from my own."[48]

After apologizing for his editorial freedom, James then spends several pages presenting, in his typical cut-and-paste fashion, assorted bits of Hegelian elements that he sees in Blood's thought. James emphasizes that these seemingly monistic components of Blood's thought are far from original, noting that in fact they echo the monism of the rationalist neo-Hegelians, such as Josiah Royce and F. H. Bradley. Then James goes on, with obvious relish, to quote from Blood's more pluralistic utterances:

> Reason is neither the first nor the last word in this world. Reason is an equation; it gives but a pound for a pound. Nature is excess; she is evermore, without cost or explanation. . . . Go back into reason, and you come at last to fact, nothing more—a given-ness, a something to wonder at and yet admit, like your own will. And all these tricks for logicizing originality, self-relation, absolute process, subjective contradiction, will wither in the breath of the mystical fact. . . . The monistic notion of oneness, a centred wholeness, ultimate purpose, or climateric result of the world, has wholly given way. Thought evolves no longer a centred whole, a One, but rather a numberless many, adjust it how we will. . . . The pluralists have talked philosophy to a standstill—Nature is contingent, excessive and mystical essentially.[49]

Having by this time experienced for himself the mystical insights that can arise during an anaesthetic trance, James accepts Blood's post-trance proclamations as those of a seasoned mystic. Blood himself also has no doubts about his own mystical status. He writes that after twenty-seven years of anaesthetic experiences: "I [am] now not only firm and familiar in this once weird condition, but triumphant—divine. . . . I know, as having known, the meaning of Existence: the sane centre of the universe—at once the wonder and the assurance of the soul."[50]

By establishing his friend as an authentic mystic, James is then able to draw upon Blood's mystical "authority" by linking Blood's perspective with his own. James emphasizes that both he and Blood agree that facts and experiences have priority over rationalistic, abstract conceptual systems. He enthusiastically endorses Blood's stress on the intellect's inability to claim philosophical primacy. Blood speaks for James when he says: "*We do not know*. But when we say we do not know, we are not to say it weakly and meekly, but with confidence and content. . . . Knowledge is and must ever be *secondary*—a witness rather than a principal—or a 'principle'!—in the case."[51]

This emphasis on the centrality of experience (and the corresponding denigration of monistic rationalism) does not indicate an anti-rationalism in either thinker's philosophy, but rather, demonstrates that both James and Blood believe that reason should rest on experiential foundations. James demonstrates his alignment with Blood's mystically inspired pronouncements on the priority of experience by quoting from a letter Blood wrote to James announcing (in Blood's inimitable prose) the death of rationalistic philosophy:

> It was the long endeavour to logicize what we can only realize practically or in immediate experience. I am more and more impressed that Heraclitus insists on the equation of reason and unreason, or chance, as well as of being and not-being, etc. This throws the secret beyond logic, and makes mysticism outclass philosophy. The insight that mystery - the MYSTERY—as such is final, is the hymnic word. If you use reason pragmatically, and deny it absolutely, you can't be beaten—be assured of that. But the Fact remains, and of course the Mystery.[52]

James appears uncomfortable with the monistic implications of Blood's "Fact," and hurries to give this "Fact" a pluralistic interpretation. James stresses that this "Fact" is not a static Oneness, but rather, is a dynamic process, and that for both thinkers, there is "no more one all-enveloping fact than there is one all-enveloping spire in an endlessly growing spiral, and no more one all-generating fact than there is one central point in which an endlessly converging spiral ends."[53]

At first blush it seems as if perhaps James's pluralistic interpretation is overly strained. But a further exposure to Blood's thought demonstrates that James was essentially correct. Blood, like James, did not believe that the universe is essentially static and uniform, but rather, conceived of the universe as an embodiment of dynamic change and believed that the purpose of this ceaseless ebb and flow of life (if there is any such purpose) transcended each and every rational formulation.

It is evident that James is thrilled to finally discover a mystical writer who emphasizes the processual, non-preordained nature of life, because now the "mystical 'security,' the 'apodal sufficiency' yielded by the anaesthetic revelation" can be seen as providing an ethical foundation that is "more active, prouder, more heroic" than that given by the intellectual, logically based claims of rationalism.[54] James's attraction to Blood's understanding that the divine is ultimately beyond the grasp of philosophical rationalism's attempts to ground the universe in a mystical and/or monistic certainty and security is amplified by James's delighted realization that he is able to link his own pluralistic philosophy with the "prestige" of someone who has "been there," someone who has, as Blood puts it, "realized the highest divine thought of itself."[55] In this way, James aligns his philosophical perspective with the mystical insights of someone who (as Blood puts it) has directly experienced that "there is in [the universe] as much of wonder as of certainty; inevitable, and solitary and safe in one sense, but queer and cactus-like no less in another sense, it appeals unutterably to experience alone."[56] James's enthusiasm is almost palpable when he quotes Blood as saying:

> Certainty is the root of despair. The inevitable stales, while doubt and hope are sisters. Not unfortunately the universe is wild—game flavored as a hawk's wing. Nature is miracle all. She knows no laws; the same returns not, save to bring the different. The slow round of the engraver's lathe gains but the breadth of a hair, but the difference is distributed back over the whole curve, never an instant true—ever not quite.[57]

James exults that "Ever not quite!" (a saying that he repeated again and again in his writings) could be a herald for the pluralistic philosophical perspective. It destroys the sedate security of the rationalists, and as James stresses, underscores pluralism's emphasis on chance and uniqueness:

> There is no complete generalization, no total point of view, no all-pervasive unity, but everywhere some residual resistance to verbalization, formulation, and discursification, some genius of reality that escapes from the pressure of the logical finger, that says 'hands off,' and claims its

33

privacy, and means to be left to its own life. In every moment of immediate experience is some[thing] absolutely original and novel. . . . Philosophy must pass from words, that reproduce but ancient elements, to life itself, that gives the integrally new. The 'inexplicable,' the 'mystery' . . . remains; but it remains as something to be met and dealt with by faculties more akin to our activities and heroisms and willingnesses, than to our logical powers.[58]

James and Blood were not, however, completely aligned on every issue. Unlike Blood, James believed that mystical experience was not self-sufficient and supreme; it was merely one of numerous "contenders" in a world of various and often contradictory concrete experiences, each jostling with the others for the right to determine what the world is truly like. As will become further apparent in chapters 4 and 5, James emphasized that the insights gained in a mystical experience, no matter how convincing, were not to be automatically trusted; this information, like that gained from any other experience, had to be weighed and sifted and compared with information from other, nonmystical experiences. Ralph Barton Perry, a student and biographer of James, points out that, for James, mystical experience was justified by normal acts of perception; if "logic was rejected it was because such a rejection seemed to be warranted by the observable data of everyday immediacy."[59] Blood, on the other hand, reversed James's insistence that mystical experiences be justified by the experiences of everyday life; Perry suggests that, for Blood, "the mystical experience was the one trustworthy insight—leaving no doubts, and superseding both philosophy and normal experience."[60]

Back on the Ladder of Mystical Experience

James was refreshingly candid concerning his doubts about mystical experience. For instance, early in the *Varieties*, James mentions: "There are moments of sentimental and mystical experience . that carry an enormous sense of inner authority and illumination with them when they come. But they come seldom and they do not come to every one; and the rest of life makes either no connection with them, or tends to contradict them more than it confirms them."[61] James's ambivalence about mystical experience also appears, if somewhat indirectly, at the tail-end of his discussion of mystical experiences that occur during anaesthetic trances. After his descriptions of his own experiences with nitrous oxide, James once again describes an experience narrated by J. A. Symonds, the same person who had the invasive trance which James includes on a lower rung of the mystical ladder. Symonds, while under the influence of chloroform, had an experience of God, not as a theological concept, but as an ecstatic "intense personal present reality . . . streaming in like light"[62] upon him. Unfortunately, however, this ecstatic awareness was short-lived, and when Symonds emerged out of this drug-induced trance, he leapt off the table, screaming, "it is too horrible, it is too horrible, it is too horrible"—not because of anything he had experienced while anaesthetized, but rather, because, as he puts it: "I could not bear this disillusionment. . . . To have felt for that long dateless ecstasy of vision the very God, in all purity and tenderness and truth and absolute love, and then to find that I had after all had no revelation, but that I had been tricked by the abnormal excitement of my brain."[63] In a sense, Symonds's reaction acts as a mask for James's own doubts, as do Symonds's later intellectual oscillations, in which his immediate disillusionment was somewhat tempered, leading him to wonder whether it really was so evident that his experience was delusive— whether it indeed might have been "possible that [he], in that moment, felt what some of the saints have said they always felt, the undemonstrable but irrefragable certainty of God."[64]

After relating Symonds's experience, James moves on to the final rung of his mystical ladder, which is devoted to "religious mysticism pure and simple."[65] James points out that many of these profound mystical experiences appear to have been inspired by the beauty of natural settings, a correspondence to which James, with his love of nature and his own "Walpurgis Nacht" experience, is especially receptive. James quotes from several literary figures and philosophers to help illustrate the role of nature in mystical experiences. For instance, below is one excerpt from the journal of the Swiss writer and philosopher Henri Frederic Amiel:

> One day, in youth, at sunrise, sitting in the ruins of the castle of Faucigny; and again in the mountains, under the noon day sun, above Lavey, lying at the foot of a tree and visited by three butterflies; once more at night upon the shingly shore of the Northern Ocean, my back upon the sand and my vision ranging through the milky way;—such grand and spacious, immortal, cosmogonic reveries, when one reaches to the stars, when one owns the infinite! Moments divine, ecstatic hours . . . instants of irresistible intuition in which one feels one's self great as the universe, and calm as a god.[66]

Exploring Unseen Worlds

James's decision to place Ameil's narrative (along with his other examples of "nature mysticism") on the rung of "religious mysticism" is both puzzling and enlightening. It is puzzling, since, as R. C. Zaehner would (much later) forcefully emphasize in his provocative text *Mysticism: Sacred and Profane*, most descriptions of experiences of "nature mysticism" have very little overt "religious" language associated with them.[67] However, it is also enlightening, since it clearly demonstrates the casual manner in which James is constructing this "mystical ladder." Although we might wish otherwise, it appears that his task at this point is neither to identify and categorize definitively the varieties of mystical experience, nor to give any conclusive and clearly articulated justifications for the placement of these experiences on the different rungs of the mystical ladder. Where particular experiences should go on the ladder and why they should be placed at one particular rung and not another were questions that seemingly were not that important to James. What he *does* do is to demonstrate, in a loose-limbed fashion, the overall spectrum of mystical experiences. In the construction of his ladder, James remains faithful to his aversion to overabstraction and hypersystematization, and prefers to let the experiences, in a sense, speak for themselves. Their specific placement on one rung or another is certainly of secondary importance, and seems to rely primarily on James's own intuitive sense of which experiences seem more clearly mystical than others, rather than on a precisely formulated rationale.

James concludes his discussion of spontaneous religious mystical experiences and, perhaps, the ladder of mysticism as well with the mystical experience of Dr. R. M. Bucke.[68] This experience of what Bucke terms "cosmic consciousness" occurred while Bucke was riding home in a hansom after an evening of philosophical discussion with friends. With his mind at peace, Bucke suddenly, without warning, found himself "wrapped in a flame-colored cloud."[69] At first, Bucke thought that the world around him was on fire, but he then realized that the fire was actually burning inside of himself. He then felt a powerful "sense of exultation, of immense joyousness accompanied or immediately followed by an intellectual illumination impossible to describe," in which he directly perceived that "the universe is not composed of dead matter, but is, on the contrary, a living Presence."[70] As part of his illumination, Bucke also became assured that he had "eternal life"—then and always, and "that the cosmic order is such that without any peradventure all things work together for the good of each and all; that the foundation principle of the world, of all the worlds, is what we call love, and that the happiness of each and all

36

is in the long run absolutely certain."[71] Bucke's vision lasted only a few seconds, but left him with an absolute conviction of its truth and instilled in him a permanent and abiding faith in that truth—a faith that, according to him, was never lost, even in moments of deep depression.

The Reality of the Unseen

Dr. R. M. Bucke's experience (a favorite with later philosophers of mysticism) is incredibly rich. Not only is it a wonderful demonstration of each of James's four marks of a mystical experience (it is difficult, if not impossible, for Bucke to adequately describe; it contains a wealth of noetic content; it lasted "only a few seconds"; and it descended upon him with very little overt preparation), but it also exemplified James's repeated argument that religious beliefs are created and sustained by powerfully transformative experiences. As James put it in his essay, "The Pragmatic Method," which was composed several years before the *Varieties:*

> What keeps religion going is something else than abstract definitions and systems of logically concatenated adjectives, and something different from faculties of theology and their professors. All these things are after-effects, secondary accretions upon a mass of concrete religious experiences, connecting themselves with feeling and conduct, that renew themselves *in saecula saeculorum* in the lives of humble private men. If you ask what these experiences are, they are conversations with the unseen, voices and visions, responses to prayer, changes of heart, deliverances from fear, inflowings of help, assurances of support, whenever certain persons set their own internal attitude in certain appropriate ways. The power comes and goes and is lost, and can be found only in a certain definite direction, just as if it were a concrete material thing. These direct experiences of a wider spiritual life with which our superficial consciousness is continuous, and with which it keeps up an intense commerce, form the primary mass of direct religious experience on which all hearsay religion rests, and which furnishes that notion of an ever-present God out of which systematic theology thereupon proceeds to make capital in its own unreal pedantic way. What the word 'God' means is just those passive and active experiences of your life. . . . Like all other human experiences, they too certainly share in the general liability to illusion and mistake. They need not be infallible. But they are certainly the originals of the God-idea, and theology is the translation.[72]

In the above compressed, succinctly worded early summation of James's belief in the experiential foundation of religion, it becomes clear that many of the religious experiences that James lists are examples of religious mysticism: they are powerful, transforming, personally interpreted experiences of an unseen, yet very real, spiritual world. This spiritual world is not understood by James to be *ganzander;* it is not a completely separate reality divorced from our everyday world. Instead, this unseen world is intimately connected with who we are, it is present in the deepest levels of our selfhood, and can never be known except in and through our psyche. But this often unacknowledged interface of the spiritual world with our psyche does not imply that this unseen world is therefore simply a creation of our mind. For James, this "deeper world" is as much discovered as it is created. Like the material world, it has a directionality; it can be found in particular "places" when we orient ourselves to its "magnetic" influence. Yet unlike the material world, the spiritual world appears to be both conscious and benevolent; it makes itself known as an influx of powerful, beneficent energy. In a sense, the spiritual world is the raw material of divinity, which manifests itself within an almost infinite number of forms: the fallible, mutable vessels of our different psyches. As such, "God," for James, can only appear to us in and through our consciousness; but this does not mean that "God" is *confined* to these experiences. James affirms that "God" can certainly, in theory, be understood to exist beyond the experience of each individual ego (in much the same way that James believes that the material world is there, in some form, prior to our cognition of it). But just as James believes that data from the senses, while inevitably interpreted differently by each person's selective interests and background, gives us a basically trustworthy picture of the material world, in the same way, he thinks that these experiences of the spiritual world, molded and shaped as they are by each individual's expectations, interests, and cultural patterning, are also a reliable bedrock upon which any further theological conceptual elaborations should be based.

James is clearly convinced that personal religious experiences are the root of most major world religions. He asserts that Christ, the Buddha, Muhammed, as well as the charismatic originators of less influential sects (i.e., George Fox for the Quakers, Joseph Smith for the Mormons, and so on) "owed their power originally to the fact of their direct personal communion with the divine."[73] James also insists that if we are going to understand what the essence of religion is, what makes it a different phenomena, for instance, from morality, then "we must search for original experiences which were the pattern setters to all this mass of suggested feeling and imitated conduct"; furthermore, he goes on to say that we must focus our attention on those experiences, which "we can only find in individuals for whom religion exists not as a dull habit, but as an acute fever," individuals who are the "geniuses" of each religion.[74] These "geniuses" (who do not have to be well-known) are what keep each religion alive; it is their religious mysticism that keeps religions from becoming merely another corrupt social institution or abstract theological system.[75] It is their religious mysticism, their powerfully felt, transforming, personally interpreted experiences of an unseen spiritual reality that can rejuvenate a religion, that can instill within different individuals the strong, unshakable faith in the reality and goodness of that unseen world.

In the chapter of the *Varieties* entitled "The Reality of the Unseen," James emphasizes the crucial role mystical experiences play in creating a strong faith in the existence of this unseen spiritual world. Time after time, James offers accounts of individuals whose faith has been transformed by an unexpected contact with this spiritual level of reality. One particularly profound experience that James includes is the following narrative of a clergyman:

> I remember the night, and almost the very spot on the hilltop, where my soul opened out, as it were, into the Infinite, and there was a rushing together of the two worlds, the inner and the outer. . . . I stood alone with Him who had made me, and all the beauty of the world, and love, and sorrow, and even temptation. I did not seek Him, but felt the perfect unison of my spirit with His. The ordinary sense of things around me faded. For the moment nothing but an ineffable joy and exaltation remained. It is impossible fully to describe the experience. It was like the effect of some great orchestra when all the separate notes have melted into one swelling harmony that leaves the listener conscious of nothing save that his soul is being wafted upwards, and almost bursting with its own emotion. The darkness held a presence that was all the more felt because it was not seen. I could not any more have doubted that *He* was there than that I was. Indeed, I felt myself to be, if possible, the less real of the two. . . . My highest faith in God and truest idea of him were then born in me. . . . Then, if ever, I believe, I stood face to face with God, and was born anew of his spirit. There was, as I recall it, no sudden change of thought or of belief, except that my early crude conception had, as it were, burst into flower. There was no destruction of the old, but a rapid, wonderful unfolding. . . . My most assuring evidence of his existence is deeply rooted in that hour of vision.[76]

James also quotes a Swiss individual who describes a similar experience of a direct and overwhelmingly convincing apprehension of God's presence while hiking:

> All at once I experienced a feeling of being raised above myself, I felt the presence of God . . . as if his goodness and his power were penetrating me altogether. The throb of emotion was so violent that I could barely tell the boys to pass on and not wait for me. I then sat down on a stone, unable to stand any longer, and my eyes overflowed with tears. . . . The state of ecstasy may have lasted four or five minutes, although it seemed at the time to last much longer. . . . The impression had been so profound that in climbing slowly the slope I asked myself if it were possible that Moses on Sinai could have had a more intimate communication with God. I think it well to add that in this ecstasy of mine God had neither form, color, odor, nor taste; moreover that the feeling of his presence was accompanied with no determinate localization. It was rather as if my personality had been transformed by the presence of a spiritual spirit. But the more I seek words to express this intimate intercourse, the more I feel the impossibility of describing the thing by any of our usual images. At bottom the expression most apt to render what I felt is this: God was present, though invisible; he fell under no one of my senses, yet my consciousness perceived him.[77]

These experiences (which James in a footnote also indirectly included in his ladder of mysticism as examples of "religious mysticism") illustrate James's contention that some human beings apparently have the ability, as it were, to perceive or feel the objective, yet amorphous presence of "something" not perceptible or felt by any of the other more specialized senses. According to James, this "reality-feeling," as inarticulate and vague as it often is for those who experience it, imbues religious beliefs with an impregnable certitude and allows these beliefs to withstand any and all logical criticisms. As James puts it:

> We may now lay it down as certain that in the distinctively religious sphere of experience, many persons (how many we cannot tell) possess the objects of their belief, not in the form of mere conceptions which their intellect accepts as true, but rather in the form of quasi-sensible realities directly apprehended. As his sense of the real presence of these objects fluctuates, so the believer alternates between warmth and coldness in his faith.[78]

An Hallucinatory Interlude

In essence, for James, mysticism is simply a vivid sense of the reality of the unseen.[79] This "sense" gives an individual a particular "cluster" of information, but this information, which itself varies, can also be interpreted differently by different individuals, and not necessarily always in a religious manner. Hallucinations, for instance, as James mentions in the *Varieties*, are not always religious, yet they provide some of the best illustrations of the sense of the reality of the unseen, since during an hallucinatory experience many people "will feel a 'presence' in the room, definitely localized, facing in one particular way, real in the most emphatic sense of the word . . . and yet neither seen, heard, touched, nor cognized in any of the usual 'sensible' ways."[80]

James's brief mention of hallucinations in the *Varieties* is the end result of earlier extensive theorizing, most of which appears in *The Principles of Psychology* in the chapter, "The Perception of Things." In this chapter, James presents a detailed discussion of the possible physiological causes of hallucinations, as well as their philosophical implications. The physiological hypotheses are extremely complex, but a highly simplified (yet basically faithful) summarization of these hypotheses could be phrased in the following way: James believed (at least at this point in his career) that hallucinations, contrary to the way in which they are ordinarily understood, have an objective sensory stimulus. In this way, hallucinations are closer to illusions (which are false interpretations of sensory images) than to delusions (which do not necessarily involve sensory images—for example, people can be deluded about their religious beliefs, their own importance, and so on). James claims that hallucinations are not just mental images that lack objective sensory stimuli, but rather, they are states of consciousness in which the cerebral activity of the brain is wildly disproportionate to the incidental sensory stimulus that initially prompted the hallucination. As James puts it: "*An hallucination is a strictly sensational form of consciousness, as good and true a sensation as if there were a real object there.* The object happens not to be there, that is all."[81]

To help illustrate this contrary-to-common-sense hypothesis, James uses the analogy of an empty bucket with a hole in the bottom. In the analogy, the bucket is described as leaning against a support in such a way that it tips over if it is ever filled with a greater amount of water than the hole can release. This bucket, which represents an individual's quiescent state of consciousness, has two separate streams of water flowing through it. One stream, which is the raw material of our concepts, is typically such a slow trickle of water that it easily flows through the hole in the bottom of the bucket, thereby producing the conceptual activity that we experience. However, the other stream of water, the raw material of our sensations, is much more copious, and ends up filling and overturning the bucket, regardless of the hole in the bottom, thereby producing our experience of sensations. What happens in hallucinations, according to this hypothesis, is that if the hole in the bucket is plugged by drugs, fainting, falling asleep, and so on, then the flow of "water" from the conceptual source (along with a severely reduced stream from the sensory source) can eventually fill the bucket and upset it, producing an experience of sensations similar to that produced from the sensory source alone. In other words, hallucinations seem to be as real as more ordinary sense experiences, because sense experiences and hallucinatory experiences ultimately arise from the same sensory source, even though the way in which hallucinations are produced is different from ordinary sense experiences.

James emphasizes that there are several distinct categories of hallucinatory experiences. For instance, in the *Principles*, James makes a point of phenomenologically distinguishing hallucinations from what he calls "pseudo-hallucinations." True hallucinations are those hallucinations which the individual interprets as giving accurate information about reality, whereas "pseudo-hallucinations," although just as vivid as true hallucinations, are recognized, even by the individual who experiences them, to be illusory. To help illustrate this distinction, James gives an example of a mentally disturbed individual who at one point saw and felt a (nonexistent) lion putting its paws on his shoulders. James tells us that this man felt no fear, because he knew the lion was not really there, and recognized that the hallucination of the lion was a purely mental phenomenon. Using James's terminology, this aspect of the man's experience was pseudo-hallucinatory. However, at the same moment that this man saw and felt the lion, he also heard a loud voice from his imagined "persecutors" speaking from a hole in the wall telling him to change his nationality. The man was convinced that this voice, unlike the lion, was objectively real, and he therefore resolved to switch his Russian nationality and become a citizen of England. This aspect of the man's experience is, from James's perspective, a *true* hallucination.

Unlike our ordinary experiences of memory or fantasy, the vision of the lion was consistent, highly detailed, vivid, and almost impossible to create by an act of will; however, even though it was, in this sense, hallucinatory, the vision of the lion was only a pseudo-hallucination, since unlike the voice, it lacked the essential characteristic of a real hallucination: the strong conviction by the "subject" of this alteration of consciousness that the vision was objectively real. The voice was also hallucinatory, in that it had all the qualities that distinguish it from memory or fantasy, but the mentally ill man interpreted (and thus experienced) it very differently from the vision of the lion; for him, this voice was real. Because of this conviction of the reality of the voice, the man was willing to act on the information he had received, whereas the vision of the lion was ignored.

Psychical Research

James was unwilling to dismiss hallucinations as "unreal" not only because his understanding of "reality" was extremely fluid, but also because he was impressed by the numerous accounts of various "psychical" experiences that he obtained during his decades of work with the Society for Psychical Research. In the section on hallucinations in the *Principles,* James gives many examples from the "Census of Hallucinations," a research survey that James participated in as part of his work for the American branch of the society. In one case that James mentions in the *Principles,* a man describes how he was sitting at his desk doing math problems. His pregnant wife was fifty miles away. The man felt a touch on his left shoulder, turned his head, saw his wife, and heard her say, "It is a little Herman; he has come."[82] The man got up, pinched himself to make sure he was not dreaming, and the figure disappeared as he walked towards it. The man did not tell anyone of this peculiar event. The next morning, having a feeling that he should go to the telegraph office (and yet resisting that intuition), he (eventually) decided to investigate, and at the telegraph office he found waiting for him a telegram telling him that he had that night become a father of a nine pound boy.

James was not naive; he was aware that accounts like the one above could be fraudulent, but as he collected more and more similar accounts, he became increasingly open to the possibility that these experiences, like experiences of religious mysticism, could in fact be reliable indicators of the existence of an unseen spiritual world.

James's interest in psychical research was not peripheral to his better known philosophical concerns. As Robert A. McDermott says in his valuable introduction to the *Essays in Psychical Research:*

For James psychical research was central in that it put to the test religious and scientific claims which were at the core of his philosophy and typical in its sympathetic curiosity concerning the varieties of experience. Despite its being at once the most controverted and neglected area of his thought, it is also one that presents James's philosophical method and goals in sharp outline and detail. Fidelity to fact, avoidance of abstract categories, patient attention to ultimate questions, and preference for complexities over the dogmatism of either the skeptic or the believer are all evident in James's work of nearly three decades as a psychical researcher.[83]

James's philosophy as a whole did not directly arise out of his interest in psychical research (or from his interest in mysticism). However, these interests are in many ways similar (or at least complementary) to James's wider philosophical project. As McDermott makes clear, philosophy and psychical research were *complementary* for James in that "philosophy, as the older and more developed enterprise, needs enthusiasm for the novel and marginal, whereas psychical research, which is more on the cutting edge, needs the intellectual scope and patience of philosophy."[84] McDermott adds that James's philosophy and his psychical research were *similar* in that they both "sought to show, by argument and example, that religious experience could be illuminated by a sympathetic science, and that science could be rendered a more powerful servant of truth by recognizing the reality of religious experience."[85]

Despite James's often vocal distrust of the excesses of science, his interest in psychical research was in actuality (as McDermott and many other Jamesian scholars have repeatedly pointed out) an attempt to integrate harmoniously the most important aspects of both science and religion, while simultaneously overcoming their respective weaknesses. James was an ardent supporter of most aspects of the scientific method, and attempted, as much as possible, to investigate psychical phenomena using scientific methodology. He did not want to be seen as someone who naively believed in all of the claims about psychical phenomena that were being made at that time by a thriving "spiritualist" subculture, and he hoped that this critical approach would help to establish the credibility of his conclusions within the academic world. James was extremely aware of the ever-present possibility of fraud, and was often dismayed by the crudity and contradictions inherent in the phenomena he encountered in his psychical research. At the same time, as Ralph Barton Perry points out, James was convinced that just as the new science of psychopathology had offered scholars and clinicians new theoretical ways to understand sympathetically "phenomena such as hypnotism, hysteria, and multiple personality . . . he saw no reason why the phenomena that were still outlawed should not undergo a like change."[86] According to McDermott, James was dismayed by the reluctance of scientists of his time to investigate psychical phenomena, and argued strongly that science could and should include within its purview "the study of phenomena that are random, nonrepeatable, and dependent on unusual personal capacities and dispositions."[87] James spent much of his life attempting to convince the scientific establishment that these types of psychical (and religious) events were valid "objects" of study, and that a critical examination of personal narratives (both in psychical research and in the study of religious experiences) was an appropriate methodological strategy, arguing that such events by their very nature could not be experimentally replicated in a controlled setting.

James's attempt to justify this stretching of the boundaries of acceptable scientific methodology was not based on a passion for methodological discussion, but rather, emerged out of James's deepest religious and philosophical convictions. In a sense, it could be said that James's writings on psychical research were designed to foster two complementary goals. First, if narratives of personal, nonreplicable, experiences of nonordinary reality could become acceptable material for scientific and philosophical investigation, then the results of psychical research, as well as data from mystical experiences, could be used as evidence for the reality of a spiritual level of existence. Second, if the reality of a spiritual level of existence could be seen as justified by empirical evidence, then this "supernatural" worldview could serve as a viable alternative to the philosophically unsophisticated materialism that was presumed by the majority of the scientists of James's time.

Probably the most clear-cut example of the rhetorical strategy James used to accomplish these two goals appears in a chapter in *The Will to Believe* entitled, "What Psychical Research Has Accomplished." This adroitly constructed essay begins by emphasizing the difficulties science has accommodating information that does not fit within the boundaries of its carefully constructed understanding of the nature of reality. James points out that exceptions to the norm disrupt the neatly packaged and taken-for-granted worldview of the reigning scientific paradigm, and that the scientific establishment responds to any philosophical irritations by either ignoring the anomalies or by aggressively denying their validity. As James further notes:

> No part of the unclassified residuum has usually been treated with a more contemptuous scientific disregard than the mass of phenomena generally

45

called *mystical*. . . . [i.e., such phenomena as] divinations, inspirations, demoniacal possessions, apparitions, trances, ecstasies, miraculous healings and productions of diseases, and occult powers possessed by peculiar individuals over persons and things.[88]

For James, the almost complete disregard of such a large body of information is scientifically reprehensible, especially since science avoids stagnation primarily by paying attention to anomalous phenomena. In James's opinion, if science continued to cling to a "certain fixed belief—the belief that the hidden order of nature is mechanical exclusively, and that non-mechanical categories are irrational ways of conceiving and explaining such things as human life,"[89] if it continued to proclaim that this "mechanical rationalism" is the only viable way of understanding the world, then Western culture would become severely impoverished. According to James, this "mechanical rationalism" denies the value of religion, ethics, poetry, and any other perspective that gives credence to the "personal and romantic view of life"; it negates our stubborn intuition that "oracles and omen, divinations, and apparitions, miraculous changes of heart and wonders worked by inspired persons, answers to prayer and providential leadings" can and do occur; and it refuses to accept that events in the external world can take place not just as a result of a blind clashing of molecules, but also as a consequence of the benevolent promptings of a powerful force or forces acting for our benefit.[90]

James is convinced that the scientific pronouncement against this "romantic" perspective is premature, since this more personalized worldview is based on concrete experiences (regardless of how these experiences are ultimately understood in light of further scientific and philosophical investigations). Unfortunately, as James concedes, these experiences are also "capricious, discontinuous, and not easily controlled; they require peculiar persons for their production; [and] their significance seems to be wholly for personal life,"[91] thereby making replicable scientific experimentation almost impossible. However, James stresses that if these experiences were acknowledged by the academic community to be valid sources of information about the nature of reality, then a romantic, nonmaterialistic perspective would no longer seem preposterous, but rather, might actually appear to be the preferable option.

It is not as far-fetched as it seems for James to have believed that science might ultimately acknowledge the existence of a nonmaterial reality, since, as he points out, science has never remained static. As a result of its constant self-transformation, the scientific understandings of the nature of reality that were held by previous eras always seem, from our present point of view, incredibly naive and limited. James realizes the implications of this ongoing scientific revision—that there was every likelihood that the scientific paradigm of his own era would also suffer the same fate. As James notes: "This rigorous belief [by science] that in its own essential and innermost nature our world is a strictly impersonal world, may, conceivably, as the whirligig of time goes round, prove to be the very defect that our descendants will be most surprised at in our own boasted science."[92]

James makes a similar point in the *Varieties*. In a discussion on the contrast between the scientific and religious understandings of the world, James, after once again emphasizing the mutable nature of what counts as a fact, stresses that scientists, by dogmatically refusing to recognize the "facts" described by mystics and mental healers, often leave out much that is worth investigating. James notes that "miraculous healings" used to be dismissed by scientists as "figments of the imagination," but that, because of information from the field of hypnotism, science "allows that such healings may indeed exist, provided that they are expressly designated as the effects of 'suggestion'."[93] James humorously wonders aloud, "how far this legitimation of occultist phenomena under newly found scientist titles may proceed—even 'prophecy,' even 'levitation,' might creep into the pale."[94] In his opinion, it is even possible that in the future the "personalism and romanticism" of the religious point of view may be adopted by science itself, in which case "the rigorously impersonal view of science might one day appear as having been a temporarily useful excentricity [sic] rather than the definitively triumphant position which the sectarian scientist at present so confidently announces it to be."[95]

However, just because James was opposed to the dogmatic materialism of science, it does not mean that he denounced every aspect of the scientific perspective. In "What Psychical Research Has Accomplished," James hastens to tell his audience that a balance between romanticism and "mechanical rationalism" is needed, unless we want (in one of James's more unfortunate and provincial statements) "Central African Mumbo-jumboism."[96] James attempts to harmonize the "scientific-academic mind" with the "feminine-mystical mind" (another unfortunate phrasing) by emphasizing that a person's subjective preferences will often determine which "facts" that person will notice.[97] But in many ways, James's *own* preference is clearly aligned with the academy. He finds the "mystical style of philosophizing" aesthetically unappealing and prefers to let the critical and analytical perspective have priority when it comes to investigating and theorizing about any "wild facts," since "to pass from mystical to scientific speculations is like passing from lunacy to sanity."[98] Yet, as James candidly observes, the mystics often do provide correct information (even if that data has to be reinterpreted through the theoretical framework of science); so, in James's mind, it is important to develop an overarching methodology that can balance the "academic" and the "mystical" elements in our philosophical or scientific investigations, a methodology that can enable us to "pay attention to facts of the sort dear to mystics, while reflecting upon them in academic-scientific ways."[99]

That this harmonious interaction of scientific inquiry and mystical facts is indeed possible is proved, in James's opinion, by the investigations of the Society for Psychical Research.[100] The task of the members of the Society (who, as James never failed to emphasize, were highly critical and skeptical men and women with impeccable academic credentials) was "to carry on systematic experimentation with hypnotic subjects, mediums, clairvoyants, and others; and, secondly, to collect evidence concerning apparitions, haunted houses, and similar phenomena" which occur randomly and cannot be subject to experimental control.[101] James personally found the minute, painstaking, and detailed work of the Society "insufferably tedious" and the evidence itself also incredibly dull, "contextless and discontinuous";[102] but at the same time, he was proud of the efforts of those in the Society, since he knew of no other in-depth attempt to assess the validity of these phenomena. Every other faction either blindly adhered to an unsupported belief in every aspect of psychical phenomena or else dogmatically denied even the possibility that psychical events could occur.

In the end, however, James confessed that he was disappointed in the results of the investigations of the Society. In "Confidences of a 'Psychical Researcher'," an essay published the year before his death, he confessed his dissatisfaction after twenty-five years of interest and involvement in psychical research. James writes: "I am theoretically no 'further' than I was at the beginning; and I confess that at times I have been tempted to believe that the creator has eternally intended this department of nature to remain *baffling*, to prompt our curiosities and hopes and suspicions all in equal measure."[103] However, James's frustration with the lack of any overwhelmingly conclusive evidence for the reality of psychical phenomena was not so severe that he could not also feel an equally powerful frustration with the unwillingness of scientists to acknowledge the information gathered by the Society. For instance, even as early as 1896, in his essay, "Psychical Research," James asserts:

The concrete evidence for most of the "psychic" phenomena under discussion is good enough to hang a man twenty times over. The scientist's
objections . . . are either shallow on their face (as where apparitions at the
time of death are disposed of as mere "folk-lore," or swept away as a
mass of fiction due to illusion of memory), or else they are proved to be
shallow by further investigation.[104]

So while James admitted in "Confidences of a 'Psychical Researcher' " that he was baffled and frustrated by the lack of conclusive
evidence for the existence of the supernatural, he also went on to
emphasize that, "weak sticks make strong faggots; and when the stories fall into consistent sorts that point each in a definite direction, one
gets a sense of being in presence of genuinely natural types of phenomena."[105] James was clearly, in the end, personally convinced that
psychical and mystical phenomena offered reliable evidence for the
existence of an "unseen" world.[106] He was also the first to admit that
unequivocal proof is difficult, if not impossible to come by. But he was
nonetheless willing to defend his own personal belief in the reality of
this unseen world, even if that belief, in the last analysis, was based
primarily on his "personal sense" of the "dramatic probabilities of
nature,"[107] that is, on his intuitive and usually unarticulated assumptions of what can actually take place in the universe (assumptions
that, in James's opinion, affect the process of all theoretical evaluations, even those of the most "objective" scientists).

In "What Psychical Research Has Accomplished," James discusses
the psychological factors that prompted his publicly acknowledged
belief in the "supernatural" world.[108] James frankly admits that if investigators of allegedly supernatural occurrences became convinced
through a painstaking investigation of evidence and/or through their
own experience that at least one type of supernatural phenomena
existed (as he did), then they might "begin to relax their vigilance as
to evidence, and throw the doors of their minds more or less wide
open to the supernatural along its whole extent."[109] He concedes that
just because belief in one type of supernatural event has been validated, this does not imply that every other supernatural occurrence
has also been confirmed; however, he goes on to insist that simply
because an individual comes to believe in the supernatural through a
less-than-ideal logical process, it does not necessarily follow that the
end result of this less-than-ideal logical process is incorrect (since a
supernatural world might indeed exist). James stresses that underneath this less-than-ideal process of reasoning lies a logically valid
inference. As James is quick to point out:

49

If you wish to upset the law that all crows are black, you must not seek to show that no crows are; it is enough if you prove one single crow to be white. My own white crow is Mrs. Piper. In the trances of this medium, I cannot resist the conviction that knowledge appears which she has never gained by the ordinary waking use of her eyes and ears and wits. What the source of this knowledge may be I know not, and have not the glimmer of an explanatory suggestion to make; but from admitting the fact of such knowledge I can see no escape. So when I turn to the rest of the evidence, ghosts and all, I cannot carry with me the irreversibly negative bias of the "rigorously scientific" mind, with its presumption as to what the true order of nature ought to be. I feel as if, though the evidence be flimsy in spots, it may nevertheless collectively carry heavy weight. The rigorously scientific mind may, in truth, easily overshoot the mark. Science means, first of all, a certain dispassionate method. To suppose that it means a certain set of results that one should pin one's faith upon and hug forever is sadly to mistake its genius, and degrades the scientific body to the status of a sect.[110]

If James has to choose between faithfulness to his own experience and faithfulness to the scientific worldview, the choice is clear:

The trances I speak of have broken down for my own mind the limits of the admitted order of nature. Science, so far as science denies such exceptional occurrences, lies prostrate in the dust for me; and the most urgent intellectual need which I feel at present is that science be built up again in a form in which such things may have a positive place. Science, like life, feeds on its own decay. New facts burst old rules; then newly divined conceptions bind old and new together into a reconciling law.[111]

There is a striking resemblance between, on the one hand, James's attempt to reconcile the new facts discovered by psychical research with the old laws of science, and, on the other hand, his attempt in *Pragmatism* to formulate a new understanding of the nature of "truth." In *Pragmatism*, "truth" is not seen as a static property inherent in an event or phenomena, but rather, is envisioned as a dynamic process in which a person (or group), in the face of new evidence, struggles to retain the maximum amount of old conceptions with a minimum amount of rearrangement. It is conceivable that this pragmatic conception of truth could be linked, at least in part, to James's own personal struggle with how to harmonize his previous scientific and materialistic worldview with those anomalous events which he (almost reluctantly) had to admit took place during spiritualist sessions with Mrs.

Lenora Piper, the trance medium he conscientiously studied for many years.

Meetings with a Remarkable Woman: Lenora Piper

James met Mrs. Lenora Piper (1859–1950), the woman whose pronouncements so forcibly rearranged his mental furniture, in the autumn of 1885. He was introduced to her by his wife, who, accompanied by her mother, had visited Mrs. Piper the previous summer. Prior to this meeting, in July of 1885, the Jameses had suffered the tragic death of their infant son Herman, and it is quite likely that James's interest in exploring the "supernatural" was heightened by this tragedy (as well as by the earlier death of his father in December 1882). However, it is also apparent that these personal tragedies were not the only stimuli for James's interest in psychical phenomena. Not only had James reviewed a book on spiritualism as early as 1869, his interest had already been kindled by his unorthodox upbringing. He was raised in a family that was exceedingly open to a wide variety of unconventional belief systems. It is probable that James's own fascination with mediums, mesmerism, ghostly visitations, clairvoyance, and other psychical phenomena were nourished by the open-minded environment in which he grew up—one in which his father, and his father's friends, supported women's rights and the abolition of slavery, explored the socialistic ideas of Charles Fourier, experimented with the alternative medical system of homeopathy, and were attracted to the visionary inspirations of Emanuel Swedenborg.

Alongside of this exposure to unconventional ideas, James as a young man was also attracted to more mainstream belief-systems. He was trained in physiology; he was sympathetic to agnostic and materialistic philosophies; and he was highly supportive of Darwinian ideas. These components of James's worldview led him to temper his initial receptivity to marginal (cutting edge?) beliefs and prompted him to approach spiritualist claims with a great deal of caution. On the whole, James's preference was to remain uncommitted until he had thoroughly explored as many "conventional" theoretical avenues as possible.

James's initial visit with Mrs. Piper was informed with just this combination of receptivity and theoretical caution. In 1890, James discussed that first visit in a letter to Fredrick Myers, an important member of the British branch of the Society for Psychical Research. In the letter, he stressed the care that he and Mrs. James took not to ask leading questions. He went on to say that, despite the numerous minor inaccuracies in Mrs. Piper's pronouncements, he nevertheless had to admit that he was struck by Mrs. Piper's ability to know a number of "very intimate or very trivial"[112] details from his family life—details that she could not have had access to through normal channels. Sharing with Myers some of the specific information Piper ascertained, James writes:

> She said that we had lost recently a rug, and I a waistcoat. . . . [S]he told of my killing a grey-and-white cat, with ether, and described how it had "spun round and round" before dying. She told how my New York aunt had written a letter to my wife, warning her against all mediums. . . . (Of course no one but my wife and I knew the existence of the letter in question.) . . . She told how the crib creaked at night, how a certain rocking-chair creaked mysteriously, how my wife had heard footsteps on the stairs, &c., &c. Insignificant as these things sound when read, the accumulation of a large number of them has an irresistible effect.[113]

At first, James struggled to find possible "non-supernatural" explanations for Mrs. Piper's apparent clairvoyant capacity, but later had to conclude that "Mrs. P. was either possessed of supernormal powers, or knew the members of my wife's family by sight and had by some lucky coincidence become acquainted with such a multitude of their domestic circumstances as to produce the startling impression which she did."[114] However, by the time of the letter, James's initial skepticism had disappeared and he confessed that "later knowledge of her sittings and personal acquaintance with her has led me absolutely to reject the latter explanation, and to believe that she has supernormal powers."[115]

After years of association with Mrs. Piper, James felt sure that she was someone incapable of fraud, and he began to embrace emphatically the "supernaturalistic" hypothesis to explain the information that Mrs. Piper would communicate while in a trance state. James did not, however, accept this hypothesis easily. But, as he mentions in an 1898 review of a book by another member of the Society, Richard Hodgson, he also found it difficult to claim that Mrs. Piper was a fraud. He trenchantly observes:

> The medium has been under observation . . . as to most of the conditions of her life, by a large number of persons, eager, many of them, to pounce upon any suspicious circumstance, for fifteen years. During that time not only has there not been one single suspicious circumstance remarked, but not one suggestion has ever been made from any quarter which might

tend positively to explain how the medium, living the apparent life she leads, could possibly collect information about so many sitters by natural means.[116]

James's conviction that Mrs. Piper's abilities were trustworthy was not shaken by the inaccuracies of the messages transmitted by any of Mrs. Piper's "controls" (the primary spiritual personality that acted as a type of "switchboard operator" for the numerous other "spirits" wanting to speak through Mrs. Piper); he was not bothered by their lack of specific details, the names they did not quite get correct, the descriptions of events that were vague and open-ended enough to be interpreted in many different ways. In fact, he felt that these mistakes or the apparently willful blurring of specifics in the accounts given by the different controls actually *enhanced* Mrs. Piper's veracity. His reasoning was as follows: If Mrs. Piper was consciously attempting to be deceptive, if she was cleverly trying to impress others, then it would seem that she would go out of her way to present only that information which would be dramatically convincing. However, since she (through the control) seems to have had no compunctions at all about making mistakes or about openly contradicting herself, then it is doubtful that she was, consciously at least, deceitful.

There is certainly a possibility, however, that James was overly trusting of Mrs. Piper. Ignas K. Skrupskelis, a Jamesian scholar, in his substantial notes to the *Essays in Psychical Research*, points out that Mrs. Piper could have gathered some of her information from the "gossip of servants"; Skrupskelis further emphasizes the extent to which Mrs. Piper's sessions were financially quite lucrative.[117] However, Skrupskelis's suspicions are themselves not heavily documented, and his account offers no decisive evidence that Mrs. Piper was consciously deceptive. The source of Mrs. Piper's abilities seems to resist any definitive answer, and once again, we are forced, as James was, to rely on a sense of life's "dramatic possibilities."

Although James was convinced that Mrs. Piper did indeed have access to "supernormal knowledge," he was never content with any of the various hypotheses he formulated to account for the source of this knowledge and the process by which it was transmitted. In fact, he periodically expressed the wish that fraud *would* be a satisfactory explanation: at least then there would be some theoretical clarity!

Of all the various hypotheses that were offered, the one that James was the most reluctant to accept, at least in any simplistic form, was the spiritualistic hypothesis that the actual spirits of the dead spoke directly through Mrs. Piper. James, in a letter to Myers, stated

53

that he believed that "Phinuit" (one of Mrs. Piper's earlier controls) was actually a fictional creation and not as "he" claimed, a French doctor born in Marseilles. (Phinuit's credentials appeared particularly dubious to James in light of the fact that his French seemed limited to a few stock phrases and he never seemed to understand James's own excellent French.) Nonetheless, James refused to be deterred by Phinuit's "rough and slangy style" of speech. For him, Phinuit's rough edges, instead of indicating conscious showmanship on the part of Mrs. Piper, demonstrated the power possessed by culture to shape spiritualistic phenomena. As James pointed out to Myers, the "Spiritualistic tradition here in America is all in favour of the 'spirit-control' being a grotesque and somewhat saucy personage. The *Zeitgeist* has always much to do with shaping trance-phenomena, so that a 'control' of that temperament is what one would naturally expect."[118]

Even though James did not believe Phinuit was literally who he claimed to be, James *was* tremendously impressed by the complexity of "Phinuit" as a personality, seeing him as someone who possessed "immense tact and patience, and great desire to please and be regarded as infallible."[119] James was also astonished by Phinuit's powers of memory. In contrast to Mrs. Piper's own rather ordinary everyday memory, Phinuit was, years after having seen hundreds of people, most of whom were complete strangers, able to recapitulate numerous details from earlier meetings.

However, even though James had considerable respect for the positive qualities demonstrated by Phinuit (as well as for the other controls that later spoke through Mrs. Piper), James, unlike other members of the Society, continued to express his reluctance to accept the theory that a spirit of someone who had died was actually speaking through Mrs. Piper. One of the primary reasons James gave for this reluctance was aesthetic: the information transmitted was usually exceedingly trivial. As James points out, "What real spirit, at last able to revisit his wife on this earth . . . [could not] find something better to say than that she had changed the place of his photograph?"[120] This is not to say that James had a negative evaluation of *all* of the information that Mrs. Piper communicated. For instance, James at one point mentioned to Myers that he had a very favorable impression of Phinuit's messages to him and his wife "about our inward defects and outward shortcomings," finding them "very earnest, as well as subtle [sic] morally and psychologically, and impressive in a high degree."[121] James had to concede, however, that most of the information given in the sessions with Mrs. Piper was often not only trivial, but also foggy and at times incoherent, so that if a person accepted the reality of the spirit's presence, then he or she was forced to postulate that "although the communicants probably are spirits, they are in a semi-comatose or sleeping state while communicating, and only half aware of what is going on."[122] James felt that it was much more likely that the controls were "secondary and automatic" personalities created by Mrs. Piper in trance and "consolidated by repetition into personalities consistent enough to play their several roles."[123] He did not believe that these "secondary personalities" generated the "supernormal knowledge" demonstrated by Mrs. Piper. Instead, James preferred the hypothesis that this knowledge is "flashed, grafted, inserted—use what word you will—" onto (or into) this "secondary personality"; the secondary personality then acts as an "intermediating condition" for the supernormal knowledge, which itself comes from another source.[124]

James was also open to the possibility that "thought-transference" might be an explanation of Mrs. Piper's abilities; but he insisted that if thought-transference was to be a respectable hypothesis in her case, then the meaning of the term would have to be broadened to include information gathered not only from the conscious or subconscious minds of those present during the "sittings," but also information gathered from the minds of those who were far away. James's stress on the "long-distance" telepathic ability of Mrs. Piper came from a number of the sittings he participated in with Mrs. Piper. In one of these sittings, for instance, a former aunt spoke through Mrs. Piper about the health of two members of James's family who lived far away. Even though James and his wife had heard nothing recently from these family members, Mrs. Piper's information was later verified, leading James to theorize that "if the supernormal element in the phenomenon be thought-transference it is certainly not that of the sitter's *conscious* thought. It is rather the reservoir of his potential knowledge which is tapped; and not always *that*, but the knowledge of some distant living person."[125]

A related hypothesis to account for Mrs. Piper's abilities was that perhaps Mrs. Piper's "supernormal knowledge" welled up from the depths of her subliminal mind. But this theory was also problematic for James in that it would imply that the subliminal self of Mrs. Piper was "using its preternatural powers of cognition and memory for the basest of deceits"—that this "humbugging and masquerading extramarginal self" was really only "a ghastly and grotesque sort of appendage to one's personality."[126]

James's most explicit and detailed ruminations on the origins and nature of Mrs. Piper's abilities occur in a document prepared in 1909, the "Report on Mrs. Piper's Hodgson-Control." This lengthy and

55

often tedious account prepared for a general meeting of the Society for Psychical Research summarizes James's investigation of one of Mrs. Piper's most controversial controls. James had been especially eager to determine the true identity of this control, since it claimed to be the spirit of Richard Hodgson, a close friend of James (as well as a highly active and respected member of the Society) who had died unexpectedly on 20 December 1905, and then (apparently in a hurry to get back to his friends with information about the after-life) had begun speaking through Mrs. Piper a few days later.

James was aware that, if Hodgson really was speaking through Mrs. Piper, then the Society was presented with a unique research opportunity: Unlike other controls who claimed to be people for whom biographical details were lacking, Hodgson was intimately known by James and many others in the Society, and therefore, could be asked highly specific questions about events in his life about which Mrs. Piper could not possibly have known. If "Hodgson" was actually able to pass this test successfully, then the Society might, for the first time, have fairly conclusive evidence of the reality of the spiritual world and of life after death. This possibility was made even more tantalizing by the fact that Hodgson "had often during his lifetime laughingly said that if he ever passed over and Mrs. Piper was still officiating here below, he would 'control' her better than she had ever yet been controlled in her trances, because he was so thoroughly familiar with the difficulties and conditions on this side."[127]

Unfortunately, the Society never received its incontestable evidence. "Hodgson's" communications were often strikingly convincing, but mixed in with tidbits of excitingly accurate information was a stream of confused or exasperatingly vague replies. This mixture of fact and fantasy made it necessary for James, once again, to wrestle with various hypotheses that could conceivably account for this confusing (and frustrating) combination. James begins his report with a list of possible explanations for "Hodgson's" *accurate* communications through Mrs. Piper:

1. Lucky chance-hits.
2. Common gossip.
3. Indications unwarily furnished by the sitters.
4. Information received from R. H., during his lifetime, by the waking Mrs. P. and stored up, either supraliminally or subliminally, in her memory.
5. Information received from the living R. H., or others, at sittings, and kept in Mrs. Piper's trance-memory, but out of reach of her waking consciousness.

56

6. "Telepathy," *i.e.,* the tapping of the sitter's mind, or that of some distant living person, in an inexplicable way.
7. Access to some cosmic reservoir, where the memory of all mundane facts is stored and grouped around personal centres of association.[128]

James indicates that the first five explanations are "natural," whereas the last two are "supernatural" or "mystical." (The fact that James uses the term "mystical" during a discussion of psychical phenomena indicates, once again, that James's interests in psychical research and in mysticism were not as divorced as even he himself at times maintained, but rather that there was an intimate link between his fascination with psychical events and his investigations of mysticism.)

After reaffirming his loyalty to scientific principles, stressing that "no mystical explanation ought to be invoked so long as any natural one remains at all plausible,"[129] James lets his readers know that some of the naturalistic explanations are, in fact, quite plausible in many instances. He emphasizes that Mrs. Piper would have enormous resources from which to construct a believable facsimile of Hodgson's personality because of her own intimate knowledge of Hodgson during his lifetime. James's doubts about the authenticity of the material seem to be especially pronounced when, after presenting an amazingly detailed and comprehensive transcript of several sessions with the "Hodgson-control" (nearly one hundred pages in the Harvard edition), James concludes that there is "so much mere mannerism, so much repetition, hesitation, irrelevance, unintelligibility, so much obvious groping and fishing and plausible covering up of false tracks . . . that the stream of veridicality that runs throughout the whole gets lost as it were in a marsh of feebleness."[130]

However, it is apparent that James's skepticism is more a rhetorical ploy than a genuine reflection of his final assessment. In his report of the Hodgson control, he goes on to emphasize:

> Nevertheless, I have to confess also that the more familiar I have become with the records, the less *relative significance* for my mind has all this diluting material tended to assume. The active cause of the communications is on any hypothesis a will of some kind, be it the will of R.H.'s spirit, of lower supernatural intelligences, or of Mrs. Piper's subliminal.[131]

Further on, James notes that the difficulties in the communication could conceivably indicate that this "will to communicate" was simply not adequately received and relayed to the sitters by Mrs. Piper. James conjectures:

57

Dramatically, most of this 'bosh' is more suggestive to me of dreaminess and mind-wandering than it is of humbug. . . . That a "will to personate" is a factor in the Piper-phenomenon, I fully believe, and I believe with unshakeable firmness that this will is able to draw on supernormal sources of information. It can "tap," possibly the sitter's memories, possibly those of distant human beings, possibly some cosmic reservoir in which the memories of earth are stored, whether in the shape of "spirits" or not.[132]

James realized that it is impossible to demonstrate conclusively that this "will to communicate" exists above and beyond Mrs. Piper's psyche, but (in a typically Jamesian fashion) his awareness of the lack of conclusive evidence does not stop him from publicly asserting his belief in its transnatural origins. He realizes full well that his conclusion might conceivably be incorrect, but he is also aware that in this area of investigation it is highly unlikely that there ever will be any completely irrefutable proof that a supernatural world (of whatever shape) either does or does not exist above and beyond the trance medium's particular consciousness.

James is also willing to speculate rather freely about the possible forms that this "will to communicate" could take. For instance, James hypothesizes that it conceivably *could* actually be Hodgson's spirit, or it could also be a manifestation of "daimons" or "inferior parasitic spirits."[133] In both of these cases, the control would have a degree of permanence. James takes both of these possibilities seriously, and even adds a third: Mrs. Piper's controls might even be the end-result of a cooperation between the spirits of the dead and these "inferior parasitic spirits." For James, possession is a workable hypothesis, and he scoffs at the refusal of the science of his time, despite the enormous amount of evidence throughout history in numerous different religious traditions in favor of possession, even to consider possession as a possible theory for spiritualistic communications. Even as early as his Lowell lectures on "Exceptional Mental States," James was willing to discuss possession as a viable hypothesis. In his lecture on the issues surrounding multiple personalities, he admitted that most of the cases that were originally described as "possession" could probably be explained using psychological theories on dissociation, hysteria, obsession, and so on. However, James then went on to emphasize that there may be instances that could not be accounted for by standard psychological theories, but which could be explained by the more traditional theories of possession. In the end, James attempts to reconcile modern psychological theories with more historically enduring, religiously based diagnoses of possession; as James suggests: "we might

58

have hysteric mediums; and if there were real demons they might possess only hysterics. Thus each side may see a portion of the truth."[134]

In his discussion of the Hodgson control, James theorizes that the "will to communicate" in spiritualistic sessions might also take on a less permanent form than either a "spirit" or a "daimon." Drawing on a theory originated by the German psychologist and philosopher, Gustave Fechner, James speculates that the "will to communicate" could possibly be the end-result of "a limited process of consciousness arising in the cosmic reservoir of earth's memories," a level of consciousness which, if the conditions were favorable, might jump the gap between that cosmic reservoir and Mrs. Piper like a current of electricity crossing the space between two poles of different potential.[135] Fechner posits that after death, a person leaves behind a changed world due to her or his mental and physical actions—a world that has becomes imprinted by that person's existence. If this is the case, James goes on to reason, then the bodies (including the brains) of Hodgson's friends would have been altered by Hodgson's actions while he was alive; in this sense, these friends themselves would serve as a continuing register of Hodgson's presence. Conceivably then, his friends could, when gathered together during these sessions, radiate the traces of Hodgson's consciousness that were embedded in their own bodies; in this way, his "spirit" might be revived, giving these disparate traces of his consciousness the opportunity to momentarily coalesce into a unified presence. James perceived that a major strength of this theory was that it would "account for the 'confusion' and 'weakness' that [were] such prevalent features" of the communications with the Hodgson control, because, in theory, each individual friend would emanate only a fragmented, "imperfectly aroused" trace of Hodgson's consciousness.[136]

To the end, James remained puzzled by Mrs. Piper's psychic powers. He was impressed enough by what he saw and heard during sessions with her that he had not been able, in good conscience, to ignore the phenomenon, and strove to develop a theoretical structure that was sufficiently nuanced to cope adequately with the complexities inherent in spiritualistic communications. But, finally, even if none of these theoretical formulations felt completely satisfactory to James, he still maintained that the phenomenon itself provided evidence that undermined the naturalistic materialism of science, as well as the idealistic monism of his philosophical opponents. James was certain that the data provided by psychical research supported his own philosophical vision of the world—a world consisting of a complex, multilayered, plurality of existents that, at bottom, were part of a deeper, unseen world. In the conclusion of "Confidences of a 'Psychical Researcher'," James's acknowledges:

> Out of my experience, such as it is (and it is limited enough) one fixed conclusion dogmatically emerges, and that is this, that we with our lives are like islands in the sea, or like trees in the forest. The maple and the pine may whisper to each other with their leaves, and Conanicut and Newport hear each other's fog-horns. But the trees also commingle their roots in the darkness underground, and the islands also hang together through the ocean's bottom. Just so there is a continuum of cosmic consciousness, against which our individuality builds but accidental fences, and into which our several minds plunge as into a mother-sea or reservoir. Our "normal" consciousness is circumscribed for adaptation to our external earthly environment, but the fence is weak in spots, and fitful influences from beyond leak in, showing the otherwise unverifiable common connexion.[137]

James recognizes that this type of "panpsychic" belief is only the bare bones of a theoretical structure that needs fleshing out, and that many questions remain:

> What is the structure of this common reservoir of consciousness . . . it's inner topography? . . . What are the conditions of individuation or insulation in this mother-sea? . . . Are individual "spirits" constituted there? How numerous, and of how many hierarchic orders may these then be? How permanent? How transient? and how confluent with one another may they become?[138]

James concludes that these extremely complex and difficult questions will never be solved unless the facts of psychical research are acknowledged to be worthy of study. However, if psychical research *could* be taken seriously by the scientific community, then James (quite optimistically) predicts that the most important scientific discoveries in the near future would emerge out this openness to nonmaterialistic realities.

"A Suggestion about Mysticism"

In many ways, James's belief in a "mother sea" of cosmic consciousness links his interest in psychical research to his philosophy of mysticism. In chapter 3 we will investigate James's speculations about the possible connection between mystical experiences and this mother sea of consciousness; but at this juncture it might be helpful at least to provide a brief introduction to this concept, especially since it appears in "A Suggestion about Mysticism," an important essay written by James which was published in 1910 (the year of James's death).

This essay opens with some rhetorical sleight-of-hand. James claims that hé is a mystical innocent, that he has had no direct experiences to draw upon in order to back up his psychological theories about mysticism. But as we have already seen, this statement is somewhat misleading; and by the end of the essay, after reading James's narratives of several recent puzzling experiences of his own (and especially after reading his detailed defense of the mystical qualities of these puzzling experiences), we have to wonder just how seriously we should take this initial disclaimer. While it is obvious that James is by no means a "professional mystic," at the same time, it is also apparent that he has had many, often quite dramatic, and typically unasked for, experiences that struck *him* at least as being "quasi-mystical." After all, as James himself admits in this essay, it was several of these recent personal experiences that prompted him to propose once again a theory that could account for these sudden and powerful alterations of consciousness.

James hypothesizes that, perhaps "states of mystical intuition" are actually "very sudden and great extensions of the ordinary 'field of consciousness'" in which the "margin" of the field expands to such an extent that "knowledge ordinarily transmarginal would become included" within it.[139] Drawing once again on Fechner's work, James speculates that one way to picture a person's present moment of awareness is to imagine it as a wave in an ocean—a wave that, while perhaps momentarily rising above sea level, also remains in its depths connected with the ocean (and with all the other "waves" of awareness). James suggests that "sea level" in this model could be seen as the base level of human consciousness, the "threshold" of waking awareness. A person's moment-to-moment "wave" of conscious awareness includes everything that appears above this threshold, while below it there exists the oceanic depths of "subliminal" awareness—depths not normally conscious to the person, but which, nonetheless, contain an enormous amount of psychic activity. James's hypothesis is that in mystical states of awareness, the threshold is lowered, producing surprising results. James writes:

> A fall of the threshold, however caused, would, under these circumstances, produce the mental equivalent to what occurs in an unusually flat shore at the ebb of a spring-tide. Vast tracts of what is usually covered are then

revealed to view, but nothing rises more than a few inches above the water's bed, and great parts of the scene are submerged again whenever a wave washes over them.[140]

In this hypothesis, mystical awareness is viewed as a sudden and dramatic opening of ordinary consciousness to the vast quantity of information in the subconscious—a powerful influx of previously hidden data breaching the seemingly secure boundaries of the self. However, James would say it is not just in moments of mystical ecstasy that these boundaries shift. According to James's field conception of consciousness, our awareness is *always* in a state of flux. James summarizes this theory when he asserts:

> The field is composed at all times of a mass of present sensation, in a cloud of memories, emotions, concepts, etc. Yet these ingredients, which have to be named separately, are not separate, as the conscious field contains them. Its form is that of a much-at-once, in the unity of which the sensations, memories, concepts, impulses, etc. coalesce and are dissolved. The present field as a whole came continuously out of its predecessor and will melt into its successor as continuously again.[141]

In this continuous ebb and flow of our awareness, the "horizons" or "margins" of consciousness lack specific boundaries; further, what is central in consciousness can rapidly shift to the margins and vice versa. According to James, this shifting of our field of consciousness is "like the field of vision, which the slightest movement of the eye will extend, revealing objects that always stood there to be known."[142] James suggests that these shifts in our field of consciousness are very similar to the lowering of the threshold of consciousness that occurs in mystical experience, but in a mystical experience, new sensations do not enter into consciousness. Instead, what is revealed is another, larger "much-at-onceness" of previously hidden memories, impulses and beliefs that have always been operative either on the margins of our awareness or within our "transmarginal" awareness. James concludes:

> If this enlargement of the nimbus that surrounds the sensational present is vast enough, while no one of the items it contains attracts our attention singly, we shall have the conditions fulfilled for a kind of consciousness in all essential respects like that termed mystical. It will be transient, if the change of the threshold is transient. It will be of reality, enlargement, and illumination, possibly rapturously so. It will be of unification . . . [because the enlargement of consciousness unites normally unaccessible psychic

elements within one field of consciousness]. Its form will be intuitive or perceptual, not conceptual, for the remembered or conceived objects in the enlarged field are supposed not to attract the attention singly, but only to give the sense of a tremendous *muchness* suddenly revealed.[143]

In this essay, James does not give a rationale for his assumption that these particular characteristics (transiency, reality, enlargement, illumination, rapture, unification, and intuition) are inherent qualities of what makes an experience "mystical." Although several of these qualities were listed earlier in the *Varieties* (i.e., transiency and noetic quality—if noetic quality can be seen as containing "illumination" and "reality"), two qualities (ineffability and passivity) no longer "make the cut ." James gives no explanation for this change. He also does not discuss why he includes "enlargement," "unification," "rapture," or the intuitive/perceptual nature of mystical experience as essential characteristics of a mystical experience. Perhaps he does not think that he needs to justify the addition of these new phenomenological characteristics (even though they were not *explicitly* listed in the *Varieties*), since he does allude to them quite frequently, either implicitly in the *Varieties* or explicitly in other less well known texts.

It is also possible that James did not provide a detailed rationale for this brief listing of the phenomenological characteristics of mystical experience because he was less concerned with the descriptive task than he was with creating a workable explanation of mystical experience. In "A Suggestion about Mysticism," James attempts to create a viable model of the processes active below the surface of consciousness that help to catalyze a mystical experience. Yet, at the same time, James realizes that his model is tentative, at best, and that many mystics might well have problems with his psychological theories on the underlying dynamics of mystical experience. It is highly probable that this cautious assessment is correct. For instance, James's theory does not seem particularly helpful when it is applied to mystical experiences that are apparently devoid of objective content (for instance, the *nirvikalpa samādhi* of the Hindu yogi). It is difficult to see how getting flooded with information from the subliminal depths of one's consciousness could produce the acute awareness, profound stillness, and apparent lack of mental activity that characterize the "pure consciousness events"[144] so often described in different mystical traditions.

However, certain types of mystical experiences do appear to lend themselves particularly well to James's "suggestion" about the psychological processes that may generate a mystical expansion of consciousness. Mystical transfigurations of nature, for instance, seem particularly amenable to this level of explanation. Typically, in these types of mystical experiences, the mystic is swept up by the beauty of nature and perceives with great joy his or her union with the natural world. The "outer" scene is unchanged; it is still the same trees, ocean, mountains, sunset, and so on, that the mystic sees, hears, smells, touches, and tastes; however, he or she experiences this outer beauty in a radically new way. If we use James's hypothesis to help us understand the underlying dynamics of this experience, then two different, yet interrelated possibilities present themselves.

First, the transfiguration of nature can be seen as the result of previously unaccessible emotions, memories, and beliefs surging up from the transmarginal areas of the mystic's psyche and superimposing themselves upon the mystic's more commonplace perceptions of the external world. According to this hypothesis, during moments of mystical awareness, the mystic's sensory data remains constant, but that data is perceived very differently since it is "filtered" through an enormously expanded gestalt of newly felt emotional and cognitive "lens."

The second, less prosaic, possibility is that in the transfiguration of nature the mystic not only is flooded with newly felt *personal* memories and impulses, but also experiences a joyous recognition of a *transpersonal* underlying connection with nature, a connection that already existed in the mystic's subliminal depths.[145]

If James's "suggestion" about mystical experience can be seen to include an openness to transpersonal input, then the ability of his hypothesis to account for other types of mystical experiences, such as highly detailed visionary experiences, is enormously strengthened. In other words, if the mystic's transmarginal awareness could be understood to contain not only personal memories and buried emotions, but also transpersonal or transnatural "raw material" ("raw material" that is, inevitably, molded by one's psychological and cultural background), then James's hypothesis could easily account for the powerfully felt, intricately detailed sense of the "otherness" and "newness" inherent in many visionary experiences. According to this reading of James's hypothesis, if the mystic's psychic threshold suddenly lowers, it would uncover and release into awareness preexistent, highly structured "gestalts" of transpersonally generated, but psychologically and culturally shaped, information—gestalts of information that would then catalyze and form the mystic's numinous visionary experience.

Unfortunately, in this essay, James's hypothesis suffers from an overly sparse depiction of the nature of the contents of the mystic's subliminal awareness. It seems, at first, as if James depicts the subliminal or transmarginal awareness in strictly personal terms, as if it were only an amalgam of each particular individual's unavailable memories, beliefs, and impulses. But as will become apparent in chapter 3, James's conception of our subliminal awareness is typically not so circumscribed; in fact, it is specifically constructed in such a way as to allow for both psychological and theological interpretations of the dynamic processes that underlie mystical states of consciousness. James did believe that each person's transmarginal awareness contains transpersonal as well as personal "contents"; however, this expanded understanding of the nature of each individual's transmarginal awareness is not readily apparent in this essay.

Perhaps, "A Suggestion about Mysticism" focuses more on the *personal* components of the subliminal awareness because the essay was prompted by several unusual experiences in which James perceived himself as being flooded with specifically personal (not transpersonal) components of his subliminal consciousness. Three of these experiences were very similar. In each case, in middle of ordinary activities, James would suddenly remember an event that happened in the past. This memory in turn would connect with another memory or idea, which then would connect to something else, and so on. The whole process happened very rapidly, too quickly for him to be able to label what it was that he was undergoing. This bewildering chain of interconnected thoughts and memories had a powerful effect on James. As he put it: "The feeling—I won't call it belief—that I had had a sudden opening, had seen through a window, as it were, distant realities that incomprehensibly belonged with my own life, was so acute that I can not shake it off to-day."[146]

James did not claim that his own experiences fit the typical pattern of religious mystical experiences in every respect, but they did have features that were at least "quasi-mystical": first, they came with an inner assurance that what had been experienced was not simply imaginary; second, the experience was primarily perceptual rather than conceptual (a distinction that is based on the vivid imagistic content of his memories?); and third, the experience was difficult to describe adequately. (Here "ineffability" surfaces again as a quality of what defines a mystical experience.) The primary difference James saw between his own experiences and those described in religious texts was that his experiences only uncovered select portions of reality, "whereas in classical mystical experiences it appears rather as if the whole of reality were uncovered at once."[147]

James's fourth experience was very different than the other three. One night in February 1906, while at Stanford University, he awoke suddenly and was extremely disoriented. In the middle of one dream, two other separate dreams had "shuffled themselves abruptly in between the parts of the first dream."[148] James began to get frightened and confused, because it seemed to him as if he had dreamed all three, not in succession, but at the same time. He began to have difficulty distinguishing which dream he had "really" dreamed, and it seemed to him as if he belonged to "three different dream systems at once."[149] In a panic, he attempted to account rationally for this bizarre experience: Perhaps the mental confusion was brought on by heart trouble; more disturbing yet, perhaps this experience was the beginning of a mental breakdown; perhaps he was dreaming other people's dreams via a telepathic contact; perhaps he was being invaded by a some sort of dual (or triple) mental presence; or finally, perhaps he was merely remembering dreams from a previous night's sleep. Ultimately, James's panic was soothed somewhat by the recognition that his rational facilities were at least sufficiently present to be able to create these various theories, and he was eventually able to go back to a restless night of confusing (but not panic-arousing) dreams.

It is unclear why James considered this experience of interconnected dreams to be mystical. Even James admits that "the distressing confusion of mind in this experience was the exact opposite of mystical illumination."[150] But James (straining somewhat) defends the mystical status of these dreams; he emphasizes that, just as mystical experiences create an increased awareness of unity, these dreams, too, created an increased awareness of interconnectedness, since they "*both did and did not belong in the most intimate way together*"; he also stresses that, similar to the heightened sense of reality so commonly found in mystical experiences, his dreams conveyed a vivid sense that "*reality was being uncovered.*"[151] These peculiar dreams remained, nonetheless, very puzzling to James—so much so that he concludes by saying that "to this day I feel that those extra dreams were dreamed in reality, but when, where, and by whom, I can not guess."[152]

"On a Certain Blindness in Human Beings"

In these accounts of James's own "mystical" experiences, as well as in certain sections of the *Varieties,* James struggles both to *describe* the most prominent phenomenological characteristics of mystical experiences and to *explain* their mechanics using psychological constructs. But James is equally concerned to *assess* the normative status of mystical experiences by investigating their potentially transformative personal and social effects. James does not just want to know what mystical states are, and how they came to be, he also wants to determine whether they are worthwhile (and as we will see in chapter 5, this assessment of value is integrally linked with the determination of the truth of mystical experiences as well).

One of the texts in which James most overtly focuses on the positive value of mystical experiences is the essay, "On a Certain Blindness in Human Beings," included in James's *Talks to Teachers*. This essay has not received a great deal of attention by Jamesian scholars. There is a tendency to consider the essay as a piece of well-intentioned, but lightweight rhetoric, designed more to inspire and uplift than to be part of James's more serious philosophical investigations. Up to a point, this criticism is valid. James himself, in the preface to *Talks to Teachers*, expresses his regret that he had not made "On a Certain Blindness," as he puts it, "more impressive."[153] However, James was also convinced that the essay was not just "sentimentalism," but instead, was actually a demonstration of his "pluralistic or individualistic philosophy."[154] In fact, James several times mentions that he is especially fond of this essay, and goes so far as to say that it is "better loved by [him] than any of [his] other productions."[155]

In addition to the lack of serious attention given to "On a Certain Blindness" by most Jamesian scholars, there has been a rather more puzzling development: the shortage of commentary regarding the essay's focus on the positive value of mystical states of awareness. This lacuna is, again, up to a point, understandable. The central contention of this essay is that "the truth is too great for any one actual mind, even though that mind be dubbed 'the Absolute,' to know the whole of it."[156] At first glance, this contention seems to have little to do with mystical states of consciousness, and in fact, appears to be in tension with some of the most important characteristics of many mystical experiences, especially the mystical perception of unity and the conviction held by many mystics that they have directly known the absolute Truth. It is also true that, although James does from time to time use the term "mystical" to refer to the altered states of consciousness that are at the heart of the essay, he also does not ever directly point out the extent of his emphasis on mysticism. But if we look carefully at "On a Certain Blindness" it becomes clear that practically every major claim that James makes in the essay is illustrated by, or defended with, numerous examples of mystical experiences.

In the course of the essay, James also goes to great lengths to demonstrate that mystical insights can actually help to establish a pluralistic philosophical perspective; he makes several interrelated, and almost audacious, claims about the philosophical, psychological and cultural value of mystical states of consciousness. First, James believes that mystical experiences take us beyond our everyday, prosaic reality, and thereby force us to acknowledge that alternative perspectives of reality are possible. Second, mystical experiences, by concretely revealing our intimate connection to others, can generate an empathetic feeling of the "innerness" of another person, which thereby allows us to value the other person's uniqueness and individuality. Third, mystical experiences vividly demonstrate how difficult and dangerous it is to impose our own limited set of values and judgments on the life of another, in that they possess a deeply personal, and often hidden, joy and richness that resists any arbitrary external critical assessment. Fourth, the powerful, self-contained inner joy of mystical experiences can also relativize our conventional, taken-for-granted assumptions of what a "good life" really is and can provide the mystic with an unseen, but potent, reason to live that does not depend upon external standards and rewards. And, finally, mystical experiences open us up to a renewed and revitalized vision of the world; they give us the gift of seeing the world in a different, deeper, and truer way than the routinized and mechanical vision of life that we typically receive from our modern culture.

James begins his exploration of these themes by first emphasizing that our supposedly "objective" ideas about the world around us are always inextricably connected with our subjective interests and feelings. Unfortunately, these (usually unconscious) subjective assessments lock each of us into an often extremely narrow perspective of the world. This psychological and cultural tunnel vision prevents us from truly knowing others, and in turn, prevents them from truly knowing us, since they also have a particular set of interests that are very different than ours. James cautions us that this "blindness" often leads us to make unfair and arrogant opinions about the inner world of another person; he emphasizes that in order to overcome these limiting prejudices, it is crucially important to recognize the fragile and extremely circumscribed perspective that we bring to any of our attempts to assess another's world. James stresses that if we can begin to acknowledge the impossibility of completely knowing another person's experience, then perhaps this recognition of our limits will impress upon us not only the need for a tolerance of differences, but also the value of methodological modesty, as well as a certain bottom-line respect for the sacredness of the individual.

James repeatedly underscores the difficulties inherent in making an accurate assessment of another person's level of happiness, especially if that assessment is based simply on the external elements in that person's life. For instance, drawing upon an essay by Robert Louis Stevenson (an essay that James describes as being "the best thing I know in Stevenson"),[157] we are told a story of how a group of boys, simply for the joy of it, would gather together, often in the cold and the rain, with smelly, hot tin lanterns hidden under their topcoats. As the story goes, these boys were not using the lanterns for any practical purpose; in fact, what gave them joy was keeping these lanterns completely hidden from view underneath their topcoat. Had some outside observer been watching these boys, that observer would merely perceive these boys as cold and drenched by rain. But if the boys' point of view were included, then a very different story would emerge, since for them, nothing could be more joyous than meeting together in the rain and cold, bound together by the secret knowledge that only those within their circle were aware that a hot, foul-smelling tin lantern burned underneath each of their topcoats. James uses this story to illustrate just how difficult it is to discover the roots of another person's joy, especially if we focus exclusively on external factors. James stresses that if we see only the outer difficulties of a person's life (the rain and cold) and miss that person's inner, and often hidden joy (the tin lantern), then we have missed what is most important in that situation.

James believes that our concern with the external, practical, day-to-day details of our life tends to harden our hearts to anything that is different than what we are used to experiencing. According to James, only the dreamers, poets, philosophers, and mystics of a culture are given the degree of freedom from mundane responsibilities necessary to break through this hardened crust of conventionality. Only they are given the chance to see "the vast world of inner life beyond us"; only they are granted that empathetic unitary vision that can catalyze a dissolution of our carefully guarded boundaries—a vision that can subvert "the whole scheme of our customary values," a vision that can prompt us to search for "a new centre and a new perspective."[158] This mystical insight into another person's inner world keeps us from making an "it" out of that person and forces us to recognize that, instead, he or she is a "thou"—someone like ourselves, someone to be treated with respect and understanding.[159]

James stresses that "this higher vision of an inner significance in what, until then, we had realized only in the dead external way, often comes over a person suddenly; and when it does so, it makes an epoch in his history."[160] This vision is not something nebulous. Instead, James emphasizes (while paraphrasing Ralph Waldo Emerson, a close family

69

friend): "There is a depth in those moments that constrains us to ascribe more reality to them than to all other experiences."[161] For James, these mystical experiences can be a pivotal moment in a person's existence; even though the externals in that person's life may give little or no clue that such a momentous event has occurred, the person's perspective on life (and consequently his or her responses to life) may be revolutionized by that single moment of both sensing an underlying connection to another person and coming to cherish another's irreducible uniqueness.

According to James, this revolutionary "mystic sense of hidden meaning starts upon us often from non-human natural things."[162] To illustrate how this mystical insight often emerges via our contact with the natural world James quotes from a French novel of the nineteenth century (which he apparently thought was, at least in part, autobiographical). This novel tells the story of a melancholy person in Paris who, one dark, cold day went for a walk and saw a jonquil blooming on a wall. Without warning, that person was swept up in a powerful, ecstatic experience:

> I felt all the happiness destined for man. This unutterable harmony of souls, the phantom of the ideal world, arose in me complete. I never felt anything so great or so instantaneous. I know not what shape, what analogy, what secret of relation it was that made me see in this flower a limitless beauty. . . . I shall never enclose in a conception this power, this immensity that nothing will express; this ideal of a better world which one feels, but which it would seem that nature has not made.[163]

James's own appreciation of natural beauty responds to this nature-inspired mysticism, which he sees echoed in the life experience of yet another writer, William Wordsworth, to whom "every natural form, rock, fruit or flower" gave "authentic tidings of invisible things."[164] James compares Wordsworth's experience to that of the French novelist and points out that Wordsworth's experience was also ineffable in that he could not articulate "what this hidden presence in Nature was" that he "so rapturously felt."[165] But James realizes that ineffability does not halt poetic inspiration, much less mitigate the value of a mystical apprehension of nature. For James, Wordsworth's poetry may not be able to conceptualize logically such an experience, but his poetry can serve an important function: it can enable others who have also shared in this mystical vision of a transfigured natural world to recognize fragments of their own experience in the inspired words of another, thereby reaffirming the truth and value of that previously inchoate and often socially illegitimate experience.

James also uses Wordsworth's life to demonstrate once again the futility of attempting to assess the value of the inner life of another based merely on the externals of that person's life. James points out:

> As Wordsworth walked, filled with his strange inner joy, responsive thus to the secret life of Nature round about him, his rural neighbors, tightly and narrowly intent upon their own affairs, their crops and lambs and fences, must have thought him a very insignificant and foolish personage. It surely never occurred to any one of them to wonder what was going on inside of *him* or what it might be worth. And yet that inner life of his carried the burden of a significance that has fed the souls of others, and fills them to this day with inner joy.[166]

According to James's uniquely individualistic reading of mystical experience, Wordsworth's inner revolution is truly known only by Wordsworth himself; no combination of subtle laboratory instruments, no crude external calculus of objective observations can adequately describe this transformed inner vision, nor do justice to its possible personal and social impact. For James, Wordsworth, like all mystics, is the ultimate judge of his own joy; he alone truly knows the significance and worth of this transformation of consciousness.

James does not use only Wordsworth to illustrate the value of mystical insights. He also draws upon the autobiography of another mystic, Richard Jefferies, to reaffirm the inviolability of mystical perceptions. In *The Story of My Heart*, Jefferies pictures himself on a hilltop; he writes:

> I was utterly alone with the sun and the earth. Lying down on the grass, I spoke in my soul to the earth, the sun, the air, and the distant sea far beyond sight. . . . With all the intensity of feeling which exalted me, all the intense communion I held with the earth, the sun and sky, the stars hidden by the light, with the ocean—in no manner can the thrilling depth of these feelings be written—with these I prayed, as if they were the keys of an instrument. . . . The inexpressible beauty of all filled me with a rapture, an ecstasy. . . . The prayer, this soul-emotion, was in itself, not for an object; it was a passion. I hid my face in the grass, I was wholly prostrated. . . . I was rapt and carried away. . . . Had any shepherd accidentally seen me lying on the turf, he would only have thought that I was resting a few minutes. I made no outward show. Who could have imagined the whirlwind of passion that was going on within me as I reclined there![167]

71

James points out that Jefferies's inner drama, if measured by purely commercial standards, is basically worthless. No time-saving technology was invented, no scientific theory was verified, no architectural marvel was constructed. However, as James emphasizes, if life was utterly devoid of such moments, would it really have any meaning? Is not the value of our life truly measured by the subtle, yet enduring, significance inherent in variations of just these highly personal, if outwardly impractical, experiences?

While James is perhaps excessive in his construction of an antithesis between mystical vision and practical life (the Tantric and Sufi belief that a mystic could also be highly successful in the everyday work-world was never part of James's understanding of the possibilities of mysticism), James at least helps to undercut the often-held simplistic and overly utilitarian understanding that mystical experiences are worthless since they appear to generate nothing of measurable value in the external world.[168] James insists that mystical experiences are often innately valuable, and indeed, it is frequently just these kinds of experiences that act as a benchmark to establish what exactly in life is actually valuable and what is not. Mystical experiences in this sense have the potential to catalyze a crucial relativization of our conventional normative assumptions. James once again draws upon a poet and mystic to support his case: Walt Whitman. This famed "loafer" would often spend his day doing nothing more than watching the panorama of sights from the top of an omnibus (a style of life often mirrored by James's younger brother, Henry). James, no lover of wasted time, comments:

> Truly a futile way of passing the time, some of you may say, and not altogether creditable to a grown-up man. And yet, from the deepest point of view, who knows the more of truth, and who knows the less—Whitman on his omnibus-top, full of the inner joy with which the spectacle inspires him, or you, full of the disdain which the futility of his occupation excites? When your ordinary Brooklynite or New Yorker, leading a life replete with too much luxury, or tired and careworn about his personal affairs, crosses the ferry or goes up Broadway, *his* fancy does not thus "soar away into the colors of the sunset" as did Whitman's, nor does he inwardly realize at all the indisputable fact that this world never did anywhere or at any time contain more of essential divinity, or of eternal meaning, than is embodied in the fields of vision over which his eyes so carelessly pass. . . . To the jaded and unquickened eye it is all dead and common, pure vulgarism, flatness and disgust. . . . That eternal recurrence of the common order, which so fills a Whitman with mystic satisfaction, is

72

to a Schopenhauer, with the emotional anaesthesia, the feeling of "awful inner emptiness" from out of which he views it all, the chief ingredient of the tedium it instils.... [Yet] to be rapt with satisfied attention, like Whitman, to the mere spectacle of the world's presence, is one way, and the most fundamental way, of confessing one's sense of its unfathomable significance and importance.[169]

According to James, this re-vision of one's perception of the world, this transfiguration of the most mundane aspects of life, carries with it an innate and profound importance. But, unfortunately, James would add, it also seems that there is no way in which we can nourish and stimulate this type of experience. He believes that "there is no receipt one can follow. Being a secret and a mystery, it often comes in mysteriously unexpected ways. It blossoms sometimes from out of the very grave wherein we imagined that our happiness was buried."[170] But James insists that this unanticipated upsurge of spiritual joy carries with it enormous power: the power to turn an outer hell into an inner heaven on earth. According to James, even if a person is in prison, suffering from rotting teeth, a broken leg, and voracious hordes of rats, he or she can still rise above that outer suffering through the redemptive grace of religious joy and religious visions. For such a person, this spontaneous influx of mystical awareness can be the miracle that makes any life worth living.

James's discussion of the innate value contained within many mystical experiences is thought-provoking. Nonetheless, his account is weakened by a conspicuous omission: James's Protestant emphasis on the miraculous, unexpected visitation of mystical awareness prevents him from sufficiently exploring the tantalizing ethical ramifications of his claim that mystical experiences are often linked with numerous positive and potentially transformative effects. It is clear that, at least in "On a Certain Blindness in Human Beings," James does offer a glowing assessment of mystical experiences. For instance, James attempts to establish that mystical states of awareness have the capacity to revitalize life, and he seeks to show that mystical experiences can also provide standards by which a meaningful and valuable life is measured. He also tries to demonstrate that mystical experiences can serve the function of questioning a culture's encrusted assumptions. However, if mystical experiences, in James's eyes, contain this wealth of positive repercussions, what then keeps James from an active endorsement of the mystical life? It is difficult to second-guess James at this juncture, but it would seem plausible that this absence of support for the value of a life in which mystical experiences are actively nurtured comes about, in part at least, because of James's lack of exposure to those religious traditions that stress that each individual can, and should, cultivate regular mystical experiences. If, from James's perspective, mystical experiences come unexpectedly and infrequently, then it would indeed appear to be futile to emphasize the value of any attempts to nurture the onset of these transformative states of awareness. If, however, James's emphasis on the spontaneous nature of mystical experiences is incorrect, if there are indeed reliable, effective methods available to access these mystical states of awareness (a claim that many meditative and contemplative traditions would endorse), then it would appear that James could have, and perhaps should have, made a strong case for the social acceptance, if not active support, of these practices.

Nonetheless, even though James prefers to focus on the spontaneous emergence of mystical awareness, he does briefly touch upon some of the factors that can either facilitate or block this transformative vision. One circumstance that, in James's opinion, often stifles mystical awareness is one's level of education. If a person is overly educated, alienated from nature, excessively refined, filled with intellectual, abstract conceptions and divorced from the "simpler functions" of mankind, then he or she, according to James, is in danger of drying up and growing "stone-blind and insensible to life's more elementary and general goods and joys."[171] The solution that James advocates is to re-immerse oneself in nature (like James himself would do almost routinely in his hikes in the Adirondacks) in order to "descend to a more profound and primitive level."[172] James posited that certain types of mystical experiences appear to be prompted by renouncing sophistication, by returning to a simpler, more elemental type of existence. In an almost Zen-like fashion, James describes the "intense interest that life can assume when brought down to the non-thinking level, the level of pure sensorial perception."[173] He spends several pages quoting at length from a book by W. H. Hudson, who describes how he would go riding for hours in the wilderness, doing nothing but "listening to the silence" and watching the grey, cold landscape with a type of alert elation.[174] James comments that while this story might seem to be "a mere tale of emptiness, in which nothing happens, nothing is gained, and there is nothing to describe [except] meaningless and vacant tracts of time . . . to him who feels their inner secret [of the vacant tracts of time], they tingle with an importance that unutterably vouches for itself."[175] According to James, this hypersensorial awareness carries within itself an innate sense of fulfillment and pleasure and produces a magic invisible to anyone outside of its spell.

Establishing Foundations

James concludes the essay by stressing, once again, that the existence of this type of imperceptible, yet crucially significant mystical re-visioning of the world has several important consequences:

> It absolutely forbids us to be forward in pronouncing on the meaningless-ness of forms of existence other than our own; and it commands us to tolerate, respect, and indulge those whom we see harmlessly interested and happy in their own ways, however unintelligible these may be to us. Hands off: neither the whole of truth, nor the whole of good, is revealed to any single observer, although each observer gains a partial superiority of insight from the peculiar position in which he stands.[176]

Diabolical Mysticism: Mystical Experience and Psychopathology

James's depictions of mysticism were rarely so rhapsodic as in "On a Certain Blindness." More typically, James's positive comments on mysticism were accompanied by a cautionary note or by some mention of the less appealing repercussions of mystical experiences. One of the most striking examples of this alternation between positive and negative assessments of mysticism occurs in the *Varieties*. After spending a prolonged period discussing the ladder of mysticism and filling page after page with quotes from various individuals who proclaim the intrinsic value of mystical experience, James sets down his conclusions on an extremely difficult question in the philosophy of mysticism: to what extent can mystical experiences legitimately authorize specific theological positions? His conclusion (which will be more carefully examined in chapter 4) is broken down into three sections. The first and third sections are extremely supportive of mystical experience. (The first section asserts that individuals who have mystical experiences have every right to believe that these experiences reveal the truth. The third section claims that mystical states of awareness clearly demonstrate that our everyday waking consciousness is only one among many possible types of consciousness.) But the second section is a stern reminder of the limitations of mysticism's authority and prestige (it argues that non-mystics are under no obligation to accept the revelations proclaimed by different mystics). In the middle of this sobering second section, after demonstrating the contradictions inherent in the different theological claims of mystics from various traditions, James further undermines mysticism's prestige by pointing out that religious mysticism is really "only one half of mysticism,"[177] also noting that the mirror image of the ecstasy, oneness, and wisdom of classical mysticism is the terror, fragmentation, and delusions of insanity. According to James, this "diabolical mysticism" is "a sort of religious mysticism turned upside down."[178] Regarding diabolical mysticism, James observes:

> The same sense of ineffable importance in the smallest events, the same texts and words coming with new meanings, the same voices and visions and leadings and missions, the same controlling by extraneous powers; only this time the emotion is pessimistic; instead of consolations we have desolations; the meanings are dreadful; and the powers are enemies to life.[179]

It is clear to James that mysticism and psychopathology both arise out of the subliminal region of the mind, but recognizing that this area of psychological investigation was still in its infancy, James does not attempt to generate explanatory theories to account for this subliminal connection between mysticism and psychopathology. (In a sense, this work was left to James's "successors" in the field of psychology—e.g., Sigmund Freud and Carl Jung, as well as other less well-known psychological theorists.)

Besides this realization that the subliminal areas of the psyche were, at that point, almost completely unmapped, James's reluctance to create detailed explanatory theories on the connection between mysticism and psychopathology springs from yet another reason. James is ultimately less interested in creating explanatory models of mystical experience than he is drawn to the philosophical task of how to assess the *value* of these mystical experiences. For James, this normative task (which James refers to as the "spiritual judgement") appears to have been much more appealing than the equally important explanatory and descriptive tasks (which James refers to as the "existential judgement").[180] Unfortunately, however, many theorists of mysticism of his time unknowingly confused these tasks and ended up practicing versions of what James terms "medical materialism": the attempt to undermine the validity and value of mystical experiences by pointing out their biological antecedents; in other words, the process of asserting that mystical experiences are nothing but repressed sexuality, epilepsy, and so on.[181] James does not deny the value of attempting to formulate various explanations for mysticism, but, at the same time, he does not think that the biological, psychological (or spiritual) origins of mystical experiences have any relationship to the final determination of whether mystical experiences are worthwhile or not. So, to use some quick and dirty contemporary comparisons, James, unlike Freud and most of his followers, does not believe that the similarities between mystical visions and paranoid delusions automatically undermine the value of mysticism, and unlike Jung and most of *his* followers, James does not think that simply because mysticism arises out of the subliminal areas of the psyche that it is therefore especially significant. Instead, James uses the idea of the common subliminal genesis of mystical experiences and psychopathology to demonstrate the futility of attempting to assess the value of *any* experience by simply pointing to its origins. In the final analysis, James believes that "so long as we are not mystics ourselves" our assessment of the value of a mystical experience cannot automatically be positive simply because of its genesis in the subconscious and cannot be automatically be negative simply because of its similarity to the delusions of insanity. Instead, any assessment of the value of a mystical experience must be based on a complex and ongoing process in which the mystical experience is "sifted and tested," and forced to "run the gauntlet of confrontation with the total context of experience."[182] Mystical experiences in this way are not understood as privileged cases to be singled out for special treatment, but rather, their validity and value, like all other information about the world (including the data from the senses), is determined by the overall effect of their interaction with the rest of life.

James's emphasis on the pragmatic evaluation of mystical experiences does not mean that he is unwilling to speculate on the relationship between psychopathology and mystical experiences. In fact, earlier in the *Varieties*, James emphasizes that "it always leads to a better understanding of a thing's significance to consider its exaggerations and perversions, its equivalents and substitutes and nearest relatives elsewhere."[183] James makes use of this comparative methodology early in the *Varieties*, noting that the "geniuses" of religious life, the saints and mystics of the different traditions, often showed signs of being psychologically unstable. But James refuses to draw the conclusion that the possession of a neurotic personality automatically nullifies the viability of mystical revelations. In fact, for James, the melancholy, obsessiveness, and emotional upheavals that are such prominent features in the biographies of many saints and mystics might well be the very personality traits that could grant someone access to "inspiration from a higher realm."[184]

Without a doubt, James overemphasized the discordant, psychopathological elements in the personality structure of the religious "genius." James is much more fascinated with the dramatic and colorful biographies of mystics such as George Fox, John Bunyan, or Heinrich Suso, than he is with the radiant, centered, serene, and compassionate personalities of Buddhist bodhisattvas or the dynamic, courageous, and judicious personalities of Sikh gurus or Sufi saints.[185] James's emphasis on the extreme emotional oscillation that is so often encountered in the lives of religious "geniuses" may, in part, be due to his lack of distinction between the initial phases of a mystic's spiritual development (during which time psychic strife is indeed prominent) and the later stages of mystical life (during which time, according to most traditions, the mystic has transformed most, if not all, of his or her negative traits into highly positive psychological characteristics). It is also possible that James's stress on the discordant emotional elements of a mystic's life arose from his intimate knowledge of the life of the mystic he knew best: his father, Henry James, Sr.

Saintly Fathers and Suffering Sons

In the *Introduction to the Literary Remains of the Late Henry James*, James's filial and adulatory assessment of his father's theological treatises, James describes his father as "one member of that band of saints and mystics, whose rare privilege it has been, by the mere example and recital of their own bosom-experience, to prevent religion from becoming a fossil conventionalism, and to keep it forever alive."[186] Henry James, Sr., in the eyes of his son, William, was a living exemplar of mysticism and saintliness and was the model on which James, consciously or not, patterned much of his understanding of what a genuine and deeply felt religious life should ideally be.[187] For instance, in the *Introduction to the Literary Remains*, explicitly drawing upon the pattern of his own father's personal experience, James describes the stereotypical process of a profound spiritual life as that which moves from "an acute despair, passing over into an equally acute optimism, through a passion of renunciation of the self and surrender to the higher power."[188] James knew the family myths well, and these mythic themes (dark despair, the self offered on the divine altar, and miraculous saving grace), which emerge from stories told time after time in the gatherings of the James family, form the backbone of his thinking on the religious life, particularly in the *Varieties*.

Henry Sr.'s moment of "acute despair" was especially vivid, and is most fully described in his book *Society the Redeemed Form of Man*. In this text, Henry Sr. describes how, in 1844, he and his family lived in England, not far from the royal castle near Windsor, in a beautiful cottage surrounded by parks and gardens. Henry Sr. was in good health, both physically and mentally. But life did not remain so idyllic. The highly stylized recollection of his theologically significant moment of despair is as follows:

> One day . . . towards the close of May, having eaten a comfortable dinner, I remained sitting at the table after the family had dispersed, idly gazing at the embers in the grate, thinking of nothing, and feeling only the exhilaration incident to a good digestion, when suddenly—in a lightning-flash as it were "fear came upon me, and trembling, which made all my bones to shake." To all appearance it was a perfectly insane and abject terror, without ostensible cause, and only to be accounted for, to my perplexed imagination, by some damned shape squatting invisible to me within the precincts of the room, and raying out from his fetid personality influences fatal to life. The thing had not lasted ten seconds before I felt myself a wreck; that is reduced from a state of firm, vigorous, joyful manhood to one of almost helpless infancy. The only self-control I was capable of exerting was to keep my seat. I felt the greatest desire to run incontinently to the foot of the stairs and shout for help to my wife,—to run to the roadside even, and appeal to the public to protect me; but by an immense effort I controlled these frenzied impulses, and determined not to budge from my chair till I had recovered my lost self-possession. This purpose I held to for a good long hour, as I reckoned time, beat upon meanwhile by an ever-growing tempest of doubt, anxiety, and despair, with absolutely no relief from any truth I had ever encountered save a most pale and distant glimmer of the divine existence, when I resolved to abandon the vain struggle, and communicate without more ado what seemed my sudden burden of inmost, implacable unrest to my wife.[189]

Jamesian biographers have, understandably, made considerable mileage from this narrative. R. W. B. Lewis is especially perceptive in his analysis of "the damned shape" that Henry Sr. envisions during this moment of abject terror. Lewis points out that this masculine presence ("*his* fetid personality") could have been interpreted by Henry Sr. in numerous ways:

> *This* is what he really was: not the righteous, virtue-seeking, family-loving man he had striven to be, but a nauseous, hateful, corrupted being that poisoned and destroyed everything he touched. At the same time, this was Henry James as he lay exposed to the spectral, all-perceiving eye of God. And finally—if this *was* an active element, it was one that [Henry] James did not allow himself to acknowledge—the shape was the son in

79

the outraged view of the father; a fulfillment of the father's furious prophecy, passed along by his surrogate years before, [when Henry Sr. had as a
young man in college spent the father's money frivolously] that he would
"become a loathing to himself and his best friends."[190]

Regardless of the particular interpretive gloss given to this
"damned shape," it is undeniable that after this experience Henry Sr.
suffered, on and off for two years, from the "rays" from its "fetid
personality." His immediate response was to approach several physicians in an attempt to get relief from the overwhelming, irrational fear
that he felt, but these physicians were somewhat less than helpful,
telling him that he was simply overly tired from his theological work
and recommending that he take a "water cure" at a nearby resort.

Apparently the "water cure" provided little immediate relief, but
Henry Sr.'s time at the resort was not wasted, for it was here that he
met a woman who was to prove crucial to his psychological and spiritual rejuvenation: a relatively obscure figure named Mrs. Chichester.
Mrs. Chichester, during one of their frequent meetings, heard Henry
Sr. narrate his experience at Windsor and then offered the following
insight: "It is, then, very much as I had ventured from two or three
previous things you have said, to suspect: you are undergoing what
Swedenborg calls a *vastation*; and though, naturally enough, you
yourself are despondent or even despairing about the issue, I cannot
help taking an altogether hopeful view of your prospects."[191] Prompted
by this intriguing, spiritually optimistic divination, Henry Sr. quickly
located two volumes of Emanuel Swedenborg (a Swedish mystic who
lived from 1688–1772) and began the philosophical/religious study to
which he later credited his cure.

Henry Sr. took to Swedenborg's writings almost immediately.
The texts of the mystic's thought became such a part of the James
family that, according to Henry James Jr., the family never felt fully
settled in their numerous journeys during the 1850s until Henry Sr.'s
Swedenborg volumes were safely placed on the bookshelves of their
new home.[192] It is important to note, as Lewis points out, that Henry
Sr. was not being overly eccentric in attaching himself so quickly to
the teachings of Swedenborg, since at that time, Swedenborg's influence permeated the philosophical world of England and America. For
instance, although disagreeing with Swedenborg's overly narrow
Christian perspective, Henry Sr.'s close friend, Ralph Waldo Emerson,
still referred to Swedenborg as "a colossal soul."[193] Swedenborg's teachings were also, to one degree or another, utilized in the flurry of
radical religious experimentation—the communitarianism, free-love,

faith-healing, mesmerism, and so on—that was sweeping across America at that moment in history. But in the final analysis, Henry Sr. wasn't a strict disciple of the Swedish mystic. He was much more interested in utilizing Swedenborg's insights for his own theological work than he was in passing them on verbatim to would-be converts. Even though he had enormous respect for Swedenborg's visionary experiences, he was much less enthusiastic about Swedenborg's philosophical and literary acumen (a complaint that others, including William, often directed to Henry Sr. himself as well).

In Henry Sr.'s opinion, Swedenborg had one key insight: selfhood is the only real evil in the universe. That this insight was central to Henry Sr. is not surprising, since its truth was so dramatically impressed upon him during his own "vastation" experience. According to Swedenborg, it is during these "vastations" that the soul, out of God's love and compassion, is emptied of its self-assurance and comes to experience directly its own inherent lack of substance and worth. Henry Sr. clearly connects his experience at Windsor with a radical transformation in his feelings of self-worth when he writes:

> It was impossible for me . . . to hold this audacious faith in selfhood any longer. When I sat down to dinner on that memorable chilly afternoon in Windsor, I held it serene and unweakened by the faintest breath of doubt; before I rose from table, it had inwardly shrivelled to a cinder. One moment I devoutly thanked God for the inappreciable boon of selfhood; the next, that inappreciable boon seemed to me the one thing damnable on earth, seemed a literal nest of hell within my own entrails.[194]

Reading Swedenborg's writings, Henry Sr. found enormous psychological comfort in the realization that this "vastation," which had previously seemed so malignant and disturbing was, in actuality, a gracious boon bestowed upon him by a loving God who wanted to restore his connection to the divine ground of all existence. In Henry Sr.'s post-Swedenborgian understanding, nothing he could have tried would have alleviated his feeling of panic, fear, and self-loathing, since its root cause was his previous overreliance on his own efforts, his "pre-vastation" attempts to adhere rigidly to a moral code. According to Henry Sr.'s later theological vision, any feeling of satisfaction with one's own ability to act morally was symptomatic of one's inherent alienation from God—not the Calvinistic God of wrath and judgement, a God understood to be inherently different from his creation, but rather, a loving God intimately linked with mankind, a God who was, in fact, the divine substance of all human beings. Henry Sr. came to believe that mankind, in its essence, was united and divine. However, through the curse of selfhood, mankind had become tragically (although not eternally or essentially) alienated from that ground of divinity. Achieving complete selflessness then was understood as a restoration of one's hidden divine nature. As Henry Sr. wrote at one point:

> My being lies utterly outside of my*self*, lies in utterly forgetting my*self* . . . lies in fact *in honestly identifying myself with others.* I know it will never be possible for me to do this perfectly, that is attain to self-extinction, because being created, I can never hope actually to become Divine; but at all events I shall become through eternal years more and more intimately one in nature, and I hope in spirit, with a being who is thoroughly destitute of this finiting principle, that is, a being who is without selfhood save in His creatures.[195]

It is arguable the extent to which Henry Sr. was successful in his quest (for despite his genuine amiability, he was infamous for his pugnacious, argumentative nature), but for his son William, Henry Sr. was an exemplar of selflessness. As William James mentions in the *Introduction to the Literary Remains*, his father "with all the mystical depth of experience, and all the mystical unction, had not a trace of the mystical egoism or voluptuousness" that William found so often in the literature written by "the common run of mystics"—mystics who, unlike his father, were still suffering from "that perfume of spiritual sensuality, which makes it impossible to many readers, even religious ones, to get any edification from their pages."[196]

But William was typically not so appreciative of the desirability of becoming selfless. In fact, much of his life's work, both existential and academic, can be seen as an attempt to justify the need for a strong, dynamic self, a self that makes moral choices, a self that creates and risks and suffers, a self that is *not* surrendered to the divine. How to create and maintain such a strong and vibrant selfhood was the central issue of much of James's young adulthood. Indeed, it is arguable that the depression, insomnia, eye-strain, backaches, and digestive problems he suffered with throughout much of his life were brought on (according to which biographical interpretation you choose) by either the need to define himself professionally or by the struggle to establish his own identity in contradistinction to that of his father. Much of James's lifework can be seen, at least from our post-Freudian vantage point, as an attempt by James to reconcile the profound respect and love he felt for his father with his equally powerful need to claim the validity and worth of his own independent perspective.

Establishing Foundations

This dialectic of filial loyalty and rebellion against paternal authority can also be seen in James's philosophy in the form of an oscillation between the necessity of religious self-surrender and the value
of moralistic self-assertion, or in James's attempts to harmonize his
belief in a spiritual world with his desire to legitimize that belief with
scientific and philosophical criteria.

A poignant expression of James's attempt to balance his love and
respect for his father with his need for independence appears in a
letter that he wrote to his dying father:[197]

> In that mysterious gulf of the past into which the present soon will fall
> and go back and back, yours is still for me the central figure. All my intel-
> lectual life I derive from you; and though we have often seemed at odds
> in the expression thereof, I'm sure there's a harmony somewhere, and
> that our strivings will combine. What my debt to you is goes beyond all
> my power of estimating,—so early, so penetrating and so constant has
> been the influence. You need be in no anxiety about your literary remains.
> I will see them well taken care of, and that your words shall not suffer for
> being concealed.[198]

William was true to his word: his *Introduction to the Literary
Remains of the Late Henry James* is a clear demonstration of his desire
to acquaint the world with his father's teachings. Much of James's
psychical research and interest in mysticism can similarly be seen as
a desire to fulfill his father's mission, a mission vividly summarized in
a letter that William wrote to his brother Henry in 1883, in reply to
Henry's description of his father's death: "As life closes, all a man has
done seems like one cry or sentence. Father's cry was the single one
that religion is real. The thing is so to 'voice' it that other ears shall
hear,—no easy task, but a worthy one, which in some shape I shall
attempt."[199]

William would, of course, attempt to express his father's "cry" in
much, if not all, of his investigations on religion and mysticism, but
the "voice" of that cry was always his own. Like his father, William
came to believe in the reality of the spiritual world, but unlike his
father, he did not claim that these beliefs were intuitively self-evident.
Instead, William attempted to base his belief in an unseen spiritual
world on a philosophical assessment of the mystical experiences of
others. As Ralph Barton Perry points out, William James, like his father, had strong religious beliefs, and felt that lived experience was
more important than intellectual constructions, but unlike his father,
he believed "none of these things either easily or loosely, but only

after years of painstaking analysis and with their meanings scrupulously guarded and defined."[200]

The numerous similarities and differences between William and Henry Sr. are perhaps most strikingly apparent in William's own version of a "vastation," the attack of unreasoning and debilitating "panic fear" that struck him in his dressing room in Boston, sometime early in 1870. It is now well known that in the *Varieties*, when James was supposedly translating from French an account of an anonymous correspondent's experience of this type of "panic fear," he was actually giving a hidden portrayal of his own experience. The account is worth quoting at length:

> Whilst in this state of philosophic pessimism and general depression of spirits about my prospects, I went one evening into a dressing-room in the twilight to procure some article that was there; when suddenly there fell upon me without any warning, just as if it came out of the darkness, a horrible fear of my own existence. Simultaneously there arose in my mind the image of an epileptic patient whom I had seen in the asylum, a black-haired youth with greenish skin, entirely idiotic, who used to sit all day on one of the benches, or rather shelves against the wall, with his knees drawn up against his chin, and the coarse gray undershirt, which was his only garment, drawn over them inclosing his entire figure. He sat there like a sort of sculptured Egyptian cat or Peruvian mummy, moving nothing but his black eyes and looking absolutely non-human. This image and my fear entered into a species of combination with each other. *That shape am I,* I felt, potentially. Nothing that I possess can defend me against that fate, if the hour for it should strike for me as it struck for him. There was such a horror of him, and such a perception of my own merely momentary discrepancy from him, that it was as if something hitherto solid within my breast gave way entirely, and I became a mass of quivering fear. After this the universe was changed for me altogether. I awoke morning after morning with a horrible dread at the pit of my stomach, and with a sense of the insecurity of life that I never knew before, and that I have never felt since. It was like a revelation; and although the immediate feelings passed away, the experience has made me sympathetic with the morbid feelings of others ever since. It gradually faded, but for months I was unable to go out into the dark alone.
>
> In general I dreaded to be left alone. I remember wondering how other people could live, how I myself had ever lived, so unconscious of that pit of insecurity beneath the surface of life. My mother in particular, a very cheerful person, seemed to me a perfect paradox in her unconsciousness

of danger, which you may well believe I was very careful not to disturb by revelations of my own state of mind. I have always thought that this experience of melancholia of mine had a religious bearing.[201]

Having given this masked description of his own experience, James (still treating the above narrative as though it were not about himself) goes on to add:

> On asking this correspondent to explain more fully what he meant by these last words, the answer he wrote was this: "I mean that the fear was so invasive and powerful that if I had not clung to scripture-texts like 'The eternal God is my refuge,' etc., 'Come unto me, all ye that labor and are heavy-laden,' etc., 'I am the resurrection and the life,' etc., I think I should have grown really insane."[202]

In a footnote to the above passage (the only explicit reference to his father in a book that owed much to Henry Sr.), William acknowledges the connection between this experience and his father's vastation experience, citing: "For another case of fear equally sudden, see Henry James: *Society the Redeemed Form of Man*, Boston, 1879."[203]

The similarities between the experiences of Henry Sr. and his son are very pronounced: the suddenness of the attacks, the vivid imagery of the horrifying figure, the complete disintegration of self-esteem, the attempts to combat the fear by focusing on either "divine existence" or New Testament passages, as well as their shared astonishment that they had managed to live up until that point in complete ignorance of that degree of terror. But the differences between father and son are equally, if not more, compelling: Henry Sr.'s experience occurs while he is cheerful and hopeful, while William's experience emerges out of a deep depression. The father's central image is theological and barely human—the "damned shape" sending out "rays" from "his fetid personality," whereas the son's basic metaphor is clinical, perhaps based on epileptic patients William had seen in an asylum in Northampton. It is also clear that while Henry Sr. never consciously recognized that the squatting, malignant presence in the room was, perhaps, in part at least, a hidden aspect of his own being, William's terror was fueled by the acknowledgment that the catatonic patient mirrored his own potential—what he could become if he did not defeat his own immobilizing despair.[204]

How father and son both managed to recover from these devastating encounters is also illuminating. Henry Sr. finds relief through the providential guidance of a mysterious woman, who points him in the direction of the inspired words of a mystic, who, in turn, taught him the glories of self-effacement, and whose teachings, over time, radically revised his philosophical perspective. William's journey to health, although lasting approximately the same period of time (close to two years), and also based on the power of a philosophically revised worldview, takes a very different route and leads him to fundamentally dissimilar conclusions. William's path to healing was to nurture his own power of moral choice, especially the choice to believe that he had the freedom to create a vital, healthy identity through the power of his own will. William encapsulates this philosophical perspective in an often quoted diary entry on 30 April 1870, several months after the attack in the dressing room:

> I think that yesterday was a crisis in my life. I finished the first part of Renouvier's second *Essais* and see no reason why his definition of free will—"the sustaining of a thought *because I choose to* when I might have other thought"—need be the definition of an illusion. At any rate, I will assume for the present—until next year—that it is no illusion. My first act of free will shall be to believe in free will. For the remainder of the year, I will abstain from the mere speculation and contemplative Grübelei [Lewis notes that this is James's idiomatic use of the term Grübeleien, meaning, in this case, "mental rummagings"] in which my nature takes most delight, and voluntarily cultivate the feeling of moral freedom, by reading books favorable to it, as well as by acting. After the first of January, my callow skin being somewhat fledged, I may perhaps return to metaphysical study and skepticism without danger to my powers of action. For the present then remember: care little for speculation; much for the *form* of my action. . . . Not in *Anschaungen* [observings, contemplations] but in accumulated acts of thought lies salvation. . . . I will posit life (the real, the good) in the self-governing *resistance* of the ego to the world. Life shall [be built in] doing, and suffering and creating.[205]

James's heroic intentions did not immediately free him from his prolonged depression, intestinal problems, backaches, and eyestrain. As Perry insightfully points out, "the crisis of April 1870 was a turning point but not a cure."[206] In fact, for the rest of James's life, he battled with periodic bouts of varying degrees of mental and physical illness. But it is also undeniable that a corner had been turned in this particularly debilitating phase and that he never again had to wrestle with illness to quite the same degree as he had during the late 1860s and early 1870s. This positive transformation in James's emotional well-being is vividly described in a letter describing James's own awareness of his improved mental health—a letter written by Henry Sr. to Henry Jr. on 18 March 1873:

> He came in here the other afternoon when I was sitting alone, and after walking the floor in an animated way for a moment, exclaimed "Dear me! What a difference there is between me now and me last spring this time: then so hypochondriacal . . . and now feeling my mind so cleared up and restored to sanity. It is the difference between death and life." He had great effusion.[207]

Like his father, James gradually, over a period of years, managed to emerge out of a psychological abyss and found the key to successful living through philosophical inquiry. But unlike his father, James's key to vibrant life was not self-surrender to an immanent deity, but rather, was an affirmation of the value of the self and the creative powers of the will. William's salvation was found, not in mystical absorption into an all-pervasive divinity, but rather, in doing heroic battle with the forces of evil (and inertia) present in this world. However, at the same time, the son never forgot the father. Mysticism remained an alluring figure, hovering in the shadows perhaps, but always enticing him, inviting him to explore unseen worlds.

༄ 2 ༅

Experiencing Unseen Worlds: Towards a Jamesian Epistemology of Mysticism

The world sings its hundreds of millions of songs to us every minute. But our attention is on only what our habits allow us to experience. . . . We have the ability to collect our attention and aim it in any wanted direction. But it is our habit to be distracted and numbed and take no notice of the greater portion.
—Kay Cordell Whitaker, *The Reluctant Shaman*

But I must direct you to your own selves. You must apprehend a living movement. You must know how to listen to yourselves before your own consciousness.
—Friedrich Schleiermacher, *On Religion*

When the full moon is shining in the sky to gladden the hearts of all, who cares to see a picture of the moon?
—Śrī Saṅkarācārya, *Vikekacūḍāmaṇi*

Come, let us go into the body of that light. Let us live in the cleanliness of that song. Let us throw off the pieces of the world like clothing and enter naked into wisdom.
—Thomas Merton, *New Seeds of Contemplation*

During the past several decades, philosophers of mysticism have looked carefully at the philosophical status of mystical experience. Their investigation has typically revolved around a cluster of central questions: What exactly occurs in the process of having a mystical experience? What role does the mystic's cultural and psychological background play in the formation and interpretation of mystical experiences? Is there a "common core" of similar mystical experiences that transcend the inevitable doctrinal variations of different religious traditions, or are mystical experiences better understood as irreducibly pluralistic expressions of diverse and divergent cultures?

As a result of this line of questioning, some important shifts have occurred in the ways in which philosophers of mysticism understand the dynamics of mystical experiences. At the present moment within the field of the philosophy of mysticism, it is no longer possible to talk about mystical experiences as if they happen in a vacuum, cut off from the influences of the culture in which they occur. We now have a highly nuanced perception of the ways in which different cultural and religious belief systems affect not only the ways in which mystics will interpret their experiences *after* they return to ordinary consciousness, but also the ways in which these belief systems help to determine the parameters of what the mystics will likely experience *during* their mystical states. The pendulum of academic fashion has swung from the assertion made by many earlier philosophers of mysticism that mystical experiences or "feelings" are direct, nonlinguistic manifestations of an undefined (but usually vaguely Christian) Ultimate Reality[1] to the present-day assumption that every mystical experience is a highly refined, culturally produced, linguistically structured event that tells us more about the tradition in which it occurred than the transcendental realm that it supposedly contacts.[2] Claims of immediacy and intuitive certainty are now suspect. As Nancy Frankenberry, a contemporary philosopher of religion notes, "the pervasive epistemological orientation of contemporary philosophy is decidedly inhospitable to appeals to immediate experience or claims to non-inferential knowledge on the basis of experience."[3]

William James is often associated with a cluster of "classical" philosophers of mysticism and religious experience (i.e., Evelyn Underhill, Joseph Maréchal, and W. T. Stace, among others) whose theories about mystical experience supposedly have been superseded by the more sophisticated linguistic analysis practiced today by many contemporary scholars of mysticism. It will be the job of this chapter to examine James's theories on mystical experience in order to determine whether these theories are indeed so outmoded. To do so, it is necessary to unravel the complex strands of James's theories of experience (i.e., his epistemology) and in the process, answer several crucial questions: What actually is the relationship between religious beliefs and mystical experience in James's thought? How can we best understand the cognitive status of "feelings," "emotions," and "sensations" in James's epistemology, as well as the repercussions of this epistemological understanding for James's philosophy of mysticism? Finally, what is the relationship between James's more general theoretical understanding of "states of consciousness" and "experience" and his more specific study of mystical "states of consciousness" or "experience"?

Copyrighted Material

"We Feel Sorry Because We Cry, Angry Because We Strike": James's Psychology of Emotion

It is well known that James stresses the priority of felt experience in religious life. According to James, "feeling is the deeper source of religion," while "theological formulas are secondary products, like translations of a text into another tongue."[4] A genuine religious life, in James's opinion, is based primarily on "definite perceptions of fact"[5] and only secondarily on theological understandings. For James, religious perceptions indicate that "the divine is actually present," whereas theological understandings only help to interpret these religious experiences; they do "not produce them, nor . . . reproduce their individuality."[6] According to James, these intuitive, immediate apprehensions of the spiritual world can not be captured by verbal descriptions, but rather, they have to be directly experienced within oneself, since "there is always a *plus*, a *thisness*, which feeling alone can answer for."[7]

Many scholars, while commenting on the *Varieties*, have noted James's emphasis on religious feeling, but, understandably, have often assumed that in James's terminology "feeling" is equivalent to "emotion." While it is undeniable that James often does link these two terms and indeed, frequently does appear to claim that emotions are at the root of religious experience, it is important to point out that James does not equate "feeling" with "emotion."

In the beginning of *The Principles of Psychology*, James's masterpiece of psychological investigation published more than a decade before the *Varieties*, James underscores that he intends to use the term "feelings" to signify a much wider range of meanings than it typically connotes. James emphasizes that in the *Principles*, he will use the term "feeling" (as well as the term "thought") as a generic, catch-all designation of any and all states of consciousness. James's willingness to use either "feeling" or "thought" to designate any conceivable psychological event is an apt (if at times confusing) response to his insistence that every moment of consciousness is a dynamic "much-at-onceness" of cognitive, emotive, and sensory elements. James attempts to reflect this fusion of intellectual and intuitive qualities in our psychological life by stretching the significance of "thought" and "feeling" beyond the cluster of meanings that we might typically associate with these two terms. Therefore, in James's terminology "thought" is not simply cognitive and "feeling" is not just emotive or sensory.[8] In other words, in James's psychology, feelings are a much broader and inclusive category than emotions; that

91

is, for James, emotions are a special *subset* of feeling. As John Wild, a noted scholar of James, mentions, "for James, feeling is the more general term. Emotion is the name for a special kind of feeling, in which bodily changes are peculiarly evident."[9] Therefore, while James has a rich (and controversial) theory of our emotional life, his psychology of emotion has only a tangential relationship to his understanding of the nature of religious feelings.

James first articulated his theory of emotions in an 1884 essay, "What is an Emotion?" Subsequently, in the chapter on emotions in the *Principles*, he restated this theory and also acknowledged that a Danish thinker named C. G. Lange had independently formulated a basically identical theory during the same time period that James had published his initial essay. This theory, which James substantially modified later on in his career, is now designated as the "James-Lange theory" of emotions. This theory claims that our commonsense understanding of emotions is incorrect. Our common sense tells us that the process of having an emotion occurs in the following way: We perceive something (for instance, a bear in the woods). This perception then ignites an emotional reaction (in this case, fear), which then catalyzes a physical response (for example, heightened blood pressure, heart palpitations, surges of adrenaline, running, screaming, and so on). What James's radical and provocative proposal does is to jettison the idea of emotions as something separate from our physical response to a particular stimulus. For James (at least in this initial formulation of the theory), the physical response generated within us at the moment of perception *is* the emotion. According to James:

> We feel sorry because we cry, angry because we strike, afraid because we tremble. . . . Without the bodily states following on the perception, the latter would be purely cognitive in form, pale, colorless, destitute of emotional warmth. We might then see the bear and judge it best to run, receive the insult and deem it right to strike, but we should not actually feel afraid or angry.[10]

As is evident from the example above, James fought hard to embody all mental processes. For him, every state of consciousness is accompanied by or leads to a physiological response (alternations in heart-beat, gland-secretions, and so on). At first, then, it might appear that James is simply pointing out how every emotion we feel is inevitably accompanied by some sort of physical reaction, or it might seem that he merely wants to emphasize that these physiological changes are what makes every emotion distinctly "emotional." This conclusion appears to be supported by certain, isolated statements made by James, such as the following:

> What kind of emotion of fear would be left if the feeling neither of quickened heartbeats not of shallowed breathing, neither of trembling lips nor of weakened limbs, neither of goose-flesh nor of visceral stirrings, were present, it is quite impossible for me to think. . . . The only thing that can possibly be supposed to take its place is some cold-blooded and dispassionate judicial sentence, confined entirely to the intellectual realm.[11]

However, if we examine James's theory of emotions as a whole, it seems clear that this theory is, in actuality, more radical. A careful investigation of James's theory reveals that he is not merely demonstrating the inevitable physiological component present in every emotional response, but, instead, is attempting to bypass the cognitive elements in emotions altogether, so that emotions can be seen as types of reflex actions, as instantaneous responses to various perceptions. For James, these physiological responses are not generated by any specific ideas associated with what has been perceived. Rather, he theorizes that we perceive a situation and then the physical reactions set in automatically. For instance, James suggests: "If we abruptly see a dark moving form in the woods, our heart stops beating, and we catch our breath instantly and before any articulate idea of danger can arise."[12] Only later, after the fact, do we interpret these physiological sensations as being "emotions."

Understandably, James generated a storm of controversy with this rather two-dimensional understanding of emotions. In response, in an 1894 essay, "The Physical Basis of Emotion," he backed down from many of his more extreme claims. As Gerald Myers points out, in this essay James willingly abandoned his earlier "slapdash" language, claiming that "he never really believed that we are frightened because we run or are sorry because we cry, nor that any given emotion can be identified in terms of a specific act or bodily symptom."[13] However, James continued to insist that the "stuff" of an emotional experience is physiological and "denied that emotions such as anger, jealousy, and grief, which commonly exhibit physical symptoms . . . are ghostly or bodiless."[14]

In the end, James was willing to admit that emotions are not simply reflex, noncognitive responses to environmental stimuli. He conceded that emotions are intimately linked with our mental states as well (for instance, it appears that James was willing to concede that if we are *hunting* a bear, we could easily be delighted, not frightened, when we see one). In fact, if we look closely, we can see that he was already emphasizing the cognitive components of emotional life even before he wrote "The Physical Basis of Emotion." Early in his chapter on emotions in the *Principles*, he gives examples of emotional responses that are not simple reflex reactions, but instead, arise in response to our cognitive assessment of a situation. For instance, he comments that "one may get angrier in thinking over one's insult than at the moment of receiving it; and we melt more over a mother who is dead than we ever did when she was living."[15] It is clear, in these cases at least, that James is aware of the connection between thought and emotions, even if he did maintain that the "stuff" of emotions is always primarily physiological.

James's description of the cognitive elements inherent in our emotional life becomes even more pronounced by the time of the *Varieties*. For instance, early in this text he examines how a religious emotion becomes "religious." Unlike his philosophical and theological predecessors (Friedrich Schleiermacher, in particular), James does not believe that there is only one generic religious emotion that is present in all religious experiences. Instead, he suggests it is more likely that there are many different religious emotions, such as "religious fear, religious love, religious awe, religious joy and so forth."[16] For James, these different emotions are "religious" by virtue of the religious *meanings* associated with them. That is, the only difference between religious emotions and "natural" emotions is that religious emotions are understood to have a religious focus. For instance, the awe we feel in the presence of a stunning natural setting would become *religious* awe if we begin (for whatever reason) to interpret and experience this setting religiously, to understand it as being more than simply natural beauty. Therefore, religious awe (and every other religious emotion) is certainly *not* purely physiological, since in order for it to become religious at all an emotional experience must contain within it a complex cluster of implicit religious meanings.

Throughout the *Varieties*, it is, admittedly, often difficult to sort out James's distinction between emotions and feelings. James is simply not consistent in his use of "feeling" and "emotion" as technical terms. For instance, in the heat of his attempts to distinguish the experiential aspects of religion from its intellectual components, James does at times oppose "feeling" to "thought" and, unfortunately, also occasionally uses "feeling" when he apparently means "emotion." But, on the whole, when James uses the term "feeling," it should be understood to signify a much wider range of meanings than just "emotion."

Thoughts about Feelings: James's Emphasis on Religious Experience

In the *Varieties*, James typically uses the term "feeling" to refer to that which is experiential, first-hand, and direct (even though it may contain tacit cognitive elements as well). This understanding of "feeling" is rooted in a three-tiered model of how human beings interact with and respond to their environment. As several Jamesian scholars have pointed out, much of James's philosophical work was, whether consciously acknowledged or not, filtered through the grid of this triadic model, this integrated three-part process in which, (1) we perceive (sense, feel, experience) the outer world, then (2) we classify and mentally respond to that information using the intellectual "maps" that we have accumulated through our years of education and acculturation, and then (3) we act in the world guided by the results of our efforts in the first two stages.[17] "Feeling" and "experience" for James correspond to the first stage of this process, but the perceptual, immediate nature of these psychical events does not imply that feelings or experiences are therefore completely divorced from the more overtly cognitive second stage. While it is true that James does at times make a simplistic differentiation between these three components (perceptions, cognitions, and actions), more fundamentally, as he repeatedly emphasizes, these are three phases of a unified process. The psychologist or philosopher can, for analytical purposes, artificially separate out perceptions, cognitions, and actions, but in reality, they are simply different moments in an organic whole.

When James investigates religion through the lens of this triad of perceptions, cognitions, and actions, what emerges is the "holy trinity" (if you will) of religious experiences, religious beliefs, and saintly actions. A detailed discussion of saintly actions will be postponed until chapter 5, but in this section we will examine carefully the interaction between religious experiences and religious beliefs that is at the heart of James's epistemology of mysticism.

James is famous (or infamous) for his stress on the priority of religious experience as well as for his denigration of abstract theological systems that attempt to act as a substitute for a vital, living interaction with the unseen world. James, following in the path already trodden by his father, thinks that most theological work is nothing more than "a shuffling and matching of pedantic dictionary-adjectives, aloof from morals, aloof from human needs . . . [in which] verbality has stepped into the place of vision, professionalism into that of life."[18] For James, religious beliefs spring from the soil of our religious experiences; they emerge from "our passions or our mystical intuitions;"[19] they arise out of those religious "facts" which supply the data that a logically-based system of beliefs can then augment, dignify, and make plausible, but can never completely contradict nor do without. Theological speculations are seen by James's metaphor-generating mind as "buildings-out" to the "house" originally created by first-hand experience, or in other words, as helpful, logical additions that are built in accordance to the specifications originally provided by religious feelings.

It is clear that, for James, the work performed by theology and religious philosophy ultimately depends upon the raw material generated by religious experiences, and so will always be an interpretative, inductive, after-the-fact operation. However, James also stresses that since religious feeling is "private and dumb, and unable to give an account of itself," religious conceptualizations do have the important task of rescuing "religion from unwholesome privacy";[20] religious belief systems have the job of giving voice to the seemingly ineffable hints provided by various religious experiences, so that religion can emerge out of the isolation of its interiority and become a full and important component of the public sphere.

In the *Varieties*, James is not always, however, so positive in his assessment of the role of theological speculation. He frequently writes as if explicit theological work is an ignoble pretender, a puffed-up, yet essentially powerless dandy who ignores at its peril the less prestigious and articulate, yet more virile, moments of religious experience. James often writes as if rational theological constructions belong to one side of a set of neatly specified pairs of opposites—for example, the articulate versus the inarticulate, reason versus intuition, argumentation versus immediate conviction. James's rhetorical schematization of these pairs of opposites is especially apparent in the following:

> In the metaphysical and religious sphere, articulate reasons are cogent for us only when our inarticulate feelings of reality have already been impressed in favor of the same conclusion. Then, indeed, our intuitions and our reason work together. . . . Our impulsive belief is here always what sets up the original body of truth, and our articulately verbalized philosophy is but its showy translation into formulas. The unreasoned and immediate assurance is the deep thing in us, the reasoned argument is but a surface exhibition.[21]

Here, the contrast is clear: in James's opinion, our directly experienced and strongly felt religious impulses are the essential foundation for an authentic religious life, while our carefully structured, explicitly rational, theological arguments are eye-catching but basically inessential ornamentation. However, James's stress on the primacy of religious feeling does not therefore imply, as some Jamesian scholars would have us believe, that James claims that religious feelings are completely devoid of any and all religious beliefs.[22] In the previous passage, for instance, James equates "inarticulate feelings" with "impulsive beliefs." The contrast therefore is not between "feelings" and "beliefs," but between one type of knowing that is immediate and vivid (yet which may well contain "overtones" of religious beliefs in the "margins" of that experience) and another type of knowing that is logically based and explicitly thought out.[23]

James's emphasis on the priority of religious experience also does not necessarily signify that he completely denigrates the value of the more overtly intellectual aspects of our religious life. James's apparent anti-intellectualism is, in many ways, actually a rhetorical response to his philosophical opponents who at the time were attempting to give priority to the role of explicit logical argumentation in religious life. However, James's rhetorical zeal often, admittedly, does lead to an overly facile separation of reason and experience, and tends to mask James's long-lasting struggle to reconcile rationality and religious feeling. James often does tend to mock philosophical attempts to base religion on a self-sufficient and overly abstract rationality, but he also frequently praises the merits of a philosophical perspective that admits the value of our rational faculties, as long as this modest, restrained rationality acts in harmony with the information provided by religious experiences.[24]

A Contemporary Critique of James's Theories of Religious Experience

James's stress on the primacy and immediacy of powerful religious experiences has recently come under sustained criticism by different philosophers of religion. It is important, therefore, to take some time in order to examine the relative merits of these critiques. In order to limit the scope of the discussion, our attention will primarily focus on the important and influential work of Wayne Proudfoot, especially his recent book *Religious Experience* . While a complete investigation

97

of Proudfoot's entire work is obviously impossible here, it is important to single out some of the most significant aspects of Proudfoot's philosophical gameplan, especially as it relates to James's theory of the immediacy of religious experience. A analysis of Proudfoot's work will, hopefully, enable us to gain a clearer understanding of James's theories about religious experience by providing a vivid and powerful alternative to James's own insights, one that is often sharply and explicitly critical of James's work.

First, Proudfoot attempts to undermine the certainty and prestige of introspective, first-hand knowledge of inner experiences. Second, he makes the claim that emotions, including religious emotions, are not inner states that can be directly experienced, but rather are the end-result of an almost arbitrary cognitive labeling of physiological disturbances. Third, he posits that powerful religious experiences, like emotions, are perhaps nothing more than the result of the religious believer or practitioner superimposing a tacit, previously held set of religious beliefs onto a mysterious shift of physiological equilibrium. Finally, Proudfoot attempts to refute James's comparison of religious experiences to sensation and feeling—a refutation that is based on James's supposedly incorrect understanding of the true nature of sensation and emotion.

In Proudfoot's attempt to discredit the reliability of introspective knowledge, he states that "our only evidence for the claim that some moment of consciousness is immediate and intuitive is our feeling that it is."[25] Feelings alone are simply not sufficient evidence for Proudfoot. Proudfoot points out that religious experiences, like sensory experiences, can be wrongly interpreted, and therefore, the authenticity (or inauthenticity) of an experience is demonstrated not by the evidence of what that experience feels like to the person doing the experiencing, but rather by choosing which particular explanation of that experience best fits the facts. Proudfoot rejects the claim that first-hand experiential knowledge about ourselves is, theoretically at least, any more dependable, or even accessible, than what an outside observer might come to know about us. To back up this assertion, Proudfoot examines one particularly vivid example of introspective events that would seem to be known fully only from within: emotions.

Proudfoot's understanding of emotions is provocative. For Proudfoot, "emotions are not inner states or events, nor are they somatic sensations or even experiences of any kind."[26] He is willing to make this radical claim because, according to Proudfoot, "psychologists have not been able to discover peculiar physiological or mental states that are correlated with each of the emotions."[27] Our emotions, from

Proudfoot's perspective, are intimately linked with our external behavior, as well as the way in which we, and others, interpret that behavior in its particular context. For Proudfoot, emotions are better assessed by an outside observer, since "people are often mistaken about their own emotions. The person who is angry, jealous, envious, or in love may be the last one to realize it."[28] Accordingly, Proudfoot thinks that "we don't identify our own emotions by introspection, nor have we any privileged access to special inner states. . . . There is no essential distinction between first and third person attribution of emotions."[29]

In Proudfoot's model, a person does not directly perceive that he or she is, for instance, angry. Instead, that person notices certain physiological cues (increased heart rate, flushing, sweaty palms, and so on), decides what is causing these physiological reactions, and then attributes these sensations to a particular emotion, in this case, anger. The emotion chosen depends upon the context—the same physiological sensations that one person interprets as anger, in another situation might be interpreted as fear, or as sexual arousal, or as any number of other emotions. For Proudfoot, no emotion is self-evident or immediately apparent. For instance, we may think that we are directly aware of the fact that we are in love with someone, but in actuality, what happens is that we first become aware of "flutterings, consider indigestion and other possible explanations, and settle on the hypothesis that the flutterings are elicited by the person of whom [we are] thinking and conclude that [we are] in love. . . . [We] don't immediately perceive it as love and then search for a cause and an object."[30]

Proudfoot's attempt to discredit any self-apparent, internal features of religious experience allows him to reduce all emotions, especially religious ones, to cognitions which simply "explain a bit of behavior or a physiological change by setting it within a larger context."[31] If emotions can be seen as *really* cognitions in another form, Proudfoot is then in a better position to say that "the common element in religious experience is likely to be found . . . in the *beliefs* [my italics] held by the subject about the causes of that state."[32] Unlike private experiences that are inaccessible to public scrutiny, *beliefs* can be analyzed, examined, and criticized. If beliefs can be seen as the formative element of what is distinctively religious about a religious experience, then religious experience can be understood and explained in a purely naturalistic sense, without having to deal with the unnecessary, messy complication of any causality that might transcend cultural, linguistic, or historical matrices.[33]

Proudfoot's philosophical assertions about the nature of emotion and experience are rooted in a philosophical perspective that has

99

captured the loyalty of many philosophers of mysticism.[34] Robert Forman, a contemporary scholar of mysticism, calls this philosophical school "constructivism."[35] The constructivist position asserts that mystical experiences are not immediate apprehensions of some (variously construed) Absolute that are later interpreted according to the belief systems and cultural framework available in that mystic's world. Instead, according to the constructivists, mystical experiences are always filtered through, and formed by, the mystic's tacit, internalized cultural symbolic structures, structures that are operative during the experience itself.[36] Constructivism also tends to be radically pluralistic, arguing that because mystical experiences do not escape the formative influence of each mystic's cultural and psychological background, every mystical experience is inevitably different from every other mystical experience.

Forman points out that there are different versions of constructivism. "Complete constructivism" argues that mystical experiences are "one hundred percent shaped, determined, and provided by" the mystic's cultural framework, whereas "incomplete constructivism" claims that while part of every mystical experience is inevitably provided by the mystic's cultural background and psychological conditioning, other aspects of the experience are "provided by something else."[37] If that "something else" is understood to be anything more than sensory input, then Proudfoot clearly belongs within the "complete constructivism" camp. According to Proudfoot:

> [A mystical] experience is shaped by a complex pattern of concepts, commitments, and expectations which the mystic brings to it. These beliefs and attitudes are formative of, rather than consequent upon, the experience. They define in advance what experiences are possible. The terms in which the subject understands what is happening to him are constitutive of the experience; consequently those in different traditions have different experiences.[38]

In Proudfoot's theoretical model, a mystical experience is created by the interaction of two components: a shift in awareness produced by different spiritual disciplines and a cognitive labeling of that shift of awareness—a labeling in which the mystic, using the understandings he or she has acquired by immersion in a particular mystical tradition, attributes the shift in awareness to a nonnatural cause (i.e., the grace of God, the blessings of the bodhisattvas, and so on). The primary function of the cognitive labeling of a mental and physical change is to enable the mystic to identify this change as something more than just simply the result of his or her practice of various strenuous spiritual disciplines. In Proudfoot's view, this perception by the mystic that his or her experience cannot be fully explained in naturalistic terms is already encoded in the expectations of the mystic; it is already there waiting, in a sense, to rush out and greet any anomalous shift in consciousness so that this shift can then be triumphantly embraced as "mystical." For Proudfoot, these tacit expectations and beliefs given to the mystic by his or her tradition are what prompt a previously ambiguous and amorphous set of physiological and psychological changes to become a full-fledged mystical experience. Proudfoot's theoretical stance holds that it is not that a mystic has an experience which contains qualities that he or she recognizes as "mystical." Instead, the mystic is given a set of criteria of what to expect in a mystical experience and then dutifully applies this set of criteria to the various shifts in psychological and physiological equilibrium produced by the mystic's spiritual disciplines.

According to Proudfoot, ineffability is one of the most important criteria by which the mystic labels various experiences as mystical. Proudfoot claims that James is incorrect to treat "ineffability as if it were a simple property of the experience, or a phenomenological characteristic that [can] not be further analyzed."[39] For Proudfoot, mystical experiences are not beyond language. Indeed, their supposed ineffability is itself already conceptually predefined by the mystic's tradition. Proudfoot argues that the particular "Ultimate Reality" posited by almost all mystical traditions is typically said to be beyond words, thoughts or concepts. Therefore, the terms used by these traditions to designate their particular "Ultimate Reality" serve a peculiar function. Terms such as "God" in the *via negativa* of Dionysius the Areopagite, the injunction "*neti, neti*" of the Upanishadic tradition, as well as the more complex logical quandaries of Nāgārjuna and the various apophatic formulations of Taoism, Sufism, and Zen Buddhism, all act as "placeholders," that is, they are all religious terms or doctrines specifically designed to prevent the believer or practitioner from applying any labels, beliefs, or concepts to the reality or state of consciousness that they designate. In Proudfoot's opinion, would-be mystics, who have typically been immersed in an intensive study of their tradition, are on some level aware of this placeholder function and have accepted that the "object" of their spiritual search is beyond words and concepts. They are, therefore, in a sense, primed to label as "ineffable" any of the mysterious or anomalous physiological or mental experiences which are generated by their spiritual disciplines. This process in its turn leads the would-be mystics to conclude that these supposedly ineffable experiences are genuinely mystical, since ineffability is a quality that their tradition has pre-ordained to be an integral part of mystical experiences.

Proudfoot's analysis presents a striking contrast to James's understanding of the mechanics of mystical epistemology. James claims that a mystic's first-hand experience contains within it something which can only be known directly, something that is outside the sphere of intellectual categorization, something that cannot be captured by an external observer's conceptual analysis. Proudfoot strongly disagrees, claiming that "direct acquaintance is neither necessary nor sufficient for understanding religious experience. Such experience includes a cognitive component that can be analyzed and rendered intelligible even in the absence of direct acquaintance with the experience."[40] The implication of this analysis is clear: since highly trained philosophers or psychologists are often more aware of the existence of this cognitive component than the typically less educated mystics, these outside observers, in Proudfoot's eyes, actually understand the subtle nuances of the experience better than the mystics themselves.

The dispute between Proudfoot and James comes down to the following: Which has priority—the *beliefs* of the mystic or the *experiences* of the mystic? Proudfoot stresses the priority of beliefs. For Proudfoot, it is the mystic's prior beliefs that turn a neutral experience into something that can be labeled as "mystical." Although he admits that an individual can perceive internal physiological changes, he denies that an individual is given any immediately self-apparent, specific information during religious experiences themselves. Since Proudfoot is also seemingly closed to the existence of anything that transcends the natural world, his theoretical model subsequently reduces mystical experiences to a superimposition of the mystic's prior beliefs onto the passive and amorphous mold of anomalous physical or psychological changes.

On the other hand, James stresses the priority of experiences. Even though he acknowledges the important influence of the mystic's beliefs on his or her experiences, James would claim that these experiences are not simply arbitrary interpretations of neutral psychological and physiological events. In James's articulation of the complex, dialectical interaction between beliefs and experiences, mystical experiences can just as easily resist or even change a mystic's previously held beliefs as they can be molded and shaped by those beliefs. Further, since James is open to the possibility that there might indeed be a spiritual reality that actively interacts with our everyday level of existence, he is willing to posit that mystical experiences, similar to sense experiences, have a degree of integrity and objectivity, that they come to the mystic already possessing varying degrees of information prior to their "contact" with the mystic; he suggests that they have, as he puts it, a "noetic quality." James's willingness to state that mystical experiences are typically noetic is based on his recognition that mystics often claim that mystical experiences reveal truths, or that they contain reliable knowledge, or that they have an "objectivity" or "otherness" inherent within them.

Proudfoot agrees with James that mystical experiences have a noetic quality, but as with ineffability, he asserts that the noetic quality of a mystical experience is not a simple phenomenological characteristic of the experience. According to Proudfoot, the noetic quality of a mystical experience is merely the cerebral judgement made by the mystic that a certain experience is not solely his or her subjective creation. This judgement that an experience is "religious" is not made because the experience possesses certain identifiable, directly felt, intrinsic religious qualities, but instead, an experience is understood to be religious because the person who has the experience superimposes a ready-made label of "religious" onto any unexplained shift in his or her physical or psychological equilibrium.

Proudfoot argues that religious experiences are not "religious" by virtue of their subject matter, pointing out that if this were the case, then "visiting Borobodur [a Buddhist temple], listening to Bach, admiring a painting by Piero della Francesca, wishing there were a God, and tracing the history of the concept of nirvana would all be religious experiences."[41] For Proudfoot, these events could all *become* religious experiences, but only if the subject of these experiences apprehends them through the lens of his or her previously held religious beliefs.

Proudfoot attempts to underscore the validity of this analysis by contrasting two images of the Virgin Mary: an image of the Virgin consciously imagined within his mind and the vision of the Virgin which unexpectedly appeared to Alphonse Ratisbonne in a small, impoverished church in Rome (an experience that Proudfoot takes from the pages of the *Varieties*). Proudfoot notes:

> The images may be exactly the same, perhaps modeled after a certain painting with which we are both familiar, but the experiences are vastly different. I believe my image to be the deliverance of imagination and memory, and Ratisbonne took his to be the result of an external intervention that was a sign intended for him.[42]

For Proudfoot, if the external form of the Virgin stays the same, then the primary difference between these two experiences is that he and Ratisbonne each made different judgments as to the cause of these otherwise identical images. Proudfoot understands that the image is a conscious subjective creation, while Ratisbonne believes that his image was an actual appearance of the Virgin herself.

At first glance, Proudfoot's argument appears convincing. But if we look closer at his presentation, it becomes apparent that it is highly problematic. To begin with, Proudfoot's spartan, abstract depiction of Ratisbonne's experience is extremely misleading. If we go back to James's detailed account of Ratisbonne's experience,[43] it becomes immediately apparent that Ratisbonne's experience is not simply a matter of having a vision of the Virgin which, because of his previous religious beliefs, he then concludes is real. Instead, Ratisbonne's experience is a sudden, personality-transforming, emotionally complex confrontation with a powerful presence that shattered most of his previously held religious beliefs. Prior to this experience, Ratisbonne, "a freethinking French Jew,"[44] felt disdain towards Catholicism, due in part to the fact that his brother had converted to Catholicism and had become a priest. Ratisbonne at the time of the experience was in Rome, with a friend who was interested in converting him to Catholicism. This friend invited Ratisbonne for a carriage ride, but then said that he would like to spend a few moments in a church before leaving. Ratisbonne decided to amble into the church instead of waiting outside in the carriage. In the church, Ratisbonne idly glanced here and there, not thinking about anything in particular, noticing only a black dog trotting in front of him. Then, without warning, the church appeared to vanish and he had the vision of the Virgin.

Ratisbonne's description of this event is, significantly, devoid of any details of the Virgin's physical appearance. Instead, Ratisbonne focuses on the feeling-tone of the experience as well as the spiritual insights that he received:

> I did not know where I was: I did not know whether I was Alphonse or another. I only felt myself changed and believed myself another me. . . . In the bottom of my soul I felt an explosion of the most ardent joy. . . . [I]n an instant the bandage had fallen from my eyes; and not one bandage only, but the whole manifold of bandages in which I had been brought up.

> I came out as from a sepulchre, from an abyss of darkness; and I was living, perfectly living. But I wept, for at the bottom of that gulf I saw the extreme of misery from which I had been saved by an infinite mercy; and

104

Experiencing Unseen Worlds

I shuddered at the sight of my iniquities, stupefied, melted, overwhelmed with wonder and gratitude. You may ask me how I came to this new insight, for truly I had never opened a book on religion nor even read a single page of the Bible. . . . I can answer nothing save this, that on entering that church I was in darkness altogether, and on coming out of it I saw the fullness of the light. I can explain the change no better than by the simile of a profound sleep or the analogy of one born blind who should suddenly open his eyes to the day. He sees, but cannot define the light which bathes him and by means of which he sees the objects which excite his wonder. If we cannot explain physical light, how can we explain the light which is the truth itself? And I think I remain within the limits of veracity when I say that without having any knowledge of the letter of religious doctrine, I now intuitively perceived its sense and spirit. Better than if I saw them, I *felt* those hidden things; I felt them by the inexplicable effects they produced in me. It all happened in my interior mind; and those impressions, more rapid than thought, shook my soul, revolved and turned it, as it were, in another direction, towards other aims, by other paths.[45]

Ratisbonne was converted by this experience, and like his brother, went on to become a priest, and then spent much of the rest of his life working for the conversion of other Jews. Under these circumstances, a certain degree of healthy skepticism seems necessary. Although he wrote the letter containing the description of this experience only a few months after the experience, could his description have already been subtly affected by his proselytizing fervor? Was his religious instruction actually as limited as he claims? Was he really as hostile to the Catholic faith as he professes?

While it is important to take these questions seriously, I would argue that even if we approach Ratisbonne's narrative with a hermeneutic of suspicion, until there is evidence to the contrary, we have simply have to accept the basic veracity of Ratisbonne's description. And if Ratisbonne's description is basically accurate, then it is clear that not only is Proudfoot's depiction of Ratisbonne's experience misleading, but his analysis of the experience as well suffers from an inability to reflect accurately the mechanics of the experience's inner workings. It simply is not helpful to claim that Ratisbonne's experience is noetic in Proudfoot's highly restricted sense of the word. To reduce this complex, multifaceted experience to an intellectual judgement made by Ratisbonne that his vision of the Virgin was not self-generated seems to be a severe impoverishment, if not an outright distortion of the experience's phenomenology. Proudfoot would say that Ratisbonne sees the same vision of the Virgin that Proudfoot might see in his own mind's eye; however, he would add that Ratisbonne then tacks a religious casual explanation onto that image. Yet, it is apparent that this experience is much more complex and dense than Proudfoot's watered-down, cerebral account of this occurrence. Ratisbonne not only sees the Virgin, he *feels* her as well: he feels as if he has disappeared; he feels tremendous joy; he feels as if layers of ignorance are disappearing; he feels like he is awakening from the dead or from a deep sleep; he feels deep gratitude for the Virgin's infinite mercy. He feels all of these experiences quicker than any thought—as one piece, as a unified gestalt.

If we remain faithful to the phenomenology of the experience, it is clear that Ratisbonne's experience *is* noetic, but it is noetic in James's sense of the term. For Ratisbonne, at least, the experience is revelatory; it brings with it authoritative insights and truths and it imparts knowledge. This experience is not devoid of intellectual content, but according to the phenomenology of the account, that content comes with the experience itself; it is not added on by Ratisbonne. It seems philosophically imprudent, then, to claim that this experience emerged as the result of the superimposition of Ratisbonne's previous religious beliefs onto the neutral template of some physiological or psychological shift in equilibrium. Even if we indulge our skeptical academic propensities and question whether Ratisbonne was as innocent of previous religious beliefs as he claims, we would still have difficulty explaining how Ratisbonne's fragments of religious knowledge managed to transform themselves into the living, immediate, earthshaking apprehensions that characterized his experience in the church.

It is this level of direct, profoundly convincing knowledge that forms the content of Ratisbonne's religious experience, not the "external" imagery of the Virgin's appearance. Proudfoot's insistence that the content of religious experiences is not what makes experiences such as Ratisbonne's "religious" is valid only if the content is understood as limited to sensory perceptions or specifiable religious beliefs. Proudfoot's strategy is to reduce the content of religious experiences to distinctly articulated concepts or to perceptions of sounds, shapes, colors, tastes, and so on, whether these perceptions are external (as in Proudfoot's examples of temples, paintings, and pieces of music) or whether they are internal (as in discrete visionary episodes). If this strategy is successful, then Proudfoot can easily claim that something extra must be added to these concepts or perceptions in order for them to be understood as "religious." However, as the analysis of Ratisbonne's experience shows, a careful examination of the narratives of religious experiences might just as easily reveal that this "something extra" is more plausibly understood as a quality that is inherent in the experiences themselves.

"Intensely More Real Than Any Ordinary Perception": Mystical Modes of Awareness

In addition to his attack on James's discussion of the ineffability and noetic quality of mystical experiences, Proudfoot is also highly critical of James's willingness to draw an analogy between mystical perception and sense perception. Having already denied the possibility of accurate introspective knowledge during religious or mystical experiences, Proudfoot goes on to claim that mystical experiences "are testimonies not to some direct perception but to the beliefs that enter into the identification of the experience."[46] James, on the other hand, although acutely aware of the difficulty and fallibility of introspection, is willing to accept that the introspective observations of the mystics provide them with information that is at least as trustworthy as that given in any other kind of observation. For James, it would be just as unreasonable to expect a mystic to deny the information he or she has received in a mystical state of awareness as it would be to expect a person to deny the information that he or she has received through the senses.

Once again, Proudfoot disagrees. He begins his offensive by claiming (correctly) that "the theme of a sense of an unseen reality, or consciousness of a higher power, runs throughout James's characterization of religious experience in the *Varieties*."[47] But because Proudfoot is unwilling to accept that mystical perceptions can be apprehensions of anything that transcends the natural world, he attempts to refute James's understanding that this "sense" involves perceptions, on some level, of the presence of an unseen reality. As Proudfoot sees it, James's position is profoundly mistaken, since this "sense," in Proudfoot's understanding, is nothing more than "a thought that carries conviction."[48] Proudfoot defends this assertion by, once again, referring to an example drawn from the *Varieties*. He notes that James describes the experiences "of a friend who reported feeling conscious of a presence in his room one evening after he had gone to bed and again the next night while he was working on some lectures. The friend described both experiences as 'intensely more real than any ordinary perception'."[49]

According to Proudfoot, James is incorrect in assuming that his friend "perceived" anything at all. Proudfoot offers his own perspective in the following analysis:

107

Exploring Unseen Worlds

As James suggests, the experience is familiar enough. In a darkened room, or while attending to something else, I suddenly have the sense that someone is behind me. I feel a presence. In fact, however, this is not a sense or a feeling that is more like a sensation than an intellectual operation: it is a hunch, a thought, an opinion, and it has the epistemic status of a hypothesis. It may not feel like an opinion or hypothesis because of the suddenness and the element of conviction involved. But the sense that there is someone standing behind me is really the thought that someone is there. When I look over my shoulder or turn on the lights, I am engaging in inquiry in order to confirm or disconfirm the hypothesis.[50]

What are we to make of this analysis? To begin with, we have already seen in the case of Ratisbonne that Proudfoot's descriptions of the original accounts of religious experiences are often so impoverished that they end up presenting a distorted vision of what actually occurred during these experiences, a vision that, not surprisingly, is in complete accord with Proudfoot's understanding of the mechanics of mystical epistemology. Could Proudfoot, once again, be omitting important information, information that might be at odds with his analysis?

The answer is, yes. The following is the more substantial account of this experience written by James's friend:

I have several times within the past few years felt the so-called "consciousness of a presence." The experiences which I have in mind are clearly distinguishable from another kind of experience which I have had very frequently, and which I fancy many persons would also call the "consciousness of a presence." But the difference for me between the two sets of experience is as great as the difference between feeling a slight warmth originating I know not where, and standing in the midst of a conflagration with all the ordinary senses alert.

It was about September, 1884, when I had the first experience. On the previous night I had had, after getting into bed at my rooms in College, a vivid tactile hallucination of being grasped by the arm, which made me get up and search the room for an intruder; but the sense of presence properly so called came on the next night. After I had got into bed and blown out the candle, I lay awake awhile thinking on the previous night's experience, when suddenly I *felt* something come into the room and stay close to my bed. It remained only a minute or two. I did not recognize it by any ordinary sense, and yet there was a horribly unpleasant "sensation" connected with it. It stirred something more at the roots of my being than any ordinary perception. The feeling had something of the quality of a very large tearing vital pain spreading chiefly over the chest, but within the organism—and yet the feeling was not *pain* so much as *abhorrence.* At all events, something was present with me, and I knew its presence far more surely than I have ever known the presence of any fleshly living creature. I was conscious of its departure as of its coming: an almost instantaneously swift going through the door, and the "horrible sensation" disappeared. . . .

On two other occasions in my life I have had precisely the same "horrible sensation." Once it lasted a full quarter of an hour. In all three instances the certainty that there in outward space there stood *something* was indescribably *stronger* than the ordinary certainty of companionship when we are in the close presence of ordinary living people. The something seemed close to me, and intensely more real than any ordinary perception.[51]

Once again, unless we question the sincerity of the narrator, it seems apparent that Proudfoot's attempt to depict these experiences as nothing more than hunches or guesswork is simply not accurate. The narrator of these experiences goes to great lengths to emphasize that what he or she felt was not something vague, not something that could be discounted by merely "turning on the lights." The recipient of these experiences did not have a "hypothesis" that something was present. Instead, he or she *felt* a "large tearing vital pain," he or she *felt* this "horrible sensation," sometimes for as long as a quarter of an hour, he or she *knew* that "something" was present. Proudfoot's comparison of these detailed, visceral, and prolonged experiences with the hypothetical situation of himself sitting in a darkened room and "feeling" the presence of someone behind him is, at best, a misreading of the text, and at worst, a refusal to acknowledge any information that is at odds with his own epistemology.

Ironically, even through Proudfoot seems misguided in his assessment, he repeatedly attempts to convince us that the ones who are actually misguided are those individuals who trust in the accuracy of their religious perceptions. To Proudfoot, mystics are a clear example of this misplaced trust, since it is a rare mystic who does not staunchly believe in the truth of his or her mystical states of awareness. However, according to Proudfoot, although these mystical perceptions might indeed appear to be trustworthy, in reality they are not, since even ordinary sense perceptions are not always accurate (e.g., we can mistake a mirage for a real oasis, or be frightened by what we think is a bear in the woods, when, on closer inspection, the "bear" is really a log.) Therefore, Proudfoot concludes that James is overly generous

109

when he argues that "mystical states, when well developed, usually are, and have the right to be, absolutely authoritative over the individuals to whom they come."[52] In Proudfoot's opinion, not only should *nonmystics* be wary of an uncritical acceptance of the accuracy of mystical perceptions (a position that James himself embraces), but even mystics themselves have no right to accept the information that comes to them in their mystical states of awareness (a position that James would attempt to refute).

Proudfoot correctly connects James's defense of the mystic's right to trust his or her mystical perceptions to the analogy that James repeatedly draws between mystical perceptions and sense perceptions.[53] James does indeed stress that "our own more 'rational' beliefs are based on evidence exactly similar in nature to that which mystics quote for theirs. Our senses, namely, have assured us of certain states of fact; but mystical experiences are as direct perceptions of fact for those who have them as any sensations ever were for us."[54] However, James also realizes that there are limits to our ability to use the process of sensory perception as an analogy for mystical perception. He recognizes that while sense perceptions and mystical perceptions are similar in that they are both resistant to verbal description and are both felt directly only by the one experiencing them, there are also important differences. Sense perceptions deal with a fairly stable external world that is publicly shared, whereas mystical perceptions involve contact with an interior, unseen spiritual dimension of reality that is experienced only be a few select individuals. James also points out that "intellect and sense both swoon away in [the] highest states of ecstasy,"[55] so that while many mystical experiences do have a sensory-like quality, there are other types of mystical experiences in which the analogy to sense experience is not as helpful.

Yet, Proudfoot rightly points out that, on the whole, James emphasizes the similarities between mystical perceptions and sense perceptions. Proudfoot, however, then goes on to claim that James's analogy between mystical perceptions and sense perceptions is fundamentally flawed, since it is based on a mistaken, unsophisticated theory of perception, a theory that, in Proudfoot's eyes, assumes "that perceptual experience is unmediated by concepts and beliefs."[56] Yet, it is not James's theory of perception that is incorrect, but rather, it is Proudfoot's *understanding* of James's theory that is in error. James never claims that perceptions are unaffected by our prior concepts and beliefs. In fact, he was one of the earliest, and certainly one of the most articulate, defenders of the idea that our sense experience is always interwoven with our hopes, fears, expectations, and beliefs.[57]

110

Knowledge-By-Acquaintance and Knowledge-About

It is understandable that Proudfoot is confused about James's theory of sense perception. James does appear to emphasize the direct, immediate nature of mystical experiences, and he also stresses the similarities between mystical experiences and sense experiences, so it would appear logical that he would in turn claim that sense experiences as well are direct and unmediated by our thoughts and desires. However, in point of fact, James never does make such a claim. As will be shown in much more detail later in this chapter, according to James, sense experiences are, in a way, both immediate *and* mediated. On the one hand, if we analyze our perceptions, we can retrospectively acknowledge that sense experiences come directly to our experience independent of our conscious thought; they arrive already possessing a certain basic intrinsic content as well as a high degree of "otherness" and coercive power.[58] On the other hand, James also emphasizes that sense experiences as they actually occur in our day-to-day concrete life are always inextricably interwoven with our interests and belief systems; he emphasizes that we never have a sense experience that is not, in some way or another, affected by our conceptual schemes.

Other scholars of mysticism besides Proudfoot have been puzzled by the apparent contradiction in the *Varieties* between James's claim that mystical experiences are primarily affective and perceptual (which would seem to imply that they are free of concepts) and his claim that mystical experiences have a noetic quality, that is, his claim that mystical experiences contain knowledge within them as an integral part of their structure (which would seem to imply that they are *not* free of concepts). As Bernard McGinn, a noted scholar of mysticism, correctly points out, in the *Varieties* at least, James does not give us the "epistemological analysis of the relation of perceptual and conceptual knowing" that we need in order to satisfactorily resolve this tension.[59]

Fortunately, the epistemological analysis that is absent in the *Varieties* is present in many of James's earlier (and later) works, and is especially prominent in the *Principles*. It is here that James introduces "*two kinds of knowledge* [which are] broadly and practically distinguishable: . . . *knowledge of acquaintance* and *knowledge-about.*"[60] Knowledge of acquaintance (or as James also frequently terms it, "knowledge-by-acquaintance") is immediate or intuitive knowledge; it is that which is directly evident. This type of knowledge is operative when we see the color "blue" or when we taste the flavor of a pear. Knowledge-about, on the other hand, is conceptual or representational knowledge. Knowledge-about is operative when we give the blue that we are seeing or the pear that we are eating a name (let us say "navy" or "Bartlett"), and bring to these sensory experiences the wealth of cultural information that we possess about, for instance, colors or fruits.

In James's epistemology, knowledge-by-acquaintance gives us information that is qualitatively different than the information we receive in knowledge-about, even though knowledge-by-acquaintance is always, to a greater or lesser degree, tempered with knowledge-about. James illustrates this distinction with a telling example: "In training-institutions for the blind they teach the pupils as much about light as in ordinary schools. . . . But the best taught born-blind pupil of such an establishment yet lacks a knowledge which the least instructed baby has."[61] Continuing and elaborating on this theme, James states that "a blind man may know all about the sky's blueness, and I may know all about your toothache, conceptually. . . . But so long as he has not felt the blueness, nor I the toothache, our knowledge, wide as it is, of these realities, will be hollow and inadequate."[62] According to James, this type of knowledge cannot be described and it cannot be imparted to anyone who has not experienced it already.[63] As James points out, we cannot "make a blind man guess what blue is like," or give an accurate account of the taste of a pear. Instead, all that we can do to share this knowledge with others is to tell them to "go to certain places and act in certain ways, and these objects will probably come."[64]

Knowledge-by-acquaintance occurs when, as much as possible, our knowledge of an object is limited to the bare impression that it makes on the senses, or in the case of religious or mystical varieties of this type of knowledge, when we experience or feel something with an immediacy and vividness that is similar to sensory experiences. Knowledge-by-acquaintance is inarticulate, it is a pre-verbal, unmediated knowledge of the simple "thatness" of something.

Knowledge-about, on the other hand, is connected with the "whatness" of something. If we want to know how something came to pass, if we want to understand how something relates to something else, then we have to depend upon knowledge-about. Knowledge-about analyzes, compares, contrasts, explains, and describes the qualities of an object. Knowledge-about is explicit, highly articulate, linguistically-structured knowledge.

For James, the contrast between these two types of knowledge is very similar to the contrast that is present in our common sense understanding of the difference between "feeling" and "thought." As Gerald Myers points out, for James, "feelings are the vehicles of acquaintance and thoughts the vehicles of knowledge; feelings are the seeds of cognition and thoughts their fruition."[65] However, in the same way that James is willing to use "feeling" and "thought" interchangeably when referring to any state of consciousness, James repeatedly emphasizes that these two types of knowledge always appear together in any concrete moment of knowing. While they indeed represent crucial differences in the ways in which we apprehend and manipulate our environment and ourselves, "knowledge-by-acquaintance" and "knowledge-about" are relative terms for James. They are hypothetical ending points of a spectrum ranging from "some imagined aboriginal presence in experience, before any belief about the presence [has] arisen"[66] to our most explicit and abstract theoretical constructions.

According to James, we get glimpses of relatively pure varieties of knowledge-by-acquaintance when we become conscious after fainting or when we emerge from the full effects of anesthetics, or when we stare at an object until it loses most of its commonplace associations. Knowledge-by-acquaintance occurs when an object is cognized with a minimum of the "psychic fringes" or "overtones" that are present during knowledge-about, that is to say, when it is cognized with a minimum of the tacit assumptions, expectations, beliefs, and other preconscious associations that are always linked to this particular object in the background of the field of our awareness.

This way of conceiving of the distinction James makes between knowledge-by-acquaintance and knowledge-about is quite different than what other Jamesian scholars have posited. For instance, Nancy Frankenberry claims that knowledge-by-acquaintance is "concerned with the vaguely given, overabundant relations of the fringe, where resistances and tendencies in the stream of experience are immediately apprehended . . . [while knowledge-about] concerns the focal region wherein the vague relations are discriminated according to some selective interest and purpose."[67] Whereas for Frankenberry, knowledge-by-acquaintance occurs when we are *most directly in touch* with this tacit information, it seems clear, after a close reading of James, that knowledge-by-acquaintance is actually present when the tacit information located on the margins of awareness is at a *minimum.* In the *Principles,* James explicitly states that the difference between knowledge-by-acquaintance and knowledge-about "is reducible almost entirely to the absence or presence of psychic fringes or overtones. Knowledge about a thing is knowledge of its relations. Acquaintance with it is limitation to the bare impression which it makes."[68]

Frankenberry's misreading is apparently based on a conflation of James's understanding of sense impressions with his understanding of knowledge-by-acquaintance. James posits that knowledge-by-

113

acquaintance gives us information that is already vaguely structured prior to its interaction with our cognitions, but this "quasi-chaos" given to us by knowledge-by-acquaintance is *not* identical to the psychic fringes and overtones of our consciousness, as Frankenberry seems to think. For James, the fringes and margins of our awareness are components of knowledge-about, components that are, theoretically at least, separate from the felt immediacy of moments of knowledge-by-acquaintance.

James was painfully aware that every conscious investigation of moments of knowledge-by-acquaintance automatically introduces knowledge-about into that introspective moment. In other words, as soon as we attempt to become explicitly aware of the occurrence of relatively pure moments of knowledge-by-acquaintance within us, we have already brought with that reflective awareness, minimally, a tacit awareness of the self, as well as an underlying awareness of what that self is hoping to experience. In a very real sense, our explicit knowledge of these moments of knowledge-by-acquaintance can only occur in the form of a highly abstract, rarefied version of knowledge-about.

It would seem then that all moments of "knowledge-by-acquaintance" are, in actuality, nothing more than modifications of "knowledge-about," and therefore, it would appear that James fails in his argument that our experience contains immediate and non-linguistic elements within it.

However, as James is quick to point out, there is an important "difference between the immediate feltness of a feeling, and its perception by a subsequent reflective act."[69] Scholars have to be careful not to make what James calls the "Psychologist's Fallacy."[70] The Psychologist's Fallacy occurs when a investigators of states of consciousness confuse the "mental fact" that they are examining with their understanding *of* that mental fact. While it is undeniable that moments of knowledge-by-acquaintance, when studied as objects of reflective deliberation, are instances of knowledge-about, we can still logically hypothesize the existence of moments of awareness that precede any explicit, conceptually based knowledge-about. Further, even if we theorize that a completely "pure" knowledge-by-acquaintance is possible only as the theoretical end-point on the spectrum of moments of knowing, even if knowledge-by-acquaintance in all concrete moments of knowing always arrives already "mixed"[71] with knowledge-about, it seems preferable to maintain the distinction between these two types of knowing rather than collapse all knowing into knowledge-about. Knowledge-by-acquaintance provides information that knowledge-about simply cannot replicate; tasting an apple is fundamentally different than knowing-about apples, even if these two processes are fused during each bite. Analogously, seeing and feeling the Hindu God Kṛṣṇa in a visionary experience can be understood to give the visionary a categorically unique type of information, information that could never be gained from years of arduous study of Hindu (or more specifically, Vaiṣṇava) doctrine, even if Hindu theological concepts, to one degree or another, were inevitably implicated in the structure of the visionary experience itself.

It also seems crucial not to dismiss too quickly the claims made by numerous mystics to have had mystical experiences that, from a Jamesian perspective, could legitimately be understood as completely pure moments of knowledge-by-acquaintance. One type of mystical experience that might indeed qualify as a moment of knowledge-by-acquaintance that is unencumbered by knowledge-about is the experience of perceiving the world *as it is*, the experience of perceiving the *suchness* of life. Much of the spiritual discipline involved in, for instance, Zen sitting or Theravāda Buddhist insight training, is explicitly designed to strip us, bit by bit, of the layers of attachments, desires, fears, conceptual labeling, and so on (all of which are different types of knowledge-about), that, according to these traditions at least, prevent us from experiencing the world as it truly is. The claim that is often made by these traditions (as well as numerous others) is that through these spiritual disciplines we *can* come to experience the world in its purity, we *can* perceive the world free from our conceptual categorizations.

Some scholars of mysticism would disagree with these claims. For instance, Steven Katz, a contemporary philosopher of mysticism, asserts that "properly understood, yoga, for example, is *not* an *un*conditioning or *de*conditioning of consciousness, but rather it is a *re*conditioning of consciousness."[72] However, while Katz's observation might indeed be a valuable insight into the underlying dynamics of many, if not most, mystical experiences, Katz's Kantian perspective, in which *all* experiences of the world are *always* structured through our categories of understanding, might also keep us from acknowledging that a *de*conditioning of consciousness is a very real epistemological possibility. Simply because all of our everyday moments of experiencing the world are inevitably processed through our implicit knowledge-about is no reason not theoretically to acknowledge the very real possibility that we could, whether through grace or long hours of meditative effort, have moments where "we" (and all our knowledge-about) disappear, and only the world remains present as an object of consciousness. To deny this possibility outright seems rash and somewhat culturally and philosophically presumptuous, stating, in essence, that Immanuel Kant is correct, and Dōgen, for instance, is not, without ever overtly addressing *why* the Eastern philosophical perspective is wrong.

Since so many of the contemporary understandings of the dynamics of mystical experience are, on the face of it at least, indebted to Kant,[73] it is important to take a moment to point out that while James's epistemology may appear to be similar to Kant's in that both philosophers emphasize the ways in which our conceptual categories help to shape our experiences, there is a crucial difference between their respective epistemologies. According to Kant, we passively receive a formless content from our intuition of the world, a world which is unknowable in-and-of-itself. This formless content is then given a specific form by our conceptual scheme.

James, on the other hand, is not overly concerned with the theoretical existence of a world that exists in-and-of-itself (Kant's numina), but instead, focuses his attention on the world that enters into our *experience*. James emphasizes that if we pay attention, we will notice that this world-of-our-experience always comes to us already partially preformed. Even in those moments in which our knowledge-about appears to be reduced to a minimum, certain basic data is present. For instance, a woman might suddenly wake up, and for several disconcerting moments, not know where or who she is, all the while staring at a variety of forms near to her without any idea of what they are or what they do. Then, in a rapid influx of meaning and memory, the woman regains her sense of self, along with the enormous net of associations that this sense of self implies, and recognizes in a flash that the mysterious forms previously experienced are, in fact, a clock, a bed, sheets, pillows, walls, and so on. In this example, while the woman's knowledge-about who she is and what she is experiencing has momentarily vanished, or more accurately, has been extremely curtailed,[74] the knowledge-by-acquaintance of the sheer "thatness" of what she is experiencing has not: certain clusters of sense data have entered into her awareness (i.e., the "redness" of the bedspread, albeit devoid of the linguistic markers of "red" or "bedspread"). James would stress that these clusters of basic data given via knowledge-by-acquaintance can or should resist inappropriate interpretative glosses by knowledge-about (i.e., if the woman began to think of herself as a cat, or thought that the clock was really a pen, and so on, this knowledge-about would not "fit" the shapes, densities, textures, and so on, that are given to her via knowledge-by-acquaintance). For James, therefore, the world that enters our experience through knowledge-by-acquaintance exists prior to its shaping by our knowledge-about.

116

Experiencing Unseen Worlds

As Jamesian scholar John Wild perceptively comments, the world that we experience through our knowledge-by-acquaintance is not, as the Kantians might have it, a "mere chaotic manifold," but instead, "already contains the germs of meaningful patterns,"[75] patterns that are unfolded and elaborated, but *not* created by our knowledge-about.[76] According to James, knowledge-by-acquaintance provides our experience with the "raw material" that our knowledge-about can refine, place in a context, give meaning to, and so on, but the "raw material" provided by knowledge-by-acquaintance is not completely malleable. Instead, it enters our experience with a certain cluster of basic qualities that knowledge-about has to work with, qualities that limit the range of interpretations and meanings that knowledge-about can legitimately superimpose upon it.

In many contemporary epistemologies of mysticism, the contrast that is often drawn between "experience" and "interpretation" mirrors, at least to some extent, the complex interaction that takes place between knowledge-by-acquaintance and knowledge-about. It is instructive, however, to note the differences between a Jamesian understanding of the dynamics of mystical experience and the epistemological assumptions that underlie the ways in which mystical experiences and interpretations are understood by, for instance, Steven Katz and many of the scholars that have contributed to his various edited volumes on mysticism. These "neo-Kantian" philosophers of mysticism emphasize (correctly, for the most part) that mystics of different traditions do not merely interpret their experiences through the conceptual framework of their culture *after* the experiences themselves; instead they argue that each mystic's interpretative framework is actively present in every mystical experience at every moment. This otherwise laudable epistemology becomes problematic, however, when examined more closely. As Frankenberry notes:

> A critical issue in this discussion is whether and to what extent the data of experience exercise any influence on the interpretations. If there is no self-evident, uninterpreted datum of any sort of experience, is there, nevertheless, a distinctive otherness or objectivity to the data? Is interpretation *derived* from experience as much as it is *added* to it? How far can we assume that human interpretations provide evidence of the actual nature of things? . . . Are our theories constructed only to satisfy our intellectual and emotional demands or do they in some sense, however problematically, "fit" the nature of the reality they claim to render intelligible?[77]

117

A Jamesian epistemological analysis of mystical experiences offers us an opportunity to resolve these important questions by positing a dialectical relationship between experience and interpretation. In a Jamesian mystical epistemology, the knowledge-by-acquaintance aspect of experience maintains a degree of theoretical autonomy and coerciveness, and is not pushed out of the picture by the jostling insistence of the mystic's culturally based interpretative framework. From a Jamesian perspective, we can theorize that a mystical experience is formed in roughly the following way: A preexisting, "objective," partially structured, unnamable "something" appears within the consciousness of the mystic.[78] This knowledge-by-acquaintance aspect of experience, however, does not appear alone, but rather, comes into consciousness fused with the mystic's knowledge-about, and structured by the mystic's cultural and psychological categories. Furthermore, this mystical experience is not a static moment frozen in time, but rather, it shifts and reforms, with different "percentages" of these two types of knowledge prevalent at different moments in the process. Let us envision, for example, a Hindu yogi immersed in an ecstatic meditation on the form of Kālī. Over a period of time, this meditation becomes so profound that the form of Kālī disappears. Meanwhile, the yogi's sense of identity also begins to dissolve, and only an ineffable sense of unity and oneness remains. If we analyze this process using James's epistemological categories, we could say that during the time that this yogi was meditating on the form of Kālī, he or she had an experience that was a fusion of knowledge-by-acquaintance and knowledge-about. The knowledge-by-acquaintance components of the experience were those elements of the experience that entered the yogi's awareness with a high degree of objectivity, that came without the conscious instigation of the mystic, that shone with what James calls "immediate luminosity." And yet, this mystical experience also possessed important elements of knowledge-about. For instance, knowledge-about was present in the cultural constructs that helped to create a visionary form of Kālī instead of Jesus or Muhammad, or in the tacit egoistic identifications present within the yogi during this experience, or in the yogi's preconscious understanding of the functions and goals of meditation, and so forth. However, when the visionary form of Kālī disappeared, and the yogi's experience shifted to a non-dual state of oneness, it could be theorized that the "percentage" of knowledge-about that was previously present during the yogi's mystical experience was significantly lowered. It is even possible, if we accept the claims made by the yogic tradition, that during these moments, the yogi's egoistic identification completely disappeared, his or her conceptual activity totally ceased, and there was a radical disappearance of any sense of separate existence. If these claims can be taken seriously, then we would have to say that knowledge-about disappeared altogether during these moments of mystical union. However, to describe what remains during these non-dual experiences as knowledge-by-acquaintance is perhaps philosophically imprudent, since the category of knowledge depends upon an implicit duality of the knower and the known, and it is this very duality which has purportedly disappeared during unitive mystical experiences.[79]

James would almost certainly recognize the difficulties inherent in using the term "knowledge" for unitive experiences. For James, at least during the time of the *Principles*, knowledge is always intentional, that is, it is always knowledge *of* something, there is always an implicit duality between the knower and what is known.[80] For James, it is a philosophical mistake to conceive of consciousness as some sort of aboriginal "stuff" apart from its contents. And yet, even if we do acknowledge James's emphasis on the inevitable intentionality of consciousness, it is difficult to say conclusively whether James would have objected to another, less Western, nondual understanding of the nature of consciousness. James's critique of philosophical conceptions of a consciousness that is free from any intentional content are primarily directed to Western, academically framed formulations that attempt to describe consciousness in a purely logical, abstract, nonempirical manner, as opposed to James's own epistemology, which is rooted in a penetrating analysis and reinterpretation of the richness of concrete, day-to-day experiences of ordinary life.[81] It seems that James was basically ignorant of most of the arguments of Buddhism or Hinduism in favor of the philosophical validity of a nondual awareness in which the subject and object fuse, arguments that often draw upon the empirical data and assumptions generated by mystical experiences to buttress their highly technical and sophisticated logical argumentative structure. It is therefore an open question whether James would have abandoned his opposition to the concept of a contentless consciousness if he had been exposed to these technically sophisticated, yet empirically grounded, arguments in favor of the philosophical validity of the notion of a consciousness free from any and all intentional content.[82]

Perhaps more seriously, there have been questions raised as to whether moments of knowledge-by-acquaintance can be designated as a moment of "knowledge" at all. For instance, while Myers concedes that the phenomena of acquaintance serves a function that knowledge-about cannot replace (e.g., being acquainted with a

119

particular shade of blue or a certain aroma);[83] he then goes on to claim that this type of phenomena is not actually a form of knowledge at all. For Myers, and for many other current philosophers, in order for knowledge to occur "some activity of naming, noticing, or classifying must take place."[84]

There has been such a stress on the linguistic nature of experience in recent philosophical thought that any claims to immediacy or to a knowledge that is not structured linguistically are instantly suspect. But the battle over what range of phenomena are eligible for promotion into the cognitive pantheon is far from over, primarily because there are differing ideas about what exactly constitutes a moment of cognition. A cognitive moment is typically said to be one that is factual, or truthful, instead of illusory or false, but the criteria used to determine what actually constitutes factuality or truth are themselves highly controversial.[85]

In the *Principles*, James avoids confronting this issue by stating that as long as psychology posits a knower separate from the known, psychologists simply have to accept the cognitive moment as a basic, and ultimately mysterious, given. According to James, psychologists can describe the brain-states that underlie shifts in consciousness, but they cannot adequately account for how a state of consciousness manages to transcend itself in every moment of knowing. James believes that it is philosophy's task to explain how the epistemological chasm between knowledge of a thing and the thing itself is crossed. Therefore, if psychologists do not become metaphysicians and simply assume the commonsense distinction between the knower and the known, they are forced to accept, without explanation, that somehow a mental state of awareness is able to reach out and know a fact that is seemingly made of such different "material" than itself. The psychologist's task then is to pay close attention to the dynamics of what occurs *during* this continuously occurring, "miraculous" event. James claims that what the psychologist will discover through an introspective observation of this cognitive moment is the distinction between the two different "types" of knowing, which he labels "knowledge-by-acquaintance" and "knowledge-about."

Many investigators of mysticism and religious experience, however, often limit what qualifies as "cognitive" to moments of explicit, discursive knowledge (i.e., knowledge-about) and are therefore often unclear as to how mystical experiences, in James's understanding, can be simultaneously moments of knowledge and moments of feeling. This apparent contradiction is the source of McGinn's terse and insightful comment that "mysticism for James is both cognitive and not cognitive, but we are never sure how."[86] If we limit "cognitive" to moments of knowledge-about, then clearly many of the religious experiences that James describes are not cognitive, since they are primarily instances of knowledge-by-acquaintance.[87] However, if we, like James, admit immediacy, feeling and sensation into the exclusive club of cognition, then it is easy to understand how James could argue that *all* religious and mystical experiences are cognitive, albeit in often radically different ways.

Carving the Statue Out of the Stone: Sensing and Perceiving

A clearer grasp of the distinction between knowledge-by-acquaintance and knowledge-about and its possible application to issues in the philosophy of mysticism can be gained if some time is taken to examine the distinction that James makes in his psychology between sensation and perception. For James, a sensation is a relatively pure variety of knowledge-by-acquaintance, whereas a perception is, loosely, a sensation in which concepts (i.e., "knowledge-about") have been, so to speak, "added into the stew."

However, using this "stew" metaphor is not without its problems. If taken too literally, it might lead us to think that James understands perception to be a moment of consciousness that contains several isolated, easily discriminated components (i.e., sensations and different concepts) floating around like carrots or celery in a binding sauce of consciousness. In fact, however, James fought hard to replace this "atomistic" understanding of consciousness with a theory that could do justice to the unity and simplicity of each moment of consciousness. James did not think that perception is best understood as the end result of concepts "mixed together" with several discrete "chunks" of sensation. Instead, each moment of perception, like all other moments of consciousness, is a "much-at-oneness"; it is a total, unified gestalt.

James illustrates his claim that every moment of consciousness is a "much-at-onceness" by analyzing what takes place within us when we think of the phrase, *"the pack of cards is on the* table."[88] James recognizes that it takes time mentally to articulate the whole phrase, but he claims that careful introspection reveals that each of these "time-parts" does not appear in our consciousness as a collection of separate thoughts ("cards" and "table," for instance). Instead, each of these moments of consciousness apprehends the total thought *the pack of cards is on the table* "in a unitary, undivided way."[89] According to James, each word is not cut off and isolated from the rest of the thought, but rather, is "suffused with the whole idea."[90] In a similar way (to use another rather pertinent Jamesian example), when we say, "Columbus discovered America in 1492," each word is "fringed and the whole sentence bathed in the original halo" of the often obscure, or only vaguely felt meanings that we associate with these words.[91] Any educated Westerner simply cannot think the word "Columbus" cut off from its association with "America" and "1492." To make matters even more complex, each individual will have a unique "horizon" of meanings associated with this sentence. In explicating James's understanding, a contemporary interpreter could point out that the phrase "Columbus discovered America in 1492" will be understood in one way by an Italian-American who is fiercely proud of his connection to Columbus, and in quite another way by a Native-American who is upset at the seeming glorification of an imperialistic terrorist.

According to James, every moment of perception comes to us carrying a vaguely felt conceptual fringe. In the same way that knowledge-by-acquaintance is inevitably, to a greater or lesser degree, accompanied by knowledge-about, sensations are always accompanied by some sort of conceptual background. From a Jamesian perspective, what is referred to as "sensations" are moments of comparative stillness in the on-going flow of the "stream of consciousness" (a phrase that James inaugurated). According to James, psychologists can dip the buckets of their introspective attention into this ever-moving stream and confine within these buckets seemingly isolated moments of sensation, but such analytic attempts succeed only at the cost of ignoring the rest of the stream that flows around the non-fluid containers of these theoretical efforts. Because the stream, as a stream, cannot be captured within the containers of theoretical investigation, there is a tendency to overlook the confused tumult of associations, memories, and concepts that swirl around, and are integrally linked with, the seemingly more stable moments of sensation. As James points out:

> Every definite image in the mind is steeped and dyed in the free water that flows round it. With it goes the sense of its relations, near and remote, the dying echo of whence it came to us, the dawning sense of whither it is to lead. The significance, the value, of the image is all in this halo or penumbra that surrounds and escorts it,—or rather that is fused into one with it and has become bone of its bone and flesh of its flesh; leaving, it is true, an image of the same thing it was before, but making it an image of that thing newly taken and freshly understood.[92]

For James, while "part of what we perceive comes through our senses from the object before us, another part, (and it may be the larger part) always comes . . . out of our head."[93] James points out that when we look at a "big solid rectangular walnut library-table," the initial sensory image is of a "brown eye-picture with lines not parallel, and with angles unlike. . . . It is a distorted perspective view of three of the sides of what [we] mentally perceive (more or less) in its totality and undistorted shape."[94] We do not actually see the back of the table or its square corners, or feel its heaviness and solidity, or sense its name and function. All of these features of the table are imperceptibly added to our initial sensations by our tacit conceptual network to produce the "final product" of our perception of the table.[95]

To further illustrate this complex perceptual process, it might be useful to analyze what happens when we pick up a book and look at it. When we pick up a book and look at it, we tend to imagine that nothing more is occurring than a simple process in which our eyes and hands are relaying information to our brain, telling us that the book is such and such a height, weight, color, texture, and so on. A careful examination of this process, however, will reveal that much more is occurring "below the surface" than we might assume. When we look at the book, on some preconscious level we know what the book's function is; we associate the book with past experiences of reading similar books; we link this book with our experiences in libraries, with our interactions with particular teachers, with our time in elementary school or on our mother's laps. When we look at the book's title, we don't just see shapes of ink on paper; we see letters, words, and meanings. When we pick up the book, we are subtly aware, on some level, of our role as readers; we sense our hopes of what we intend to accomplish by reading the book, we may even feel our reluctance to begin the task based on previous all-night cram sessions in college. None of these conceptual associations occur in isolation. Instead, they are fused with the information that comes through our senses in such a way that is impossible, except retrospectively, to determine which part of the final perceptual "package" comes from the senses, and which part comes from our conceptual background.

As James repeatedly stresses, we do not passively receive information through the senses. Rather, we are, in a very real sense, co-creators of the world that we experience. In "Remarks on Spencer's Definition of Mind as Correspondence," an early essay that set the stage for his later psychological work, James argues that the mind plays a very active role in the process of perception:

123

The knower is not simply a mirror floating with no foot-hold anywhere, and passively reflecting an order that he comes upon and finds simply existing. The knower is an actor, . . . he registers the truth which he helps to create. Mental interests, hypotheses, postulates, so far as they are bases for human action—action which to a great extent transforms the world—help to *make* the truth which they declare. In other words, there belongs to mind, from its birth upward, a spontaneity, a vote. It is in the game, and not a mere looker-on.[96]

According to James's psychology, one of the most important ways in which we help to create the world that we experience is through the process of "selective interest." Our selective interests insure that we create a livable and coherent world by deciding which aspects of "an undistinguishable, swarming continuum, devoid of distinction or emphasis"[97] to notice, and which aspects to ignore—in other words, which parts to accentuate and which parts to suppress. In much the same way that a sculptor carves a statue out of stone, we shape a mass of indistinct sensations into our own personal experience by choosing which of these sensations to reject and which to accept. As James points out, "millions of items of the outward order are present to my sense which never properly enter into my experience. Why? Because they have no interest to me. My experience is what I agree to attend to. Only those items which I notice shape my mind—without selective interest, experience is an utter chaos."[98]

While our own personal desires and interests are an important factor in this process of selective interest, for the most part the activity of molding a mass of chaotic sensory data into a coherent world happens automatically and without conscious effort on our part since, to a large extent, this process is rooted in the previous choices made by our culture as a whole. According to James, our understanding of the ebb and flow of time, our sense of the significance of space, even our assumption that the world consists of discrete "objects" are all the results of generalizations from our prior experiences, either through individual maturation or through our cultural "memory." These concepts are human achievements that allow us to act more efficiently; they permit us to predict how our environment is going to respond to our actions; and they enable us to communicate with each other in specific ways. Because of their practical value, these basic ideas, as well as other significant cultural assumptions, are internalized during childhood and have become an ingrained, seemingly fixed part of an individual's mental life. They have become the basic cognitive building blocks that allow us to gain new experiences, the memories of which are then added to our previous store of beliefs and assumptions, which in turn determine which aspects of the world we will notice; these selective perceptions then affect our actions in the world, which give us new experiences, and so forth and so on. This interactive process of experiences, beliefs, and actions, which mutually affect each other, is never-ending. It perpetually creates an ever-new, ever-changing, personal, and idiosyncratic worldview, a worldview that is rarely noticed—a worldview that operates under the surface of our perceptions to help create the taken-for-granted world that seems so prearranged, so external, and so separate from our minds.

Mystical Discoveries

As James puts it, "we add . . . to reality. The world stands really malleable, waiting to receive its final touches at our hands."[99] But it is important to understand that James does not think that the world is *completely* malleable. For James, even though "we carve out everything, just as we carve out constellations, to suit our human purposes,"[100] we are always given something to carve; we discover the world as much as we create it. James argues that the world exists prior to our creative epistemological endeavors, a world that can often stubbornly resist our inaccurate and fumbling attempts to understand it, a world that is often frustratingly independent of our wishes and interests, however "selective" they might be. According to James, "there is something in every experience that escapes our arbitrary control. . . . There is a push, an urgency, within our very experience, against which we are on the whole powerless."[101] From James's perspective, we *find* the world as much as we *make* our experience of that world, and what we find is a world that is actually only a "quasi-chaos," since it is "all shot through with regularities."[102] James admits that we can never be certain what shape this world might possess apart from our conceptually-altered experience of it, and concedes that "reality *per se* . . . may appear only as a sort of limit;"[103] but James also emphasizes that, within our own experience, we do discover that the world seems to come to us containing certain inherent tendencies, patterns, and consistencies.

James's epistemological stress on this preexisting, partially formed world that can at times resist our attempts to encapsulate it arbitrarily within our conceptual framework has important implications for our understanding of the dynamics of mystical experience. For instance, a "complete constructivism" such as Proudfoot's has difficulty accounting for any mystical experiences that appear to contradict the mystic's theological and cultural assumptions, since these experiences are understood as completely constituted by those very assumptions. James's "incomplete constructivism," however, can easily account for mystical experiences that contradict the mystic's theological and cultural background, since it postulates the existence of an extra "something" that is operative within mystical experiences in addition to the mystic's psychological and cultural categories, "something" that the mystic finds (or that finds the mystic), "something" that is not under the volitional control of the mystic's ego, "something" that has an integrity of its own, "something" that has sufficient power not only to coerce the mystic's attention, but also the power necessary to transform the mystic's self-understandings and tacit worldviews. This "something" is malleable; it can and does appear to mystics in forms that they are most easily able to comprehend, but it also can and often does appear to mystics in ways that they never imagined, in ways that confound the mystics' personal expectations and cultural assumptions, in ways that surprise and disturb them.

By way of illustration, I would like to narrate a personal experience that I believe supports James's mystical epistemology. But, beforehand, because I am acutely aware that personal testimony is often frowned on in academic philosophical discussions, it seems vital that I take a moment and attempt to justify this transgression of academic orthopraxy.

I would begin by arguing that attempts to "ghettoize" the religious experiences of scholars of religion to the safely guarded parameters of their private life, cut off from any explicit contact with the public arena of their academic enterprise, is overly restrictive and methodologically unsound. While a fervent proselytizing missionary zeal is obviously misplaced within the academy, the endeavor to emulate the natural science paradigm of complete neutrality and objectivity is equally misguided. I believe that James is correct: we will inevitably approach any philosophical project, including the study of religious phenomena, guided and empowered with our passions, our personal interests, and our idiosyncratic perspectives. Pretending that this is not the case is not only impractical, but also leads to an impoverished grasp of the material that we are studying, since a study of that which we have experienced and which passionately concerns us will arguably produce more fruitful and nuanced observations than a study of that which we only observe from a disinterested distance.

Aligning myself with James once again, I believe that the study of religious phenomena needs to be broadly empirical, and personal religious and mystical experiences, if examined with appropriate rigor, can and should become a rich source of empirical data for further philosophical reflection. If we become overly dependent upon texts to provide all of our data about mystical experiences and overlook, or more seriously, censor, the information available through personal introspective work (or even careful, in-depth discussions with living mystics), then it is perhaps inevitable that we will be tempted to reify mystical experiences—that we will forget the very real limits to the accuracy and completeness of retrospective, textual accounts of mystical experiences, limits that are often overlooked when, as has become fashionable, we restrict our sources of information on mystical experiences to narratives written by mystics who lived in centuries and cultures that are far removed from our own. If we focus our attention to such an extent on the substantive, more apparent aspects of the experiences that are encoded within the words of historical narratives, we will quite possibly overlook the less obvious, but equally tangible, elements of the experiences that might well exist in the interstices and margins of the verbal formulations. An overreliance on descriptions of mystical experiences that are neatly packaged in precise, beautifully crafted phrases can, if we are not careful, lead us to imagine that mystical experiences really do have such carefully delineated borders, really are something static and frozen in time. Including personal mystical experiences within our methodological parameters, we are less likely to forget that mystical experiences are actually dynamic, on-going, subtly shifting, complex, and often obscure processes of awareness that, instead of being completely constituted by our concepts as the "full-constructionists" would have us believe, can often shatter the rigidities of our previously held conceptual framework—can expose us to something novel, something unexpected, something not captured in the web of our words.

Keeping the points raised in this methodological digression in mind, it seems worthwhile at this point to demonstrate the ways in which at least one personal experience of my own leads me to support James's hypothesis that not all mystical experiences are created from previous theological assumptions.[104]

When I was thirteen years old, I was walking to school in Gainesville, Florida, and without any apparent reason, I became obsessed with the idea of what would happen to me after my death. Throughout that day I attempted to visualize myself as not existing. I simply could not comprehend that my self-awareness would not exist in some form or another after my death. I kept trying, without success, to envision a simple blank nothingness. Later, I was returning

127

home from school, walking on the hot pavement next to a stand of pine trees less than a block from my home, still brooding about what it would be like to die. Suddenly, without warning, something shifted inside. I felt lifted outside of myself, as if I had been expanded beyond my previous sense of self. In that exhilarating, and yet deeply peaceful moment, I felt as if I had been shaken awake. In a single, "timeless" gestalt, I had a direct and powerful experience that I was not just that young teenage boy, but rather, that I was a surging, ecstatic, boundless state of consciousness.

In relating this description of my experience, I am conscious of the fact that my narrative is itself a reification of the experience; yet, at the same time, I would argue that this awareness of the difference between the verbal narrative and the experience itself is highlighted precisely because it *was* my own experience. I am vividly aware of the vast difference between what I experienced and what I have just described, and my awareness of this difference can then itself become the basis for theoretical observations that would be problematic, if not impossible, if I was simply reading a preexisting narrative written by a mystic who lived hundreds of years ago. For instance, I would claim that the difference between my experience as a thirteen-year-old boy and my narrative of that experience is not simply due to the difficulties inherent in describing any mystical state of awareness. As a child of thirteen, I had no words with which to make sense of this experience, no "knowledge-about" with which to give my "knowledge-by-acquaintance" a context, nor even to give this knowledge-by-acquaintance a specific, describable shape. I just knew that "something" profound had occurred. What little religious training I had been exposed to during my brief, and to me incredibly boring, Sundays in church did not help me in my subsequent attempts to come to grips with this mysterious and yet powerful event. It was not until many years later, after several years spent practicing meditative disciplines and studying Eastern philosophical scriptures, that I was able to give this experience a viable interpretative structure. The "thatness" of the experience was always there, but this "thatness" was primarily operative as a goad prodding me to find some philosophical framework that could do justice to the inchoate content that had been so powerfully present to me in that brief, but transformative, moment.

I would argue that an epistemology of mystical experience that is based on "complete constructivism" does not adequately reflect the dynamics of this experience. My previous religious and cultural conceptual background was not sufficiently dense and nuanced enough to constitute completely this experience. Instead, I first had an experience, without any real religious preparation, that possessed inherently "mystical" qualities; then *after* having this experience (because it was sufficiently puzzling), I began to search for an intellectual framework that could accurately reflect the content that was latent in that experience. Undeniably, at thirteen years of age, I was not a completely blank slate: I knew that the experience had something to do with awareness (and I knew enough to remain quiet about this experience with my parents and even friends). But to claim, as complete constructivists would, that this highly rudimentary conceptual framework created that experience seems woefully inadequate.

It is clear that a Jamesian "incomplete constructivism" is better equipped to handle the dynamics of this experience. James's willingness to claim that we discover the world as much as we create our experience of it, his theoretical openness to a preexisting, partially-formed, autonomous "otherness" appearing within experience, can account for the fact that I did experience "something" that came to me possessing certain specific and inherent "mystical-like" qualities (i.e., loss of personal boundaries, feelings of extreme joy and peace, vivid and convincing metaphysical knowledge), even though I possessed no prior religious or cultural preparation. However, James's corresponding emphasis on the ways in which our tacit interests, assumptions, and intellectual constructs continually shape our experience in specific ways can theoretically justify why my initial experience was so inchoate and vague, as well as why that vagueness differs from the current, highly polished, intellectually informed nature of my memories of that experience. A Jamesian epistemology, however, would not be forced to claim that this difference is radical, since it could legitimately affirm that my current memories of that experience are still, in some very real sense, faithful to the initial experience itself.

Something Old and Something New: Religious Geniuses and Cultural Change

The Jamesian understanding that mystical experiences emerge out of a dialectical interaction between previous religious beliefs and a preexisting, amorphous, but vividly felt spiritual reality allows us to account for the ability of mystical experiences to bring something new into existence, something that was not previously present, either in an individual's personal life, or in his or her culture. A complete constructivist, on the other hand, who posits that mystical experiences are completely constituted by a particular culture's interpretative framework, has much more difficulty accounting for the appearance of anything within mystical experiences that was not previously present in the culture itself. In addition, a complete constructivist is extremely limited in his or her ability to explain how mystical experiences have time and time again managed to initiate profound transformations within the structure of the mystic's culture. (For instance, think of the changes that can, arguably, be traced back to the mystical experiences of Muhammad, Jesus, or the Buddha, to say nothing of the less-apparent, but highly significant cultural changes initiated by the mystical experiences of the multitude of less well-known religious mystics of different cultures and time-periods.)

James himself never presents a detailed argument that specifically addresses the ability of mystical experiences to change a culture's stock of beliefs, even though he does, from time to time, indicate that this is a significant function of mystical experiences, as when, in the *Varieties*, he claims that all major religions were founded by "religious geniuses," who, in James's mind, were inevitably mystics of some sort or another. However, even though this detailed argument is absent from James's work, in "Great Men and Their Environments," an essay in *The Will to Believe*, James does describe in more general terms his understanding of the dynamics of cultural change; this understanding has, as shall soon be shown, important implications for an understanding of the dialectical relationship between a mystic's experiences and his or her beliefs.

According to James, cultural change does not take place as the necessary result of environmental, economic, or institutional factors. Instead, James argues that cultural change is primarily due to an interaction between two separate components: the initiatives, decisions, and ideas of specific influential and creative individuals[105] and the willingness or unwillingness of the social environment of these individuals to adopt their original contributions. According to James, "both factors are essential to change. The community stagnates without the impulse of the individual. The impulse dies away without the sympathy of the community."[106]

Underlying much of James's work is an assiduous attempt to validate the freedom and social importance of an individual's contributions to his or her culture. James strenuously opposes any theory that attempts to portray novelty as being predetermined by unseen political, economic, or psychological forces. James claims (based on his own experience with acute bouts of depression) that not only do such theories insidiously strip individuals of their ability to make difficult moral choices by picturing them as unwitting puppets of impersonal and all-powerful forces, but such theories also overly simplify the complex give-and-take that occurs between creative individuals and their social environment. James acknowledges, although perhaps not to the degree that he could have, that powerful and creative individuals such as Napoleon and Grant, or Galileo and Newton, were, to a great degree, influenced by the culture in which they lived; but at the same time, he refuses to support the notion that every decision and insight of these social leaders and geniuses was the predetermined product of their social environment.

For James, as for many other thinkers in the turn-of-the-century Western world, the process of on-going social transformation could best be understood through a neo-Darwinian lens. For instance, James asserts that the inexplicable flashes of insight that arise in geniuses are analogous to Charles Darwin's notion of spontaneous variation, whereas the ability of the social environment either to adopt or to reject the genius's flashes of insight is comparable to Darwin's conception of selection of the fittest. In the same way that spontaneous variation emphasizes the unpredictable nature of genetic transformations, James claims that every major discovery, technological improvement, philosophical system, social institution, and religious innovation can be traced back to "flashes of genius in an individual head,"[107] flashes that the external environment surrounding that individual showed no signs of possessing before these insights appeared. The social philosopher, in James's opinion, will never be able to ascertain clearly the original cause of these insights, but instead, "must simply accept geniuses as data, just as Darwin accepts his spontaneous variations."[108] Of course, as James himself asks: "as for Darwin, the only problem is, these data [i.e., the geniuses] being given, how does the environment affect them, and how do they affect the environment?"[109] James believes that in order for these flashes of genius to have concrete and long-lasting social repercussions, the culture to which these insights are directed must be willing and able to accept and adopt these insights, it must *select* them. Then, if these insights are translated into specific and enduring components of the cultural and social environment, they become, in turn, part of the cultural and social background that influences, but does not produce, still more flashes of genius.

Because James quite frequently describes the saints and mystics of different cultures as "religious geniuses," it is legitimate to extend his analysis of social and cultural change to the changes provoked by mystical experiences as well. From a Jamesian perspective, it can be postulated that mystical insights are influenced by, but not produced from, the culture and social environment in which the mystic is situated. These insights and experiences can be understood not as

131

predetermined effects of a variety of quantifiable environmental, economic, and social factors, but rather, as unpredictable, novel gifts to the social and cultural nexus of the mystic. These mystical offerings are inevitably adapted to the contours of this nexus and arise in response to its particular configurations, but if accepted and adopted by the mystic's social and cultural environment, then these unexpected communications from an unknown source can become a ferment that transmutes the contours and configurations of that environment from within. The mystic's new insights and revolutionary perspectives can then, over the course of time, if successful, become themselves fairly stable and accepted components of the culture. These newly established cultural components will in turn, at a later time, be addressed by a new series of mystical insights—mystical insights that are influenced by, and are responding to, and perhaps, at a later time, are even adopted by, these now fairly taken-for-granted components of the culture.

Countless Radiant Windows

James himself was not reluctant to apply his interactive, dialectical epistemology to a deeper understanding of mystical states of awareness. In a letter written in 1904 to James Henry Leuba, an American psychologist whose work James periodically refers to in the *Varieties,* James explicitly utilizes his epistemological understanding of the relationship between the senses and an individual's intellectual background to comment on the nature of mystical perceptions:

> Just as the foundation of "natural" knowledge is sensation due to immediate non-rational influence of either body on body (or if you are an idealist, of mental fact on mental fact), so there might be a similar direct influence from God, and our knowledge might be partly at least founded thereon. . . . The mystical and the rational spheres of life are not absolutely discontinuous. It is evident that our intellectual stock in trade plays a suggestive part in our mystical life, and that this suggestive part changes with the progress of our thoughts, so that Vedantic and Christian mysticism have slightly different forms.
>
> If mystical states with all their differences have a common nucleus, then this nucleus should be reckoned a coordinate factor with reason in the building of religious belief. The intellect is interpretative, and critical of its own interpretation, but there must have been a thesis to interpret, and

that thesis seems to me to be the non-rational sense of a "higher" power. Religious men largely agree that this sense has been that of their 'best' moments—best not only in passing, but when looked back upon. The notion of it has leaked into mankind from their authority, the rest of us being imitative, just as we are of scientific men's opinions. Now may not this mystical testimony that there is a God be true, even though his precise determinations, being so largely "suggestive" contributions of our rational factor, should widely differ? It seems to me that to throw out, as you do, the whole mystical life from a hearing, because of the facility with which it combines with discrepant interpretations, would be like throwing out the senses, for a similar reason.[110]

In this letter, James makes it clear that while he would agree that the cultural and psychological background of a mystic is an inevitable and important factor in the construction of that mystic's experiences, he would also argue that every authentic mystical experience has a "core" of "raw material" that the intellect operates "upon." According to James, this undefinable, but directly felt, "'higher' power" will always be perceived differently, but "its" energy is what catalyzes every mystical experience; "its" presence is what informs every mystical experience.[111]

To further illustrate James's mystical epistemology, we could use a metaphor, which although not originating from James, is nonetheless respectably Jamesian. Picture a radiant light shining out from inside a beautiful building. The walls of the building are covered with many windows, each a different shape. Each window is made of thousands, if not millions, of uniquely shaped panes of a specially tinted, photo-active glass that changes color in response to the shifting pulsations of the brilliant light shining from within the building. For observers viewing the building from the outside, it seems as if a constantly changing rainbow of different colors is emerging from each pane of glass, even though each window as a whole tends to produce a fairly predictable range of hues. In each window, some panes of glass tend to remain, for the most part, almost opaque, letting very little light emerge, whereas other panes of glass seem to be continuously and almost completely transparent, letting so much light emerge that the outside observers are dazzled. These observers are also astonished at how the brilliance of the light emerging from the transparent panes of glass of one window is so similar to the brilliance of the light emerging from the transparent panes of glass of the other windows. The observers also notice that there are other panes of glass which alternate, seemingly unpredictably, between dark, murky shades of

133

color and shimmering pastels, with perhaps occasional unexpected surges of resplendent luminosity, while still other panes appear to change color following a noticeable pattern, and over the course of time, appear to be growing steadily more and more transparent, and are thereby increasingly able to let greater amounts of light emerge from the interior of the building.

In this metaphor, the light is James's "higher power." The observers are those individuals who are interested in, and knowledgeable about, mystical experiences from different cultures. Standing outside the building, the walls of which represent the boundaries of our everyday experience of reality, the observers can only speculate as to the nature of the source or sources of that light, but the fact that there is light coming through the windows is undeniable. The differently shaped windows symbolize the world's different religious traditions, while the panes of glass that make up these windows are the individuals within these traditions. The photo-active quality of the glass within each window-pane symbolizes the ability of these individuals to sense and respond to the light of the "higher power," each according to his or her cultural framework and psychological background, while the different colors of light are the different spiritual experiences of these individuals.[112] The almost completely opaque panes represent those individuals who, for whatever complex reasons, have few overt spiritual experiences, while the continuously and almost completely transparent panes of glass represent those individuals (the great saints and spiritual guides of different traditions) who have had powerful spiritual experiences—experiences that often seem to be astonishingly similar, at least in power, if not always in their specific features. The panes that alternate unpredictably between dark and pastel colors represent the day-to-day alternations of spiritual dullness and receptivity within most individuals, while the occasional bursts of radiance are indicative of the possibility of a sudden, unexpected mystical experience. Finally, the panes that appear to be growing steadily more transparent represent those individuals who are involved in conscious spiritual disciplines and who, over the course of time, have an increasing ability to let that "higher power" emerge into this world.[113]

It is necessary to be careful at this point, however. By using such a concrete metaphor, it is almost not possible to avoid imagining that this "higher power" is something objective, something definable, something that is a transcendent, unchanging foundation for every mystical experience. However, simply because James does not reduce all mystical experiences to natural causes and is willing to admit a sense of a "higher power" into his epistemology, does not imply that James is an advocate of what has recently come to be known in philosophical circles as "objectivism." Richard Bernstein, a contemporary philosopher, defines objectivism as "the basic conviction that there is or must be some permanent, ahistorical matrix or framework to which we can ultimately appeal in determining the nature of rationality, knowledge, truth, reality, goodness, or rightness."[114] James was an early and powerful opponent to any and all such attempts to ground the knowledge or the claims to truth in any indubitable, unchanging metaphysical foundation. But, at the same time, James was not a relativist or an advocate of skepticism. He never argued that all knowledge and claims to truth are simply variations of competing, humanly created, linguistically based webs of beliefs. For James, our concrete experience in the world is a rich and important testing ground for knowledge claims. While never static or clear-cut, and always interwoven with human desires and beliefs, our concrete experience in the world provides us with a nonhuman, partially objective referent that often stubbornly refuses to mold itself into the shapes that we might desire. Therefore, in many ways, it can be said that James is interested in articulating a position that avoids the rigidity and dogmatism of an objectivist perspective, while at the same time, he wants to leave a space in his philosophical model for the existence and power of the translinguistic and transcultural modes of reality that relativism denies.

James most certainly believes in the existence of an unseen spiritual world, but he also adamantly resists any temptation to describe its contours conclusively or to ground the legitimacy of particular beliefs on a dogmatic affirmation of its existence, even if that affirmation emerges out of a powerful mystical experience of that spiritual level of reality. Although James occasionally does imply that he believes that there is a single source to all mystical experiences, he is just as likely to claim that the "unseen world" is at least as pluralistic and complex as the world we experience in our everyday life. Additionally, contrary to the assumptions of some theorists, James is most certainly *not* an advocate of the "common core theory." This theory claims that although the mystics of different traditions interpret their experiences differently according to the religious and cultural environment in which they live, the mystical experiences in-and-of-themselves are basically the same. While James most certainly does believe that powerful religious experiences and saintly actions are often strikingly similar from one cultural system to the next, and while James does work hard to articulate some basic commonalties between different mystical experiences, he also emphasizes that each mystical experience is unique. As he says in the *Varieties*: "I imagine that these experiences can be as infinitely varied as are the idiosyncrasies of individuals."[115]

This emphasis on the continual variety and plurality of mystical experiences reflects James's emphasis in the *Principles* on the ever-changing nature of experience in general. For James, consciousness is dynamic, ever-new, perpetually in motion. No state of consciousness ever repeats itself, nor is it ever identical to what came before. According to James, we mistakenly think that we hear the same sounds or see the same sights simply because we confuse the apparent "sameness" of the objects (e.g., blades of grass) with our *perceptions* of those objects (e.g., the colors and feel of the grass). Even if the objects themselves managed somehow to remain completely static (which James would deny is actually possible), the ways in which we perceive them will inevitably change from moment to moment since every new perception changes the mass of memories, expectations, and so forth, that form the background context that surrounds and suffuses our perception and understanding of these objects. As James puts it: "experience is remoulding us every moment, and our mental reaction on every given thing is really a resultant of our experience of the whole world up to that date."[116] In a similar way, if these observations were extended to mystical states of consciousness, it could be argued that, from a Jamesian perspective, no two mystical experiences will ever be the same, even though it is quite possible that all of these different experiences do come from the same trans-natural catalyst.

However, some recent philosophers of religion have produced evidence that seems to belie this Jamesian emphasis on the plurality of mystical experience.[117] They point out that many different traditions have descriptions of a mystical state of consciousness that appears to be phenomenologically identical. This state of mystical awareness (which has been termed by these philosophers as "the Pure Consciousness Event," or "PCE") is described as simple, contentless awareness itself, a state of consciousness that is free from thoughts and that does not contain a subject/object distinction.[118] Therefore, they argue, while it may indeed be true that mystical experiences with specific content differ from mystic to mystic, it would seem reasonable that mystical experiences without any specific content would share the same quality of emptiness and would thus be phenomenologically identical.

However, from a Jamesian perspective, we might question whether this apparent sameness is actually masking more subtle differences. Even though it is undeniable that many mystical experiences do appear to contain striking phenomenological similarities, especially

136

as they become less visionary and move towards the reported subject/object merger or identity that characterizes so many unitive mystical experiences, it is an open question whether emptiness of apparent content implies complete phenomenological sameness. As James points out, "there are innumerable consciousnesses of emptiness, no one of which taken in itself has a name, but all different from each other. The ordinary way is to assume that they are all emptinesses of consciousness, and so the same state. But the feeling of an absence is *toto coelo* other than an absence of a feeling: it is an intense feeling."[119] James gives us a concrete illustration of this phenomena from our everyday experience:

> Suppose we try to recall a forgotten name. The state of our consciousness is peculiar. There is a gap therein; but no mere gap. It is a gap that is intensely active. A sort of wraith of the name is in it, beckoning us in a given direction, making us at moments tingle with the sense of our closeness, and then letting us sink back without the longed for term. If wrong names are proposed to us, this singularly definite gap acts immediately so as to negate them. They do not fit into its mould. And the gap of one word does not feel like the gap of another, all empty of content as both might seem necessarily to be when described as gaps. . . . Our psychological vocabulary is wholly inadequate to name the differences that exist, even such strong differences as these. But namelessness is compatible with existence.[120]

The argument that is being made here is *not* that searching for a memory is identical to a PCE. Instead, James's illustration demonstrates that just as our everyday experience clearly shows us that moments devoid of mental content do not all feel the same, analogously, there is a strong possibility that PCEs, while sharing the same absence of mental content, might well differ from each another, based on felt qualities that are transverbal in nature.

James underscores how often we make the mistake "of supposing that where there is no name no entity can exist. All dumb or anonymous psychic states have, owing to this error, been coolly suppressed; or, if recognized at all, have been named after the substantive perception they led to."[121] In the same way, while the phenomenological emptiness of the PCE's described in different religious traditions might indeed appear to be identical, it is also quite likely that a more subtle introspective phenomenology would reveal other, less obvious (since unnamed or even unnamable) differences from one PCE to the next. The territory of these unitive experiences is still relatively unmapped in the Western philosophical tradition; thus, it seems premature to make any firm philosophical conclusions, especially when we are dealing with states of awareness in which the subject and object distinction has apparently dissolved. All philosophical observations, as well as the narratives of the mystics who have described their PCEs, are inevitably structured in a linguistic system which is rooted in the very subject/object distinction that is said to be overcome in these states of awareness; it may be quite some time before we can recognize, and perhaps overcome, some of the philosophical perils that are inherent in using dualistic categories of understanding to explore nondualistic experiences.

Pure Experiences and a Radical Empiricism

Until this point, a direct investigation of James's philosophical exploration of the subject/object distinction has been postponed. Until now, James's epistemology has been discussed in fairly standard dualistic terms: there is a knower, there is something known, and there is a mysterious process of knowing that somehow connects these apparently disparate realms of being. This dualistic terminology is faithful to James in that the discussion so far has focused on his work in the *Principles* and the *Varieties*. In these works, James openly refuses to confront the mind's ability to transcend itself in the process of knowing. In the *Principles*, James is quite explicit about the fact that his underlying approach to the metaphysical status of cognition is that of "a thoroughgoing dualism. It supposes two elements, mind knowing and thing known, and treats them as irreducible."[122]

But James was never truly satisfied with this theoretical standoff, and in the years following the publication of the *Principles*, he struggled to articulate a conceptual framework that could account for the mystery of cognition. Classical empiricism had not solved the puzzle of how mental and physical modes of existence manage to become united in the moment of knowing, and James was determined not to accept rationalism's postulate of a transempirical "Absolute," whose all-encompassing knowledge bridged the chasm between the knower and the known. In the end, James decided that the solution to the dilemma of knowledge was not to be found by somehow jumping outside of our experience and logically deriving the existence of a transcendental Knower, but rather, the key to how the knower and the known are united was to be found by a reimmersion into the depths of experience itself—it was to be found by drawing out and articulating the metaphysical implications inherent in a detailed study of the complex and yet fruitful ways in which our concrete experience reveals itself to us moment by moment.

In his psychological work, James had already demonstrated that there are not disjunctions between one moment of consciousness and the next. Instead, as James illustrated, consciousness flows seamlessly from moment to moment. James held that the British empiricists (i.e., David Hume, David Locke, and James Mills) made the critical mistake of acknowledging only the more substantive moments of our conscious experience, especially the sense impressions. This focus on the easily observed, and apparently atomistic, elements of our experience was the basis of the British empiricist claim that each unit of consciousness is isolated and cut off from every other unit of consciousness. According to James, however, careful introspective work reveals that these classical empiricists were incorrect: the transitions between each moment of consciousness are not empty, but rather, contain specific, if difficult to articulate, felt qualities of tendency, directionality, and so forth. James repeatedly pointed out that the quickly flowing connections between one moment of awareness to the next may indeed be less apparent than the more obvious "resting places" of our awareness; but these vaguely felt transitive relations between one part of our experience and the next are indeed present in our experience. James concluded, therefore, that there is no need to accept the judgement made by classical empiricism that our consciousness is disjointed and fragmented. Further, since our consciousness can be demonstrated to be inherently connected from one moment to the next, there is also no theoretical need to depend upon a Kantian transcendental ego to bind together all of these supposedly disparate components of our consciousness.

James's philosophical strategy after the *Principles* was to make a daring link between his psychological investigations and his metaphysical speculations. What James did was to claim that the connectivity that is present within our consciousness is not limited to the confines of our consciousness, but is also an inherent ontological quality of the universe itself. Therefore, in James's radical empiricism, psychology becomes a doorway into ontology.

James's "radical empiricism" was rooted in the methodological presupposition that the only universe that is theoretically available to us is manifested within and through the thickness and concreteness of our lived experience. The initial methodological postulate of James's radical empiricism states that "the only things that shall be debatable among philosophers shall be things definable in terms drawn from experience."[123] This postulate underscores the fact that philosophers cannot legitimately discuss "the universe" as something external, since the only universe that can be directly experienced is always nothing more than different forms of experience itself. And what does this experience reveal? Not just "things," but also connections and relations between things. Therefore, according to radical empiricism, the world of our experience (the only world that we know) is itself joined together, and there is no need to import some "higher unifying agency"[124] to serve as a sort of cosmic glue.

James's methodological admonition that radical empiricism must deal only with that which is directly experienced does not mean that he is unwilling to speculate on the possible existence of God or other spiritual realities. James's radical empiricism has a much broader definition of what constitutes a legitimate experience than classical empiricism's limitation of "experience" to "sense experience." Religious, psychical, mystical, pathological, and sensory experiences: all of these are equally valid forms of data from a radical empiricist's perspective.[125] Furthermore, while James recognizes that it is not theoretically acceptable to move directly from the specific information revealed in a mystical experience (even if it were authentic) to specific theological assertions about the nature of God, he nonetheless asserts that metaphysical speculations are still acceptable as long as the spiritual realities they postulate have, in some way or another, observable effects within our experience. As James puts it: "I am perfectly willing to admit any number of noumenal beings or events into philosophy if only their pragmatic value can be shown."[126]

Some of the metaphysical and theological speculations about these noumenal beings or events are, however, decidedly less appealing to James than others, especially those formulations that conceive of God as a monistic Absolute whose universal presence and overarching omniscience is supposedly needed to provide a cohesive substratum in which apparently disparate subjects and objects can be united. James recognizes that the idealism of neo-Hegelians, such as Josiah Royce and F. H. Bradley, is theoretically possible, but his radical empiricism attempts to provide a viable (and perhaps superior) alternative, one that can not only connect the knower and the known together without having to jump outside of our experience, but an alternative which can also account for the felt moments of disconnection that appear within our experience—a theoretical difficulty for any monistic philosophical system.

In one of James's more colorful metaphors, he gleefully contrasts the pristine perfection of the universe as seen from the perspective of absolute idealism with the messy, tangled, and complex universe that is pictured by radical empiricism:

> If you should liken the universe of absolute idealism to an aquarium, a crystal globe in which goldfish are swimming, you would have to compare the empiricist universe to something more like one of those dried human heads with which the Dyaks of Borneo deck their lodges. The skull forms the solid nucleus; but innumerable feathers, leaves, strings, beads, and loose appendices of every description float and dangle from it, and save that they terminate in it, seem to have nothing to do with one another. Even so my experiences and yours float and dangle, terminating, it is true, in a nucleus of common perception, but for the most part out of sight and irrelevant and unimaginable to one another.[127]

As will become clear in chapter 4, James is repelled by any monistic philosophical system that unifies the universe to such an extent that there is no room for novelty, human initiatives, or a coherent ethical response to the felt reality of evil and suffering. Radical empiricism is James's metaphysical response to the "block universe" of the monists; he sees it as a metaphysical framework that can legitimately account for the process of knowing (which meant somehow uniting the knower and the known), and yet which could, at the same time, do justice to our felt sense of separateness from each other and the world around us. James claims that this combination of unity and separation does not need to be justified or artificially created by some logical sleight-of-hand, but instead, is constantly present if we only look carefully and deeply enough into each concrete moment of our experience.

James at one point attempts to illustrate the underlying connection that is to be found from one moment of our experience to the next by referring to radical empiricism as a "mosaic philosophy"; but he quickly points out that this metaphor is misleading, since "in actual mosaics the pieces are held together by their bedding, for which bedding the substances, transcendental egos, or absolutes of other philosophies may be taken to stand. In radical empiricism there is no bedding; it is as if the pieces clung together by their edges, the transitions experienced between them forming their cement."[128] James then goes on to say that even this way of expressing the dynamics of our experience is misleading; since "in actual experience the more substantive and the more transitive parts run into each other continuously, there is in general no separateness needing to be overcome by an external cement."[129]

It is important to remember that in radical empiricism, James is no longer confined to describing the connections between one moment of *consciousness* and the next. Instead, he is describing moments of *experience*, and experience is, as James put it, a "double-barreled" term—it is "subjective and objective both at once."[130] James develops this controversial (and at times maddeningly difficult to comprehend) claim that experience itself is inherently neither mental nor physical, but is potentially both, in his discussion of "pure experience."

As Marcus Ford, a Jamesian scholar, has perceptively suggested, much of the controversy surrounding James's discussion of pure experience is rooted in the fact that when James explicated his understanding of this already highly abstruse subject, he was unknowingly articulating two separate and perhaps even mutually contradictory, philosophical positions.[131] On the one hand, pure experience appears to be an extension and continuation of James's psychological discussion of knowledge-by-acquaintance. Pure experience in this sense is what Ford refers to as "prereflective experience;"[132] it is, as James admits, only "another name for feeling or sensation."[133] Pure experience from this perspective is the term that James uses to describe "the immediate flux of life which furnishes the material to our later reflection with its conceptual categories. Only new-born babes, or men in semi-coma from sleep, drugs, illnesses, or blows, may be assumed to have an experience pure in the literal sense of a *that* which is not yet any definite *what*, tho ready to be all sorts of whats."[134] From this point of view, pure experience is really more of a psychological insight than a metaphysical position, since its focus is primarily on the psychical state of awareness of the experiencer, and does not explicitly wrestle with the connection of that psychical state with the "external" world.

James's alternate conception of pure experience, however, is specifically metaphysical.[135] James claims that in the immediate, initial moment of knowing and experiencing anything, the object that is seen and "the seeing of it are only two names for one indivisible fact, which, properly named, is the datum, the phenomenon, or the experience."[136] Pure experience in this sense is James's recognition that in experience *per se*, "there is no self-splitting . . . into consciousness and what the consciousness is 'of'."[137] Pure experience in this way is understood as a nondual "primal stuff" which is potentially either physical or mental depending upon its particular functional context.[138] However, by referring to pure experience as a "primal stuff," James does not mean to imply that it is some sort of general, underlying substance which takes the form of everything we experience. Instead,

142

James views pure experience as the "thatness" of each *particular* experience. Pure experience in this sense consists of "just what appears, of space, of intensity, of flatness, brownness, heaviness, or what not."[139] In this conception, pure experience is simply "the instant field of the present . . . [a] plain unqualified actuality, a simple that, as yet undifferentiated into thing and thought,"[140] a "thatness" which can and does become both what we perceive and our perceptions themselves.

To illustrate this "doubling-up" of experience, James analyzes what occurs when we perceive the room in which we are presently sitting. On the one hand, the objects in the room are specific items in our external environment. On the other hand, at the same time, these objects are perceptions in our mind. The question is, how can one reality be both places at the same time? How can physical objects simultaneously be mental perceptions? James answers that this simultaneity is possible in the same way that one point can be on two lines at once if it is "situated at their intersection."[141] Experience, like the point existing on the intersection of the two lines, can be "counted twice over"; once as a "field of consciousness" and once as "the room in which [we] sit," all the while remaining "a numerically single thing."[142] In the example of the room, the two processes that intersect in the single moment of pure experience are, first, our subjective stream of "sensations, emotions, decisions, movements, classifications, expectations, etc. ending in the present" moment of the pure experience of the room (and continuing on into the future), and second, the previous, external, "physical operations, carpentering, papering, furnishing, warming, etc." which finally terminate as well in the present moment of the same pure experience of the room (and also continue on into the future).[143] James recognizes that the "physical and mental operations form curiously incompatible groups. As a room, the experience has occupied that spot and had that environment for thirty years. As [our] field of consciousness, it may never have existed until now."[144] The question remains, therefore: If these two operations are indeed so incompatible, how is it possible to justify any claim that they are somehow different ways of experiencing the same "stuff"?

James's answer to this question is straightforward: our categorization of experience as "subjective (or mental) " and "objective (or physical)" is a secondary, post-facto operation based on a preconscious, retrospective assessment of the *consequences* of the experience. Objective/physical experiences are those experiences that "act," whereas subjective/mental experiences are those that do not. In his typically colorful and down-to-earth fashion, James specifies how this "post-partum" sorting out process operates:

143

> As the general chaos of all our experiences gets sifted, we find that there
> are some fires that will always burn sticks and always warm our bodies,
> and that there are some waters that will always put out fires; while there
> are other fires and waters that will not act at all. . . . Mental fire is what
> won't burn real sticks; mental water is what won't necessarily (though of
> course it may) put out even a mental fire. . . . With "real" objects, on the
> contrary, consequences always accrue; and thus the real experiences get
> sifted from the mental ones, the things from our thoughts of them.[145]

Unlike most other theorists, James does not believe that the
decision as to whether an experience is "subjective" or "objective" is
predetermined. This understanding that experience is classified as
subjective or objective according to its context or function, rather
than according to its inherent, predetermined qualities, has important implications for the reality status that is assigned to mystical
experiences. From a philosophical perspective that accepts the sub-
ject/object distinction as a given, mystical experiences are inevitably
seen as "subjective" because they occur within an individual's psyche
and cannot be observed, weighed, measured, and quantified like other
more overtly "objective" aspects of our experience. Unfortunately,
from this particular philosophical perspective, when an event is
determined to be "subjective," it is also, by default, "illusory," "arbitrary," "unreal," and so on. From a Jamesian perspective, however,
the reality status of mystical experiences is not preordained. If it can
be demonstrated that mystical experiences have important effects on
other aspects of our experience, if it can be shown that they heal,
they enliven, they guide, they inspire, they illumine, then we have
every right to claim that they are "objective" or "real."[146] On the
other hand, James would say that if mystical experiences make no
viable connections with the rest of our experience, then we can and
should shrug them off as being nothing more than fanciful products
of our imagination.

In many ways, mystical experiences are very similar to what
James describes in his discussion of "affectional facts."[147] James points
out that it is unclear whether certain types of feelings are "inner" or
"outer." For instance, if we hurt our arm, it is difficult to determine
whether this is a painful experience or an experience of something
that is painful. As James puts it: "sometimes the adjective wanders as
if uncertain where to fix itself. Shall we speak of seductive visions, or
of visions of seductive things? Of wicked desires or of desires for
wickedness?"[148] This class of experiences remains equivocal, since "in
practical life no urgent need has yet arisen for deciding whether to

144

treat them as rigorously mental or as rigorously physical facts."[149] They seem to be "inner" in that they do not affect the physical world beyond our body, but they are "outer" in that they do, most certainly, produce alternations in the experience we have of our bodies (i.e., changes in heart-rate, glandular secretions, pulse, rate of breath, and so on).

Mystical experiences seem to share a similar ambiguity of status with "affectional facts." Does a mystic experience "higher states of consciousness" or does he or she have experiences of "realms of higher consciousness"? If a shaman has a visionary experience in which he or she is shown a previously unknown herb that is later located in the physical world and is efficaciously used to cure the illnesses of a patient, is the shaman's visionary experience "subjective" or "objective"?[150] If a !Kung healer dances the Giraffe dance, and feels the *num* energy "boiling" inside him, and then gets into a state of *kia* in which he "sees" the illnesses within someone's body in the form of different noxious objects (such as pieces of wire, insects, and so on), and if that healer, trembling and crying out in pain, then "pulls" those illnesses from the "patient's" body, is the healer's altered state of awareness "physical" or "mental"?[151] (This question would seem to be especially pertinent if that "patient" feels substantially better afterwards.) A philosophical perspective such as James's radical empiricism, which can be utilized to demonstrate the ways in which mystical experiences are not exceptional in their subjective/ objective ambiguity, seems infinitely preferable to a philosophical stance that neatly divides the universe into easily discernible "mental" and "physical" realms. If the "subjectivity" or "objectivity" of all experiences is understood to be only a functional and retrospective determination, then it becomes exceedingly difficult to disparage mystical experiences as being "merely subjective."[152] Conversely, the theological tendency to speak of "God" as being an external "object" is undercut when we are forced to question the status of the entire subject/object distinction itself.[153]

For James, nothing in life is clear-cut. In the jostling give-and-take of our ordinary experience, *and* in the numinous depths of mystical experience, borderlines and boundaries are hard to draw. Experience always presents itself to us, moment by moment, as a complex, densely textured whole. It is difficult, therefore, from a Jamesian point of view, to say precisely to what extent we make our experience, and to what extent experience makes us. However, even this recognition of the difficulties that are inherent in any philosophical investigation of mystical experience can move us towards a more subtle, and nuanced, understanding of the interactive nature of mystical experience, can let us speak convincingly about mystical experiences, while, at the same time, providing mystical experiences with the opportunity to speak back to us in their own, often surprising, ways.

꧁ 3 ꧂

"Fields within Fields within Fields":
Mysticism and a Jamesian Psychology of the Self

There is ablaze from the center, the heart of each and all things—life. From galaxies to photons. Life is conscious, intelligent energy that can collect itself into any function or shape. . . . When it collects into something, that is an individual. Its matrix has a unique pulsing, a rhythm, that belongs only to it. It sings to the universe and life pours through it carrying its little song. It tells everybody around about its existence. This is life energy itself being scattered out as a gift from the heart. An individual's song is its joy. And we share them with each other continually. This is our web.

—Kay Cordell Whitaker, *The Reluctant Shaman*

I went into my courtyard. The walls of the building were dancing in Her Fire, like starlit smoke. Everything was dancing in time with everything else, the walls, the windows, the stars, my dirty wet hands, my mind. *One dance. One dance. One dance.* Somehow I walked up the stairs to my room. I went in, not turning on the light. *Turn and look in the mirror.* There is a mirror all along the small wall above my bed. I turned. I was not in the mirror. There was only a Dance in the mirror, only a light hilarious spiral of drunken leaping atoms, a Dance of Fire in which everything was swirling—the bedspread, the chair, my hands moving up and down, the strict classical railing of the outside window. All was Myself, dancing in Fire in Myself. Then a Peace descended, of which I remember nothing.

—Andrew Harvey, *Hidden Journey*

Every philosophical, social-scientific, or theological investigation of mystical experience operates with certain assumptions about the nature of the self. All too often, however, these assumptions go unexamined; consequently, a detailed exploration of the give-and-take between our theoretical understanding of mystical experience and our preconceptions about the nature of the self never takes place. It is rare that scholars of mysticism explicitly deal with questions such as the following: Who exactly is it that undergoes mystical experiences? What do mystical experiences suggest about the nature of the self? Which doctrines of the self are most amenable to the range of mystical experiences? Is the self of the mystic an ever-changing, organically based amalgam of memories, thoughts, emotions, and social roles centered around a physical body? Or is the soul the true self of the mystic—that unique inner essence of an individual, that underlying substance that preserves personal identity even after death? Or, in actuality, is the self of the mystic something more, something grander, perhaps an all-pervasive, eternal, cosmic Consciousness?

While William James never offered detailed and systematic answers to these questions, nonetheless, a close reading of his work as a whole reveals that he did generate some extremely insightful and provocative proposals about the relationship between mystical experience and the nature of the self. However, any attempt to uncover James's understanding of the interconnection between mystical experience and selfhood is made more complex by the fact that James articulated several seemingly incompatible conceptions of the self during the course of his career. In the *Principles*, James claimed that the self is epiphenomenal, transitory, and completely intertwined with the physical body. In his essay "Human Immortality," James explored the tantalizing possibility of the self's connection with a mother-sea of consciousness. In the *Varieties*, James explicitly investigated the self-transformations that take place as a result of mystical experiences; and in order to bridge the chasm between the scientific and theological understandings of the dynamics of religious experience, he offered the mediating theoretical construct of the subliminal self. In the *Essays on Radical Empiricism*, the self dissolved into a nondualistic fusion of subject and object, but then later, in *A Pluralistic Universe*, the self reemerged, this time cosmic in scope.

How should a scholar approach these strikingly different conceptions of the self? Do these theories represent dramatic alternations in James's thought that can never be reconciled or are there, perhaps, certain thematic patterns that repeat themselves during this onrush of conceptual mutations? A viable argument could be made for either conclusion, but I suggest that a careful examination of James's conceptions of the self demonstrates that certain key themes do emerge again and again: an antipathy towards any conception of the "soul"; an ongoing attempt to explain how personal identity can be maintained without rigid individual boundaries; and perhaps most importantly, a continuing struggle to envision the self in ways that overcomes dualistic modes of understanding the mind and the body, the human and the divine, and the many and the one.

These threads of consistency indicate that the shifts that occurred in James's theoretical understandings of the self were neither as radical nor as arbitrary as they might at first appear. James's proposals on the nature of the self were always rooted in a methodological stance that emphasized empirical, introspectively based observations augmented by analogical, carefully disciplined, speculative elaborations. However, as his career progressed, his loyalty to scientific exactitude was increasingly tempered by his moral and religious predispositions, resulting in a corresponding openness to conceptions of the nature of the self that were increasingly, and overtly, "mystical"; that is to say, more and more, James began to stress the theoretical possibility of an underlying connection between the self and a transnatural dimension of reality, as well as to emphasize a corresponding permeability of personal boundaries.

The Psychology of the Self: From the Outside In and From the Inside Out

James's earliest, and most detailed, discussion of the nature of the self occurs in the *Principles*. In the chapter "The Consciousness of Self," James explicitly contrasts his vision of the self with several other philosophical alternatives: Hume's skepticism about the possibility of personal identity, Kant's belief in a transcendental ego, and the theoretical constructions of neo-Hegelians such as T. H. Green and Edward Caird, who posit that the Absolute is identical with the self. James's proposal is that the self is, instead, a shifting, multilayered continuum in which bodily awareness, internalization of social roles, subtle feelings of effort and attention, and an evanescent "Thought,"[1] all combine to form the ever-changing basis of our personal identity.

The foundation of this multidimensional self is what James refers to as the "empirical self." The empirical self is protean in scope; it includes everything that a person might typically label as "me," that is, the body, personality traits, memories, ideas, social roles, and so on. However, as James notes, the "me" is not limited to these commonsense identifications in that "we feel and act about certain things that are ours very much as we feel and act about ourselves. Our fame, our children, the work of our hands, may be as dear to us as our bodies are."[2] Seen from this perspective, our possessions and our family are just as much a part of our "me" as are our bodies. James suggests that we would be mistaken if we too quickly assume that simply because our family and our possessions (what James calls "the material self") appear to be external to us, that they are not also integral parts of our being. He offers several examples of the ways in which the externals in our lives are inextricably connected with our sense of personal identity: we feel differently when we wear different types of clothes; if someone insults a family member, it is as if we were personally insulted; furnishing and decorating our home is a highly individual and intimate activity; and if the external components of our life prosper, then we feel expanded, whereas if they diminish, we feel as if we are losing a part of ourselves. Thus, for James, the empirical self is not only a person's body, memories, emotions, habits, intelligence, morals, interests, and social roles, but it is also that person's clothes, spouse, family, home, possessions, and artistic creations. The empirical self is the sum total of everything with which a person could possibly identify.

The self for James, therefore, is not just something which is hidden deep within us, something utterly private and interior. Rather, as Don Browning points out: "to see the self as a me spread out before the world with certain public and observable dimensions . . . means the self is accessible from two perspectives."[3] We not only know ourselves by looking inwards, we also become acquainted with a very real part of ourselves by observing our behavior in the "external"[4] world. In a very real sense, we not only know ourselves from the inside out, but also from the outside in.

It is often easy to forget that James's well-known stress on the individual was not, in actuality, individualistic, since, for James, a large part of who we are is determined by our interactions with the "external" world. This public dimension of ourselves is not just limited to our clothes, our jobs, our family, and so on. It is also constituted, in part, by the recognition that we receive from significant individuals in our social world. According to James, every interaction we have with someone creates a corresponding social self within us. Although strictly speaking, we have "as many social selves as there are individuals who recognize [us] and carry an image of [us] in their mind,"[5] the most important of these social selves are created out of interactions with individuals who mean a great deal to us. James argues that we actually take on a different self when we play the numerous, and often discordant, roles that our modern society demands of us. For instance, a man can be a stern father and yet a loving husband; a woman can be a gentle mother and yet a demanding school teacher;

and so on. From this point of view, we are not a unified substance, but rather, a jostling plurality of sub-selves created and maintained by our emotional and behavioral interactions with others. This transactional understanding of the self was revolutionary for its time, and as Browning rightly points out, not only did it have a profound effect on the psychological understandings of John Dewey and George Herbert Mead, but also, through Mead, shaped the psychological conceptions of Harry Stack Sullivan, Carl Rogers, Heinz Hartmann, and Erik Erikson.[6]

The task of harmoniously integrating these various sub-selves is often exceedingly difficult, especially if the demands of one social self are in opposition to those of another. At certain points in our lives, this task is especially arduous, particularly when we feel impelled to go against the expectations of social groups that define us in important ways, for example, when a teenager fights for civil rights in opposition to his or her parents' racial prejudices, when a Protestant converts to Catholicism, or when a homosexual comes out of the closet. During these confrontations, we are, in essence, destroying a former social self in favor of a new one.

James points out that we are able to endure the loss of these former social selves "by the thought of other and better possible social judges than those whose verdict goes against [us] now."[7] James believes that we grow as social and moral human beings by substituting "higher tribunals for lower," and he claims that the "ideal social self" to which we can appeal, the "true, the intimate, the ultimate, the permanent Me" from whom we can gain the nourishing sustenance of "approving recognition," is "God, the Absolute Mind, the 'Great Companion'."[8] Bracketing for the moment James's later theological and metaphysical speculations, at this point he makes the daring suggestion that God is, to some extent at least, both a social creation and a potentially crucial component of our psychological structure. God is pictured as simultaneously the idealized Other and the idealized Self; God is understood as that internalized social and moral presence that enables "the humblest outcast on this earth" to feel "real and valid"; God is seen as an "inner refuge" against an "abyss of horror" that can well up within us "when the outer social self" fails in its task of sustaining our psychic cohesion.[9]

James is not attempting a Feuerbachian reversal here; he does not believe that God is simply a human projection. But in these brief, albeit suggestive, passages, James is already beginning to press against several dualistic assumptions. Not only are the inner (self) and the outer (social interactions) pictured as intimately related to one another, but the conventional view of the human and the divine as completely separate ontological categories is also challenged by this fusion, on one level at least, of God and our ideal "me."

This understanding that the self is to be discovered in the interstices between inside and outside, this notion that the self is not just limited to the clear-cut boundaries of the physical form, but rather extends outwards into the universe, is astonishingly congruent with what is unveiled in many unitive mystical experiences. In certain respects, it is as if the mystical experience of feeling one's connection with other human beings and the surrounding environment is simply a more vivid way of experiencing who we always have been, but have tended to overlook or to deny because of the distorting effects of our ingrained sense of ourselves as inherently disconnected from others and from the world.[10] In addition, James's radical notion that the self incorporates the divine as an integral part of its psychic structure could easily point to the possibility that the overwhelmingly joyous merger of self and God that characterizes many mystical experiences may perhaps be, in some respects, an amplification of the psychological nurture and sustenance that a person receives from the often unconscious and indistinct, yet crucially important, internalization of the God-images that are present within his or her self-structure.[11]

James's notion of the self in the *Principles* is inherently syncretic and pluralistic. For James, we are not isolated monads cut off from other human beings, the world, or the divine. Instead, the Other is already discovered within us (or we are discovered to exist within the Other). Every exposure to another human being, another culture, or another religious worldview enlarges us and expands our boundaries. Each new experience that comes to us (including mystical experiences) interacts with the stock of previous experiences that we use to define ourselves, creating a selfhood that is spread out into our world, a selfhood that is a loosely knit, often shockingly discordant, pattern of cultural, psychological, and religious experiences. We are constantly re-adjusting, re-forming, renewing this volatile and tentative selfhood— but rarely smoothly or without pain. According to James, our selfhood is inseparable from continuous struggle, it is bound up with perpetual choices: what to include and to exclude, what to accept and what to reject, what is essential and what is irrelevant. Our autonomy and integrity emerges as we attempt to give a rough order to this cacophony of life-experiences, conflicting cultural assumptions, and opposing ideals.

We are given crucial assistance in this project, James believes, by the images of the spiritual world that we, often unknowingly, carry within us. These tacit images, based as much on vivid, enlivening religious experiences as on prior religious indoctrination, give us a glimpse of our potential as human beings; they offer us a vision of what the self could and should become; they establish a teleological framework which not only assists us in our efforts to establish priorities in life, but which also gives life a sense of purpose and value. As we will clearly see from an investigation of the *Varieties*, James believes that mystical experiences challenge us to go beyond our previous sense of limitations; they reveal our inherent, and yet often hidden, connection with deeper levels of ourselves and the world. Mystical experiences also often catalyze dramatic transformations in our notions of who we are and how we wish to express ourselves in the world by shattering old images of ourselves, images that then coalesce around a new religious center of gravity, a center defined in part by our previous religious backgrounds, but also in part by the nature of that which is mystically revealed.

Thinking through the Body and Seeing with an Ever-Changing I

James's conceptions of the self in the *Principles* not only dissolve the differences between inside and outside, and the boundaries between the human and the divine, but also subvert the clear-cut distinction between the body and the mind. This body/mind dualism is implicitly challenged throughout James's discussion of the "spiritual self."[12] For James, our empirical "me" not only consists of our material selves and our social selves, but it also includes our spiritual self, that is, our "inner or subjective being," that part of us which includes within its purview our powers of reason, our ethics, as well as that subtle, but perceptible, "active element in all consciousness" that "welcomes or rejects" the input of our senses, and which is "the home of interest" as well as "the source of effort and attention."[13]

Interestingly, however, James denies that this spiritual self is "spiritual" at all. Although this spiritual self would seem to consist of exclusively mental processes, James reports that in his own introspective efforts he experienced nothing that was specifically mental about his reasoning, his efforts of attention, and so on. He claims, instead, that when he remembered something, reflected on something, used his will, and so on, he was only able to observe subtle, yet apparently physical, movements in his eyeballs, jaw, throat, chest, eyelids, and eyebrows; he noticed nothing exclusively mental during these

153

processes. For instance, James pointed out that he could not visualize any image without feeling "a fluctuating play of pressures, convergences, divergences, and accommodations" in his eyeballs.[14] Similarly, James associated reasoning with "a kind of vaguely localized diagram" in his head, where oscillations in his attention from one idea to the next were felt as movements from one point on this diagram to another.[15] He also noted that the acceptance or rejection of an idea was linked with changes in respiration, whereas feelings of effort were associated with contractions of the jaw muscles. James quickly states that, because of the difficulty of introspective work, he is not claiming that our spiritual self is *nothing but* these physiological processes, but it is clear that James is inclined to think that "our entire feeling of spiritual activity, or what commonly passes by that name, is really a feeling of bodily activities whose exact nature is by most men overlooked."[16]

Here, James is seemingly advocating a type of behaviorism in which mental phenomena are denied, replaced instead by the physiological activities of the body. How are we to square these rather extreme claims with James's previous emphasis that psychologists need to accept as a given the introspective evidence that thinking is occurring? Several recent Jamesian commentators have attempted to overcome this apparent contradiction.[17] They point out that James's emphasis on the physicality of consciousness should not be understood as an attempt to reduce consciousness to the activities of inert matter. Instead, James's stress on the physicality of consciousness is a rhetorical emphasis on the embodied nature of consciousness, in which the commonsense, dualistic distinction between mind and body is dismantled and replaced with a vision of the inevitable physicality of every moment of consciousness. According to this interpretation, James is attempting to persuade us that the terms "body" and "mind" are simply heuristic concepts, different points on a common continuum rather than radically separate phenomena. If this understanding of James is correct, then James is not so much reducing consciousness to the body as he is stretching the limits of what we are willing to include within the boundaries of the terms "physical" and "mental"; he is replacing the commonsense understanding that our bodies are inert matter mysteriously connected with mental states of consciousness with the idea that our mind is spread out through our bodies, that every thought and emotion is "enfleshed" and physically expressed.[18]

John Wild is one of the most active advocates of this interpretation of James's thought. For Wild, James is not equating the activities of the spiritual self with "the body of traditional dualistic thought," but rather, according to Wild, James is demonstrating the inescapable connection of these "spiritual" activities with "the moving, living, conscious body which expresses our emotions, and is the non-objective centre of [our] world."[19] This interpretation of James, while seemingly rather anachronistic and overly influenced by the philosophical perspective of Martin Heidegger, is, nonetheless, basically sound. However, Wild does err in one aspect of his depiction of James's thought: James does *not* consider the body to be "non-objective." The body for James is the foundation of the empirical self, it is the hub of all those tenuously connected, loosely interwoven, directly experienced components of our world that are gathered together under the rubric of "me."[20] And this "me," as James clearly states in the *Principles*, is "objective," not "subjective."[21] In his discussion of the spiritual self in the *Principles*, James asserts that if the spiritual self actually does consist of these various physiological movements, then "it would follow that all that is experienced is, strictly considered, *objective* [his emphasis]; [moreover] this Objective falls asunder into two contrasted parts, one realized as 'Self,' the other as 'not-Self'."[22] This passage is, admittedly, somewhat obscure, but James appears to be arguing that if his physiological hypothesis is correct, then all the components that make up our "me" (our body, our family and possessions, our social roles, even our efforts of will and attention) are objects of experience and are therefore "objective" in the same way that other parts of our experience that are typically considered to be "not-me" (the sun, dogs barking, and so on) are also "objective" aspects of our experience.

However, if all of our experience is "objective," then just who is it that experiences this objective world? As James puts it, "the thoughts which we actually know to exist do not fly about loose, but seem each to belong to some one thinker and not to another."[23] We each possess a sense of personal identity, therefore, the question is, how can we account for this feeling of inner continuity, this subjective "I-ness"?

James tries to answer this question without having to depend upon any of the previous philosophical positions that attempted to account for the sense of personal identity and continuity: the "mind-stuff" theory of associationists, such as David Hume and Herbert Spencer; the traditional "soul" theory; and the Kantian "transcendental-ego" theory.

The mind-stuff theory holds that there is no self separate from the "atoms" of "mind-stuff" that are "added together" to form our present state of consciousness.[24] James rejects the mind-stuff theory, pointing out that our present complex state of consciousness is not the result of a straightforward combination of "simpler" psychic sensations, but rather, it is a new state of awareness in which the apparently separate components of our consciousness are united together into something unique by an additional overarching element: the act of knowing itself. James uses the example of the taste of lemonade to illustrate his objection to the mind-stuff theory. He notes that the taste of lemonade is not a simple combination of the separate tastes of water, lemons, and sugar (as the mind-stuff theory would hold). Instead, the taste of water, lemons, and sugar combine to create something new for the experiencer: the taste of lemonade. The separate tastes themselves do not combine without the experiencer. Through the awareness of this experiencer, the separate tastes are interconnected and unified into something that was not present before.

According to James, both the soul-theory and the transcendental-ego theory attempt to improve upon the mind-stuff theory by postulating the existence of a medium upon which these diverse "psychic-atoms" can be combined, a "knower" whose knowing unifies these separate elements into a single moment of consciousness. However, James believes that each of these theories has its own problems. The soul-theory is forced to postulate "another kind of substance, existing on a non-phenomenal plane";[25] as such, the "soul" is both indescribable and empirically unverifiable. For James, the soul-theory actually explains the unity of thought no better than the mind-stuff theory, since it adds nothing new to the "bald fact" of consciousness, which is that "when the brain acts, a thought occurs."[26] James argues that from a psychological perspective, the soul-theory gives no new information, and only serves to mollify our desire for personal immortality without giving us any dependable guarantees.[27]

As for the transcendental-ego theory, James in a rather uncharacteristically caustic manner, asserts that "the Ego [is] only a 'cheap and nasty' edition of the soul," in that, like the soul, it is indescribable and empirically unverifiable, all the while possessing none of the soul's "nobility."[28] James is convinced that Kant's formulations were, in essence, merely an abstract and desiccated attempt to present a more philosophically palpable version of the soul, with none of the soul's practical and aesthetic appeal.

James claims that he can theoretically account for the unification of each moment of consciousness, and for our sense of personal identity, just as effectively as the soul-theory or the transcendental-ego theory, without having to posit something (or someone) beyond that which is immediately apparent to introspection. James begins his discussion by suggesting that our present self is felt to be the same as the past selves that exist in our memory by virtue of the "warmth and intimacy" we feel towards these former selves; there is an immediacy, a "glow" that is associated with our experiences of these selves, particularly those experiences of our physical body, which give us "an unceasing sense of personal existence."[29] According to James, we collect all of the selves that have this common "animal warmth" together in our memory, separating them from the other "cattle" that do not have this "herdmark."[30] No matter how much the selves that possess this common "herdmark" of "animal warmth" might appear to differ from each other, they are still treated by us as if they were identical, as if they were actually only aspects of one self, an assumption that is amplified by the fact that each of these selves seems to have been, from moment to moment, continuous with one another, until the self of the present.

However, as James is quick to point out, the "generic unity"[31] we impose upon our memories of these different selves co-exists with equally evident and important *differences* between these "snapshot" versions of who we perceive ourselves to be. James vividly depicts several ways in which we do *not* identify with these past selves:

> We hear from our parents various anecdotes about our infant years, but we do not appropriate them as we do our own memories. . . . That child is a foreign creature. . . . Why? Partly because great time-gaps break up all these early years—we cannot ascend to them by continuous memories; and partly because no representation of how the child felt comes up with the stories. . . . It is the same with certain of our dimly-recollected experiences. We hardly know whether to appropriate them or disown them as fancies. . . . Their animal heat has evaporated.[32]

James attempts to account for why we feel that we are basically the same self, regardless of the vast difference between our present sense of ourselves and the ways in which we experienced ourselves in the past, by noting that our sense of personal identity is "only loosely constructed," it is a "relative identity, that of a slow shifting in which there is always some common ingredient retained."[33] In a note to this discussion in the *Principles*, James includes a humorous analogy drawn from Alexander Pope to illustrate why the idea of an immutable substance (like the soul) is unnecessary to explain our sense of personal continuity:

> Sir John Cutler had a pair of black worsted stockings, which his maid darned so often with silk, that they became at last a pair of silk stockings. Now, supposing those stockings of Sir John's endued with some degree of consciousness at every particular darning, they would have been

157

sensible, that they were the same individual pair of stockings both before and after the darning; and this sensation would have continued in them through all the succession of darnings; and yet after the last of all, there was not perhaps one thread left of the first pair of stockings; but they were grown to be silk stockings, as was said before.[34]

James recognizes that common sense wants a continuous, underlying "knower," an unchanging "I" that is the "owner" of the succession of different clusters of experiences that we call "me." If such an "owner" did not exist, then, to revert to the previous metaphor, the "cattle" that form our different "me's," branded or not, would simply wander here and there. James believes that it is theoretically important to provide a "herdsman" for these "cattle," but he thinks that this "herdsman" does not have to be understood as some immutable substance existing beyond that which can be observed. Instead, according to James, this inner knower can be theoretically constructed from introspective observations of the stream of our conscious experience.

James proposes that this "herdsman" is present in the form of an "onlooking, remembering, 'judging thought' or identifying 'section' of the stream . . [that] 'owns' some of the past facts which it surveys, and disowns the rest."[35] Unfortunately, however, as James realizes, this "Thought" is as transitory and mutable as the rest of the stream of consciousness, which seems to conflict with its given task of unifying all the past selves with each other and with itself. As James wryly puts it, "it is as if wild cattle were lassoed by a newly created settler and then owned for the first time."[36] Our experience seems to point to the substantial sameness of the "herdsman," a quality that James expressly denies that the Thought possesses.

It seems therefore that either the soul-theory or the transcendental-ego theory is, once again, the more satisfactory answer to the dilemma of how to account for our sense of personal identity. But James sticks to his guns:

> How would it be if the Thought . . . instead of being in any way substantially or transcendentally identical with the former owner of the past self, merely inherited his "title," and thus stood as his legal representative now? It would then, if its birth coincided exactly with the death of another owner, *find* the past self already its own as soon as it found it at all, and the past self would thus never be wild, but always owned, by a title that never lapsed. . . . It is a patent fact of consciousness that a transmission like this actually occurs. Each pulse of cognitive consciousness, each Thought, dies away and is replaced by another. The other, among the things it knows,

knows its own predecessor, and finding it "warm," . . . greets it, saying: "Thou art mine, and part of the same self with me." Each later Thought, knowing and including thus the Thoughts which went before, is the final receptacle . . . of all that they contain and own. Each Thought is thus born an owner, and dies owned, transmitting whatever it realized as its Self to its own later proprietor.[37]

James realizes that this theoretical formulation is still not without its problems. The Thought is not an object of knowledge, it is that which knows; so how can it be said with any accuracy that the present Thought "knows" its predecessor, when its predecessor is the knower, not something that is known?[38] James does not seem to have recognized that he never really provides an adequate answer as to how it is possible that the subject continually manages to turn into an object. However, he does admit that the "present moment of consciousness is . . . the darkest in the whole series," noting that the Thought "may feel its own existence—we have all along admitted the possibility of this, hard as it is by direct introspection to ascertain the fact—but nothing can be said about it till it be dead and gone."[39] He then goes on to add that "*the real nucleus of our personal* identity" in fact does not dwell in the Thought at all (since nothing specific can be said about the Thought), but rather, in the "me," especially in our awareness of the body and the physiological processes that "accompany the act of thinking."[40]

How Does the "I" See Itself?

James never really spells out the consequences of the ineffable, and yet directly experienced, nature of the Thought, but if it really is impossible to say anything specific or concrete about our present Thought, then any attempt to claim (as James appears to do) that these Thoughts are different from one moment to the next seems to be unwarranted. The only real way that James can legitimately claim that each Thought is indeed different than the Thought that it follows is to base that claim on the information that is transmitted in our intuitive knowledge-by-acquaintance of this Thought. But does there really appear to be any evidence that we feel moment-to-moment differences in our sense of "I-ness"? No one doubts that our "me" is in continual flux, but even James admits that there is a feeling of inner continuity, a sense of inner sameness in our experience of our "I-ness." It appears that perhaps James's rather convoluted attempts to

159

inject plurality into this experience of sameness is more a reflection of his distrust of traditional metaphysics than a genuine adherence to phenomenological accuracy. I suggest that if James had remained faithful to his epistemology, what he could have said, and indeed, should have said, is that we all have an immediate awareness of "I-ness," and while that awareness may indeed be inarticulate, if someone is told "look carefully into how you experience your 'I'," that person, if he or she does indeed practice a subtle introspection, will inevitably report that the most accurate description of this "I" is that "it" is a simple, contentless awareness that is continuously present "underneath" the multitude of changes continually taking place in our "me" (our body, our sense of family and possessions, our social roles, our thoughts and emotions).

In fact, exactly this sort of evocative discrimination between the ever-changing components of "me" and the seemingly unchanging, ever-present "I," is at the heart of many mystical practices. Advaita Vedānta, for instance, is famous for its *neti, neti* (not this, not this) practice, in which the spiritual aspirant is asked to contemplate the transitory nature of his or her possessions, body, emotions, and thought-processes, and is taught to recognize that these components of experience are objects witnessed by an unchanging subject, the pure Self. Likewise, the spiritual teachers of certain sects of Islamic Sufism urge their disciples to relinquish any and all identifications with social roles and egoistic aspirations in order to focus continually on the ever-present, immutable "I am" that is the inner manifestation of the unity and oneness of Allah. Similarly, although Buddhism doctrinally denies the existence of any enduring "I," many Buddhist texts urge the aspirant to contemplate the transitory flux of the "me," and emphasize the radical ineffability, or "emptiness," of anything beyond this "me," whether this "something" is termed "nirvāṇa," or the "Dharmabody of the Buddha," or the "Big Mind."[41]

The Buddhist stress on the ineffability of our experience of what (if anything) is beyond our "me-ness" is an important corrective for the philosophical tendency to overliteralize the descriptions of the experience of "I-ness," whether this experience of "I-ness" is mystical or not. It is crucial that philosophical investigators of selfhood continually reemphasize the ineffable nature of this experience of our "I." Otherwise, as was pointed out in Chapter Two, the metaphorical and fallible nature of the descriptions of this awareness that transcends words can be forgotten, and evocative language can easily become reified into definitive, analytical accounts. It may indeed be true that "simple," "contentless," and "unchanging" are the most accurate descriptions possible for our underlying "I," and it may also be true, moreover, based on numerous cross-cultural correspondences of various mystical experiences, that terms such as "blissful," "free," and "all-pervasive" might be reasonably added to this phenomenological cluster. However, given the equally insistent cross-cultural emphasis on the ineffability of these mystical experiences of our "true nature," we should be wary about positive affirmations of the specific qualities of this awareness (e.g., "it is always the same" or "it never changes"). Using metaphorical descriptions of this underlying "I" as a goad to push a diligent disciple into an experience of deep peace and a sense of unity with an all-pervasive consciousness is one thing; using this type of language as a basis for literal statements about the nature of the self and reality is quite another.

It is also important, however, to emphasize the problems connected with a rigorous reliance on introspective data alone as a basis for determining the true nature of the self. The problem with using introspection alone to gain knowledge of the self is that there is a very real possibility that our introspective efforts are themselves profoundly distorted. It is certainly the case that most, if not all, mystical traditions emphasize the unreliability of our everyday self-knowledge. These traditions typically assumes a similar cluster of premises: "Who you assume you are at the present moment is not who you really are. Who you really are is hidden from view; however, your true nature *can* be directly experienced, either through grace or spiritual disciplines or a combination of both." If these premises are indeed accurate, then correct information about who we really are is not easily available through introspective efforts alone, since these introspective efforts themselves are rooted in a state of self-awareness that itself has been systematically distorted. However, if an individual begins an introspective journey that is guided by psychological and metaphysical premises that emerge from a true apprehension of the nature of the self and reality, an apprehension that is itself rooted in a profound mystical awareness, and/or if that individual has experienced the grace that some traditions insist is necessary to overcome his or her underlying systemic distortions, then it is possible that a highly subtle introspective effort could indeed reveal to that individual his or her true nature.[42]

Within each religious tradition, the mystical quest for self-awareness inevitably begins with doctrinal propositions that claim to reveal to aspirants the true nature of the self and reality. Mystical praxis always takes place within a context permeated by these doctrinal propositions. Each member of a spiritual community is repeatedly exposed to traditionally sanctioned teachings on the nature of the self

161

and reality through scriptural study, public lectures by respected teachers, liturgical chanting, the informal web of unsystematic assumptions that circulate within the community in stories and parables, or even via affirmations that are embedded at the core of many meditative techniques. These doctrines, which are viewed not as humanly created artifacts, but rather as trustworthy, transhuman and transcultural products, point aspirants in particular directions in their introspective and meditative practice; they tell the aspirants what to expect and where to look in order to discover for themselves whether the teachings are true. These doctrines serve to shock the spiritual practitioner out of comfortable and yet, on a deeper level, limited and painful ways of self-understanding, and catapult them into a realm of previously unthinkable possibilities, providing new and compelling visions of who they are, as well as who they could and should become. These doctrines may be understood within the tradition as simply metaphorical echoes of what has been, and can be, directly apprehended via different levels of mystical experience; or these doctrines might be seen as literal manifestations of a gracious divinity; or again, paradoxically, these doctrines might even be perceived as types of conceptual timebombs designed to implode within the consciousness of the aspirants, freeing them from clinging to conceptual categories themselves. Regardless of the different functions served by these teachings on the nature of the self and reality, it is difficult to imagine that many, if any, mystical traditions would ever claim that anyone could possibly come to any worthwhile level of introspective self-knowledge without the guidance and support of these revelatory doctrines that are, in principle at least, free from the effects of systemic distortion.

James does not seem to have recognized the implications of systemic distortion in relation to introspective work.[43] Ironically, even though, as we saw in chapter 2, James repeatedly stresses the ways in which we inevitably bring our stock of previous assumptions to every moment of knowing, he nonetheless frequently appears to support the reigning model of scientific objectivity, which emphasizes that the scientist could and should free him- or herself from any and all subjective pre-conceptions during the process of investigation.[44] In the *Principles*, for instance, James explicitly states that he intends to bracket any metaphysical assumptions during his psychological investigations in an effort to rely primarily on introspection for information on the nature of the self.[45] James does not seem to have recognized that this supposedly a-metaphysical position runs directly counter to his other, more sophisticated, insights on the ways in which our personal and cultural presuppositions help us both to create and discover the world and our place in it. Indeed, it is arguable that James's desire to free himself from metaphysical presuppositions is rooted more in his desire to establish the scientific legitimacy of this newly created field of investigation than on philosophical clarity.

"A Dome of Many-Colored Glass, Stains the White Radiance of Eternity"

Despite James's sincere intentions to avoid metaphysical speculation in the *Principles*, he occasionally presents tantalizing hints about the directions his thought on the self would move if not confined within his self-imposed methodological straitjacket. For instance, drawing upon data from psychical research, James muses that perhaps our personal consciousness is not necessarily cut off from the thoughts and feelings of other individuals. Although earlier in the *Principles* James had claimed that there was an "absolute insulation, irreducible pluralism"[46] between individual minds, James began to be convinced that the evidence of "thought-transference, mesmeric influence and spirit-control" was so persuasive that it was perhaps safer to conclude that "the definitively closed nature of our personal consciousness is probably an average statistical resultant of many conditions, but not an elementary force or fact."[47]

Gerald Myers underscores the significance of James's shift towards a more "mystical" understanding of the self:

> A world of individual and substantial selves, each private and irrevocably removed from its neighbor, was not an attractive idea for James. He preferred to believe in a world where continuity prevails, including that between individual streams of consciousness; to the extent that the concept of a substantial self encourages the belief in metaphysical discontinuity between individual selves, he opposed it. It is a common judgement that James's *Anschauung* was excessively individualistic and ignored the role of community; on the contrary, he sought notions of self and reality that permit communality of the profoundest sort—in the depths of the most intimate personal experience.[48]

After the *Principles*, James appears to have become increasingly attracted to the idea that the self is not limited to the confines of our psychophysical structure, but rather, extends outwards (and inwards) in the form of broader and deeper levels of consciousness. Even in the *Principles*, James confesses: "the moment I become metaphysical and try to define the more [that is beyond what is observable], I find the notion of an *anima mundi* thinking in all of us to be a more promising hypothesis, in spite of all its difficulties, than that of a lot of absolutely individual souls."[49] Therefore, it is not surprising that after the *Principles*, no longer bound to his pledge to restrict his observations on the nature of the self to that which is immediately perceptible, James was willing to speculate in more detail on the possibility that there are dimensions of the self that transcend personal levels of consciousness and the physical body. He offers these startlingly metaphysical ruminations on the likelihood of our connection with a universal soul in "Human Immortality: Two Supposed Objections to the Doctrine."

James begins this essay with a nod towards the prevailing materialistic understanding of the interaction between the brain and the mind. He readily concedes that drugs can alter our state of awareness, and admits that stimulation of different parts of the brain can also provoke changes in our consciousness. For James, it is clear that "thought is a function of the brain."[50] However, he insists that it is not equally clear that consciousness inevitably disappears with the brain's death and decay. James points out that there are several ways in which the relationship between the brain and consciousness can be understood. First, the brain itself could produce the "stuff" of consciousness in much the same way that steam is produced by a kettle, or light is produced by an electric circuit. From this perspective, which James calls the "productive" theory, consciousness is created by the various complex chemical interactions that take place inside the brain, and consciousness ceases when the brain stops working at the moment of death.[51] He notes that there is, however, another alternative. It is also possible that consciousness preexists the brain, and that the role of the brain is to mold that preexistent consciousness into various forms.

James goes on to point out that there are two variations of this second alternative. The first version of the preexisting consciousness theory states that consciousness exists in a scattered, particle-like form. Seen from this perspective, the job of our brain would be to concentrate this "mind-dust" into useable, personal forms. James, however, does not spend much time developing and refuting this theory, since he believes that his discussion of the mind-stuff theory in the *Principles* has already performed this task.

Instead, James is much more interested in the second variation of the preexistent consciousness theory. This variation of the theory claims that the hypothetical preexisting consciousness already possesses a unified structure, perhaps that of an "absolute 'world soul,' or something less,"[52] in which case the brain's task would be to receive and

164

transmit limited forms of this consciousness in much the same way as, to use an anachronistic example, a radio receives portions of preexisting radio waves and then transmits them through the air as sound waves. James refers to this relationship between the brain and a preexisting larger consciousness as the "transmissive function," and points out that this transmissive function is operative "in the case of a colored glass, a prism, or a refracting lens," when "the energy of light, no matter how produced, is by the glass shifted and limited in color, and by the lens or prism determined to a certain path and shape."[53]

James insists that it is just as logical and scientific to postulate that the brain receives, limits, directs, and shapes pre-existent states of awareness as it is to postulate that the brain produces different states of consciousness. Both theories, in fact, have philosophical and scientific difficulty accounting for how the brain and the mind, which are completely heterogeneous, interact at all. James believes that "the theory of production is . . . not a jot more simple or credible in itself than any other conceivable theory. It is only a little more popular."[54] Indeed, James claims that, in some ways, the transmissive function has certain theoretical advantages over its more popular competitor. If the transmissive theory of consciousness is accepted, then consciousness "does not have to be generated *de novo* in a vast number of places. It exists already, behind the scenes," intimately connected with this world.[55] In this way, the transmissive theory not only avoids "multiplying miracles,"[56] but also aligns itself with quite respectable philosophical systems, such as transcendentalism or idealistic philosophy.

James points out another apparent advantage of the transmissive theory of consciousness over the productive theory: the transmissive theory is able to account coherently for a wide variety of phenomena that the productive theory has difficulty explaining. Such phenomena as "religious conversions, providential leadings in answer to prayer, instantaneous healings, premonitions, apparitions at time of death, clairvoyant visions or impressions, and the whole range of mediumistic capacities" are all more easily understood with the transmissive theory of consciousness.[57] James notes that the productive theory of consciousness is intimately linked with sense perceptions, but in the case of many of these less orthodox phenomena, "it is often hard to see where the sense-organs can come in."[58] For instance, as James mentions, a medium (like Mrs. Piper) might have knowledge of the personal life of his or her client that would be impossible to obtain from the senses, or a person might see a vision of someone who, hundreds of miles away, was at that very moment dying. James points out that it is difficult to see how the productive theory of consciousness can explain how these bits of knowledge were produced within a single brain. But if the transmissive theory is accepted, the answer is apparent: "they don't have to be 'produced,'—they exist ready-made in the transcendental world,"[59] so that in "cases of conversion, providential leadings, sudden mental healings, etc. it seems to the subjects themselves . . . as if a power from without, quite different from the ordinary action of the senses or of the sense-led mind, came into their life, as if [their life] suddenly opened into that greater life in which it has its source."[60]

James believes that psychologists and philosophers choose between the transmissive theory and the productive theory based on what type of world they are willing or able to accept (i.e., based on their metaphysical assumptions). If these thinkers are limited to a purely materialistic or naturalistic perspective, then the productive function of the brain will be all that they will acknowledge as valid. If, however, these thinkers assume that "the whole universe of material things . . . [is] a surface-veil of phenomena, hiding and keeping back the world of genuine realities," if they believe that life is similar to Percy Shelly's words in his poem "Adonais," in which "'Life, like a dome of many-colored glass, Stains the white radiance of eternity',," then they will acknowledge that the transmissive function of the brain is a legitimate possibility.[61] Utilizing Shelly's metaphor, James theorizes that our brains might indeed be places in this "dome" where the "beams" of consciousness could most easily enter into our realm of experience. In that case, as the "white radiance" of that larger preexisting consciousness enters our brains, then a type of refracting and "staining and distortion" would naturally occur, shaping that greater consciousness into the personal, imperfect, and unique forms that consciousness takes inside "our finite individualities here below."[62]

James then goes on to point out the implications for human immortality, if this transmissive theory of consciousness is basically accurate:

> According to the state in which the brain finds itself, the barrier of its obstructiveness may also be supposed to rise or fall. It sinks so low, when the brain is in full activity, that a comparative flood of spiritual energy pours over. At other times, only such occasional waves of thought as heavy sleep permits get by. And when finally a brain stops acting altogether, or decays, that special stream of consciousness which it subserved will vanish entirely from this natural world. But the sphere of being that supplied the consciousness would still be intact; and in that more real world with which, even whilst here, it was continuous, the consciousness might, in ways unknown to us, continue still.[63]

Fields within Fields within Fields

James realizes that if this "more real world" is one in which our individual consciousnesses merge into Oneness after death, then this loss of our personal boundaries conflicts with the desires of many individuals to retain the "finiteness and limitations" which appear to be the very essence of their being.[64] However, as he insightfully goes on to comment, it is an open question as to "how much we may lose, and how much we may possibly gain, if [the] finiting outlines [of our individual consciousness] should be changed."[65]

James attempts to augment his support for the transmissive theory of consciousness by drawing upon the work of Gustave Fechner (1810–87), a German psychologist and philosopher. James is especially interested in Fechner's conceptualization of the "threshold" of consciousness, a conceptualization which James, over a decade later, explicitly utilizes to envision the dynamics of mystical experiences in his essay, "A Suggestion about Mysticism."[66] Fechner postulates that consciousness can only appear after a particular psychophysical level of activity has been reached, that is, consciousness can manifest only after it has passed over a mental or physical "threshold." But, as James notes, "the height of the threshold varies under different circumstances: it may rise or fall. When it falls, as in states of great lucidity, we grow conscious of things of which we should be unconscious at other times; when it rises, as in drowsiness, consciousness sinks in amount."[67] James offers a diagram to illustrate Fechner's theory. The diagram shows a wavy line (looking somewhat like a child's drawing of three mountains) bisected by a straight horizontal line. The three sections of the wavy line above the horizontal line represent three apparently separate individual consciousnesses, whereas the parts of the wave under the threshold (the horizontal line) represent that which is unconscious in each of the three individuals. From the point of view of the three individuals, their respective consciousnesses (the peaks of the waves) are separate from one another, but underneath the threshold of consciousness, all three waves are united in a common "ocean" of awareness. As James, quoting Fechner, points out, if "we should raise the entire line of waves so that not only the crests but the valleys appeared above the threshold, then [the valleys] would appear only as depressions in one great continuous wave above the threshold, and the discontinuity of the consciousness would be converted into continuity."[68]

Fechner himself appeared to be quite dubious about our ability to catalyze this awareness of our connection with an underlying, preexisting ocean of awareness, but depending upon one's understanding of the relationship between grace and self-effort, it seems quite

167

legitimate to postulate that the spiritual disciplines in various mystical traditions function to bring about exactly this sort of recognition of our inherent connection with the deeper source of our being. It could be argued that the various chanting, fasting, and meditative practices are techniques which serve to lower the threshold of consciousness, thereby revealing to the mystic his or her underlying connection with this "ocean" of awareness. Reverting back to the previous metaphor, it could also be postulated that these spiritual disciplines expand the brain's capacity to hold increasing amounts of the light of this preexisting consciousness, while simultaneously minimizing the distortion and refraction of that light typically caused by the individual's psychological and cultural background.

James, for one, believes that mystical and psychical experiences can easily be accounted for by postulating "the continuity of our consciousness with a mother-sea, [which permits the] exceptional waves occasionally pouring over the dam."[69] However, influenced by his Protestant background, he also believes that the ultimate cause of this rising and falling of the water level of our awareness will always remain a mystery. Further, James emphasizes that this belief in our connection to the "mother-sea" of awareness does not have to be interpreted in a purely monistic fashion. He clarifies his position in a footnote:

> It is not necessary to identify the consciousness postulated in the lecture, as pre-existing behind the scenes, with the Absolute Mind of transcendental idealism, although, indeed, the notion of it might lead in that direction. . . . [Alternatively] there might be many minds behind the scenes as well as one. All that the transmission-theory absolutely requires is that they should transcend *our* minds,—which thus come from something mental that pre-exists, and is larger than ourselves.[70]

James's critics were not satisfied with this metaphysical flexibility, however, and accused James of advocating pantheistic ideas of immortality (i.e., an absorption into a higher consciousness after death) rather than the Christian idea of personal survival after death. Therefore, in the preface to the second edition of "Human Immortality," James attempted to mollify his critics, admitting that while he did "speak of the 'mother-sea' in terms that must have sounded pantheistic," nevertheless, "one may conceive the mental world behind the veil in as individualistic a form as one pleases" without reducing the viability of the transmission theory of consciousness.[71] James points out that, if this individualistic perspective on the unseen world is adopted, then "one's finite mundane consciousness would be an extract from one's larger, truer personality, the latter having even now some sort of reality behind the scenes."[72] Understood from this point of view, the experiences of one's mundane personality would register in the consciousness of one's larger personality, perhaps leaving a collection of memories that would, in effect, constitute a type of personal survival after death.

This type of substantial self, a self that exists unconnected to the physical form, a self that transcends death, a self that extends into higher levels of consciousness, coexists somewhat uneasily with James's depiction of the self in the *Principles* as an epiphenomenal, flickering, passing Thought intimately conjoined with bodily awareness and social roles. But James's willingness to postulate this more cosmic self in "Human Immortality" was perhaps driven by a deeply felt personal need to envision the shape a self might assume after death. In 1887, the year in which James published "Human Immortality," his father had been dead for five years, and by 1891, James's beloved sister, Alice, after years of life as an invalid, bedridden by aliments that seemed to defy conventional medical diagnosis and treatment, finally discovered that she was dying from a cancerous tumor in her breast, a malignancy that had most likely metastasized from her liver. Upon learning about Alice's condition, James on 6 July wrote a long and forthright letter to Alice, who was living at the time in England. The following excerpts from this letter demonstrate the close connection between James's academic hypothesis of a cosmic self and his personal need to envision a world in which his loved ones survive after death:

> I know you've never cared for life, and to me, now at the age of nearly fifty, life and death seem singularly close together in all of us. . . . Your fortitude, good spirits and un-sentimentality have been simply unexampled in the midst of your physical woes; and when you're relieved from your post, just *that* bright note will remain behind, together with the inscrutable and mysterious character of the doom of nervous weakness which has chained you down for all these years. As for that, there's more in it than has ever been told to so-called science. These inhibitions, these split-up selves, all these new facts that are gradually coming to light about our organization, these enlargements of the self in trance, etc., are bringing me to turn for light in the direction of all sorts of despised spiritualistic and unscientific ideas. Father would find in me today a much more receptive listener—all that philosophy has got to be brought in. And what a queer contradiction comes to the ordinary scientific argument against

169

immortality (based on body being mind's condition and mind going *out* when body is gone), when one must believe (as now, in these neurotic cases) that some infernality in the body prevents really existing parts of the mind from coming to their effective rights at all, suppresses them, and blots them out from participation in this world's experiences, although they are *there* all the time. When that which is *you* passes out of the body, I am sure that there will be an explosion of liberated force and life till then eclipsed and kept down. I can hardly imagine your transition without a great oscillation of both "worlds" as they regain their new equilibrium after the change! Everyone will feel the shock, but you yourself will be more surprised than anybody else.[73]

The ephemeral, fluctuating self of the *Principles*, a self that is integrally linked to the individual's physical body, might have served James's academic philosophical and psychological needs, but when faced with the death of the physical bodies of those that he loved, James's more personal philosophical and psychological needs began to clamor for a doctrine of the self that would accommodate the possibility of a continued existence, in some form or another, of the self after death. Data on the type of selfhood that could survive death could, of course, not be restricted to empirical evidence from introspection, so James became increasingly willing to look elsewhere for hints as to how the self might extend beyond the bounds of our everyday awareness. James threw his net wide: besides drawing upon the speculations of Fechner, the transcendentalists, and the Romantic poets to fashion his own notions on human immortality, James also gathered information on dreams, hypnotic manifestations, hysteria, ghostly visitations, demonic possessions, the inspirations of genius, hallucinations, witchcraft, trance mediums, and multiple personalities. These "despised spiritualistic and unscientific" areas of investigation ultimately became the basis for James's 1896 Lowell Lectures on "Exceptional Mental States," in which James for the first time began to speculate publicly and in detail on the psychology of the subconscious, thus forming an important bridge between James's work in the *Principles* and his later theories on the subconscious in the *Varieties*.[74]

The Subliminal Self

In the *Principles*, James had vigorously opposed the idea of unconscious mental processes, arguing that the claim made by certain psychologists and philosophers that mental states could possess an unconscious component "is a sovereign means for believing what one likes in psychology, and of turning what might become a science into a tumbling-ground for whimsies."[75] James asserted that, unlike an external object (e.g., a tree) which can be philosophically justified as having an existence separate from one's experience *of* it, and which can conceivably have many attributes that are not known to the experiencer (e.g., insects within the bark of the tree), the very essence of a thought or a feeling is to be experienced; it is difficult to imagine how a thought or feeling could have qualities that exist apart from the way in which that thought or feeling is experienced. A thought is only what is thought, and no more, and a feeling is what is felt—it simply did not make sense to James to conceive of a thought or a feeling that could exist without being consciously experienced.[76] James was quite clear about his position: "there is only one 'phase' in which an idea can be, and that is a fully conscious condition. If it is not in that condition, then it is not at all. Something else is in its place."[77]

However, in other sections of the *Principles*, James was quite willing to investigate hypnosis, hysteria, trance mediums, and individuals with split personalities, and based on these investigations, he concluded that a person *can* undergo a wide range of complex experiences and, on one level at least, be completely unaware that these experiences have even occurred. Therefore, as James realized, it would seem, on the face of it at least, that mental processes *can* be unconscious. James attempted to reconcile this apparent contradiction by theorizing, as did the French researcher Pierre Janet, that perhaps thoughts and feelings *can* exist outside the awareness of our conscious minds, as long as these thoughts and feelings are experienced by either an alternate, subsidiary personality or by a deeper, subconscious level of our being.[78]

It is important, therefore, to point out that James never abandoned his conviction that a thought or feeling has to be experienced in order to exist; he simply expanded his idea of who it is that has to do the experiencing. James gives several examples to illustrate this idea that a person can have experiences that are not accessible to his or her conscious mind. He claims that the conscious mind of an amnesiac, for instance, may not have access to the memory of what he or she did during a certain period of time, but the events that occurred during this time period had to have been experienced by someone— in this case, a cut off and hidden part of the amnesiac's awareness. In another example, James points out that some hypnotic subjects, after awakening from their trance, may have no memory of what happened during the trance; but the posthypnotic suggestions of the hypnotist

171

are remembered by some part of the hypnotized subjects' mind, since these subjects will act on the implanted suggestions of their hypnotist and will often be puzzled as to why they are behaving in such a mysterious fashion. In yet another example, James notes that researchers in the area of psychopathology have observed that, if hysterical patients with numbed legs or arms are aware that they are being tested, then they will typically show no reaction when they are pricked with needles in these numbed areas; however, if these patients are unaware that these tests are being performed, then the arms or legs of these patients will jerk in response to the needles, indicating that some aspect of these patients' awareness experiences the pain caused by the needle. A final example that illustrates for James the ability of certain individuals to have experiences that are not always accessible to their conscious mind centers around his observations of such mediums as Mrs. Piper. James mentions that while in trance, Mrs. Piper would have access to information that her conscious mind could not have possibly known, implying that, on some deeper level of her being, she possessed an awareness that transcended the level of her conscious mind. Numerous examples of this sort finally led James to accept the idea that individuals may indeed have experiences that are not accessible to their waking consciousness; however, he continued to insist that these experiences were *subconscious*, not *unconscious*, that is, these experiences were *experienced*, but on a subconscious level of the individual's mind.

James's conception of this subconscious awareness differed in significant respects from Freud's view of the unconscious. Gerald Myers points out some of the most noticeable differences:

> Freud, who explicitly opposed his own view to Janet's, saw the unconscious as an impersonal realm in which opposing mental forces are in conflict. . . . The idea that an item experienced unconsciously must be conscious to a secondary or subconscious self struck Freud as paradoxical. "Anyone who tried to push the argument further and to conclude from it that one's own hidden processes belonged actually to a second *consciousness* would be faced with the concept of a consciousness of which one knew nothing, of an 'unconscious consciousness'—and this would scarcely be preferable to the assumption of an "unconscious mental.' " Could James have replied, he would presumably have denied such a paradox, insisting that the secondary consciousness is indeed not known or recognized by the primary, but knows or recognizes itself in the way that any of us is acquainted with our own consciousness. . . . James would have shifted the burden of proof upon Freud, as many others have, by asking what can be

Fields within Fields within Fields

the point of calling something both unconscious and mental if it is not felt or experienced to some degree, that is, if it is not impressed on someone's consciousness at least a little bit.[79]

From James's perspective, the experiences that take place in the subconscious, as opposed to the unconscious, are registered by a "subliminal" or "transmarginal" self. While in the beginning it is apparent that James primarily derived his theories on the subliminal self from examples of "exceptional mental states," he became increasingly receptive to the concept that the subliminal self is not itself exceptional, but instead, is a deeper substratum within each of us.

This willingness to postulate that every human being possesses a subliminal self was, in many respects, a natural extension of James's theories on the "margins" of our "field" of consciousness. In the *Principles*, James had spent considerable time demonstrating how we are all "surrounded" by a vast complex nexus of tacit memories, habits, and cultural assumptions which subtly and yet continuously influence the perceptions, thoughts, and feelings that take place within our present sphere of awareness. He pointed out that we usually do not notice this "margin" of awareness, even though it is "ready at a touch to come in" and itself in turn become the present center of attention.[80] All that remained for James was to admit that beyond "the consciousness of the ordinary field, with its usual center and margin," there exists "a set of memories, thoughts and feelings which are extramarginal," and yet which are, nonetheless, "conscious facts of some sort, able to reveal their presence by unmistakable signs."[81]

James modestly assigned the "discovery" of the subliminal self, which he termed "the most important step forward . . . in psychology,"[82] to the ruminations of his friend and fellow psychical researcher Fredrick Myers (even though James, two years before Myers's formulations, had postulated the existence of subliminal aspects of the self in a essay entitled, "The Hidden Self").[83] Nonetheless, it is true that James's willingness to credit Myers with the discovery of the subliminal self was not simply a gracious concession on James's part; Myers's work considerably augmented and extended James's rather sketchy theoretical proposal.

Like James, Myers used the results of his extensive research on hallucinations, hypnotism, split personalities, trance mediums, mindcures, and other information from psychical research and psychopathology to posit the existence of subliminal aspects of the self. In a memorial assessment of Myers's contributions to psychology, James points out that Myers considered all of these "scattered phenomena, some of them recognized as reputable, others outlawed from science, or treated as isolated curiosities,"[84] as "connected parts of one whole subject . . . a vast interlocked and graded system."[85] James concludes that the very fact that Myers was able to accomplish this synthesis of previously disconnected "exceptional mental states" into a coherent theoretical whole via the overarching concept of the subliminal self should, by itself, be enough to grant Myers a place in the ranks of psychology's most important innovators.

Myers organized these numerous, seemingly unrelated phenomena, by comparing them to a spectrum of radiation waves. Seen through this model, our average waking consciousness is analogous to the visible light of the sun, while the subconscious aspects of the self are analogous to the ultrared and ultraviolet sections of the spectrum. The simplicity of this model, however, is complicated somewhat by the fact that, at certain times, Myers implied that this spectrum model of the self has a hierarchical organization, while at other times he implied that it does not. For instance, when Myers at one point in his writings associated the "lower" end of the spectrum with the physiological manifestations of the subliminal self (e.g., stigmatizations and spiritual healings), and the "upper" end of the spectrum with the "hyper-normal cognitions" demonstrated by trance mediums such as Mrs. Piper, he did not intend for this model to have hierarchical implications.[86] For Myers, the healings of the mind-cure movement were just as reputable and significant as the apparently supernormal knowledge of Mrs. Piper, and the spectrum model merely emphasized that the subliminal self manifests itself through both physical and mental aspects of our being.

However, at other times, Myers organized the manifestations of the subliminal self in a way that *was* hierarchical. When Myers's spectrum model was hierarchically organized, it typically associated the lower end of the spectrum with the unusual and often frightening experiences of the mentally ill, whereas middle range of the spectrum was linked with everyday perceptions, and the higher end of the spectrum was connected with moments of supernormal cognition.[87] To illustrate this hierarchical model, Myers at one point gave the example of an individual who mentally "hears" words that are not physically spoken. While this "word-hearing" at the lower end of the spectrum might manifest itself as the "persecuting voices" of the insane, in the middle range of normal perceptions, hearing voices could take the form of such innocuous behavior as "talking to oneself," while in the upper-levels of the spectrum, hearing voices could actually be beneficial if they were "those 'clairaudient' premonitions" that seem to come from a source that contains knowledge beyond that typically available during ordinary daily life.[88]

Aligning himself with Myers, James was willing to hypothesize that a person's typical waking consciousness is perhaps "only a small segment of the psychic spectrum,"[89] while the subliminal self is "the enveloping mother-consciousness in each of us" from which our everyday consciousness "is precipitated like a crystal."[90] James also agreed with Myers that "each of us is in reality an abiding psychical entity far more extensive than he knows—an individuality which can never express itself completely through any corporeal manifestation."[91] In addition, both men were willing to argue that many of the positive transformations that seem associated with the subliminal self, such as "the reparativeness of sleep, the curative effects of self-suggestion, the 'uprushing' inspirations of genius, the regenerative influences of prayer and of religious self-surrender, the strength of belief which mystical experiences give" are all made possible by the subliminal self's connection with the "'dynamogeny'" of an unseen, but powerfully felt "spiritual world."[92]

James did, however, indicate that he recognized certain areas of theoretical unclarity in Myers's depiction of the subliminal self. For instance, James asked:

> Are there three zones of subliminal life, of which the innermost is dissolutive, the middle one superior (the zone of genius, telepathy, etc.), and the outermost supreme and receptive directly of the impact of the spirit-world? And can the two latter zones reach the supraliminal consciousness only by passing through the interior and inferior zone, and consequently using its channels and mixing its morbid effects with their own? Or is the subliminal superior throughout when considered in itself, and are . . . hysteria and alternate personality and the curious uncritical passivity to the absurdest suggestions which we observe in hypnosis to be explained by defective brain-activity exclusively, without bringing in the subliminal mind? Is it the brain, in short, which vitiates and mixes results, or is it the interior zone of the subliminal mind?[93]

James made no concerted effort to answer these questions with any degree of comprehensiveness. Instead, James focused his attention on the rather more thankless task of attempting to persuade conservative segments of the psychological community that Myers's concept of the subliminal self was worth extended theoretical

175

consideration. These conservative psychologists (as well as, in later years, Freud and his orthodox disciples) claimed that Myers's understanding of the subliminal self incorporated too much dubious material within its boundaries. According to James, these psychologists willingly accepted the existence of "a dissociated part of the normal personality" linked to "experiences forgotten by the upper consciousness," which may "still lead a parasitic existence" and "may interfere with normal processes"; however, they were unwilling to accept those " 'evolutive,' 'superior,' or 'supernormal' phenomena" that were supported by evidence from psychical research.[94] James chastised this methodological rigidity, noting that the phenomena investigated by psychical research (such as telepathy, clairvoyance, trance states, and so on) "have a right to definite description and to careful observation."[95] Furthermore, James asserted that someday in the future, if these unorthodox phenomena were finally accepted as valid objects of study, and if sufficient evidence could be gathered to verify their existence, then a model of the self such as Myers's that accounted for psychical phenomena would actually be preferable to a model of the self that could not or would not acknowledge these unorthodox occurrences.

James claimed that philosophers and psychologists rejected the "evolutive, superior or supernormal" aspects of the subliminal self, not because of any intrinsic faults in the model itself; rather, according to James, these philosophers and psychologists refused to accept the possibility of transpersonal aspects of the subliminal self because they were clinging to one side of a frequently repeated aesthetic battleground: the clash between "the classic-academic and the romantic type of imagination."[96]

According to James, the classic-academic imagination "has a fondness for clean pure lines and noble simplicity in its constructions. It explains things by as few principles as possible and is intolerant of either nondescript facts or clumsy formulas."[97] This type of imagination lives on "a sort of sunlit terrace" populated only by that which is either clearly visible or logically pleasing, that is, by the "brain and other physical facts of nature on the one hand and the absolute metaphysical ground of the universe on the other."[98] In contrast, the romantic imagination possesses a more gothic sensibility; it acknowledges the existence of levels of reality that transcend the natural world, and yet abhors the abstraction and sterility of a logically derived Absolute. This romantic vision of the self and the universe is willing to peer into the shadows beyond the sunlit terrace of discursive rationality. Regarding this romantic vision, James writes:

Fields within Fields within Fields

A mass of mental phenomena are now seen in the shrubbery beyond the parapet. Fantastic, ignoble, hardly human, or frankly non-human are some of these new candidates for psychological description. . . . The world of mind is shown as something infinitely more complex than was suspected; and whatever beauty it may still possess, it has lost at any rate the beauty of academic neatness.[99]

James's own aesthetic preference is clear. According to his vision, even the universe of our quotidian experience "is everywhere gothic, not classic . . . [it] forms a real jungle, where all things are provisional, half-fitted to each other and untidy."[100] For James, it is unlikely, therefore, that the spiritual world revealed by our more extraordinary experiences should be classically formed. He noted that psychical research, psychopathology, and investigations of religious experiences demonstrate that the unseen aspects of our being that lie beneath the surface of our experience do not exist in a "realm of eternal essences, of platonic ideas, of crystal battlements, of absolute significance,"[101] but rather, take place in a complex, multitextured, intricately detailed, frustratingly confusing level of reality that transcends the boundaries of our personality, while simultaneously touching the depths of our being. According to James, the subliminal self is not clear, it is not pure, it is not simple. Instead, it is full of strange, unexpected shapes and mismatched combinations of utter nonsense and lucid inspirations. As such, the subliminal self denotes "a region, with possibly the most heterogeneous contents": some of the subliminal region is "rubbish" (e.g., scraps of "lapsed" memories, the "stuff that dreams are made of," odd bits of ingrained habits, and so on), while some of it is "superior and subtly perceptive" (e.g., the insights of trance mediums, the creative inspirations of artists, the revelations of mystics, and so on).[102]

In the *Varieties*, James retains the "gothic" contours of this "transmarginal or subliminal region."[103] He does not attempt to tone down its rough edges or deny its ability to contain both mental trash and psychological gems. Instead, this "area of the personality," which he terms the "B-region" (as opposed to the A-region of "full sunlit consciousness"), becomes the location of almost everything that is not immediately and easily available to our conscious attention. In the following passage, James seems to revel in the range of phenomena that he claims are located within this mysterious and subterranean expanse within ourselves:

It is the abode of everything that is latent and the reservoir of everything that passes unrecorded or unobserved. It contains, for example, such things

177

as all our momentarily inactive memories, and it harbors the springs of all our obscurely motived passions, impulses, likes, dislikes, and prejudices. Our intuitions, hypotheses, fancies, superstitions, persuasions, convictions, and in general all our non-rational operations come from it. It is the source of our dreams . . . . In it arise whatever mystical experiences we may have, and our automatisms, sensory or motor. [It is also the source of hypnosis,] our delusions, fixed ideas and hysterical accidents [as well as] our supra-normal cognitions, if such there be.[104]

It is evident to James that certain people are more fully in contact with this subliminal self than others. Psychics, the mentally ill, geniuses, saints, and mystics are all understood by James to be individuals with a strong "ultra-marginal life," they are all individuals who are frequently subject to unexpected invasions from their subliminal region which take "the form of unaccountable impulses to act, or inhibitions of actions, of obsessive ideas or even of hallucinations of sight or hearing."[105] James borrows Myers's term "automatism" to designate those mental or physical activities that seem to take place without the individual's conscious instigation. James considers hallucinations, automatic writing, the utterances of trance mediums, religious visions, and the involuntary body movements seen during revivals to be the effects of these invasive "'uprushes' into the ordinary consciousness of energies originating in the subliminal parts of the mind."[106] Unlike many psychologists of his time (and ours as well), James insists that these automatisms are not necessarily evidence of psychopathology, pointing out instead that "the whole array of Christian saints . . the Bernards, the Loyolas, the Luthers, the Foxes, the Wesleys, had their visions, voices, rapt conditions, guiding impressions, and 'openings.' "[107] For James, these automatisms are, at times, crucial to a powerful and personally transformative religious life in that they help to convince the saints, mystics, or converts that their previously held beliefs are indeed authentic. He notes:

Incursions from beyond the transmarginal region have a peculiar power to increase conviction. The inchoate sense of presence is infinitely stronger than conception, but strong as it may be, it is seldom equal to the evidence of hallucination. Saints who actually see or hear their Saviour reach the acme of assurance. Motor automatisms, though rarer, are, if possible, even more convincing than sensations. The subjects here actually feel themselves played upon by powers beyond their will. The evidence is dynamic; the God or spirit moves the very organs of their body.[108]

Fields within Fields within Fields

For the saint or mystic or convert, the spiritual world is not a matter of speculation. They see spiritual beings, they hear the angelic voices, they feel the divine touch within them. More open to information from the transmarginal region than the average person, these "religious geniuses" touch "the fountainhead of much that feeds our religion. In persons deep in the religious life . . . the door into this region seems unusually wide open; at any rate, experiences making their entrance through that door have had emphatic influence in shaping religious history."[109]

The Psychology of Conversion

James was convinced that dramatic personal transformations often occur when an individual contacts (or is contacted by) the forces that well up from his or her subliminal self by virtue of its contact with the unseen world.[110] James's student and biographer Ralph Barton Perry comments on James's fascination with these personal transformations:

> There is . . . a common thread running through James's observations on religion, neurasthenia, war, earthquakes, fasting, lynching, patriotism— an interest, namely, in human behavior under high pressure, and the conclusion that exceptional circumstances generate exceptional inner power. These phenomena have a bearing on metaphysics because such exceptional power suggest the sudden removal of a barrier and the tappings of a greater reservoir of consciousness; and they have a bearing on ethics, since this power differs in degree rather than in kind from that moral power—that fighting and adventurous spirit, that heroic quality—which gives to life the color and radiance of value.[111]

In the *Varieties*, James makes the claim that these beneficial, transpersonally catalyzed alterations in one's personality structure can be either the result of a prolonged and arduous attempt by the individual to tap into this latent reservoir of inner energy or, more frequently, they can occur when the "strenuousness" of this type of "tense and voluntary attitude" is forsaken in favor of self-surrender to the "higher powers."[112] For James, this second, "anti-moralistic" way in which human beings are able to access their reserves of inner energy is, in contrast to the first "moralistic" method, based on "passivity, not activity; relaxation, not intentness."[113] James argues that this moment of self-surrender is an essential element of most religious conversions, as well as being the primary characteristic of a purely "religious" outlook on life. According to James, self-surrender is not only a key feature of Lutheran salvation by faith and Methodist conversion experiences, but self-surrender also plays a prominent role in the "mind-cure" movement, those forerunners of many contemporary holistic health practitioners who, over one hundred years ago, stressed that positive physical and mental transformations can occur if we can manage to let go of our fears and our sense of smallness, and instead, trust in the healing that radiates from an experiential connection to the "higher powers."[114]

James correctly points out, however, that the evangelical Christians and the mind-curers would each offer radically different explanations of what takes place during these moments of self-surrender. He hypothesizes that evangelical Christians would offer a theistic explanation: divine grace creates a new personality the instant the old personality is genuinely renounced. On the other hand, he suggests that the mind-curers would, in most cases, offer a pantheistic explanation: the "narrower private self" merges into "the wider or greater self" (which is simultaneously "the spirit of the universe" as well as one's "own subconscious self") as soon as "the isolating barriers of mistrust and anxiety are removed."[115] James notes that "medico-materialistic" thinkers could also offer a third, purely naturalistic, explanatory possibility: cerebrally "lower" processes function more easily when they are not obstructed by the "higher" cerebral processes.

James does not reveal his own explanatory preference, but in a sense, these three possibilities symbolize long-standing tensions in James's own thought, tensions that were, arguably, never satisfactorily resolved. James was by no means an evangelical Christian, but for long periods of his life he advocated a unique type of theism that posited God as a loving but finite participant in the drama of salvation. James also actively fought against pantheism for much of his adult career, and was uneasy about the theological underpinnings of the mind-cure movement, but at the same time, almost as if against his better judgment, he repeatedly flirted with pantheistic doctrines (as his lecture on "Human Immortality" demonstrates); by the time of *A Pluralistic Universe*, he officially began to argue for the viability of a "pluralistic" pantheism. Finally, for much of his career, James was a strong proponent of the importance of a physiological understanding of psychological events, but his early quasi-behaviorism became increasingly muted and then finally appears to have disappeared altogether as James became an ardent spokesperson against a purely materialistic perspective that dogmatically denied the possibility of the existence of realms of existence beyond the range of the senses.

This unresolved theoretical tension in James's understanding of the nature of the contact between the self and the spiritual forces of the unseen worlds is deeply rooted in James's own existential struggle to affirm the value of individual acts of volition, while simultaneously acknowledging the value of his father's stress on the supremacy of religious self-negation. Much of the *Varieties*, in many ways, can be understood as James's attempt to reconcile these opposing tendencies in his psyche. In the *Varieties*, James often takes themes from his father's impassioned theological positions and uses them as material for his own more psychological and philosophical explorations. For instance, Henry Sr.'s theological emphasis on the necessity of self-surrender and self-negation sets the agenda for James's own psychological investigations of changes in the finite personality structures of converts, saints, and mystics; similarly, Henry Sr.'s theological monism, which James claims was "monistic enough to satisfy the philosopher, and yet warm and living and dramatic enough to speak to the heart of the common pluralistic man"[116] becomes the basis for James's own metaphysical speculations about the deeper levels of the self that are intimately connected to the divine.

James's psychological investigation of the personality changes that take place during conversion experiences can also be seen as a way in which he could theoretically come to grips with the crisis experiences that so profoundly affected both father and son (the crises described in chapter 1). It could be argued that both Henry Sr. and his son went through conversions, if conversions are understood in the expanded sense of a "process of unification," in which a relatively permanent "firmness, stability, and equilibrium" replaces "a period of storm, stress and inconsistency."[117] Both Henry Sr. and his son were, for long periods of their lives, "sick souls," a technical term James uses to describe those individuals who are prime candidates for conversion experiences, individuals who are plagued with "haunting and insistent ideas," "irrational impulses," "morbid scruples, dreads and inhibitions,"[118] individuals who at times have an "incapacity for joyous feeling," or more severely, suffer from a "positive and active anguish."[119] These sick souls, unlike "healthy-minded individuals," feel that their self is split down the middle, they undergo a type of psychological warfare in which there is a constant and anguished struggle between one part of their nature which longs to live according to certain moral and religious ideals and another part of their nature which refuses to cooperate with these idealistic demands. According to James's psychological understanding of conversion, it is possible to alleviate this "divided self" through "the normal evolution of character," which primarily consists "in the straightening out and unifying of the inner self."[120] However, even though this "volitional type" of conversion (which is "conscious and voluntary") remains a psychological option, he claims that, more typically, the discord within sick souls is so excessive that it can only be rectified through the "self-surrender type" of conversion (which is "involuntary and unconscious").[121]

These two types of conversions are not diametrically opposed. Rather, they are the end-points of a continuum in which elements of each ideal type are combined. James's own crisis experience, for instance, had certain characteristics of a "self-surrender" type of conversion (i.e., its suddenness and its unexpected quality), but his recovery from his debilitating depression was primarily an example of a volitional conversion: his self-reliance was ultimately strengthened rather than negated, his psychological improvement occurred gradually, and this improvement was the result of a conscious, deliberate cultivation of "a new set of moral and spiritual habits."[122] Henry Sr.'s crisis experience combined elements of both types of conversions as well: his psychological improvement also did not occur overnight, but his conversion experience was closer to the "self-surrender type" of conversion in that it was explicitly connected to a profound moment of self-negation, and it brought about a deep, abiding, and experiential religious faith.

James is careful to emphasize that conversions, understood in the broadest possible sense, are not necessarily religious (as his own experience demonstrates), but on the whole, James tends to describe conversion experiences in explicitly religious terms:

> To be converted, to be regenerated, to receive grace, to experience religion, to gain an assurance, are so many phrases which denote the process, gradual or sudden, by which a self hitherto divided and consciously wrong inferior [sic] and unhappy, becomes unified and consciously right superior [sic] and happy, in consequence of its firmer hold upon religious realities.[123]

Conversion for James then is the psychological reorganization of a person's personality structure, in which the "hot place in man's consciousness, the group of ideas to which he devotes himself, and from which he works . . . [i.e.,] the *habitual centre of his personal energy*" becomes religious in nature; conversions occur when, in a moment of crisis and under the impact of unexpected mystical experiences, religious ideas permanently shift from the margins of the individual's awareness to become the conscious center of the individual's life.[124]

Once again we see the interaction between religious experiences and religious ideas, with the pride of place belonging to the experiential side of the equation. James claims that an individual's religious ideas and self-understanding are dramatically reorganized by virtue of the inherent potency of these powerful mystical experiences:

> Voices are often heard, lights seen, or visions witnessed; automatic motor phenomena occur; and it always seems, after the surrender of the personal will, as if an extraneous higher power had flooded in and taken possession. Moreover the sense of renovation, safety, cleanness, rightness, can be so marvelous and jubilant as well to warrant one's belief in a radically new substantial nature.[125]

According to James, conversions are not only *catalyzed* by mystical experiences, they also tend to create a personality structure which itself revolves around a type of mystical awareness. James, following fellow psychologist James Henry Leuba, calls this mystical state of consciousness that is the new "hot-spot" of the individual, the "faith-state."[126] Quoting Leuba with approval, James notes that conversion experiences occur "when the sense of estrangement . . . fencing man about in a narrowly limited ego, breaks down, [and] the individual finds himself 'at one with all creation.' He lives in the universal life; he and man, he and nature, he and God, are one. That state of confidence, trust, union with all things . . . is the *Faith-state*."[127] Few of James's commentators have emphasized the mystical qualities of the faith-state, but James explicitly asserts that the "faith-state and [the] mystic state are practically convertible terms."[128] Furthermore, James claims that there are three primary attributes of the faith-state, all of which are mystical: (1) a loss of anxiety and fear based on the individual's felt sense of unity with the universe; (2) an apprehension of ineffable truths about the nature of reality; and (3) a transfiguration of the convert's perception of the external world. According to James, the faith-state is not a derivative of any particular set of theological beliefs, but rather, it is "a natural organic complex"; it is an affectively toned shift in a person's self-understanding which combines "religious rapture, moral enthusiasm, ontological wonder, [and] cosmic emotion" in a profoundly mystical transformation "in which the sand and grit of selfhood incline to disappear."[129]

In essence, therefore, much of James's theorizing about conversion experiences is directly related to his understanding of mystical experiences. Yet it is important to remember that James does not claim that *all* mystical states of awareness are conversions, nor does he assert that *all* conversions are mystical in nature. Instead, conversions (at least those which are deeply religious in nature) are understood to be catalyzed by mystical experiences, which then instigate a profound character transformation that is itself also understood to possess a mystical dimension: the faith-state. Thus, James's investigation of conversions primarily focus on the *results* of mystical experience on an individual's psychological structure.[130] For James, mystical experiences of this sort shift the "character to higher levels," they "show a human being what the highwater mark of his spiritual capacity is,"[131] they mark the beginning of a process that, at least potentially, can lead to sanctification.

Salvation and the Higher Self

In the *Varieties*, James focuses primarily on examples of the "self-surrender" type of conversion. These conversions, which happen unexpectedly and are typically much more dramatic than "volitional types" of conversion, intrigue James, in that they appear to provide further evidence that profound psychic activity can occur beyond the range of a person's conscious awareness. James postulates that in self-surrender conversions the individual's vivid awareness of his or her moral and/or religious defects sets in motion a vortex of subconscious activity. Whereas the individual's conscious mind typically has a vague and often inaccurate picture of what needs to occur in order to overcome his or her moral and/or religious defects, deeper forces within the individual's subliminal self have their own, and usually superior, sense of the wholeness or happiness that the individual truly needs. James postulates that prior to a "self-surrender" conversion, these "deeper forces" in the individual's psyche "take the lead," thereby allowing the individual's "better self" to direct "the operation."[132] Finally, after a period of subconscious "incubation," the individual's "new centre of personal energy" bursts forth with no apparent conscious preparation.[133] In James's thinking, the individual's ability to have access to his or her subliminal self is therefore a crucial factor in the etiology of these dramatic self-surrender conversions. According to James, the "possession of a developed subliminal self, and of a leaky or pervious margin [between the subliminal and conscious aspects of a person] is . . a *conditio sine qua non* of the Subject's becoming converted in the instantaneous way."[134]

184

Fields within Fields within Fields

The subliminal self is theoretically crucial for other areas of James's religious reflections as well. For instance, James is convinced that the subliminal self is to be found at the heart of a salvific nucleus that is present within every religion. James boils this salvific nucleus down to "two parts: 1. An uneasiness; and 2. Its solution."[135] The uneasiness, in essence, "is a sense that there is *something wrong about us* as we naturally stand," while the solution is "a sense that *we are saved from the wrongness* by making proper connexion with the higher powers."[136] James argues that, from a psychological perspective, the experience of salvation occurs when a person "identifies his real being with the germinal higher part of himself [the "evolutive" or "superior" aspects of the subliminal self]," and then "becomes conscious that this higher part is conterminous and continuous with a *more* of the same quality, which is operative in the universe outside of him, and which he can keep in working touch with, and in a fashion get on board of and save himself when all of his lower being has gone to pieces in the wreck."[137]

For James, this general depiction of the salvific process is extremely versatile in that it theoretically unites a wide variety of previously mysterious phenomena: it accounts for the pre-conversion experience of being split into two warring selves; it explains how during the process of conversion a person's center of consciousness becomes oriented around a new center of gravity through a surrender of his or her limited sense of selfhood; it gives the theorist the framework necessary to reconcile the simultaneous otherness and interiority of the power that comes to the mystic or convert; and finally, it accounts for the feelings of intense joy and emotional comfort that are commonly associated with these salvific experiences.

James is convinced that, as psychological phenomena, these salvific experiences are extremely valuable; in these experiences "spiritual strength really increases in the subject when he has them, a new life opens for him, and they seem to him a place of conflux where the forces of two universes meet"; nonetheless, James is also aware that each one of these dramatic experiences could conceivably be nothing but the individual's "subjective way of feeling things."[138] What is needed, therefore, is an assessment of the truth-status of this "more" which is the source of these experiences, this "more" that exists within us, and yet which is also, somehow, beyond us. As James puts it: "Is such a 'more' merely our own notion, or does it really exist? If so, in what shape does it exist? Does it act, as well as exist? And in what form should we conceive of that 'union' with it of which religious geniuses are so convinced?"[139]

185

James notes that, from a certain point of view, these questions are answered by theologians within the different religious traditions, but unfortunately, although these theologians all agree that this "more" does exist, and that it actively works for our benefit, they have vastly dissimilar understandings of the nature of our connection with this higher power. What James attempts to do is to use the concept of the subliminal self in a way that not only reconciles these opposing theological perspectives, but which also connects them with psychological theories of the subliminal forces associated with conversions and religious experiences.

James points out that while both psychology and theology "admit that there are forces seemingly outside of the conscious individual that bring redemption to his life," psychology understands these forces to be *merely* subconscious, and assumes that these forces do not exist beyond the boundaries of the individual's psyche.[140] Theology, on the other hand, insists that experiences of salvation are the "direct supernatural operations of the Deity," and are not the results of the individual's efforts.[141] James is convinced that this opposition between psychology and theology can be overcome via the mediation of the concept of the subliminal self. According to James, if there are indeed spiritual forces that are working for our salvation and healing, then it is quite possible that these "higher powers" primarily produce their salvific effects by entering into our life through "the subliminal door."[142] James hypothesizes "that whatever it may be on its *farther* side, the 'more' with which in religious experience we feel ourselves connected is on its *hither* side the subconscious continuation of our conscious life."[143] In this formulation, James pictures the self as a series of overlapping, interpenetrating, ever-shifting, and dynamic dimensions of awareness, in which the conscious aspects of the self merge into the subconscious, which in turn shades off imperceptibly into a spiritual source of vast and beneficent power: the "more." By envisioning the self in this manner, James aligns himself with the scientific authority and respectability of a psychological understanding of the subliminal origins of religious experiences, while simultaneously siding with the theological conviction that the "higher power" that is contacted during salvific experiences is objective and "external" to the individual. For James, the evidence in the fields of psychopathology, psychical research, and religious studies strongly suggest that there are dimensions of our being beneath the level of our conscious awareness which can operate independent of our conscious instigation, dimensions of our being that are, in a very real sense, simultaneously self and other.[144] Therefore, when we feel that something "more" is in control of the salvific process, we can legitimately claim to be united with a "power beyond us,"[145] even if that power is ultimately best understood to be deeper dimensions of the self.

The bottom line for James is that it "is literally and objectively true as far as it goes" that what is "common and generic" to every religion is "the fact that the conscious person is continuous with a wider self through which saving experiences come."[146] However, as James points out, as soon as we "ask how far our transmarginal consciousness carries us if we follow it on its remoter side,"[147] then we, once again, run into the cacophony of conflicting theological opinions:

> Here mysticism and the conversion-rapture and Vedantism and transcendental idealism bring in their monistic interpretations and tell us that the finite self rejoins the absolute self, for it was always one with God and identical with the soul of the world. Here the prophets of all the different religions come with their visions, voices, raptures, and other openings, supposed by each to authenticate his own peculiar faith.[148]

James refuses to endorse any of these theological perspectives, but he *is* willing in the *Varieties* to confess publicly his own theological predilections:

> The further limits of our being plunge . . . into an altogether other dimension of existence from the sensible and merely "understandable" world. Name it the mystical region, or the supernatural region, whichever you choose. So far as our ideal impulses originate in this region (and most of them do originate in it, for we find them possessing us in a way for which we cannot articulately account), we belong to it in a more intimate sense than that in which we belong to the visible world, for we belong in the most intimate sense wherever our ideals belong.[149]

Although James does not yet think that he is philosophically prepared to muster a strong defense for this vision of the intimate interaction between the self and the "mystical region," he is personally convinced that we are not confined to the apparent boundaries of our physical and psychological being. James believes that in some fashion we exist as well on other levels of consciousness, levels of consciousness that primarily operate independently from our everyday sense of ourselves as individuals, but which, nonetheless, from

187

another perspective, can be best understood as "deeper" or "higher" aspects of our own being. On the final page of the main text of the *Varieties*, James forcibly sums up his position:

> The whole drift of my education goes to persuade me that the world of our present consciousness is only one out of many worlds of consciousness that exist, and that those other worlds must contain experiences which have a meaning for our life also; and that although in the main their experiences and those of this world keep discrete, yet the two become continuous at certain points, and higher energies filter in.[150]

In the postscript to the *Varieties*, James offers some tantalizing hints as to how he would articulate the connection between this unseen world and our "higher" or "deeper" self. After arguing that religious experiences only unequivocally testify that "we can experience union with *something* larger than ourselves and in that union find our greatest peace," James states that from a practical standpoint a religious individual only needs to believe that "there exists a larger power which is friendly to him and to his ideals," a power that is both beyond the boundaries of the individual, and yet also, at the same time, "in a fashion continuous with him."[151] This power does not have to be "infinite, it need not be solitary. It might conceivably even be only a larger and more godlike self, of which the present self would then be but the mutilated expression, and the universe might conceivably be a collection of such selves, of different degrees of inclusiveness, with no absolute unity realized in it at all."[152]

In this passage, James is returning to the speculations that he began in "Human Immortality," playing once again with notions of a substantial, cosmic self that transcends the limitations of the physical form, a self which is neither a ghostly reproduction of the individual (like the soul), nor an all-pervasive, omniscient Absolute Self. James wants a doctrine of the self that leaves open the possibility of continued awareness after death, but his philosophical antipathy towards the soul-doctrine (inherited in part from his father's earlier antipathy towards individual selfhood) coupled with his continuing sense that aspects of ourselves exist beyond what can be empirically observed, enable him to be receptive to a version of polytheism, with the countless "higher selves" standing in the place of the former gods. And yet, alongside this polytheistic vision of the mystical region, James also articulates another possibility: that these different selves are themselves aspects of a larger, more encompassing God, a God that is not, however, infinite or all-powerful.[153]

188

Earth Angels and Cosmic Selves

At the end of the *Varieties*, as James is quite aware, numerous questions about the relationship between the self and the "mystical region" remain unanswered. Unfortunately, the texts that follow the *Varieties* do little to answer these questions. *Pragmatism* and the essays that were ultimately published in *Essays in Radical Empiricism* avoid any explicit discussion of the doctrine of the self and its interaction with the unseen world, preferring to take on the crucial task of developing James's epistemology, theories of truth, and metaphysics. However, in *A Pluralistic Universe*, James finally does return to the task of exploring the interaction between the self and the unseen world, marshaling considerable energy in order to explicate and defend his creatively vague vision of a spiritual realm populated by a multitude of cosmic selves.

James's primary job in *A Pluralistic Universe* is to provide a philosophical understanding of the relationship between the self and the divine that is a viable alternative to the choices that were prominent at the time: traditional theism and neo-Hegelian monism. In an effort to muster support for his cause, James returns, once again, to the work of the German psychologist and thinker Gustave Fechner.

Fechner's work is appealing to James because, in contrast to the "shiveringly thin wrappings" of the logically derived justifications of the Absolute offered by James's neo-Hegelian opponents (Josiah Royce and F. H. Bradley in particular), Fechner bases his religious speculations on the "intense concreteness" of sense data as well as the "fertility of detail" inherent in everyday experience.[154] Fechner's central contention is "that the whole universe in its different spans and wavelengths . . . is everywhere alive and conscious."[155] Fechner elaborates this panpsychic view of the universe by hypothesizing that in the same way that consciousness is linked to the human body, a corresponding level of consciousness may be associated with the earth, stars, and galaxies. James explains Fechner's position in more detail:

> The vaster orders of mind go with the vaster orders of body. The entire earth on which we live must have, according to Fechner, its own collective consciousness. So must each sun, moon, and planet; so must the whole solar system have its own wider consciousness. . . . [In the same way, the universe as a whole] is the body of that absolutely totalized consciousness of the universe to which men give the name of God.[156]

James realizes that, strictly speaking, Fechner is, like James's philosophical adversaries, a monist. But unlike neo-Hegelians, such as

Bradley and Royce, Fechner focuses most of his attention on the levels of consciousness that might conceivably bridge the gap between humanity and God. For James, Fechner's vision is thus much more aesthetically appealing than the "thinnest outlines" given by the neo-Hegelians:

> Ordinary monistic idealism leaves everything intermediary out. . . . First, you and I, just as we are in this room; and the moment we get below that surface, the unutterable absolute itself! Doesn't this show a singularly indigent imagination? Isn't this brave universe made on a richer pattern, with room in it for a long hierarchy of beings?[157]

James is especially pleased with Fechner's richly nuanced depictions of the "earth-soul," which Fechner believes to be a "guardian angel" that "we can pray to [just] as men pray to their saints."[158] In a way that anticipates much of the current speculations by contemporary environmentalists and theologians, Fechner notes numerous ways in which the earth could indeed be the body of a sentient being.[159] He posits that the earth, like the body of any organism, is a complex unity. It contains a teeming abundance of life-forms within itself, and yet, seen as a whole, it displays a simple, contained grace. Like a sentient being, the earth also changes from within. Unlike a piece of clay which has to be molded by an external agent, the patterns of the earth's rhythms and historical development appear to be self-propelled and governed. Yet, as Fechner points out, the earth is not identical in structure to its constituent organisms. In many ways, the earth is actually superior to human beings and other creatures, both in complexity and in self-sufficiency. Unlike human beings, the earth does not depend upon other organisms for its life: the air, water, animals, and plants that sustain us are simply constituent components of the earth's body. The earth has no need for limbs to move, no need for hands with which to grasp anything, no need for eyes with which to see, since in a very literal sense the earth moves and grasps with the fins, paws, hands, and feet of every organism and it sees through the eyes of every creature. The earth does not need a heart and blood vessels when it has the showers of rain and the flow of tides and rivers. Similarly, the earth has no need for lungs when it is in constant and intimate contact with the atmosphere itself. As James puts it, because "we are ourselves a part of the earth, so our organs are her organs. She is, as it were, eye and ear over her whole extent, seeing and hearing at once all that we see and hear in separation."[160]

190

Fields within Fields within Fields

For Fechner, the earth is the physical instantiation of the angels that are described in numerous myths of different cultures: beings that live in the light, beings that fly effortlessly, beings that are "intermediaries between God and us, obeying his commands."[161] The earth, as an angel, is understood by Fechner to be the physical body of a higher and wider awareness who lovingly looks after our best interests. This theological understanding that the earth is a manifestation of an angel apparently arouse within Fechner as a result of "moments of direct vision of this truth," moments such as the following:

> On a certain spring morning I went out to walk. The fields were green, the birds sang, the dew glistened, the smoke was rising, here and there a man appeared; a light as of transfiguration lay on all things. It was only a little bit of the earth; it was only one moment of her existence; and yet as my look embraced her more and more it seemed to me not only so beautiful an idea, but so true and clear a fact, that she is an angel, an angel so rich and fresh and flower-like, and yet going her round in the skies so firmly and so at one with herself, turning her whole living face to Heaven, and carrying me along with her into that Heaven, that I asked myself how the opinions of men could ever have spun themselves away from life so far as to deem the earth only a dry clod, and to seek for angels above it or about it in the emptiness of the sky.[162]

The primary difference between the angels as commonly portrayed in different religious mythologies and Fechner's earth-angel is that this great and benevolent consciousness is not a spiritual entity that is ontologically separate from human consciousness. Instead, the earth-angel or earth-soul is a dynamic gestalt of each of the unique and apparently separate consciousnesses that populate the earth. The perceptions of each person, animal, and plant—along with the hypothetical perceptions of the seemingly inanimate levels of being, such as rocks and rivers—combine to form the unitary, yet collective, consciousness of the earth. Fechner hypothesizes that in the same way that a leaf can be understood as having a separate existence from other leaves and from the branch to which it is connected, in the same way, each individual consciousness momentarily perceives that it is cut off from other individual consciousnesses and from the underlying earth-soul. However, just as the leaf is, in actuality, never separate from the branch, and just as the health and vitality of each leaf has repercussions on the tree as a whole, in the same way, Fechner proposes that each seemingly separate consciousness is, on a deeper level,

191

connected to all other individual consciousnesses through their collective integration as aspects of the earth-soul; and the earth-soul itself is affected by the numerous experiences of each seemingly separate individual consciousness.

For Fechner, the earth-soul, and thus by extension, the soul of the universe as a whole, or "God," is not a static, unchanging reality, but rather, is a dynamic awareness that has an inner life that is enriched and altered by the countless experiences and ideas of the individual consciousnesses that are, so to speak, its "eyes." According to this theory, the experiences and ideas of each individual consciousness are preserved in the greater memory and awareness of the earth-soul, and in a sense, take on a life of their own, combining and interacting outside of the individual's conscious awareness with the ideas and memories of other human and non-human individuals. For Fechner, the physical death of any individual is, therefore, nothing more than a closing of one of the earth's "eyes," in which, at the moment of death, the individual's awareness neither disappears altogether nor is absorbed by the larger earth-soul, but rather, survives as a preexisting, relatively independent, but radically freer and more expansive grouping of ideas and memories. This cluster of ideas and memories that is the individual's awareness after death maintains a degree of integrity, but it also possesses a new and expanded awareness of both its connection with the earth-soul and with the memories and ideas of other individuals. After the death of the individual's physical body, the individual's consciousness remains, but since it now identifies less with the physical body, its boundaries are more porous, and it is therefore more capable of freely interacting with other fields of consciousness, including those of the living. This increased freedom, fluidity, and expansiveness allows the individual's life to continue in unexpected ways, since it can now combine with other dynamic fields of consciousness to generate novel ideas and to create new and ongoing experiences.

James's discussion of Fechner's theories is always rhetorically presented in such a way as to imply that these theories are simply fascinating possibilities that are offered up to the reader as one of many alternatives. James never goes out on a limb and embraces Fechner's ideas as his own. Nonetheless, it is clear that James is implicitly giving a muted endorsement to Fechner's ideas; his reluctance to defend more actively Fechner's position seems to stem primarily from James's desire to maintain a theoretical openness on metaphysical speculations that, by their very nature, cannot be empirically confirmed or denied. James never expresses any serious qualms about

Fields within Fields within Fields

Fechner's hypotheses, and in fact, Fechner's scheme is closely aligned with James's own radical empiricism, especially with James's attempts to articulate a theory of reality that would allow for a maximum of diversity and plurality while simultaneously permitting a maximum of unity and connectedness.[163] Fechner's earth-soul can be seen as different than a person's individual consciousness; this difference thereby leaves theoretical room for genuine personal autonomy; yet, the earth-soul can also be seen as intimately connected to the individual's consciousness to the extent that it is, in some sense, the individual's deeper, truer, and wider self (ideas that are also highly congruent with James's conception of the subliminal self).

In his discussion of Fechner's ideas, James frequently draws upon explicit parallels in his own work to strengthen Fechner's analogical arguments. By far the most important of these parallels is James's depiction of the dynamics of our individual consciousness. James's psychology stresses that our consciousness always has a "hot spot," a center of gravity, a focus of attention. Surrounding this central focus of our awareness, however, is a vaguely felt, but crucially significant, penumbra of tacit assumptions, memories, hopes, and prejudices that operate below the surface of our conscious awareness and strongly influence how we perceive and interact with the world around us. In addition, encircling this fairly accessible preconscious background, there is another, deeper level of subconscious awareness, an awareness that appears to be active below the surface boundaries of our consciousness and which occasionally erupts into our lives with powerful and undeniable force.

Our attention, moment to moment, is, by definition, on the hot spot of our consciousness. According to James, this hot spot often becomes such a central part of our experience that the surrounding background of our awareness fades from view. However, in a split second, our consciousness can expand to include within its active purview material belonging to this background (e.g., vivid memories of early childhood), making the background, for the moment, the foreground, that is, the new hot spot. James beautifully describes this inherent complexity and fluidity of our inner life:

> My present field of consciousness is a centre surrounded by a fringe that shades insensibly into a subconscious more. I use three separate terms here to describe this fact; but I might as well use three hundred, for the fact is all shades and no boundaries. Which part of it properly is in my consciousness, which out? If I name what is out, it already has come in. The centre works in one way while the margins work in another, and

193

presently overpower the centre and are central themselves. What we conceptually identify ourselves with and say we are thinking of at any time is the centre; but our *full* self is the whole field, with all those indefinitely radiating subconscious possibilities of increase that we can only feel without conceiving, and can hardly begin to analyze.[164]

For James, in the same way that we are "co-conscious" with the margin of our tacit background awareness, perhaps our individual consciousnesses form a collective pool of awareness present in the margins of a more central self that is "co-conscious" with each of us. Based on this metaphor, the deeper or more extensive self that is the core reality of each of our beings would be the "hot spot" of the earth soul's consciousness that is surrounded and interpenetrated by a collective field of less extensive personal consciousnesses. Thus, for James, the dynamics of our personal consciousness can be understood as mirroring the dynamics of the relationship between each individual consciousness and the greater, more encompassing consciousness of the earth-soul. James emphasizes that if this hypothesis is accurate, if indeed "every bit of us at every moment is part and parcel of a wider self," then while our individual consciousnesses may not be cognizant of our connection to this vaster awareness, and while we might feel that we are insulated from other individual consciousnesses as well, it is still quite possible, indeed likely, that on a deeper or higher level of our being, we are "conscious, as it were, over our heads"[165] of this underlying connection with other individuals and with this wider self. From this more encompassing perspective, we may have a much broader range of knowledge and experiences than what we presently realize; we may be intimately aware of other individual consciousnesses; we may be initiating an enormous amount of activity that has a tremendous impact upon the world, all with only the slightest hint of awareness from our present, more limited perspective.

If this hypothesis of our subconscious connection with a deeper and wider spiritual level of existence is accepted, then coherent explanations of psychical and mystical phenomena begin to take shape. For instance, it is reasonable to suggest that telepathy, clairvoyance, and other psychical experiences occur when the limitations inherent within our present level of personal identity momentarily dissolve and our awareness expands and embraces within itself the knowledge possessed by other individual consciousnesses. In the same way, mystical experiences could also be seen as a letting go of our identification with our present level of consciousness in order to unite with deeper or wider dimensions of our being. Nature mysticism, from this perspec-

194

tive, would imply an experiential connection with the awareness of the earth-soul, while unitive, interior mystical experiences might well be catalyzed by a powerful sense of our underlying oneness with the universal soul itself.

While James does not explicitly develop this theory in *A Pluralistic Universe*, the overall thrust of his argument does point in this direction. For instance, James notes that Fechner's hypothesis has enormous potential to help us comprehend psychical and psychopathological phenomena:

> I doubt whether we shall ever understand some of [these phenomena] without using the very letter of Fechner's conception of a great reservoir in which the memories of earth's inhabitants are pooled and preserved, and from which, when the threshold lowers or the valve opens, information ordinarily shut out leaks into the mind of exceptional individuals among us.[166]

James also thinks that the religious experiences that he described in the *Varieties* support Fechner's ideas, claiming that "they point with reasonable probability to the continuity of our consciousness with a wider spiritual environment from which the ordinary prudential man (who is the only man that scientific psychology, so called, takes cognizance of) is shut off."[167] These religious experiences show us that our naturalistic ideas of selfhood are insufficient; they demonstrate that there are "possibilities that take our breath away, of another kind of happiness and power, based on giving up our own will and letting something higher work for us"; they "suggest that our natural experience, our strictly moralistic and prudential experience, may be only a fragment of real human experience. They soften nature's outlines and open out the strangest possibilities."[168] In James's opinion, profound religious experiences give rise to religious beliefs that are "fully in accord with Fechner's theory of successively larger enveloping spheres of conscious life"; furthermore, as James notes, Fechner's theory is congruent with James's own conception developed in the *Varieties* that "the believer is continuous, to his own consciousness, at any rate, with a wider self from which saving experiences flow in."[169]

James points out that those who have had such profound religious experiences "are quite unmoved by criticism . . . they have had their vision and they know—that is enough—that we inhabit an invisible spiritual environment from which help comes, our soul being mysteriously one with a larger soul whose instruments we are."[170] On the basis of experiences such as these, James is willing to state that

195

Exploring Unseen Worlds

Fechner's ideas have a modicum of empirical verification. In addition, he asserts that these ideas offer us a viable explanatory model that naturalism or certain varieties of theism cannot provide, since naturalism assumes "that human consciousness is the highest consciousness there is," while theism, although willing to posit the existence of a "higher mind," nonetheless asserts that this higher mind "is discontinuous with our own."[171] Interestingly, despite James's caution in the *Varieties* that we should not uncritically accept the testimony of mystics, by the time of *A Pluralistic Universe*, he is convinced that the weight of the evidence provided by psychopathological, psychical, and mystical experiences "establish, when taken together, a decidedly formidable probability in favor of a general view of the world almost identical with Fechner's," even though "the outlines of the superhuman consciousness thus made probable must remain, however, very vague;" when all is said and done, James comes down forcefully in favor of Fechner's vision of the universe:

> The drift of all the evidence we have seems to me to sweep us very strongly towards the belief in some form of superhuman life with which we may, unknown to ourselves, be co-conscious. We may be in the universe as dogs and cats are in our libraries, seeing the books and hearing the conversation, but having no inkling of the meaning of it all.[172]

The Compounding of Consciousness

That James would, in *A Pluralistic Universe*, eventually embrace a vision of the world similar to Fechner's was never a given. Even though, with the benefit of hindsight, we can easily trace a clear trajectory from his earlier work in the "Human Immortality" essay, to the *Varieties*, and then onto *A Pluralistic Universe*, James makes it clear in *A Pluralistic Universe* that he would have been unable to accept a Fechnerian worldview without a prior willingness to change his mind about a crucial, if somewhat obscure, philosophical doctrine: the "compounding of consciousness."

In the *Principles*, James had vehemently opposed the doctrine of the compounding of consciousness; now, in *A Pluralistic Universe*, he asserts that he has changed his mind, and is willing to endorse this philosophical and psychological position. It is critically important to understand the doctrine of the compounding of consciousness; unfor-

196

tunately, it is rather abstract and obscure. However, if we go slowly and carefully, its significance will hopefully become clear.

To begin with, the doctrine of the compounding of consciousness claims that complex states of consciousness are a combination of simpler states of consciousness. But what exactly is a "complex state of consciousness" and what are "simpler states of consciousness" and how do they "combine"? An example will perhaps provide some answers. Let's envision a young woman standing before an open window in early June, listening to the sounds of her two cats wrestling in the living room, smelling the stew she began two hours ago, feeling angry at her boyfriend, and wincing from the pain of menstrual cramps. All of the individual sights, sounds, smells, emotions, and bodily sensations that she is experiencing are "simple states of consciousness." However, these "simple states of consciousness" are not experienced separately. Instead, the woman experiences them within herself as a unity, as a multilayered whole, that is, as a "complex state of consciousness." According to the doctrine of the compounding of consciousness, the "complex state of consciousness" that the woman is experiencing is nothing more than a summation of the "simple states of consciousness"; that is, her unified experience is simply the sum total of what she is seeing, hearing, feeling, thinking and so on.

In the *Principles*, James had argued against this notion. He asserted that a complex state of consciousness is not *just* a combination of different simpler states of consciousness, but rather, it is something entirely new. A complex state of awareness is not, for instance, twenty-five separate simpler awarenesses added together. Instead, this complex state of awareness is itself a simple, whole, new awareness *of* these twenty-five seemingly separate awarenesses; it is a single unit; it is not made of parts; it is not a compound.

According to James's thinking in the *Principles* (which assumes a basic philosophical dualism between "thoughts" and "things"), one reason that philosophers claim that a complex state of consciousness is made of parts is that they confuse our awareness *of* something, with the thing itself. Physical things, James argued, have parts. Our thoughts do not. However, because our thoughts "know" these things, we therefore assume that our thoughts are divisible as well. For instance, for the purpose of analysis, I might presuppose that at the present moment my consciousness consists of numerous "simple" units of awareness: the awareness of my stomach rumbling as it digests food from lunch, the awareness of these words on the screen of the computer,

197

the awareness of the sounds of my wife practicing the guitar in the next room, and so on. These numerous "chunks" of awareness know certain objects: my stomach gurglings, the words on the computer screen, the sounds of the guitar. From the perspective that James defended in the *Principles*, these various objects are indeed there, and I am aware of them. But, James would add, my awareness is not a lot of smaller awarenesses joined together. Instead, my experience of these objects form a single, unified awareness in which these objects are known all together, all at once. This unified, synthetic awareness, James would argue, is very different from numerous, isolated, separate knowledges of these same objects. For instance, as James points out, in the physical world, blue and yellow pigments combine to form a green pigment, but that does not mean that seeing the color green involves joining together the perceptions of blue and yellow. The perception of green is unique; it is basic; it does not have parts.

However, even as early as 1895, in the President's Address before the American Psychological Association, James had publicly admitted that his prior opposition to the compounding of consciousness was perhaps ill-founded. His change of heart came about when he realized that there is an inner complexity to experience that *can* be introspectively analyzed. For instance, as he mentioned in the lecture, "in a glass of lemonade we can taste both the lemon and sugar at once. In a major chord our ear can single out the c, e, g, and c′ if it has once become acquainted with these notes apart."[173]

Unlike the psychology of the *Principles*, which insisted that each moment of consciousness was an indivisible, simple unity of perception, by the 1895 lecture, James had come to see that within our consciousness, unity does not have to exclude diversity. Gerald Myers underscores this shift in James's thought:

> Here we come upon a favorite idea of James's, one that especially intrigued him during his later years: unity need not be simple, unanalyzable, or utterly homogeneous. Our own experiences are unities that are also diversities. Our "knowledge of things together" is an instance: there are different things to see on the beach; of themselves they represent merely a multitude, but when we perceive them simultaneously we group them as the contents of a single state of perceptual consciousness. A state of mind such as this is not homogeneous but is rather a synthetic union of diverse elements. It is unlike anything in the physical world (James had not in 1895 eliminated psychophysical dualism) because in that world the parts of a so-called whole are separable; in a mental unity such as a state of perceptual awareness, on the other hand, the parts are distinguishable

198

Fields within Fields within Fields

but not separable, for if any are detached, the unity which they help to
constitute immediately collapses.[174]

By the time of *A Pluralistic Universe*, James had come to see that
traditional notions of identity and difference would have to be dis-
carded if a correct understanding of the nature of consciousness and
reality was ever to be reached. Traditionally, the logic of identity held
that a thing cannot be something else, and still remain itself. Or, to put
it another way, we can not say that two different things are the same
thing without contradicting ourselves. For instance, there is no logical
way in which a person can say that a dog is a cat, while simultaneously saying that it is still a dog. However, it had become increasingly evident to James that the logic of identity simply does not hold
in the realm of our consciousness where distinguishable parts of complex moments of consciousness have a felt integrity, and yet are simultaneously inseparable from the unity of the complex moment of
consciousness. For instance, in the field of my vision at the present
moment, I am seeing a computer screen. However, even though I can
conceptually separate my perception of the computer screen from my
perception of the table on which it sits, and the window behind it, and
the trees which I see outside the window, and so on, in reality, my
perception of the computer screen is inseparable from my perception
of the table, the window, the trees, and so forth. The perception of the
computer screen is not an isolated unit; it is intimately and insepara-
bly connected with my total field of vision, felt as a unity. The logic
of identity, however, would claim that this perception is impossible,
since a computer screen, in order to remain itself, has to be completely
separate from the table, the window, and the trees.

A further goad to James's willingness to abandon his previous
loyalty to the logic of identity is that, by the time of *A Pluralistic
Universe*, James had given up the dualism of the *Principles* and had
adopted the nondualism of the *Essays in Radical Empiricism*. This
nondualism claimed, unfortunately for James's previous adherence to
the logic of identity, that any single moment of pure experience can
be, simultaneously, a "physical" fact for one person and a "mental"
object for another person. For instance, as James points out to the
members of the audience listening to the lectures that ultimately came
together to form *A Pluralistic Universe*, "this very desk which I strike
with my hand in turn strikes your eyes. It functions at once as a
physical object in the outer world and as a mental object in our sundry
mental worlds."[175] The logic of identity is denied again: one thing (the
moment of pure experience) is claimed to be, in this case, two other

199

separate things (a physical object and a mental object), while remaining itself.

James did not give up the logic of identity easily. Nor did he easily surrender his prior rejection of the compounding of consciousness. He describes the difficulties he went through attempting to reconcile these related conundrums:

> Sincerely, and patiently as I could, I struggled with the problem for years, covering hundreds of sheets of paper with notes and memoranda and discussions with myself over the difficulty. How can many consciousnesses be at the same time one consciousness? How can one and the same identical fact experience itself so diversely?[176]

James, influenced by the work of the French philosopher, Henri Bergson, finally concluded that "reality, life, experience, concreteness, immediacy, use what word you will, exceeds our logic, overflows and surrounds it."[177] For James, the "secret of a continuous life which the universe knows by heart and acts on every instant cannot be a contradiction incarnate. If logic says it is one, so much the worse for logic. Logic being the lesser thing, the static incomplete abstraction, must succumb to reality, not reality to logic."[178]

By the time of *A Pluralistic Universe*, James had come to believe that concepts, unlike our concrete experience of life, are "discontinuous and fixed,"[179] they are similar to "flowers gathered, they are only moments dipped out from the stream of time, snap-shots taken . . . [of] a life that in its original coming is continuous."[180] Relying on a purely logical and conceptual approach to life, we "arrest its movement, cutting it up into bits as if with scissors," and then we mount these "dried specimens" in our "logical herbarium"[181] where "we cut out and fix, and exclude everything but what we have fixed. A concept means a that-and-no-other . . . whereas in the real concrete sensible flux of life experiences compenetrate each other so that it is not easy to know just what is excluded and what is not."[182] James stresses that in our practical life, concepts are extremely useful, but ironically, they do not allow us to really understand life. What we need to do in order to really understand life is to immerse ourselves in the immediacy and thickness of our moment-to-moment *feeling* of life. According to James, if we examine our concrete experience with care, we will make a startling discovery:

> No element *there* cuts itself off from any other element, as concepts cut themselves from concepts . . . there is literally nothing between [them]; which means again that no part goes exactly so far and no farther; that no

200

part absolutely excludes another, but that they compenetrate and are cohesive; that if you tear out one, its roots bring out more with them; that
whatever is real is telescoped and diffused into other reals.[183]

Unlike our intellectualistic analysis of life which "is a retrospective patchwork, a post-mortem dissection,"[184] the immediate feeling of
our life itself has no problems with a oneness that is also a manyness,
or with the philosophical dilemma of how something could possibly
be itself and yet still manage to be connected with something else.
"Oneness" and "manyness" may, from an intellectualistic perspective,
appear to be contradictory, but "what is immediately given in the
single and particular instance is always something pooled and mutual."[185] Therefore, James concludes that if every moment of life clearly
demonstrates the interconnectedness that he had earlier, on purely
logical principles, denied that life could possess, then he would rather
deny logic than deny life:

> Every smallest state of consciousness, concretely taken, overflows its own
> definition. Only concepts are self-identical; only "reason" deals with closed
> equations; nature is but a name for excess; every point in her opens out
> and runs into the more. . . . In the pulse of inner life immediately present
> now in each of us is a little past, a little future, a little awareness of our
> own body, of each other's persons, of these sublimities we are trying to
> talk about, of the earth's geography and the direction of history, of truth
> and error, of good and bad, and of who knows how much more? Feeling,
> however dimly and subconsciously, all these things, your pulse of inner
> life is continuous with them, belongs to them and they to it.[186]

James's willingness in *A Pluralistic Universe* to accept that the
compounding of consciousness takes place moment to moment within
the awareness of each individual had important metaphysical ramifications. James realized that a willingness to admit that the dynamic
stream of our individual consciousness, when examined closely, is a
seemingly contradictory diversity-within-unity, permitted him to extend metaphorically this diversity-within-unity to Fechner's metaphysical proposals. Because in *A Pluralistic Universe* James was willing to
accept that within our own consciousness it is possible to observe that
different "parts" of our awareness are conjoined within our awareness
as a whole, he was also willing to accept that perhaps Fechner was
correct that our individual consciousness is itself a constituent part of
a larger consciousness:

In ourselves, visual consciousness goes with our eyes, tactile consciousness with our skin. But altho neither skin nor eye knows aught of the sensations of the other, they come together and figure in some sort of relation and combination in the more inclusive consciousness which each of us names his *self*. Quite similarly, then, says Fechner, we must suppose that my consciousness of myself and yours of yourself, altho in their immediacy they keep separate and know nothing of each other, are yet known and used together in a higher consciousness, that of the human race, say, into which they enter as constituent parts.[187]

However, while it might appear that in *A Pluralistic Universe*, James was at last completely willing to accept the doctrine of the compounding of consciousness, as well as to embrace without reservation Fechner's metaphysical proposals, the reality was more complex and nuanced. James *was* willing to admit that a complex state of consciousness is not a simple unity, but rather, is an example of diversity-within-unity, but he still held tenaciously to the idea that a complex state of consciousness is more than *simply* the sum of its parts. James still held that every complex state of consciousness is something new—something which could not come together on its own without the synthesizing and unifying power of the mind of the observer. For James, it is only within the mind of each individual that the separate sights, sounds, smells and so on are woven together into something new: the individual's unified, and densely layered, state of awareness.

In the same way that James continued to deny in *A Pluralistic Universe* that a complex state of consciousness is simply the sum of its constituent parts, he also refused to accept Fechner's understanding that the earth soul is nothing more than a combination of all of the numerous individual awarenesses that are, so to speak, its "eyes" and "ears." James simply did not want to discard completely the idea that God is "a distinct agent of unification"[188] of these separate consciousnesses—an idea which is the metaphorical extension of his continuing psychological conviction that higher, complex states of awareness do not happen on their own, but instead, only occur as a result of the synthesizing ability of the individual's mind. James forcibly underscores this point:

> As our mind is not the bare sum of our sights plus our sounds plus our pains, but in adding [this sense data] together also finds relations among them and weaves them into schemes and forms . . . of which no one sense in its separate estate knows anything, so the earth-soul traces relations

between the contents of my mind and the contents of yours of which neither of our separate minds is conscious.[189]

According to James, the earth-soul is not a simple combination
of our consciousnesses, even though our consciousnesses are co-
conscious with it. It has knowledge that we, as individuals, do not
have access to, except during rare moments of mystical insight. James
argues that "we are closed against its world, but that world is not
closed against us. It is as if the total universe of inner life had a sort
of grain or direction, a sort of valvular structure permitting knowledge to flow in one way only, so that the wider might always have the
narrower under observation, but never the narrower the wider."[190]
James wants a divine being who is intimately connected with us, but
he does not wish to reduce that divine being to a simple combination
of the totality of consciousnesses in the universe. Therefore, although
James claims that his theology in *A Pluralistic Universe* is pantheistic,
in actuality, it is closer to being pan*entheistic*. For James, God is found
within the universe, but God is not reduced *to* the universe.

A Field Model of the Self and Reality

A Pluralistic Universe is a snapshot of James himself in flux. He
is attempting to jettison years of theological and psychological assumptions in order to construct an alternative psychological and theological vision; but he has difficulty completely making the transition.
For many years in his career, James was an ardent opponent of philosophers who argued that our individual consciousnesses are one
with a monistic Absolute. He had, instead, advocated the idea that our
individual consciousnesses are separate from, but known and loved
by, a theistic personal God. From this earlier theological perspective,
God was understood to be a separate being reacting and responding
to our experiences which are known within God as a totality, as a
oneness of experience. This earlier Jamesian theology had claimed that
just as a constellation is not merely a simple collection of stars, but
rather, is the result of a separate being viewing those stars as a related
unit, in the same way, God, unlike the Absolute, does not simply
consist of a combination of all of our seemingly separate awarenesses,
but rather, is an "independent higher witness" of our experiences.[191] In
A Pluralistic Universe, James changes his theology: he no longer con-
ceives of God as an ontologically separate knower of our individual

203

consciousnesses, but he still fights to maintain the distinctiveness and uniqueness of God's awareness.

As a result of his acceptance of important aspects of the doctrine of the compounding of consciousness, James realizes that he has to formulate a new theological doctrine of God, but he is still extremely reluctant to accept one obvious possibility: the monistic understanding of God as the Absolute. However, as we have seen, since James wants to accept a religious vision almost identical to Fechner's, he is forced, fighting all the way, to accept that the Absolute might indeed exist:

> The self-compounding of mind in its smaller and more accessible portions seems a certain fact, . . . [therefore] the speculative assumption of a similar but wider compounding in remoter regions must be reckoned with as a legitimate hypothesis. The absolute is not the impossible being I once thought it. Mental facts do function both singly and together, at once, and we finite minds may simultaneously be co-conscious with one another in a superhuman intelligence.[192]

Nonetheless, James remains more open to Fechner's monistic vision of reality than to Royce's or Bradley's, not only because, unlike these neo-Hegelians who claim that we are forced by logical necessity to believe in the Absolute, "Fechner treats the superhuman consciousness he so fervently believes in as an hypothesis only," but also because Fechner's vision is much more concretely and thickly articulated than the abstract conceptual system of the philosophers of the Absolute.

Nonetheless, James is not completely happy with Fechner's theological vision. He still does not agree with the monistic implications of Fechner's conception of God as the hypothetical end of the hierarchy of larger consciousnesses enveloping smaller consciousnesses. James claims that, "as we envelope our sight and hearing, so the earth-soul envelopes us, and the star-soul the earth-soul, until—what? Envelopment can't go on forever . . . so God is the name that Fechner gives to this last all-enveloper. But if nothing escapes this all-enveloper, he is responsible for everything, including evil."[193] James prefers to "assume that the superhuman consciousness, however vast it may be, has itself an external environment, and consequently is finite."[194]

This concept of the "finite God" is a puzzling irritant within James's basically promising theo-metaphysical hypothesis: pluralistic pantheism.[195] Pluralistic pantheism (admittedly, an apparent contradiction in terms) is James's attempt to avoid the rigid, static, completely monistic "block universe" that he claims is portrayed in the various neo-Hegelian philosophies of the Absolute. At the same time, pluralistic pantheism is James's attempt to align himself with the understanding that the divine is constituted, at least in part, by our own finite individual consciousnesses. James's religious impulses want a God that is extremely intimate, so much so that he understands God to be, from a certain perspective at least, our deepest self; yet, James's ethical needs mandate that this God not be completely all-pervasive in order to allow real moral choice for each individual. Unfortunately, James never adequately harmonizes these often contradictory temperamental requirements, leaving his finite God to end up at times looking suspiciously like a weaker, younger brother of the older theistic God, and his alleged pantheism looking very much like a revamped version of polytheism. (Chapter 4 will explore the notions of the finite God and pluralistic pantheism in considerably more depth.)

Nonetheless, the general contours of James's model of the interaction between the self and the divine is enormously suggestive and appealing. Eugene Fontinell, a creative and thorough Jamesian scholar, suggests that we might best envision this interaction and indeed James's entire vision of reality, as "fields within fields within fields."[196] This field model of reality sees individual selves not as self-contained monads with an unchanging, essential core, but rather, as swirling vortices of interpenetrating, interdependent fields whose boundaries are, according to Fontinell, "open, indefinite, and continually shifting such that other fields are continually leaking in and out."[197]

From the perspective of the *Principles*, which primarily focuses on the observable components of the individual, these fields can be seen as the continually shifting elements of the empirical self: our moving, breathing, eating, excreting body in continuous interaction with the surrounding environment; our ever-changing emotional bond to our possessions, friends and family; the different degrees of social approval and rejection superimposed and churning within us as we play the numerous roles thrust upon us by our social circumstances; as well as the slowly shifting background of our memories, hopes, dreams, and cultural assumptions, the surging tides of our emotions, and the sharp influx of unexpected inspirations or volitional decisions.[198]

The *Varieties* depicts a world in which these fields within fields not only take the form of our ongoing stream of consciousness, but are themselves surrounded by another whirling miasma of interpenetrating fields: the subliminal self, that bubbling cauldron of intuitions, passions, delusions, fantasies, paranormal cognitions, and mystical ecstasies that from time to time spills over into our consciousness, and yet which, in many ways, appears to have a dynamic life of its own above, or below, our conscious awareness.

Finally, a still further extension of this field vision of reality is briefly touched upon in the *Varieties*, and then dealt with more fully in *A Pluralistic Universe* with James's qualified acceptance of the compounding of consciousness. Here we find a hierarchy of different interpenetrating fields of awareness: not only the collective fields of our conscious and subliminal selves, but also the earth-soul, the solar-soul, the galaxy-soul, and so on—a veritable pantheon of cosmic consciousnesses that are not ontologically separate divine beings, but rather, are our very own deeper and wider selves.

Ignoring for the moment the problems inherent in James's conception of the finite God, it would seem that Fontinell is essentially correct when he claims that this field model of the self and reality provides a coherent, persuasive vision of a world in which, although "all fields are 'incomplete' and continuous with others, they are not so continuous that reality is reduced to an undifferentiated monistic flux"; a vision of reality that provides "ground for the recognition of individuals while avoiding any atomistic individualism or isolating egoism."[199] This field model of reality has enormous metaphysical and ethical advantages, in that it posits a self that is connected with the divine, with the selves of others, and with nature, without allowing that self to be swallowed up into an unchanging, all-pervasive Oneness. In this vision of the self and of reality, the individual is seen as deeply connected to the divine and yet also able to maintain a very real degree of autonomy. In similar fashion, the divine is understood to be neither purely other nor purely the same as the self. The divine is seen as intimately united with humanity and nature, but not so closely united as to dissolve operative, if not ontological, distinctions between humanity and the spiritual world.

Unlike the purely logical justifications of the Absolute asserted by neo-Hegelian philosophers, and unlike the dogmatic denial of anything beyond the senses that is insisted upon by materialism, this field understanding of reality can be seen as offering a hypothetical, yet coherent and reasonable extrapolation from the concrete experience of life itself, buttressed by the data gathered from psychical and mystical experiences.[200] If James is correct and the diversity-within-unity that appears to be present within our conscious experience of reality is also the structure of reality itself, and furthermore, if the existing accounts of mystical and psychical experiences are reasonably trustworthy, then this model would appear to offer a relatively secure starting point for extremely productive philosophical work.

Fields within Fields within Fields

Even though I recognize that it is impossible, within the confines of the present context, even to begin the detailed and careful work that is necessary to support any of the claims that I might make about this field model's alleged philosophical advantages, I believe that it is legitimate, and necessary, to indicate the valuable contributions that a revised Jamesian field model of the self and reality could make to several contemporary philosophical discussions. Therefore, bearing in mind that in the future I intend to amplify and support the following set of philosophical proposals, I ask that they be considered, for the moment at least, as intriguing suggestions that bear careful consideration.

To begin with, I propose that we modify Fontinell's field model in a nondualistic direction,[201] in order to make the claim that the overlapping, ever-changing fields of reality and the self consist of different vibratory rates of conscious energy.[202] If we do so, then a number of provocative possibilities for philosophical reformulation offer themselves to us.

First, modifying the model in a nondualistic direction opens up the possibility that the model can be aligned explicitly with James's radical empiricism, which is also a nondual metaphysical position. As noted in chapter 2, James's radical empiricism posits that the commonsense separation between mental and physical reality is a postpartum functional distinction, not an ontological chasm. From the perspective of James's radical empiricism, our mental and physical spheres of experience, which on the surface seem so heteronomous, actually emerge from a prior, nondual "pure experience" that is neither physical nor mental, but potentially both.[203]

Second, a nondual reworking of this field model of the self and reality creates numerous points of connection between James's work and several other nondual metaphysical systems (of which the Tantric metaphysical understandings, with their focus on unity-within-diversity and the vibratory nature of reality and consciousness, are perhaps the best "match").

Third, using an energetic metaphor for consciousness underscores James's claim that consciousness is not static, empty, unchanging, and devoid of contents, but rather, that it is a dynamic, rich, mutable flux (a notion that, once again, aligns quite nicely with Tantra's own emphasis on the creative and fluid nature of consciousness).

Fourth, because this nondual field model of the self and reality posits that the mind, body, and spirit are not heteronomous substances, but rather, are mutually interacting and interdependent fields of energetic awareness, then the mind/body interaction itself is much easier to account for and justify, than if reality is understood to consist of a mysterious fusion of opposing mental and physical substances.

Finally, a field model of the self and reality in which everything and everyone is understood to possess individual integrity, and yet which also sees all of life as intimately connected and interdependent, offers a persuasive and valuable framework for cultivating a reverent respect for nature and for each other.[204]

This neo-Jamesian field model of the self and reality also has important implications for the philosophy of mysticism. To begin with, it often appears as if each of the reigning theological paradigms (monism, theism, and polytheism) has difficulty accounting for a particular range of mystical experiences.[205] For instance, any theism that posits a God who is totally Other than humanity often has to contort itself into numerous uncomfortable and awkward theological positions in order to accommodate mystical experiences of complete identity with the divine. (Christian devotional mystics, for instance, frequently extol their union with God, while simultaneously insisting that God and the soul are completely different substances. This claim is perhaps legitimate, but most Christian mystics rarely address the philosophical issue of how two heteronomous substances can interact at all, preferring instead to rely upon evocative metaphors—for instance, the image of the iron bar thrust into the fire, which takes on the qualities of fire, while remaining different than the fire itself.) Similarly, any polytheistic position that considers the gods or spirits or ancestors to be ontologically separate beings from humanity would appear to have the same kind of problems accounting for unitive mystical experiences as a theistic stance that insists on the complete Otherness of the divine. (It is rare to see shamans philosophically address, for instance, how their souls are both united with, yet distinct from, their totem or power animal during shamanic out-of-body journeys). On the other hand, any monistic worldview that denies the reality of diversity and of the individual often has to resort to a type of metaphysical sleight-of-hand to account for why the mystical experience of unity is not our universal and perpetual experience. (Advaita Vedānta's reliance on the concept of *māyā* seems particularly dubious in this regard, in that *māyā*, as the illusory source of separation from Brahman, is itself seen to be both real, since it projects the changing world of appearances, and unreal, since it does not exist separate from Brahman.)[206]

A field model of reality, however, could conceivably accommodate both our everyday experience of alienation and separation as well as mystical experiences of oneness with the divine. If reality indeed is a network of overlapping, shifting vortices of energy and

Fields within Fields within Fields

awareness vibrating at different rates, then we could easily picture our normal awareness of separation from the divine as an identification with those fields that vibrate within a rather narrow portion of the entire spectrum of energy. These fields might include especially dominant and taken-for-granted cultural assumptions, such as "I am a physical body"; "I am completely separate from other human beings and from the world around me"; and "reality is nothing more than matter in different combinations." These fields might also consist of the individual, traumatic events that every person endures in the process of maturation that tend to manifest as defensive and painfully contracted internalizations, such as "I am unloved and unlovable"; "The world is an untrustworthy place"; and "I am weak and alone." Mystical experiences of oneness with the divine, however, could be pictured as moments when, for a variety of reasons, our self-identification suddenly opens up to a broader spectrum of the fields of energy and awareness always present and operative within us, thereby catalyzing an experience of joy, freedom, expanded vision, and fulfillment.

These unitive mystical experiences (as well as the perhaps more common "visionary" experiences) would naturally vary from person to person, and from moment to moment, because within a field model of reality, nothing is static, including the deeper, broader fields of our being that constitute the different dimensions of spiritual reality. Therefore, each mystical experience would take on a unique, culturally and psychologically appropriate shape, since it would be formed by the interaction of the ever-changing fields that create our quotidian awareness with the ever-changing fields that create the deeper levels of our being. The differences from one mystical experience to the next could therefore be understood as coming from both "directions": either these differences would emerge because different "strata" of the deeper fields of our being were contacted, or because there were alternations in the fields that constitute our individual sense of ourselves, or more likely, because both of these alternations took place simultaneously. From this perspective, mystical experiences could be understood as catalyzed by a variety of interrelated causes: the disciplined, steady transformations in our ego-sense that are nurtured by an immersion in various spiritual practices, or by the violent, sudden alternations of our everyday awareness that lead to a collapse of ego boundaries and the individual will, or by the spectacular "subterranean" initiatives of the deeper strata of our being that are experienced as unforgettable, wondrous moments of grace, compassion, and unasked-for spiritual openings.

Furthermore, even though several philosophical and theological perspectives would have difficulty coexisting with this field model of the self and reality, it could easily be aligned with a broad range of other spiritual traditions. Although a field model would conflict with any theistic claim that the divine is totally Other than humanity, or with different varieties of naturalism, or with certain versions of monism in which the reality of the individual is completely denied, there is still room under its extremely flexible roof for a multitude of mystical and visionary experiences: becoming lost in the nondualistic flashes of satori, perceiving the radiant manifestations of Christian and Islamic angels, experiencing the gracious presence of the celestial bodhisattvas of Mahāyāna Buddhism, hearing the sacred words of the spirits and ancestors of tribal peoples, or having the beneficent visitation of the Taoist and Hindu gods. Each of these spiritual experiences would have a legitimate and understandable place within a field model, as long as the levels of reality apprehended within these experiences were not understood to be completely ontologically distinct from human consciousness.

As Fontinell points out, a field model of the self and reality is eminently congenial with a perspective that emphasizes the worth of a plurality of religious traditions:

> The divine life, understood as the widest field, enriches and is enriched by the variety of fields with which it is related. Thus, the plurality of religions may not be a necessary evil to be endured until the one true religion is formed; rather this plurality may be the necessary and only means by which the richness of the divine life can be lived and communicated.[207]

A field model of the self and reality could actually go further and say that while important, practical, and fascinating differences can be observed from one religious tradition to the next, from one religious person to the next, and from one religious experience to the next, these traditions, people, and experiences are not hermetically sealed off from one another, but rather, overlap and interact with one another. From this perspective, personal and cultural identity would not be understood as any sort of static, indivisible essence, but rather, it would be seen as a relatively stable, yet complex, cluster of dynamically interrelated experiences that is open to, and affected by, other clusters of experiences. If a field model of the self and reality were accepted, it would be impossible to claim that there is any such thing as a purely "Hindu" mystical experience or a purely "Jewish" mystical experience. Instead, as scholars of mystical experience, we would be forced to accomplish the much more complex task of describing and assessing the numerous vortices of influences present within each mystical experience (whether psychological, physiological, historical, cultural, linguistic, or economic), while remaining open to the very real likelihood that each mystical experience is also shaped, in ways that we may never be able to determine, by a wide variety of transcultural and transnatural influences as well. A field model of the self and reality would, therefore, be receptive to, and even encourage, a wide variety of theoretical approaches to mystical experiences, respecting and valuing the countless different ways in which we each choose to explore the unseen worlds that surround and interpenetrate our being.

❧4❧

Beyond Words, Beyond Morals: The Metaphysical and Ethical Implications of Mysticism

O, how may I ever express that secret word? O how can I
say He is not like this, and He is like that? If I say that He is
within me, the universe is ashamed. If I say that He is without
me, it is falsehood. He makes the inner and the outer worlds
to be indivisibly one. The conscious and the unconscious,
both are His footstools. He is neither manifest nor hidden,
He is neither revealed nor unrevealed. There are no words to
tell that which He is.

　　　　　　　　　　　　　　　—Kabir, *Songs of Kabir*

A Saint is beyond good and evil. But Saints are people of
highest morality and will never give a bad example.

　　　　　　　　　　　　　　—Irina Tweedie, *Chasm of Fire*

So much depends on our idea of God! Yet no idea of Him,
however pure and perfect, is adequate to express Him as He
really is. Our idea of God tells us more about ourselves than
about Him.

　　　　　　　　—Thomas Merton, *New Seeds of Contemplation*

In most contemporary philosophical discussions of mysticism, it
is automatically assumed that every mystical experience is shaped by
the underlying cultural and religious assumptions of the mystic. What
is less frequently discussed, however, is that underlying this neo-
Kantian "constructivist" perspective is a tacit metaphysical agnosti-
cism.[1] Many contemporary scholars of mysticism might, if pressed,
admit that it is logically possible to claim that mystical experiences are
constituted by something other than *just* the mystic's cultural assumptions; however, even those scholars who are philosophically open to
the possibility that mystical experiences might indeed originate from
contact with a transcultural reality often claim that this level of reality
is beyond the grasp of conceptual categories—an assumption that

appears to turn metaphysical formulations into, at best, idle guess-work. Many philosophers of mysticism have therefore tended to avoid pursuing any in-depth explorations of the metaphysical implications of mystical experiences and have, instead, preferred to direct their energies towards categorizing and examining the characteristics of mystical experiences in and of themselves.

This studious refusal to make even tentative metaphysical claims based on mystical experiences is in vivid contrast to the mystics themselves, who are often quite willing to assert that their mystical experiences form the basis for valid, trustworthy insights into the nature of reality. Numerous mystics did not shy away from making detailed and often highly provocative metaphysical claims based on their mystical experiences; and even those mystics who were less metaphysically inclined commonly claimed that they had been given direct, if ineffable, knowledge of the true nature of reality. What are we to make of these claims? Do mystical experiences tell us anything about the nature of reality? If so, what? How do we account for the numerous, and at times, seemingly contradictory, metaphysical systems presented by the mystics? Can any metaphysical system be articulated that overcomes most, if not all, of these apparent contradictions? What are the philosophical and ethical advantages and/or hazards of formulating a metaphysics based on mystical experiences?

William James, unlike many recent philosophers, was convinced that it was important to address these questions. Due at least in part to his own "mystical germ," James was a staunch believer in the reality and goodness of an unseen spiritual world and was convinced that accounts of powerful religious experiences were some of the best indicators of this transnatural reality. However, James was also philosophically and ethically dissatisfied with the monistic implications of many, if not most, mystical experiences and fought to establish the possibility of a more pluralistic interpretation of these altered states of awareness. Moreover, James was disturbed by the religious dogmatism implicit in many mystical assertions and was determined to establish clear boundaries of what the mystics could and could not legitimately tell us about the nature of reality, especially the reality of the unseen spiritual world. James argued that any claims that mystically derived metaphysical speculations were immutable and infallible revelations of the true nature of reality only served to stifle the give-and-take of philosophical discourse. Nonetheless, he was willing to defend the importance and legitimacy of metaphysical speculations about the unseen world and our relationship to it, as long as these

214

speculations were acknowledged as fallible, constantly changing, and incapable of adequately representing the complexity and richness of the unseen world.

The Authority of Mystical Consciousness

In the *Varieties*, James claims that a religious worldview, in essence, amounts to "the belief that there is an unseen order, and that our supreme good lies in harmoniously adjusting ourselves thereto."[2] It is important to note that this claim is not a neutral observation. James expends considerable energy in the *Varieties* in a dogged attempt to provide evidence that this unseen order does indeed exist and that our deepest and truest purpose is to harmonize ourselves with this spiritual level of reality. One of the most powerful weapons James uses in his rhetorical assault on the academic unwillingness to give credence to any level of reality beyond our day to day experience is his in-depth exploration of the metaphysical implications of powerful mystico-religious experiences.[3] James himself insists that these experiences are typically "ineffable," which would seem to imply that nothing metaphysically significant could emerge from a comparative analysis of their most typical phenomenological characteristics. Nonetheless, James also claims that this ineffability does *not* undermine our ability to make certain, very general metaphysical conclusions based on such an analysis. For James, it is clearly the case that the majority of mystical experiences are *not* metaphysically neutral. Instead, in James's opinion, mystical experiences on the whole support two very distinct philosophical options: monism and optimism. James is struck by the fact that, time after time, mystics from numerous religious traditions claim to have experienced states of union with some sort of "Absolute," and further, that these mystics frequently stress that underneath the world's apparent suffering and discord, there is a deeper level of harmony and perfection. James argues that the sheer numbers of these accounts is highly suggestive, easily tempting the philosopher to assume that mystical experiences, taken as a whole, support a pantheistic worldview in which the individual is understood to be, under the surface, one with the divine, and therefore, always protected, always safe, always whole and fulfilled.

However, as James is aware, a very important question remains unanswered: to what extent are these mystical experiences of oneness and perfection trustworthy and authoritative? James breaks down his own answer to this question into three parts:

1. Mystical states, when well developed, usually are, and have the right to be, absolutely authoritative over the individuals to whom they come.

2. No authority emanates from them which should make it a duty for those who stand outside of them to accept their revelations uncritically.

3. They break down the authority of the non-mystical or rationalistic consciousness, based upon the understanding and the senses alone. They show it to be only one kind of consciousness. They open out the possibility of other orders of truth, in which, so far as anything in us vitally responds to them, we may freely continue to have faith.[4]

After introducing this three-part response, James goes on to discuss each part in turn. James first argues that mystical experiences should be understood as highly specialized types of perception. While mystical states of consciousness might not be based entirely upon sensory data, if at all, nonetheless, these states of awareness are as much "direct perceptions of fact . . . as any sensations ever were for us. . . . They are face to face presentations of what seems immediately to exist."[5] As we saw in chapter 2, while James makes no attempt to claim that sense data is infallible, he does point out that, as a matter of psychological fact, most people, rightly or wrongly, typically trust the information that they receive through their senses, especially if this information enables them, on a regular basis, to deal more effectively with the surrounding environment. In much the same way, according to James, it is quite reasonable to expect that mystics would trust their own mystical perceptions, especially since these mystical experiences are "as convincing to those who have them as any direct sensible experiences can be, and they are, as a rule, much more convincing than results established by mere logic ever are."[6]

However, as James emphasizes in the second part of his response to the question of the alleged authority and trustworthiness of mystical experiences, while mystics have every right to believe their *own* perceptions, especially if those perceptions give meaning and purpose to their lives, they have absolutely no right to foist these perceptions, or more specifically, the worldview that these perceptions seem to authenticate, upon those individuals who have not had similar experiences. James stresses that mystical states of awareness offer only metaphysical possibilities, not certainties, to those who are not mystics themselves. James is an ardent opponent of religious intolerance, and he is vividly aware that history repeatedly demonstrates that there is a very real danger that the absolute certainty engendered by mystical experiences can, in the wrong setting, become the basis for religious fanaticism, and as such, can provide a pious sanction for religious hatred, persecution, and violence.[7]

James, therefore, is no friend of mystical univocity. He rather mischievously points out that his earlier claim that mystical states of awareness speak with "the same recurring note . . . perpetually telling of the unity of man with God" was perhaps somewhat premature.[8] As he notes, it is simply not true that all mystics are inevitably pantheistic in their outlook. For instance, most Christian mystics were not pantheists, and even in India, the source of several important mystically based monistic philosophical systems, many influential mystics were staunch philosophical dualists. Thus, James stresses that the generic mystical feeling "of enlargement, union, and emancipation," has "no specific intellectual content of its own."[9] This metaphysical neutrality, in James's view, permits mystical experiences to form "matrimonial alliances with material furnished by the most diverse philosophies and theologies."[10] According to James, it is illegitimate to attempt to use the "prestige" of mystical experience to justify any set of metaphysical beliefs, "such as . . . in absolute idealism, or in the absolute monistic identity, or in the absolute goodness, of the world," although James does admit that the mystical experience of enlargement, union, and emancipation does indeed seem to be "relatively in favor of all these things—it passes out of common human consciousness in the direction in which they lie."[11]

Granting for the moment the rather controversial assertion that most mystical experiences can be said to manifest, to some degree, the characteristics of "enlargement, union, and emancipation," what are we to make of James's concurrent claim that these generic mystical feelings have no "specific intellectual content"? Are we to understand that James is assuming that this sense of "enlargement, union and emancipation" is a type of "knowledge-by-acquaintance," and is, therefore, a directly perceived, but inarticulate, component of mystical experiences which is analytically distinct from the discursive, linguistically structured "knowledge-about" aspects of mystical experiences? This way of reading James is an interpretative possibility; but, on closer inspection, it becomes clear that James actually is implying that this sense of "enlargement, union and emancipation" is *some* sort of generic, "feeling-based" substratum of every mystical experience, a type of affective essence that is completely devoid of any intellectual components.

Unfortunately, this implied split between the affective and intellectual components in mystical experiences is extremely difficult to reconcile with James's previous, and more subtle, understanding that every instance of "knowledge-by-acquaintance" is always intertwined,

217

to some extent, with elements of "knowledge-about."[12] Even if these nebulous, but powerfully sensed, feelings of enlargement, union, and emancipation actually do come to the mystic already partially structured, already carrying with them innate qualities of expansion, fusion, and liberation prior to any contact with the mystic's network of tacit conceptual assumptions, these moments of "knowledge-by-acquaintance" will be inextricably fused with elements of "knowledge-about," when they become part of the total gestalt of the mystical experience.

Furthermore, if the "knowledge-by-acquaintance" components of every mystical experience actually do manifest themselves in ways that are best described as "enlargement," "union," and "emancipation," then it is not helpful or accurate to claim that they are metaphysically neutral. While James is correct to point out that the powerful religious experiences that occur in different faiths "corroborate incompatible theological doctrines," it is philosophically sloppy to claim that these mystical experiences therefore "neutralize one another and leave no fixed result."[13] Simply because mystical experiences are used to justify contradictory theological positions does not automatically cancel out the truth of these theological positions. Instead, one theological or metaphysical system may be more accurate than another, or alternately, it may be possible to formulate a wider, more inclusive theometaphysical viewpoint that can reconcile these numerous doctrinal differences.

In addition, as James himself recognizes, mystical states of awareness, at the very least, are not supportive of certain types of metaphysical positions, most notably materialism or naturalism. While accounts of mystical experiences do not conclusively prove the existence of nonmaterial levels of existence, they do at least undermine the taken-for-granted reductionism of naturalistic worldviews, in which "ideals appear as inert by-products of physiology," and in which "what is higher is explained by what is lower and treated forever as a case of 'nothing but.' "[14] As James stresses in the elaboration of his third point regarding the authority and trustworthiness of mystical experiences, "the existence of mystical states absolutely overthrows the pretension of non-mystical states to be the sole and ultimate dictators of what we may believe."[15]

As an ardent opponent of any form of dogmatic close-mindedness, James is especially perturbed when scientists and philosophers, who should exemplify a nonprejudiced examination of empirical data, refuse to acknowledge the existence of any information that happens to go against the prevailing naturalistic paradigm. In the essay "Is Life Worth

Living?" James points out that "our science is a drop, our ignorance a sea. Whatever else be certain, this at least is certain—that the world of our present natural knowledge *is* enveloped in a larger world of *some* sort of whose residual properties we at present can frame no positive idea."[16] While we certainly do not need to "define in detail [this] invisible world, and . . . anathematize and excommunicate those whose trust is different,"[17] at the same time, it is important to acknowledge that "the counting in of that wider world of meanings, and the serious dealing with it, might, in spite of all the perplexity, be indispensable stages in our approach to the final fullness of the truth."[18]

For James, therefore, while mystical experiences do not conclusively prove the existence of these levels of reality beyond the senses, they at least offer reasonable hypotheses. He notes:

> It must always remain an open question whether mystical states may not possibly be . . . windows through which the mind looks out upon a more extensive and inclusive world. The difference of the views seen from the different mystical windows need not prevent us from entertaining this supposition. The wider world would in that case prove to have a mixed constitution like that of this world, that is all. It would have its celestial and its infernal regions, its tempting and its saving moments, its valid experiences and its counterfeit ones, just as our world has them; but it would be a wider world all the same.[19]

The Transformative Power of Religious Beliefs

According to James, the indispensable bedrock of religious faith is belief in the existence of a wider, unseen world that is integrally connected with, but distinguishable from, the world that we ordinarily experience. James argues that most of the doctrinal assertions affiliated with different religious traditions are optional, even if they are aesthetically and emotionally important. However, James insists that, in order for an individual to be considered genuinely "religious" (as opposed to "moral"), he or she would have to affirm, at bare minimum, "that the so-called order of nature, which constitutes this world's experience, is only one portion of the total universe, and that there stretches beyond this visible world an unseen world of which we now know nothing positive, but in its relation to which the true significance of our present mundane life consists."[20] James argues that a religious person does not need to possess a detailed knowledge of

219

this unseen world, but he or she does need to possess, at the very least, "the bare assurance that this natural order is not ultimate but a mere sign or vision, the external staging of a many-storied universe, in which spiritual forces have the last word and are eternal."[21]

According to James, this assurance that the unseen world is real and beneficent (an assurance which is often catalyzed by powerful religious experiences) may be the only difference between "the wild-eyed look at life—the suicidal mood" and a radiant, vital conviction that life is worth living.[22] Having himself emerged out of a period of deep depression by virtue of, in part at least, a profound philosophical conversion, James is convinced that a person's faith-stance has enormous repercussions on the way in which he or she grapples with suffering. He argues that a bare-bones religious faith, if nothing else, provides a psychologically powerful antidote against the debilitating effects of nihilism and skepticism, and moreover, can nurture a courageous willingness to deal effectively with life's hardships.

In James's opinion, if we believe that our lives "lie soaking in a spiritual atmosphere, a dimension of being that we at present have no organ for apprehending," then we can quite reasonably assume that our struggles in this world are somehow "bearing fruit somewhere in an unseen spiritual world," even if we have no indubitable proof that this is indeed the case.[23] James illustrates the connection between this faith in the reality of the unseen world and an increased ability to cope effectively with suffering with an example guaranteed to infuriate modern-day animal rights activists (an example which, ironically, ultimately stems from James's own empathy for the sufferings of animals). James notes that a dog, shrieking from the agony that it endures while being vivisected, can, understandably, give no meaning to the pain that it feels. However, if the dog could somehow step outside of its own limited experience of the world and come to understand the possible humanitarian benefits brought about as a result of its suffering, then its pain, if not diminished, would at least be ennobled, to the point that, if it were capable of doing so, the heroic and altruistic aspects of the dog's being might voluntarily acquiesce to this redemptive suffering.

James ruefully points out that there is a good likelihood that humanity is in a somewhat similar position to that of the dog. Just as the dog can physically see the world in which we live—a world that is unseen by the dog, since its deeper meanings and inner workings are not within the range of the dog's understanding—in the same way, "in human life, although we only see our world, and [the dog's] within it, yet encompassing both these worlds a still wider world may

be there, as unseen by us as our world is by [the dog]."[24] The beliefs
that we hold about this unseen world are in themselves crucial components of the total gestalt of our everyday experience. Like the dog,
we cannot avoid suffering; yet unlike the dog, we can choose how we
will respond to, and even to a degree experience, our present sufferings. If we choose to have faith that our sufferings are part of an
ultimately positive, if at present unseen, purpose, then the quality of
our suffering shifts. We are no longer strapped onto a table of forced,
inevitable, and senseless pain. Instead, we have chosen to respond to
our suffering from a position of broader understanding, a position
that itself catalyzes new abilities, enabling us to unlock "innumerable
powers, which, but for the [new perspective], would never have come
into play."[25]

According to James, our beliefs, experiences, and actions are always intimately intertwined. James is famous (infamous?) for his claim
that there are innumerable situations in our life "where faith in a fact
can help create the fact."[26] While James never goes so far as to claim
that our personal beliefs have an effect upon every aspect of our lives
(since, as he points out, "throughout the breadth of physical nature
facts are what they are quite independently of us"), he nonetheless
insists that there are numerous situations in which our personal faith
in ourselves, or in others, has a crucial impact on how we experience
and respond to life.[27] To illustrate the point James uses the analogy of
a mountain climber. In the analogy, the mountain climber is trapped
on a ledge from which he can escape only with a great leap. James
argues that this mountain climber is more likely to succeed if he has
faith in his ability to jump over the chasm to safety, than if he mis-
trusts his ability. Similarly, in our personal relationships, James would
say that we increase the chances of being treated in a loving manner,
if we trust that others will indeed treat us lovingly. Along the same
lines, James suggests it is also quite likely that, if we have faith in the
existence and goodness of the unseen world, this faith might, in and
of itself, transform the unseen world from an abstract possibility into
a living reality. Our receptivity to the possibility that a transnatural
reality might be actively and lovingly working within us, may be all
that is necessary for us to notice the presence of that which was previously too amorphous to attract our attention. Indeed, as James suggests, it is quite possible that "the very existence of an invisible world
may . in part depend on the personal response which any one of us
make to the religious appeal."[28]

According to James, vivid and compelling experiences of this
unseen world do not happen in a vacuum. From a Jamesian perspective,

221

our beliefs, experiences, and actions are simply three moments in a complex, interactive process: our faith is rooted in religious experiences, but our religious experiences are themselves prompted and partially molded by our faith. Our actions, in turn, emerge out of this rich inter-relationship between faith and experience, and then serve to set the stage for further experiences and a deeper faith. Up to a point, James agrees with contemporary constructivists (i.e., with those philosophers who claim that mystical experiences are "constructed" by the prior beliefs of the mystic): we do help to create our mystical experiences, not only by our prior religious understandings, but also by the ways in which we chose to structure our lives in light of these historically formed and culturally mediated patterns of beliefs.

If James is correct and our beliefs and life-choices not only mold the "raw material" of our mystical experiences into culturally specific forms, but also provide a religiously charged context out of which mystical experiences could potentially emerge, then there is a tantalizing, but typically unmentioned corollary to any and all "constructivist" philosophical perspectives on mystical experience: choosing to believe in the existence and beneficence of an unseen world, and acting upon that belief, will enormously increase the chances that we will actually experience this spiritual dimension of reality. Theorists such as Wayne Proudfoot have been eager to utilize the malleability of human consciousness to suggest that powerful religious experiences are perhaps nothing but misguided attributions of prior religious patterns of belief onto amorphous physiological sensations. However, these constructivist philosophers overlook an alternative possibility: if, as James believes, a transnatural dimension of reality actually does exist that is simultaneously objective enough that it is not simply the product of an individual's consciousness, yet which is subjective enough that it must always be experienced in and through that individual's consciousness, then nurturing an active faith in this spiritual world via immersion in traditional religious texts, meditative disciplines, ritual praxis, and so forth, could be understood as a legitimate and important way of structuring one's consciousness in order to increase the likelihood of an authentic contact with this unseen world. In addition, if, as numerous religious traditions claim, this spiritual dimension of reality is a source of vast love, wisdom, and power and if contact with this level of existence actually is the *telos* of human life, then having faith in its existence would not be evidence of the delusional suggestibility of human consciousness, but would, instead, be an essential component of a successful, joyous, and fulfilled life.[29]

Beyond Words, Beyond Morals

Even if, as James emphasizes in the *Varieties*, there are numerous cases of spontaneous religious experiences that do not appear to be directly linked to the individual's prior religious beliefs, the structure of that individual's *future* religious experiences, if any, would be dramatically affected by the subsequent beliefs that he or she chooses to adopt. For instance, picture a woman with no overt religious background who is walking along a beach and suddenly has a joyous and prolonged sense of her oneness with the beauty that surrounds her. In light of this dramatic experience, it is quite possible that this woman would begin to search for a belief-system that could put this unexplained occurrence into a meaningful context. From a Jamesian perspective, the subsequent life choices that this woman makes will have tremendous repercussions on what types of mystical experiences, if any, that she will have in the future. For instance, joining a charismatic Christian church is more likely to provide a context in which certain religious experiences, such as feeling God's love or having visions of Jesus, are more likely to happen than the *satori* experiences that one would expect if she chose to spend a prolonged period of time in a Zen monastery; *both* of these options, however, would be far more likely to nurture further religious experiences than if she chose, for example, to immerse herself in the frequently cynical and secular environment of a typical university graduate program.

However, while these various contexts of belief and practice would most certainly affect the parameters of this woman's future mystical experiences (if any), it is equally important to point out that, from a Jamesian perspective, the types of mystical experiences that this woman might undergo would not *necessarily* be limited to the expectations encoded within these communities. From a Jamesian point of view, she could conceivably have a "*satori*-like" experience within a charismatic Christian context, just as she could conceivably have a sense of divine love within a Zen monastery. However, there is a strong likelihood that these more unorthodox mystical experiences would typically occur far less frequently than the types of mystical experiences one would normally expect in such settings, primarily because these experiences would have little or no support within their given communities of interpretation and praxis. Furthermore, if these experiences *did* repeatedly occur, then it is quite likely that they would be intensely disturbing. It is even possible, from a Jamesian perspective, that if these unsettling experiences were persistent enough, they could catapult the woman outside of her initial community and initiate a further search for a setting that would offer her a system of beliefs and practices that *could* help her make sense of these puzzling

223

and stubbornly insistent experiences. This new community would potentially not only serve to validate her previous experiences, but it would also serve to nurture and catalyze new experiences—experiences which would, in turn, be filtered through a new interpretative grid, thereby further validating the correctness of her choice and encouraging the faithful practice of the religious activities appropriate to that community.

The Science of Religions

From a Jamesian point of view, there is no escaping this swirling vortex of interactions that take place between experiences, beliefs, and actions, especially within a religious context. However, the complex and interactive nature of our religious life does not necessarily imply that profound mystical experiences tell us absolutely nothing about the nature of reality. Even if the information we receive from mystical experiences is often ambiguous and multivalent, it does not mean that this information is completely neutral. Instead, as James points out, mystical experiences "point in directions to which the religious sentiments even of non-mystical men incline. They tell of the supremacy of the ideal, of vastness, of union, of safety, and of rest. They offer us *hypotheses*, hypotheses which we may voluntarily ignore, but which as thinkers we cannot possibly upset."[30] Mystical experiences give us a range of data that is relatively circumscribed, a body of information that points in specific directions, even if the metaphysical possibilities to be found in those directions are themselves quite numerous. For James, mystical experiences are facts. Not univocal, self-evident facts, not facts that pronounce unimpeachable truths, but still, facts, facts that support some hypotheses better than others, facts that nudge and cajole.

As an empiricist, James wants to follow these facts wherever they lead. James is suspicious of both the logical deductions of rationalistic philosophy and the unquestioned dogmas of traditional theology. He argues that a more dependable source of evidence for the existence of a spiritual universe is his "thicker and more radical empiricism,"[31] which "would depend for its original material on facts of personal experience . . . [and] would never get away from concrete life, or work in a conceptual vacuum."[32] He argues that if empiricism could be expanded to include the information given in accounts of religious experiences and psychical phenomena, then philosophy would be given an "additional set of facts to use,"[33] a cluster of data which, when sifted through and assessed, could enable a "philosophy of immediate

Beyond Words, Beyond Morals

experience . . . using all the analogies and data within reach, to build up the most probable approximate idea of what the divine consciousness concretely may be like."[34]

James realizes that "superstitions and wild-growing over-beliefs" could easily arise if the concepts of "higher consciousnesses" and "fechnerian earth-souls" ever became acceptable, and still more, "if science ever puts her approving stamp" on psychical research; nonetheless, in James's opinion, this jungle of flourishing and competing theological elaborations and speculations is infinitely preferable to the "thin inferior abstractions" of scholastic theology or monistic idealism, as well as the un-self-critical materialism of many anthropological, psychological, and sociological analyses of religious life.[35] James is convinced that it is possible to study human religious life in a way that does justice to its complexity and particularity, without denying either the philosophical urgency of a subsequent normative evaluation of the world's religious options or the necessity to concurrently construct a theo-metaphysical framework that would ideally adjudicate and reconcile the world's numerous and often opposing religious beliefs and practices. James designates this complex, multileveled methodological alternative as the "science of religions."[36]

As James envisions it, the science of religions is not just an academic exercise, it is not simply gathering knowledge for the sake of knowledge. He argues that the science of religions, as an inductive, comparative, and normative approach to religious beliefs and practices, should ideally not *just* give descriptive accounts of the rituals and worldview of different religious traditions. Instead, while it must begin with this sort of empirically based "thick description," it must then go on to attempt the more arduous and delicate task of normatively assessing the relative merits of different religious positions as well as attempting the equally difficult work of a constructive theology. While a Jamesian perspective would certainly support the nuanced descriptive work currently undertaken by scholars within the field of the History of Religions, nonetheless, inherent in a Jamesian methodological understanding is the insistence that if the world's rich variety of religious traditions is ever going to cease being regarded as simply items of "objective" study and become, instead, potentially invaluable resources for personal and cultural transformation, then the science of religions has to be willing to take the risk of losing a degree of academic purity and objectivity; the science of religions has to be willing to let its own Eurocentric and secular metaphysical and psychological assumptions be challenged and confronted by the worldviews and practices of other cultures and other times.[37]

James emphasizes that if the study of religions is ever to become a vital cultural resource, and not simply the machinations of ivory-tower academics, it is crucial that it address the psychotherapeutic task of fending off the depression and despair caused by nihilism as well as the cultural need to combat the intolerance and hatred caused by bigotry and religious dogmatism. James thinks that the science of religions can confront the debilitating effects of nihilism by offering qualified support for the reality of a wider, beneficent spiritual level of existence and by establishing a reasonably satisfactory sketch of the most important features of this unseen world. To accomplish these tasks, James claims that the science of religions must take the risk of seeming imperialistic and must judiciously proceed to eliminate "doctrines that are now known to be scientifically absurd or incongruous" as well as those beliefs and practices that are simply "local and accidental," in order to ultimately appropriate from these differing traditions "a residuum of conceptions" that it can then use as testable hypotheses.[38] Having carefully examined these various hypotheses, the science of religions can then "perhaps become the champion of one which she picks out as being the most closely verified or verifiable,"[39] and offer this "gem from clay"[40] as a workable outline of a theological metaphysics that is congruent with the conclusions of natural science and psychology—an outline which after further refinement via the jostling give and take of philosophical discourse might even "offer mediation between different believers, and help to bring about consensus of opinion."[41]

The careful practitioner of the science of religions, in James's eyes, is therefore someone who immerses him- or herself in the rich, tumultuous, and often confusing accounts of differing religious experiences, doctrines, and practices, and then sifts through these accounts with attentive and respectful humility in order to construct a tentative, but reasonable, metaphysical model that could act as an effective resource for those individuals struggling to integrate varying perspectives into a single coherent worldview—a task that, arguably, could be especially important in the contemporary Western cultural landscape in which an individual is buffeted by an often overwhelming variety of "live" religious options.

James is quite clear that the science of religions should never claim that its decisions are authoritative: the science of religions should not become a new, only slightly more respectable, source of dogmatism and intolerance. In fact, James insists that the science of religions is inevitably fallible: it can never conclusively determine the truth of varying religious hypotheses. According to James, metaphysical work only becomes totalitarian if it forgets that truth is always ongoing, partial, and mutable. Further, even if the science of religions *could* somehow construct a synthetic metaphysical model that addressed and overcame the doctrinal differences inherent in the multitude of metaphysical perspectives offered by the world's religious and philosophical traditions, then there would still be a human need for a rich variety of religious systems. As James points out:

> If an Emerson were forced to be a Wesley . . . the total human consciousness of the divine would suffer. The divine can mean no single quality, it must mean a group of qualities, by being champions of which in alternation, different men may all find worthy missions. . . . We must frankly recognize the fact that we live in partial systems, and that parts are not interchangeable in the spiritual life.[42]

As James presents it, in order to successfully fulfill its function, the science of religions would need to be perpetually alert to two dangers: the danger of becoming so overtly supportive of religious ideas that it would lose any semblance of objectivity, and conversely, the danger of becoming subtly infected by the antipathy of science in general towards religious conceptions, to the extent that those within the science of religions could conceivably end up denying the validity or value of any aspect of religious life. In addition, James emphasizes that those practicing the science of religions would constantly need to remind themselves that "knowledge about a thing is not the thing itself."[43] While, ideally, the science of religions could offer a philosophically justifiable starting place for further religious reflection and practice, it should not pretend to be a substitute for the transformative power of genuine religious experiences. For James, just "as every science confesses that the subtlety of nature flies beyond it, and that its formulas are but approximations," the science of religions as well should continually reaffirm its own fallibility and limitations.[44]

According to James, "philosophy lives in words, but truth and facts well up into our lives in ways that exceed verbal formulation. There is in the living act of perception always something that glimmers and twinkles and will not be caught, and for which reflection comes too late."[45] He goes on to add that the philosophically informed practitioner of the science of religions must, of course, use concepts, but "he secretly knows the hollowness and irrelevancy" of each and every philosophical formulation, all of which, no matter how subtle or profound, lack "the depth, the motion, the vitality" of personal experience.[46] James repeatedly underscores the assertion that our full-

227

bodied, multitextured, concrete experiences resist any and all philosophical attempts to encapsulate and codify them with words; they flow effortlessly around the webs of concepts set out to snare them; they mock the hollow claims made by philosophers and theologians who pretend that personal experiences are ultimately less important than grammatical rules, logical presuppositions, and conceptual systems. For James, the science of religions, at its best, is fueled by an engagement with an irreducible facticity—it is driven by an encounter with the basic givenness at the core of every experience. Although James recognizes that tacit belief structures are interwoven with each and every experience, he nonetheless stresses that there is something in the heart of every experience that comes to us unbidden, something that initiates changes in our assumptions and actions, something that refuses to be coerced. In *religious* experiences that "something" is that which allows itself to be clothed in the metaphysical and theological garb of different cultures, yet still manages to resist the imposition of arbitrary philosophical and doctrinal constructs upon itself; that "something" is that which prompts philosophical and theological discourse, even while it eludes the grasp of the most subtle philosophical and theological formulations.

James's emphasis on the limitations inherent in a philosophically grounded science of religions does not mean that he believes that philosophy is unimportant to the empirical study of religions. According to James, a nuanced philosophical perspective is a crucial component of any investigation of religious experiences:

> We are thinking beings, and we cannot exclude the intellect from participating in any of our functions. Even in soliloquizing with ourselves, we construe our feelings intellectually. Both our personal ideals and our religious and mystical experiences must be interpreted congruously with the kind of scenery which our thinking mind inhabits. The philosophical climate of our time inevitably forces its clothing on us. Moreover, we must exchange our feelings with one another, and in doing so we have to speak, and to use general and abstract verbal formulas. Conceptions and constructions are thus a necessary part of our religion; and as moderator amid the clash of hypotheses, and mediator among the criticisms of one man's constructions by another, philosophy will always have much to do.[47]

In addition to its contributions to the study of religions, James argues that philosophy, taken as a whole, can serve a number of other important functions as well. For instance, the study of philosophy ideally should instill within us the "habit of always seeing an alternative, of not taking the usual for granted, of making conventionalities fluid again, of imagining foreign states of mind."[48] Philosophy, at its best, "rouses us from our native 'dogmatic slumber' and breaks up our caked prejudices,"[49] it calls into question our habitual ways of envisioning ourselves and our world, it encourages a constant reexamination of those preconceptions that distort our vision and keep us locked into destructive patterns of interaction. In addition, James observes that philosophy has the remarkable ability to turn its critical spotlight upon itself. It can come to question its own assumptions, it can become aware of its own hypothetical nature, it can remind itself that every conclusion it makes is tentative and that no theory ever comes "armed with a warrant."[50]

But as James also points out, philosophical work does not have to be *exclusively* critical. While these deconstructive, analytical, and critical tasks are a crucial component of philosophical work, James argues that they need to be complemented and enriched with a more constructive, synthetic, and creative response to life. Philosophy, in James's opinion, must "always be something of an art as well as of a science"; it is a personally shaped, passionately felt vision that, ideally, draws upon the widest possible variety of empirical and intellectual data in order to produce alternate sketches of the world; it is a way in which to paint "our more or less plausible pictures" of our world and our place within it in order to energize an active and engaged response to that world.[51] For James, philosophy at its best, can make a difference: it can create a vivid and compelling sense of human potential; it can make a persuasive case that there is more to existence than might be immediately apparent; it can convince those suffering from a loss of meaning and purpose that there is an underlying, intimate, powerful, loving connection between each individual and the unseen world; it can prompt human beings to re-vision, to re-enchant the world, themselves, other humans, and nature; and it can help to rough out workable, flexible, open-ended worldviews that can serve to orient each individual to the ongoing process of spiritual and personal exploration.

From a Jamesian perspective, the "metaphysical myths"[52] that arise out of the philosopher's creative response to his or her feeling for life as a whole are neither reflections of stable, immutable foundations, nor are they arbitrary, bodiless, rhetorical wordplays emerging out of a web of linguistic and social patterns. Instead, they are best understood as artistic reenvisionings of previous philosophical and religious attempts to re-present in words those experiences and sensations that impel and precede language, they are centers of momentary stability where we can catch our breath before plunging once again into the maelstrom of creative, yet fluidly structured, possibility. While these hypothetical ontologies will always come shaped by the aesthetic, temperamental, and ethical sensibilities of the philosopher, they are not simply fanciful whimsies or idle speculations with little or no concrete significance. Instead, these metaphysical myths have the potential to become cultural seeds, vortices of profound change. Since all experience is filtered through the interpretative grid provided by the culture's underlying assumptions, if these metaphysical myths succeed in becoming integrated into the philosopher's culture, they can have a subtle, yet revolutionary, effect on the ways in which individuals within that culture interpret, and thus experience, events in their lives.[53]

Philosophers, therefore, have an implicit ethical responsibility: not only must they unearth and critique the harmful and restrictive prejudices that limit and distort the ways in which we understand ourselves and the world around us, but they must also articulate and promote that metaphysical vision that they believe is best able to shape and support the sort of world in which they would ultimately prefer to live. Seen in this way, philosophical work is ideally a spiraling alternation between prophetic challenges and poetic creativity, it is an on-going dialectic in which we arduously attempt to analyze and deconstruct the complacent and comfortable underlying assumptions of our culture, only to then, playfully, yet carefully, construct tentative metaphysical myths that can not only embody the widest possible range of experiences (both quotidian and mystical), but that can also act as potent catalysts for personal and social change. Seen in this way, the details of each theo-metaphysical formulation are far less crucial than philosophy's ability to catalyze and encourage a renewed openness to continuing personal and communal transformation.

What Sort of Oneness?

One of the primary targets of the critical and analytical component of James's own philosophical work is the relationship between mysticism and monism. On the one hand, James is clear that there is a strong congruence between the accounts of powerful mystical experiences and the philosophical perspective articulated by most monistic philosophies. On the other hand, James is reluctant to conclude that mystical experiences therefore offer unambiguous support for monistic philosophical perspectives. James goes out of his way to emphasize that "the only thing that [mystico-religious experience] unequivocally testifies to is that we can experience union with *something* larger than ourselves and in that union find our greatest peace."[54] As an empiricist, James wants to maintain the evidential weight of mystical experiences, but he insists that the metaphysical conclusions that can be drawn from a careful examination of the broadest possible range of mystical experiences are, at best, extremely circumscribed and multivalent. Based on the evidence that he has available to him from his own study of powerful mystico-religious experiences, James is willing to make only two relatively firm conclusions. First, he concludes that a powerful spiritual dimension of reality does indeed appear to exist—a spiritual dimension that is experienced, from one perspective, as the deepest and truest level of our selfhood, and from another perspective, as an "objective" level of existence that is analytically distinct from our conscious personality. Second, he concludes that mystical union with this unseen world gives every indication of being a joyous, transformative, enlivening, and salvific event.

James's conclusions appear to offer a powerful endorsement of the value of a genuine spiritual life, but the metaphysical specifics of these conclusions are kept purposefully vague and open-ended. He does *not* want to endorse the conclusion that an examination of mystical experiences can give us a detailed, trustworthy map of the exact nature of this spiritual dimension of reality. He also refuses to support any claims that mystical experiences can give us specific information about the ways in which we, as individual selves, are related to this spiritual dimension of reality. James emphasizes that mystical experiences can offer an unambiguous endorsement of neither monism nor pluralism; for James, it is simply not clear from the evidence whether the unseen spiritual world is an all-pervasive Oneness that underlies all of the apparent differences of the cosmos, or alternately, whether profound mystical experiences are indicative of many higher spiritual powers, powers that are not subsumed by an absolute Oneness.

James argues that, depending upon our philosophical preferences, we can examine any range of experiences and focus either on oneness or manyness. In every cluster of experiences, there will be differences and similarities, ways in which these experiences can be said to be "One," and ways in which they can be said to be different. If we wish, James suggests, we can claim that the obvious differences contained within any range of experiences render all apparent similarities merely accidental and unimportant. However, within the same range of experiences, he adds, we can just as easily claim that any apparent differences mask a deeper, more essential sameness.[55]

James's reluctance to commit himself forcefully to either a monistic or pluralistic interpretation of mystico-religious experience is
indicative of his own philosophical ambiguity.[56] As Marcus Ford has
perceptively noted, "James is usually regarded as a pluralist. . . . However, James is not a pluralist through and through. He is attracted to
some of the implications of metaphysical monism, and at times he
himself endorses a type of metaphysical monism."[57] A close examination of James's work reveals that James is particularly intrigued with
the *religious* connotations of metaphysical monism (especially the
understanding that God and the self are intimately conjoined); such
an examination also reveals that he is at times drawn to the *epistemological* implications of monism (e.g., the nonduality between subjects
and objects that he explores in *Essays on Radical Empiricism*). Nonetheless, throughout his career, James demonstrates his reluctance to
accept the *ethical* implications of metaphysical monism (in particular,
the difficulty monism has reconciling the presence of evil within the
all-pervasive Oneness of the Absolute).

James's philosophical ambiguity is also reflected in his discussion of the interaction between mystical experiences and monistic
philosophies. For James, a monistic perspective receives its strongest
support from mystical experiences, rather than from the abstract, logical arguments used by neo-Hegelian philosophers, such as Josiah Royce
and F. H. Bradley. As James puts it, the authority of monism "draws
its strength far less from intellectual than from mystical grounds. To
interpret absolute monism worthily, be a mystic."[57] However, James's
support for the mystical foundations of monism is, at best, lukewarm.
According to James, while mystically prompted monistic insights may
be tantalizing and emotionally satisfying, they remain intellectually
feeble, since they are inspired by experiences that are too private to
carry much weight in public philosophical discourse. Furthermore, in
James's opinion, these monistically flavored mystical experiences can
actually at times undermine philosophical discourse in that philosophers who have had such experiences may tend to hide the fact that
these experiences are at the root of their monistic philosophies. This
tendency to resist stubbornly any critical appraisal of their own monistic philosophical assertions in essence puts a stranglehold on philosophical debate, since these mystically inspired philosophers refuse to
admit that "the palpable weak places in [their] intellectual reasonings
are protected from their own criticism by a mystical feeling that, logic
or no logic, absolute Oneness must somehow at any cost be true."[59]

However, as a pragmatist, James also recognizes that mystical
experiences of complete oneness with the universe quite often have

very positive psychological consequences. He argues, for instance, that mystically based monistic systems, such as the Vedānta expounded by Swami Vivekananda, provide individual practitioners with "a perfect sumptuosity of security."[60] According to James, Vedantic mystics, via a structured set of disciplines (that are often much more intellectually based than James seems to have realized) come to a direct realization that there is nothing in the world for them to fear, or hate, or envy, since they are at all times intimately united with the entire universe. James quotes with obvious relish Swami Vivekananda's rhapsodic endorsement of the numerous psychological benefits of monistic illumination:

> When man has seen himself as one with the infinite Being of the universe, when all separateness has ceased, when all men, all women, all angels, all gods, all animals, all plants, the whole universe has melted into that oneness, then all fear disappears. Whom to fear? Can I hurt myself? Can I kill myself? Can I injure myself? Do you fear yourself? Then will all sorrow disappear. What can cause me sorrow? I am the One Existence of the universe. Then all jealousies will disappear; of whom to be jealous? Of myself? Then all bad feelings disappear. Against whom will I have this bad feeling? Against myself? There is none in the universe but me.[61]

James willingly admits that there is something aesthetically pleasing about this type of monistic discourse; Vivekananda's words seem inspiring and uplifting, they seem somehow more noble and lofty than depressingly frank discussions about the world's pain, differences, and conflict. As James points out, "we all have some ear for this monistic music: it elevates and reassures. We all have at least the germ of mysticism in us. . . . [And] this mystical germ wakes up in us on hearing the monistic utterances, acknowledges their authority, and assigns to intellectual considerations a secondary place."[62]

However, as a critical philosopher, James refuses to let the alleged pragmatic and aesthetic advantages of mystically based monism deter him from a hard-nosed analysis of the intellectual advantages and disadvantages of a monistic perspective. James is willing to concede that the universe may indeed prove, in the end, to be more essentially "One" than many, but he insists that before any such an assessment can be made, it is critical that we philosophically define the exact parameters of what we mean when we claim that the universe is "One."

As James points out, there are many different sorts of oneness. For instance, simply calling the universe by a single term ("universe")

unifies it as a subject of discourse, but this limited degree of acknowledging unity is quite a bit less substantive than the oneness argued for
by monistic philosophers. However, as James goes on to note, there
are also more comprehensive types of unity. For instance, both "space"
and "time" act as unifying principles in the universe, since we can
move, without discernible breaks, from one part of space or time to
another part. We can also trace "lines of influence" from one piece of
the universe to the next through the unifying capacity of natural forces,
such as gravity and electricity, as well as through the more culturally
processes of unification, such as interlocking networks of acquaintan-
ces or the intricate patterns of connection found in political and economic systems.[63] According to James, the end-result of this rather
prosaic, yet extensive, process of unification, is that there are many
"little worlds" within the larger universe that are connected to each
other—there are many networks of influence superimposed upon one
another that, when added together, manage to create a piecemeal type
of comprehensive unity.[64] Undeniably, there is also enormous disconnection between these different systems of influence, but James stresses
that, if we look carefully enough, we will discover that "everything
that exists is influenced in *some* way by something else."[65] Therefore,
James argues that the universe has, at the very least, a "strung-along"
type of unity, a unity that James is philosophically quite willing to
accept, since it permits the universe to be both one and not one at the
same time, in contrast to the monistic vision of a "through-and-through
unity of all things at once."[66] For James, within this "reticulated
or concatenated" unity (the sort of unity postulated by radical
empiricism), "the oneness and the manyness are absolutely co-
ordinate. . . . Neither is primordial or more essential or excellent than
the other."[67]

According to James, the monistic notion of a complete and systematic unity, in which everything is known, all-at-once, by an "All-
Knower" is, at best, on the same logical level as the pluralistic
perspective adopted by James's own radical empiricism, in which
knowledge about the world is "strung along and overlapped," a perspective that views the world as a place in which "everything gets
known by some knower along with something else; but the knowers
may in the end be irreducibly many, and the greatest knower of them
all may yet not know the whole of everything."[68] However, in James's
mind, even if monism and pluralism are both equally valid metaphysical possibilities, the political implications of pluralism are decidedly preferable to those of monism. To James, monism's depiction of
an infinite, completely unified, and omniscient Consciousness smacks

234

of imperialistic absolutism, whereas pluralism's vision of the world as "a sort of republican banquet . . . where all the qualities of being respect one another's personal sacredness, yet sit at the common table of space and time,"[69] seems to possess respectably democratic and egalitarian qualities.

James is also disturbed by the dogmatic claim made by numerous neo-Hegelian monistic philosophers that the Absolute is a logical necessity of all thought; he is also appalled by the highly abstract philosophical arguments used by the neo-Hegelians to promote their cause. From James's perspective, the neo-Hegelian monists demonstrate a disturbing philosophical rigidity when they assert that "the theory of the Absolute . . . [has] to be an article of faith, affirmed dogmatically and exclusively . . . [since] the slightest suspicion of pluralism, the minutest wiggle of independence of any one of its parts from the control of the totality, would ruin it."[70] In contrast, James depicts his own radical empiricism as eminently flexible, in that it allows for a tremendous amount of unity, as long as there is theoretical space provided for "*some* separation among things, some tremor of independence . . . some real novelty or chance, however minute."[71]

Despite James's numerous reservations about monism, however, he attempts to give its arguments an unbiased presentation. In order to accomplish this task, James summarizes several of the neo-Hegelian "proofs" of monism—not, however, without several rather humorous complaints, not only about the abstract nature of these proofs, but also about the consequent abstract nature of his own summation of these proofs. (Unfortunately, and yet unavoidably, the following delineation of James's summary of Rudolph Lotzes's proof of the existence of the Absolute is also itself rather abstract.) James structures his summation of Rudolph Lotze's proof of the existence of the Absolute by using a series of rhetorical questions and logical arguments designed to show that the process of causation cannot be adequately accounted for without positing an underlying cosmic unifying principle. Essentially, James's summation takes the following shape: How can one thing (a) ever influence or act upon another thing (b), if they are indeed truly separate from each other? Does *this* "influence" somehow separate itself from *a*? If so, then this influence itself must be a third separate thing, which we can call c. The problem then is, how does this third separate thing c influence b without *this* influence becoming a fourth thing, which we can call d, and so on into infinity. We are therefore faced either with an eternal regress or we are forced to conclude that these two things (a and b) cannot, in actuality, be truly separate from each other, since they do manage to influence one another. Therefore, *a* and *b* must have belonged "together before-hand," they must have been "co-implicated already . . . as parts of a single real being, *M* [the Absolute]."[72] If we believe that *a* and *b* were never actually separate to begin with, but were linked as parts of a common substratum, *M*, then it is simple to see how *a* influences *b*: through the underlying being *M* that they both share.

For James, this alleged proof of monism is nothing more than a rhetorical chimera: "*Call* your a and b distinct, they can't interact; *call* them one, they can. For taken abstractly and without qualification the words 'distinct' and 'independent' suggest only disconnection."[73] However, James argues that simply calling a thing "distinct" or "in-dependent" does not make it so in actuality. He goes on to add that what is needed, instead, is a more careful investigation of what actu-ally occurs in the rich, multitextured, concrete process of interaction and change. To label a thing in such a way as to imply that it pos-sesses just one particular quality (for instance, "distinct from other things") and by that process of labeling, to leave out all of the numer-ous other qualities of the thing (for instance, its connections with other things) is what James calls "vicious intellectualism."[74] James asserts that the flux of life itself contains an internal, organic unity, a unity that is overlooked when we attempt to analyze our experience of life by using concepts, since concepts are inherently either one thing or another, they are never both/and. From a logical perspective, then, "disconnection" cannot also contain within it "connection," but life itself may be able to reconcile this opposition, if we only look carefully and closely enough within our own experience.

According to James, the Absolute would not be needed as a type of philosophical "glue" to unite the alleged fragmentation of the world, if we could only recognize that the world was never fragmented to begin with. James insists that the Absolute is not a logical necessity, since our concrete experience of life demonstrates time and time again that "one part of our experience may lean upon another part," which in turn implies that "experience as a whole is self-containing and leans on nothing."[75] Therefore, James concludes that, with the notable ex-ception of the mystic (who experiences monistic oneness as an "imme-diate certainty"), monism is not forced upon us as thinkers, and *"reality MAY exist in distributive form in the shape not of an all but of a set of eaches, just as it seems to."*[76]

James is willing to speculate that there might be a "total one-ness" at "the end of things rather than at their origin," in which case "the notion of the 'Absolute' would have to be replaced by that of the 'Ultimate.' "[77] However, for James, the world in its present form ap-

236

pears to be "neither a universe pure and simple nor a multiverse pure and simple."[78] James stresses that it is philosophically crucial to acknowledge the obvious fact that "each part of the world is in some ways connected, in some other ways not connected with its other parts, and the ways can be discriminated."[79] James concedes that we may eventually discover that the world is far more unified than is immediately apparent, but he insists that if we disregard "the authority which mystical insights may be conjectured eventually to possess [and] treat the problem of the One and the Many in a purely intellectual way" then it is clear that, from a pragmatic point of view, the best option is to "equally abjure absolute monism and absolute pluralism."[80]

Mystical Nondualism

Unfortunately, monism and pluralism, as seen through James's eyes, each imply a cluster of rather stereotypical assumptions. Monism for James is a dogmatic, rigid, rationalism cut off from ethics and the concrete experiences of daily life; it is a mystically tinged, abstract, academic absolutism which posits a static, omnipresent, omniscient, all-controlling Oneness that utterly transcends our ordinary level of reality. Pluralism, on the other hand (along with its champions, radical empiricism and pragmatism), is said to provide us with a flexible, open-ended, and tolerant philosophical perspective based on the widest range of concrete experiences; it is a practical, empirical, moderate metaphysics that offers support for moral decision-making by its willingness to posit a "partial community of partially independent powers" that is influenced, but not controlled, by a finite, loving God who is deeply involved with the day-to-day affairs of humanity.[81]

However, even if these characterizations of monism and pluralism are accurate, it is questionable whether monism and pluralism are the only metaphysical options available. It is quite possible to have a distinct philosophical emphasis on metaphysical oneness without adhering to the doctrines expounded by the neo-Hegelian philosophers of James's time. Assuming for the moment that James's description of neo-Hegelian monism is basically sound (a point that Royce, Bradley, and others would often hotly deny), there are, nonetheless, numerous other "nondual" philosophical systems that easily escape most, if not all, of James's critique against monism. Although James does occasionally allude to the fact that there are overtly mystical and salvific nondual perspectives that are not identical to the more academic, neo-Hegelian monisms that he typically focuses upon, his

237

tendency is to group together casually any and all positions that emphasize an underlying Oneness as "monistic." Moreover, James appears to be completely unaware of the existence of many nondual philosophical and religious options (for instance, he never refers to Mahāyāna Buddhism or Taoism); further, his knowledge of the non-Western, nondual systems that he *does* refer to (Vedānta is his most frequent example) is, at best, somewhat sketchy.

While it is crucial to recognize the numerous and important differences between various nondual traditions (e.g., Zen, Yogācāra Buddhism, Mādhyamika Buddhism, Advaita Vedānta, the different varieties of Tantra, and Taoism, to name only a few), nonetheless, these traditions arguably possess enough underlying similarities to justify speaking of them as a readily identifiable nondual alternative to James's typical depiction of monism.[82] As a group, these nondual traditions share enough common features that it is possible to use them as a collective rebuttal of James's lamentable tendency to assume that all nondual philosophical perspectives suffer from the same problems as he ascribes to neo-Hegelian monism.[83]

It is important to emphasize at the outset that these Eastern philosophical systems are directed to a different audience and serve different goals than neo-Hegelian monism. These Eastern nondual philosophical traditions are not primarily intended to convince an existentially uninvolved audience. Their basic purpose is not to satisfy professorial egos or to improve the social status of a particular cluster of academics. Instead, these Eastern nondual philosophical traditions are primarily soteriological; they are teachings offered in a context of ritual and meditative praxis to those individuals who are committed to an arduous search for existential liberation; they are conceptual intimations of a reality that transcends concepts; they are solutions to the problems of suffering that are meant to be repeatedly pondered, digested, and then, in the end, directly realized.

These Eastern nondual systems are not simply academic intellectual exercises as is often the case with the monistic philosophies that James criticizes. In fact, for many of these soteriological nondual traditions, the use of the intellect itself is the primary problem that needs to be overcome. According to these traditions, it is the subconscious superimposition of our conceptual and logical categories upon the nondual, primal "suchness" of experience that results in the duality (and consequent suffering) of our ordinary experience of life. Therefore, the meditative efforts and ritual praxis within these traditions are designed to facilitate a rediscovery of this inherent nonduality via a systematic deconditioning and deconstruction of our taken-for-granted assumptions of the world, assumptions that are rooted in our subconscious superimposition of cultural and intellectual constructs onto the originally nondual "raw material" of our experience.

Nonetheless, even though these nondual traditions often stress that our intellectual categories lie at the root of our ordinary sense of duality and suffering, it is important to emphasize that the use of the intellect and logic is often highly prized in these soteriological nondual traditions. (Many of the most important figures in these traditions were devastating debaters.) However, the skillful use of the intellect is typically understood as a means to an end, not as an end in itself. For instance, the intellect may be used to provide a piercing analysis of the presence of nondual consciousness in everyday life (as in many Tantric traditions), or as a way to examine the distinction between dual and nondual consciousness (as in Vedānta), or as a vehicle of its own destruction (as in the dazzling logical dilemmas of Mādhyamika Buddhism or in the koans of Zen). Regardless of what strategy is utilized, the ultimate goal is not to demonstrate intellectual brilliance. Instead, the goal is to transcend the intellect altogether in a direct and transformative mystical realization of nonduality; the goal is to be released from one's limited and contracted ego-sense in order to respond to life continuously and effortlessly with a consciousness that no longer bifurcates reality into seer and seen, knower and known, subject and object.

This emphasis on the limits of intellectual knowledge allows these salvific nondual traditions, unlike neo-Hegelian monism, to be strikingly nondogmatic. Rooted in an experiential (not merely intellectual) grasp of nondual awareness, and dubious about, if not flatly hostile to, doctrinal propositions about the specific nature of this consciousness, these Eastern traditions display an empirical grounding and metaphysical flexibility that James would surely have valued. These traditions are nondual rather than monistic in that they refuse to say that the world is ultimately one, or not one, or both, or neither; instead, in their most philosophically rigorous moments, they advocate a ruthless apophatic negation of any and all conceptual structures, even nonduality itself. The result of this basic apophatic understanding is that these traditions offer, theoretically at least, an extremely flexible metaphysical stance.

In fact, James's desire to defend an equal philosophical emphasis on plurality and oneness could easily be accommodated by many of these nondualistic traditions. Although thinkers in these traditions often make what appear to be specific descriptive propositions about the nature of Ultimate Reality, using such conceptually loaded terms as

Exploring Unseen Worlds

"oneness," "true nature," "pure consciousness," and so on, this use of conceptually impregnated terminology, as well as any other concrete propositional statements about nondual awareness, is always framed by the taken-for-granted understanding that any and all "positive" statements about "Ultimate Reality," whether called Brahman, the Tao, or the Dharmakāya, are, if not an ultimately delusive clinging to conceptual categories, then either simply metaphorical indicators or compassionate strategies (or *upāya*, as it is called in the Mahāyāna Buddhist tradition) offered to those in need of more concrete and colorful language.

When these nondual traditions make use of seemingly descriptive language, the "goal" of meditative and ritual praxis is rarely pictured (especially by the Tantric traditions and Zen), as an awareness of simple unity. More commonly, these nondual traditions emphasize the value of a simultaneous consciousness of diversity and unity, a paradoxical fusion of dual and nondual awareness, limitation and freedom, *saṁsāra* and *nirvāṇa*. From this perspective, the enlightened being (the *siddha* or *bodhisattva* or immortal) is not someone who escapes from this world's suffering and limitations in order to plunge into a transcendent world of joy and freedom, but rather, he or she is seen as someone who perceives this joy and freedom in the *midst* of the world's suffering and limitations. While, admittedly, some of these traditions (Advaita Vedānta in particular) so strongly emphasize the underlying *unity* of reality (with a concurrent stress on the unreality of everyday existence) that the particularities and differences of experience become subsumed within this more fundamental (and seemingly more valuable) oneness; nonetheless, there are other nondualistic traditions (especially much of Mahāyāna Buddhism, as well as Taoism and the Tantric traditions) in which an awareness of simple unity, again understood metaphorically, is not the pinnacle of enlightened consciousness, but rather, is a necessary stage on the way towards a deeper (higher?) awareness: unity-within-diversity.

Typically, those traditions which emphasize this unity-within-diversity awareness do not claim that a trance-like, thought-free, introspective unity awareness is the highest and most desirable state of consciousness. Instead, these traditions claim that enlightenment is attained (or recognized) when one is rooted in an ineffable, nondual state of awareness, a state of consciousness in which each moment, as it is, is recognized and responded to as a perfect manifestation of one's true nature. This mystically charged, and yet utterly natural, state of awareness is said to be continuously and effortlessly present regardless of what actions the enlightened being performs. According to these traditions, those who are rooted in this nondual awareness have

240

no need or desire to close their eyes and sit for hours in meditation in order to plunge into a superconscious state of unity-awareness free from thought-constructs, since this world, in all of its complexity, diversity, and chaos, is experienced and valued as whole and perfect—not *in spite* of its complexity, diversity, and chaos, but *because* of it. The claim, which is repeated in different ways in Zen, Taoism, and the Tantric traditions, is that whether eating, drinking, making love, or talking with friends, the enlightened being continually swims and dances in the ecstasy of this natural state, a state in which a consciousness of underlying unity is fully interwoven with an awareness of the uniqueness and wonder of diversity.

A Dual Allegiance

Since James was, on the whole, unaware of these salvific, mystically based nondualistic traditions, it is difficult to predict how he would respond to their attempts to reconcile oneness and plurality. However, James did at times comment on other philosophical endeavors to overcome the apparent differences between unity and diversity, and his comments were, for the most part, highly unfavorable. For instance, in *Pragmatism*, James makes the following biting characterization of those "philosophical amateurs" who wish to be both monists and pluralists: "Most of us have a hankering for the good things on both sides of the line. . . . The world is indubitably one if you look at it in one way, but as indubitably is it many, if you look at it in another. It is both one and many—let us adopt a sort of pluralistic monism."[84] According to James, the average philosophical layman thinks that he or she can legitimately vacillate between pluralism and monism, "never being a radical, never straightening out his [or her] system, but living vaguely in one plausible compartment of it or another to suit the temptations of successive hours."[85] James argues that while this intellectual waffling can be condoned in the thought of philosophical laymen, it is completely unacceptable for professional philosophers who are bothered by too much inconsistency. In James's eyes, both philosophical clarity and intellectual consistency demand that philosophers openly and publicly align themselves with either monism or pluralism, those two philosophical options, which, according to James, are "genuine incompatibles."[86]

James is also extremely suspicious of the commonly found Hegelian philosophical tendency to reconcile opposites within a higher synthesis:

241

Exploring Unseen Worlds

In the exceedingness of the facts of life over our formulas lies a standing temptation at certain times to give up trying to say anything adequate about them, and to take refuge in wild and whirling words which but confess our impotence before their ineffability. . . . "Nothing is near but the far; nothing true but the highest; nothing credible but the inconceivable; nothing so real as the impossible; nothing clear but the deepest; nothing so visible but the invisible; and no life is there but through death."[87]

For James, while these "wild and whirling words" might legitimately serve "as a mystical bath and refuge for feeling when tired reason sickens of her intellectual responsibilities," nonetheless, James adds that Georg Hegel's dubious distinction was that he attempted to make this type of paradoxical merger of opposites "the very form of intellectual responsibility itself."[88] James recognizes that paradoxical language is commonplace in mystical literature, where "such self-contradictory phrases as 'dazzling obscurity,' 'whispering silence,' 'teeming desert,' are continually met with,"[89] and where the "dialectical use, by the intellect, of negation as a mode of passage towards a higher kind of affirmation" is connected to the "denial of the finite self and its wants" as a "doorway to the larger and more blessed life."[90] However, in *Pragmatism*, James expresses his distrust of this sort of paradoxical language and stresses that an "either/or" mentality is essential, unless one wishes to become someone who attempts "to have all the good things going, without being too careful as to how they agree or disagree."[91]

This hard-headed insistence on the necessity of an "either/or" mentality is actually fairly uncharacteristic of James. In fact, James frequently chastises the philosophers of the Absolute for just this sort of "either/or" mentality, especially when they attempt to assert, almost by sheer force of will, that the universe must either be completely rational and coherent or completely irrational and chaotic. Ironically, James's own willingness to lash out at the neo-Hegelians for their insistence that the universe must be either completely coherent or completely chaotic masks the fact that his own insistence on the necessity of an "either/or" mentality is just as naive, just as rigid as the outlook of the neo-Hegelians whom he opposed. Similarly, if we keep in mind James's own attempts, several years later, to articulate a pluralistic pantheism in which he attempts to overcome the dichotomy between manyness and oneness, then James's perplexing assertion that monism and pluralism are the only alternatives available and that only "amateur philosophers" would attempt to create a philosophical system that recognizes the legitimacy and truth of both diversity and unity can be understood in a different light. A recognition of James's own philosophical ambivalence alerts us to the possibility that his hard-headed methodological stance is perhaps, in actuality, indicative of a deeper internal struggle between the tough-minded, "either/or" James and the James for whom "the commonest vice of the human mind is its disposition to see everything as yes or no, as black or white, its incapacity for discrimination of intermediate shades."[92]

In many ways, this internal struggle is a variation of the battle that raged within James for years, as he oscillated wildly back and forth between the poles originally mapped out by his father. Henry James Sr. had, years before, envisioned a God that was "monistic enough to satisfy the philosopher, and yet warm and living and dramatic enough to speak to the heart of the common pluralistic man";[93] he had proclaimed the distance and difference between God and each person's egoistic sense of self, while ardently opposing any theological conceptions that pictured God as a being that was completely alien from mankind. James himself spent much of his philosophical career negotiating the terms of his dual allegiance to the "double character"[94] of his father's thought, with the result that he often careened recklessly back and forth from the hard-nosed pluralistic moralist to the tender-hearted, religiously inclined pantheist.

In James's "Introduction to *The Literary Remains of the Late Henry James*," we are given an early preview of the parameters of the battlefield in which these two opposing philosophical camps fought against each other within James for the rest of his life. On one side of this battleground James situates the pluralist, someone who does not adhere to the naive pluralism of the common person, but rather someone who is a "*philosophic* pluralist . . [someone who advocates] a pluralism hardened by reflection." James pictures this philosophical pluralist as a vibrant, healthy-minded moralist, tingling with moral energy, fully able to struggle against the evils that he or she encounters with no need at all to ask for help from any deeper or higher spiritual source. On the other side of the battlefield, however, James situates the person who needs religious faith, someone who sympathizes with the "*morbid* view" of life, someone who cannot summon sufficient personal resources of will to battle the day-to-day occurrences of evil and suffering, someone who has been paralyzed with fear, someone for whom "morality appears but as a plaster hiding a sore it can never cure, and all our well-doing as the hollowest substitute for that well-*being* that our lives ought to be grounded in, but, alas! are not."[96] For James, this morbid individual is religious because he or she desires consolation and recognition from "the Powers of the

243

Universe," a desire that can never be satisfied with the occasional and external moments of moral action that are sufficient for the moralist.[97]

For James's father, and thus implicitly for James as well, moralism and religion are only apparently in accord; on a deeper level, morality and religion are actually bitter enemies because morality depends upon a person's self efforts, whereas religion is rooted in self surrender. Moreover, this enmity is reflected on a philosophical level, for "any absolute moralism is a pluralism; any absolute religion is a monism,"[98] with the result that "the deepest of all philosophic differences is that between this pluralism and all forms of monism."[99] James muses, almost as if he is talking about himself, that the "the battle is about us, and we are its combatants, steadfast or vacillating, as the case might be."[100] He goes on to assert that in this battle between pluralism and monism, and between moralism and religion, an inconsistent vacillation may, from a practical point of view, be sufficient, but ultimately, this inconsistent vacillation must give way to a radical adherence to one side or the other. In his own life, James attempted to support the most hardened philosophical pluralists in what would appear to be a covert rebellion against his father; but time and time again, this prodigal son returned home and openly extolled the merits of religious salvation and pantheistic union with God.

The Moral Holidays of Monistic Mysticism

Because of this internal polarization between the pluralistic and pantheistic aspects of James's being, there are occasional moments when James's public opposition to monism softens. For instance, as a pragmatist, James is willing to claim that if someone believes in the Absolute, and if these beliefs can be demonstrated to have useful consequences, then a belief in the Absolute appears to be justified, at least for that individual and to that limited extent. Therefore, James concedes that belief in the Absolute at times seems to be "indispensable, at least to certain minds, for it determines them religiously, being often a thing to change their lives by, and by changing their lives, to change whatever in the outer order depends on them."[101] According to James, the primary "cash value" of belief in the Absolute, "pragmatically interpreted," is that "since in the Absolute finite evil is 'overruled' already," we do not have to believe that evil and suffering are the last word; we are given the opportunity to see perfection shining in and through the admittedly imperfect actions in this world and we can trust that whatever happens in our lives is aligned with this deeper, underlying perfection.[102] Therefore, in James's mind, belief in the Absolute permits us "to take a moral holiday"; it enables us to stop worrying; it allows us to give up our fear and our sense of responsibility for the results of our actions; it warrants our desire to feel that the affairs of the world "are in better hands than ours and are none of our business."[103] The monist, unlike the Jamesian pluralist, is given the luxury of having faith in "the absolutely Real"; he or she can trust in that which is unalterable and eternal; he or she can rest in that which "alone makes the universe solid. . . . This is Wordsworth's 'central peace subsisting at the heart of endless agitation.' This is Vivekananda's mystical One. . . . This is Reality with the big R, reality that makes the timeless claim, reality to which defeat can't happen."[104]

James admits that his own more pluralistic philosophy has a marked inability to catalyze the sorts of "quietistic raptures" often associated with a belief in an underlying perfection and Oneness, but James is adamant that such an inability is not a serious defect.[105] According to James, the philosophical optimism of monism and mysticism, an optimism which is distinguished by a deeply felt faith in the underlying perfection of each moment, is in many ways actually an indication of psychological immaturity. James asserts that this monistic optimism is, in reality, closely linked to "moments of discouragement in us all, when we are sick of self and tired of vainly striving," moments when "our own life breaks down," moments when "we mistrust the chances of things" and "want a universe where we can just give up, fall on our father's neck, and be absorbed into the absolute as a drop of water melts into the river or sea."[106] According to James, monistic optimism, much like the Hindu or Buddhist desire for _nirvāṇa_, is based on fear, a fear of more experience, a fear of life. Moreover, monism, in James's opinion, encourages fatalism and antinomianism; it engenders a "nerveless sentimentality or a sensualism without bounds. . . . It makes those who are already too inert more passive still; it renders wholly reckless those whose energy is already in excess."[107]

What are we to make of this flailing attack on the alleged debilitating effects of monism? Unfortunately, it seems clear that James's suggestion that we can automatically connect a particular set of beliefs with a corresponding set of ethical and psychological consequences is overly facile. In fact, James's claim that monism encourages fatalism and antinomianism, juxtaposed with his argument that the Hindu and Buddhist longing for _nirvāṇa_ is based on fear, appears to be little more than an effort to score some quick and dirty rhetorical points by drawing upon an unsupported and stereotypical collection of clichés that are deeply rooted in Western fears and misapprehensions of

Eastern systems of belief and praxis. It is simply not accurate to claim that antinomianism and fatalism are confined to the East as James, infected by a lingering cultural imperialism, seems to believe.[108] Christians, Jews, and Muslims, as well as hedonists and nihilists of all varieties, have all, at one time or another, been smeared by the same brush that James uses against monism. Alternatively, and perhaps more importantly, there is simply no automatic one-to-one connection between monism and its alleged fatalistic and antinomian consequences. While it is almost undeniable that there are casual connections between the beliefs of individuals and their consequent behavior, it is extremely difficult, if not impossible, to demonstrate that one particular set of beliefs automatically generates only one particular set of results. Although there might well have been numerous monists throughout history who have used their metaphysical beliefs to justify passivity or amoral actions, that does not imply that monism, in and of itself, was the direct cause of their behavior. In fact, a case could just as easily be made that, historically, monism has frequently been associated with highly energized and ethical individuals.

James is also blatantly simplistic and one-dimensional in his assessment of the psychological reasons why a person would choose to adopt a monistic belief system. While the desire to give meaning to personal suffering and the need for solace and comfort may indeed be catalysts for adopting a monistic worldview, any number of religious belief systems could conceivably satisfy an individual who is seeking a workable theodicy and psychological sustenance. James himself even admits as much when he says that ethical breathing spaces are not the exclusive possession of monistic philosophies, since "any religious view" has the ability to grant us "moral holidays."[109]

Furthermore, James's attempt to claim that individuals choose to adopt a monistic perspective as a way to avoid life's difficulties is, at best, naive, and at worst, indicative of a prejudicial blindness. There are numerous, and more positive, reasons why different individuals adopt monist beliefs.[110] For instance, monistic beliefs could be linked to a longing to break free from the sufferings brought on by the ego's sense of limitation and separation; monistic beliefs could signal a desire to incarnate more fully the love and clarity that is sensed at the root of one's nature; monistic beliefs could reflect a need to serve humanity more deeply by gaining access to the depths of power, wisdom, and compassion that are allegedly found in unity awareness; or finally, monistic beliefs could arise out of an urgent need to destroy illusion and gain direct access to a clear and undistorted perception of the true nature of reality.

Beyond Words, Beyond Morals

James, when pressed by William Adams Brown, a theologian who objected to the "narrowness" of James's depiction of the moral effects allegedly linked with a belief in the Absolute, concedes that monism can indeed inspire strenuous and active ethical behavior, but he maintains that monism's "affinities with strenuousness are less emphatic than [pluralism's affinities]."[111] From James's perspective, while both pluralism and monism can provide a philosophical foundation for ethical choice, there is, nonetheless, a very real difference between the two: pluralism "demands" strenuous behavior, whereas monism merely "permits" it.[112] According to James, pluralism actively encourages ethical choices and makes "the very life we lead seem real and earnest";[113] pluralism is the philosophical option for those among us who have a more hardy constitution, those of us who possess a "certain willingness to live without assurances or guarantees."[114]

James argues that just as monism is linked with optimism, pluralism is closely aligned with "meliorism," the doctrine that understands salvation to be "neither inevitable nor impossible."[115] Unlike the ethical complacency allegedly engendered by monistic optimism, James asserts that the meliorism promoted by a pluralistic worldview allows us to envision a world with "real adventure" and "real danger," yet nonetheless, a world in which salvation may occur through one's own efforts combined with those of others in "a social scheme of cooperative work genuinely to be done."[116] James stresses that this pluralistic understanding of a world in which there might "be real losses and real losers, and no total preservation of all that is," does not necessarily imply that human beings are alone with their struggles.[117] James is willing to entertain the hypothesis that in the process of working towards the world's salvation we can expect cooperation not only from our fellow human beings, but also from the beneficent forces that populate the unseen world. For James, pluralism by no means precludes a belief in transnatural assistance:

> If we drop the absolute out of the world, must we then conclude that the world contains nothing better in the way of consciousness than our consciousness? Is our whole instinctive belief in higher presences, our persistent inner turning towards divine companionship, to count for nothing? . . . Such a negative conclusion would, I believe, be desperately hasty, a sort of pouring out of the child with the bath. Logically it is possible to believe in superhuman beings without identifying them with the absolute at all.[118]

247

Exploring Unseen Worlds

James is convinced that there are higher and more wide-ranging forms of consciousness in the universe than human consciousness, and he even goes so far as to speculate that we might "stand in much the same relation to the whole of the universe as our canine and feline pets do to the whole of human life."[119] Just as our cats and dogs form an important part of our lives, but presumably have little specific understanding of the reasons behind many of our actions, similarly, as human beings, we might also be working harmoniously with unseen "higher powers," with little, if any, conscious understanding of the numerous ways in which our decisions and struggles are aligned with the salvific efforts of these spiritual beings.

James goes on to add that these spiritual beings may, in turn, be in harmony with a more inclusive divinity, who, unlike the Absolute, "is no absolute all-experiencer, but simply the experiencer of the widest actual conscious span."[120] Although James's melioristic universe has no place for an omniscient, omnipresent, and omnipotent God, nonetheless it *can* permit the loving assistance of a God who has sufficient power to change life for the better, while not so much power as to render all of our choices and struggles unnecessary and ultimately trivial. This Jamesian God, who "is finite, either in power or knowledge, or in both at once,"[121] is pictured by James as an extremely loving and powerful personal divinity who is willing and able to assist humanity in its struggles, and yet who, simultaneously, may be in need of human assistance in order to successfully carry out its purposes. James emphasizes that God, as conceived in this way, may actually "draw vital strength and increase of very being from our fidelity."[122] He goes on to say: "For my own part, I do not know what the sweat and blood and tragedy of this life mean, if they mean anything short of this."[123] Clearly, this sort of mutual dependence between God and humanity leaves little room for either a belief in the underlying perfection of the universe or an optimistic faith in the world's inevitable salvation. The universe, for James, even with divine assistance, remains a dangerous, adventurous place, a place where our struggles really count for something, a place where salvation comes with no guarantees:

> If this life be not a real fight, in which something is eternally gained for the universe by success, it is no better than a game of private theatricals from which one may withdraw at will. But it feels like a real fight—as if there were something really wild in the universe which we, with all our idealities and faithfulnesses, are needed to redeem.[124]

Beyond Words, Beyond Morals

For James, the tumultuous process of living calls upon those who are consistent and clear in their thinking to make a commitment, both morally and philosophically. Intellectual and ethical ambiguity may be fine for those who have not hammered out what they believe, but a philosopher should take a firm stand: either "the world *must and shall be* [saved]" or "the world *may be* saved."[125] For the "tough-minded" James, there is no middle ground: monistic optimism simply cannot be reconciled with pluralistic meliorism. However, as we saw earlier in this chapter, James did not always advocate this sort of "either/or" mentality. In fact, during the years in which James worked out his radical empiricism and his pluralistic pantheism, he struggled to find some way to escape the straightjacket of exactly this type of thinking; he looked for some way in which he could avoid the logical assertion that the world can be *either* one *or* many, but not both at once. In the end, by the time of *A Pluralistic Universe*, James chose to deny that logic had precedence over concrete experience, arguing, for instance, that the compounding of consciousness that we constantly observe in our daily life gives us countless examples of manyness conjoined with oneness. In *A Pluralistic Universe*, James decided that he could no longer deny the evidence of concrete experience simply because it did not coincide with the demands of the logic of identity. This willingness to renounce the hegemony of abstract logic, in turn, provided sufficient philosophical freedom for James to articulate his pluralistic pantheism—a theo-metaphysical stance in which finite individual consciousnesses are conceived to be both separate from each other and yet united within a higher or deeper cosmic consciousness.

However, even though James ultimately was willing to relinquish the authority he had previously bequeathed to logic when dealing with the philosophical problem of the one and the many, in other philosophical arenas James's loyalty to logic proved much more intractable. For instance, when arguing against his neo-Hegelian opponents, James often points out that perfection cannot logically coexist with imperfection. Therefore, his argument continues, those philosophers who attempt to claim that the Absolute is consubstantial with this phenomenological reality must also claim, contrary to logic, that the Absolute (which is perfect) itself takes the form of all imperfect phenomena, including evil and suffering. For James, it is simply not acceptable for the monists to try and wiggle off the hook of this dilemma through the clever rhetorical ploy of contrasting the Absolute's "eternal and the temporal 'points of view' " or contrasting the "truth" of the Absolute in-and-of-itself with its "appearances."[126] As James pointedly observes, the use of such blatantly dualistic terminology is nothing more than an illegitimate attempt to resolve the logical problem of how it is possible that perfection and goodness can be the source of imperfection and evil. From James's perspective, if the monists wish to claim that the Absolute is One, then they should cease their philosophical wordplay, and simply admit the logical and ethical repercussions of such a claim.

According to James, the problem of evil only arises if we conceive of the world from a monistic perspective. He argues, therefore, that instead of blindly accepting the claims of monism, we should align ourselves with a "popular or practical theism," which is always "more or less frankly pluralistic, not to say polytheistic."[127] If we acknowledge the claims of this "commonsense theism," in which there are countless, ontologically separate beings in the universe (i.e., "God, the Devil, Christ, the saints"[128] and human beings) instead of one (i.e., monism), then it is legitimate to conceive that evil might also be an ontologically distinct reality that has no inherent need to exist, a reality that might conceivably be destroyed in the future through our own collective efforts supported by God's loving power. If we choose to accept this pluralistic metaphysical position, then we are free to reject the neo-Hegelian attempt to resolve the problem of evil (in which evil is understood to be an essential part of the universe that is ultimately "overcome" within the Absolute); a pluralistic metaphysical position allows us to focus our energies on "dropping [evil] out altogether, throwing it overboard and getting beyond it, helping to make a universe that shall forget its very place and name."[129]

For James, one of the primary advantages of a pluralistic philosophical system is that it can energize an individual's concrete struggle against suffering and evil, since from the perspective of a pluralistic metaphysics, "the problems that evil presents are practical, not speculative. Not why evil should exist at all, but how we can lessen the actual amount of it, is the sole question we need there consider."[130] But this seeming disavowal of the importance of theoretical concerns about the nature of evil is belied by James's own life. James was obsessed with the theoretical problems that surround any attempt to juxtapose evil with a religious faith, obsessed to such a degree that he frequently suffered severe bouts of disabling depression, as well as a host of related psychosomatic disorders (such as backaches, eyestrain, indigestion, and so on), when the contradiction between visible evil and an invisible spiritual world remained beyond the grasp of a logical solution. James was haunted by the specter of the intellectual conflict between his day-to-day experience of the reality of evil and suffering and his religious desire to believe in a powerful and beneficent unseen world in which such suffering and evil was, if not denied, then at least given meaning and purpose. For James, despite his protests to the contrary, the problem of evil was intellectual in origin and his attempts to solve this problem were equally intellectual in nature. It appears that, on some level, James must have realized that if he was going to criticize the monists for their intellectual inability to deal with the problem of evil, then it was simply not legitimate for him baldly to assert that pluralistic metaphysics, unlike monism, is exempt from the speculative and intellectual problems associated with the existence of evil. A theological argument would have to be fashioned that could provide a logically credible solution to the problem of evil.

A Literally Finite God

James's theological answer to the problem of evil is strikingly simple, but theologically daring: God is *not* all-powerful, all-knowing, or all-pervasive, but rather, is finite. In James's opinion, God is "the name not of the whole of things, heaven forbid, but only of the ideal tendency in things, believed in as a superhuman person who calls us to cooperate in his purposes, and who furthers ours if they are worthy. He works in an external environment, has limits, and has enemies."[131] James believes that this unique depiction of the divine avoids the logical contradictions that plague the philosophers of the Absolute, since, if the divine is understood as finite, if it can be seen to possess specific, almost mathematically measured boundaries, then it can escape the taint of including evil within itself. This finite God may be an almost inconceivably vast consciousness; he (using James's masculine term) "may conceivably have almost nothing outside of himself; he may already have triumphed over and absorbed all but the minutest fraction of the universe; but that fraction, however small, reduces him to the status of a relative being";[132] that fraction means that God is not an all-inclusive being, and therefore, in theory at least, need not be understood as ontologically connected to evil and suffering.

For James, this finite God offers numerous theo-metaphysical and ethical advantages. First, the finite God, as a theological construct, reflects the moral intuitions of many individuals that God is willing and able to assist in humanity's moral struggles, but not to such an extent that human ethical responsibility is undercut. Second, the finite God offers a theological understanding of the divine that is more concrete, and more personal, than the abstract, impersonal Absolute

251

of nineteenth-century philosophical idealism. James's finite God is a loving, interactive God, a God who is related to us, who cares about us, who is intimately linked with us. Third, because the theological understanding of the finite God stresses the loving, personal nature of the divine, it maintains a type of continuity with other theistic speculations, even if it breaks with those theological speculations that emphasize God's complete ontological otherness. James's finite God may be distinct from other individual beings, but it is not ontologically separate from them. Fourth, and perhaps most importantly, the finite God, who is understood to be "finite, either in power or knowledge, or in both at once," is a bold attempt to solve the logical dilemma that plagues classical theism: how to resolve the fact that God is both all-powerful and all-good, and yet still permits evil to exist.[133] If, as James proposes, God is *not* understood as all-powerful, yet nonetheless is still conceived to be all-good, then there is no need to saddle God with the responsibility for evil. Evil, from this perspective, could simply be a distinct ontological reality that God, in tandem with our own ongoing human efforts, is attempting to eradicate.

James's finite God reflects a God that is fully in line with the "either/or" aspect of James—the James that insists that reality is *either* monistic *or* pluralistic, the James that insists that the world *either* shall be saved, *or* may be saved. The idea of the finite God is the creation of James the hard-nosed pluralist, the tough-minded philosopher who insists on a logically congruent understanding of God that is consistent with his moral intuitions. However, as was previously emphasized, there is another aspect of James: the "both/and" James. This James has his own, often opposing, intellectual needs. This is the James who possesses the quasi-Hegelian desire to reconcile opposites; this is the James who finally decides, if with the greatest reluctance, to surrender the unbridled hegemony of logic; this is the James whose methodology is rooted in a subtle analysis of the "both/and" nature of experience—whether the nondualism of pure experience, the compounding of consciousness inherent in our everyday experience, or the paradoxical fusion and distinction of self and divinity found in countless mystical experiences. This is the James that developed pluralistic pantheism, a theo-metaphysical vision in which reality is *both* many *and* one, a vision in which an open-ended series of interlapping, interpenetrating fields allows for *both* diversity *and* unity, a vision in which an ontological nondualism merges with a functional dualism.

Unfortunately, the "either/or" and the "both/and" aspects of James's nature were never harmoniously reconciled, leading, inevitably, to several ongoing unresolved oppositions in James's philosophical perspective. In particular, James never explicitly deals with the tensions that are created when, in *A Pluralistic Universe*, he conjoins his arguments for the necessity for a finite God alongside his advocacy of a pluralistic pantheism. While it might be philosophically possible to reconcile the profound difference between the visions of reality endorsed by the finite God and pluralistic pantheism, James never really makes the attempt. On the whole, James seems strangely unaware of any need to deal consciously with the differences inherent in the metaphorical imagery generated by his pluralistic pantheism (e.g., his depictions of interpenetrating levels of cosmic consciousness, his flirtations with earth-souls and mother-seas of awareness, his speculations that the divine is found within the depths of the human psyche, and his opposition to theism's inherent duality between God and humanity) and the metaphorical imagery associated with his finite God (who is, as he puts it, the " 'God' of the common people . . . and the creator-God of orthodox christian [sic] theology," the God of "popular Christianity," the God of "David, or of Isaiah," the God who "is an essentially finite being in the cosmos, not with the cosmos in him," the God who "has a very local habitation [in the universe], and very one-sided local and personal attachments").[134] With James's pluralistic pantheism, we are plunged into a boundless world of interpenetrating, if distinct, levels of consciousness. With James's finite God, we are introduced to an encapsulated theistic divinity with discrete borders. Just how James would have us harmonize these two dramatically different visions remains frustratingly unclear.

For the most part, it is exceedingly difficult to disentangle just what theo-metaphysical position James actually holds in *A Pluralistic Universe*. At the beginning of the text, James gives the rather misleading impression that he has fully embraced a pantheistic, rather than theistic, position, but by the end of the text, James's theistic finite God manages to surface right within the heart of his pantheism.

It appears at first that, based on his acceptance of the compounding of consciousness as well as his desire to posit a spiritual reality that is intimately connected with the deeper levels of human consciousness, James reverses years of theistic advocacy, in order to devote considerable energy to touting the superiority of pantheism over a theistic perspective. For instance, James claims that pantheism is "more intimate" than theism, since in pantheism the person is "substantially fused" with God, whereas in theism "God and his creation [are seen] as entities distinct from each other."[135] James goes on to add that theism makes every human being "an outsider and a mere subject to God," since it advocates a God that is "not the heart of our heart and reason of our reason, but our magistrate."[136] However, even though pantheism wins James's approval at this point in *A Pluralistic Universe*, since the pantheist sees "God as the indwelling divine rather than the external creator, and . [sees] human life as part and parcel of that deep reality," James ultimately reverses his own reversal and readmits a theistic, if finite, God back into his pantheistic metaphysics.[137]

Granted, James's pantheism is rather different than most versions of pantheism, in that it is pluralistic. James's pantheism is *not* a doctrine that posits God as all-inclusive (even though this is the most common understanding of the term). Instead, James's pantheism is pluralistic in that it attempts to allow for a multitude of functionally distinct, if ontologically inseparable, conscious entities—entities that have moral independence, but are metaphysically connected. From this perspective, God is both ontologically fused with the depths of human consciousness *and* possesses an independent identity that is distinct from each individual. James's pluralistic pantheism is willing, like monism, to posit that "we are indeed internal parts of God and not external creations," but unlike monism, James's understanding of the relationship between the self and God tries desperately to avoid the implication that God is an all-pervasive principle.[138]

James is reluctant to endorse the notion that God is all-pervasive because this would, in effect, signal a complete capitulation to the monistic pantheism that he had been battling for many years. James chooses his pluralistic brand of pantheism over the monistic varieties, not only because of the ethical difficulties that he links with monism, but also because, for James, the overtly monistic varieties of pantheism are actually *less* intimate than pluralistic pantheism, in that they picture the Absolute as divorced from the everyday life of humanity. James's advocacy of pluralistic pantheism in no way implies an acceptance of the monistic Absolute, this "metaphysical monster" who, according to James, "neither acts nor suffers, nor loves nor hates," this abstract philosophical entity who "has no needs, desires, or aspirations, no failures or successes, friends or enemies, victories or defeats," this principle of logical necessity that is "neither intelligence nor will, neither a self nor a collection of selves, neither truthful, good nor beautiful, as we understand these terms."[139] For James, every aspect of the Absolute is utterly opposed to our day-to-day experience of imperfection, finitude, and change; this "stagnant felicity" of the Absolute is simply too perfect, too cut off from humanity's sufferings and struggles to promote any feelings of sympathy or intimate connection on our part.[140]

James believes, however, that the finite God can capture our sympathies. Like us, the finite God not only has "an environment," but it can also be understood as existing "in time and working out a history just like ourselves."[141] However, as we have already pointed out, James never explicitly wrestles with just how this finite God, with its metaphors of discrete boundaries and explicit limitations, fits within the open-ended, interpenetrating fields of pluralistic pantheism. This rather jarring mixture of incongruous metaphors, this insistence on retaining the finite God within a pluralistic pantheism, presents us with an intriguing possibility: perhaps even though James was consciously intending to renounce his theism for a pantheistic perspective, on a deeper level, he was simply unable to abandon his years of loyalty to a theistic God, his years of combative insistence that God is best understood as a being who is separate from humanity and the universe.

James's deeply rooted theistic dualism is perhaps best seen in *The Will to Believe*, where James argues that "it is essential that God be conceived as the deepest power in the universe; . . . conceived under the form of a mental personality," a personality that "is to be regarded, like any other personality, as something lying outside of my own and other than me, and whose existence I simply come upon and find."[142] In this earlier understanding of God, James stresses the otherness of God, God's separateness from humanity. However, James seems to have realized that the monistic overtones of many mystical states of consciousness appear to contradict this duality between God and humanity, since, as he notes, it is undeniable that the "highest moments of the theistic consciousness" generate intense feelings of oneness.[143] Nonetheless, James still asserts (with little or no specific arguments to back up his claim) that "this consciousness of self-surrender, of absolute practical union between one's self and the divine object of one's contemplation, is a totally different thing from any sort of substantial identity."[144] As James goes on to say: "Still the object God and the subject I are two. Still I simply come upon him, and find his existence given to me."[145]

James's advocacy of a dualistic theism in *The Will to Believe* is firmly entrenched in an equally dualistic epistemology: for James, it is clear that even theistic mystical union "is based unchangeably on the empirical fact that the thinking subject and the object thought are numerically two."[146] James realizes that this dualistic epistemology creates numerous difficulties for his theology, since from a dualistic perspective it is almost impossible to explain "how my mind and will, which are not God, can yet cognize and leap to meet him."[147] Nonetheless, for James, this theological puzzle (and others) are problems "that for the theist can remain unsolved and insoluble forever."[148]

He goes on to argue (rather conveniently) that for those immersed in "the highest flights of theistic mysticism" it is not important to theoretically understand the relationship between God and the self, since for these theistic mystics, a loving experience of God's presence is sufficient.[149]

However, despite James's praise for the "theoretic chastity and modesty" that he insists is to be found within theistic mysticism, despite his "easy acceptance of an opaque limit to our speculative insight, this satisfaction with a Being whose character we simply apprehend without comprehending anything more about him,"[150] there are limits to James's alleged theological openness. Some metaphysical information is simply assumed: in *The Will To Believe*, "blank unmediated dualism" remains James's unwavering metaphysical presupposition.[151] Oneness with God is seen as completely unacceptable, since this oneness would dissolve the crucially important ontological distance between individuals as well as between humanity and God that James had been fighting so hard to maintain. Identity with an underlying Absolute would, according to James, abolish the crucially important understanding that "in every being that is real there is something external to, and sacred from the grasp of every other."[152] In *The Will to Believe*, therefore, James advocates a God who is always Other, a God whose "being is sacred from ours."[153]

When, many years later, in *A Pluralistic Universe*, James includes a finite God within the flowing fields of his newly developed pluralistic pantheism, it is clearly possible to surmise that James never really abandoned this emphasis on "otherness" within his theology, even after renouncing his dualistic epistemology in favor of the nondualism of his radical empiricism. But James could easily have maintained this sense of "otherness" within a pantheistic perspective without having to resort to the theological gymnastics affiliated with the notion of a finite God. James's longing for a pantheistic religious unity of God and humanity that is congruent with his moralistic desire to maintain a degree of ontological distance between the divine and human spheres of existence could be fully accommodated within James's pluralistic pantheism, if he would only let go of his tenacious, and puzzling, tendency to act as if the divine reality could be objectified, as if "it" could be precisely measured in quantitative terms, as if spatial metaphors used to depict spiritual existence should be taken literally.

Interestingly, however, in an earlier essay, James himself recognized the limitations of using spatial metaphors to depict nonordinary levels of reality:

Beyond Words, Beyond Morals

In the heart of infinite being itself there can be [no] such a thing as plethora, or glut, or supersaturation. . . . Each new mind brings its own edition of the universe of space along with it, . . . and these spaces never crowd each other, —the space of my imagination, for example, in no way interferes with yours. The amount of possible consciousness seems to be governed by no law analogous to that of the so-called conservation of energy in the material world. . . . There seems no formal limit to the positive increase of being in spiritual respects.[154]

Nonetheless, despite this insight into the limitations of using spatial metaphors to describe non-material levels of reality, James's attribution of finitude to God seems to demonstrate that, in *A Pluralistic Universe*, James thinks it is legitimate to conceive of God as circumscribed and existing within an "environment." In addition, when James attacks the theo-metaphysical constructions of his philosophical opponents, he (along with the philosophical idealists he opposes) inevitably treats "the Absolute" as if "It" can be adequately described by using adjectives, such as "oneness" or "perfection" or "timeless" or "all-pervasive," with little or no recognition of the difficulties of using language-constructs that are rooted in a subject/object duality to depict a level of reality that purportedly transcends this dualistic structure.

James's literal-mindedness in regard to descriptions of the spiritual world appears to be the primary reason why he feels compelled to renounce monism, and in addition, is the underlying justification for his eagerness to ascribe finitude to God. It is only when terms such as "oneness" or "perfection" or "timeless" or "all-pervasive" are taken literally that the notion of the Absolute presents logical and ethical problems (i.e., How is it possible that the world can be both one and many at the same time? Or alternatively, how is it possible that the world can be innately perfect, yet be in need of salvation?). Conversely, James's claim that God is finite also depends upon a literal understanding of terms such as "finite" or "environment," and this literal understanding is what, in turn, allows James to claim that God's supposed finitude solves the problem of evil, since, for instance, if God is finite, then evil is not necessarily included "within" God.

Beyond Oneness

James is certainly not the only thinker who overliteralizes metaphysical or theological claims and then attempts to argue that these

257

theo-metaphysical conceptions, if taken seriously, are correlated with specific ethical consequences. For instance, in a thought-provoking essay, Wayne Proudfoot not only attempts to demonstrate the ethical consequences of different theological worldviews, but he then goes on, like James, to connect these worldviews with specific types of powerful religious experiences.[155] Proudfoot begins his investigation by pointing out, with considerable accuracy, that every religious tradition will inevitably interweave factual and moral beliefs to such an extent that it often becomes impossible to distinguish whether a religious symbol system is describing the way things really are or is advocating how one should ideally live one's life. For example, as Proudfoot notes, narrations of both the Exodus and of Jesus's death on the cross are not simply descriptive accounts of historical events that took place thousands of years ago, but they are also guides for how one should structure one's life in the present. Similarly, for a Hindu, *dharma* is understood to be both a description of the underlying order of the universe as well as an explicit set of instructions for correct ethical behavior. In the same way, for the Buddhist, the image of the world as a burning house from which a person should escape as quickly as possible includes within itself both descriptive and prescriptive understandings.

After having established the undeniable fact that within most religious traditions there is an inevitable fusion of "the ways things are" and "the way things should be," Proudfoot then goes on to point out, again like James, that there is a strong correlation between the interpretative accounts of many mystical experiences and the worldview presupposed by monism. According to Proudfoot, "a common element in reports of mystical experience is the sense of unity with all there is and the realization that what previously seemed to be boundaries, distinctions and distances are illusory, penultimate, or in some way finally unreal."[156] Proudfoot argues that while each mystical experience is unique, as an "ideal type," mystical experience "tends towards monism," since, in general, the interpretative framework linked with mystical experiences shares with monism a perspective in which "distinctions and boundaries are judged to be finally illusory."[157]

After pointing out the similarity between the interpretative assumptions of mystical experience and monism, Proudfoot then proceeds, following the work of Arthur Danto, to draw out the ethical implications of mystically prompted monistic beliefs:

> If distinctions are unreal and there exists only one undifferentiated unity, whether it is described as being or as emptiness, then conflict is illusory. If

there exist no boundaries between persons, things, or communities, then there can be no conflict between the interests or values of several parties, and thus there is no need for rules to adjudicate such conflict. Insofar as ethical reflection arises from the attempt to resolve conflict between different interests and alternative courses of action open to a person, or between the interests of several persons or communities, it cannot occur in a context in which no distinctions or boundaries can be drawn.[158]

Proudfoot, like James, seems to think that a theoretical emphasis on unity and oneness preempts any type of genuine ethical reflection. However, Proudfoot's argument is weakened by the fact that, while many, if not most, mystics claim that they have experienced states of unity and oneness, these claims, almost inevitably, are presented within the context of a much more fundamental claim: that these mystical experiences are *ineffable*, that any and all descriptions of what is mystically experienced should not be taken as literal descriptions of fact.[159] Mystical narratives are framed in metaphorical, evocative, or even paradoxical language; they are attempts to stretch language past its breaking point, they are impassioned efforts to point towards that which refuses to be captured within the net of words or concepts. Furthermore, ineffability is often an intrinsic aspect of mystical narratives, in that the inability to express the highest states of mystical experiences is frequently a direct result of attempting to use linguistic structures that grammatically depend upon a subject/object duality to depict a level of experience that, due to the mystical fusion of subject and object, is inherently beyond this duality.[160]

If we take seriously the ineffability of profound mystical experiences, if terms such as "oneness" or "perfection" are understood to be, at best, helpful hints or signposts along the way, rather than literally accurate accounts of the unseen world (as they are in a nondual, rather monistic metaphysics) then many of Proudfoot and James's ethical reservations about mystical experience are defused. While an argument could be made that monism (if taken literally) is incongruent with ethical reflection, nondualism is not so open to such charges. Unlike monism, nondualism can assert that distinctions are just as valid and important as unity. Distinctions and oneness may be irreconcilable opposites in a world that is tyrannized by a grammar and logic that is rooted in an assumed subject/object duality, but within a nondual level of experience different rules apply, and such forced contradictions no longer exist. Similarly, from a nondual standpoint, to say that the world is "perfect" by no means precludes an acknowledgment of the felt reality of "imperfection" in this level of experience,

259

since from a nondual perspective, neither "perfection" nor "imperfection" are understood to be literally accurate terms. At best, these terms have a relative validity as metaphorical allusions to "that" which transcends conceptual analysis.

It is important to reemphasize that a nondual understanding of the limitations of discursive language does not necessarily signify that nothing meaningful can be said about the ultimate nature of reality or the self. Instead, as was mentioned earlier in the chapter, this emphasis on the limitations of discursive thought allows us to be released from a slavish adulation of logical discourse and allows us to move into the freedom and playfulness of *symbolic* discourse. Recognizing the necessarily metaphorical nature of religious language opens up sufficient philosophical space to create metaphysical and theological models whose worth can be assessed by their ability to catalyze personal and communal transformation rather than by their capacity to adhere to rational norms. From a Jamesian point of view, our assumptions about ourselves and our world matter: we experience and respond to the world, as well as to ourselves and to others, in ways largely determined by these tacit assumptions. Our experiences, whether mystical or quotidian, are always interwoven with, and dramatically affected by, these internalized worldviews. Theometaphysical speculations, anthropological investigations, scientific experimentation, and psychological explorations are all different ways in which we can call into question these taken-for-granted worldviews and create alternate visions, which in turn can catalyze alternative possibilities of experience and action. It is, therefore, crucially important to recognize the importance of the worldviews that we internalize and to take conscious responsibility for that worldview which we believe not only most fully and accurately accounts for the widest range of experiences (both quotidian and mystical), but which also provides the most fertile ground for ongoing personal and social transformation.

Furthermore, an understanding of language that denies a one-to-one correspondence between terms and their referents does not necessarily imply (as most postmodern philosophy insists) that language refers to nothing outside of itself, and that, therefore, any and all narratives of mystical experiences are nothing more than linguistically and culturally generated, bodiless webs of words. An emphasis on the metaphorical nature of mystical narratives can and should be conjoined with an equally powerful insistence on the fluid and dynamic, yet at times, stubbornly unyielding, givenness of lived experience, experience that can not only resist inappropriate interpretations, but which can also generate new metaphors, new linguistic possibilities.

James's own methodology included within itself such an understanding of the priority of lived experience. James's pluralistic pantheism, for instance, emerged out of a creative response to experiential data—not only from a willingness to speculate that reality may be patterned analogously to the structure demonstrated by our everyday experiences of the compounding of consciousness, but also from a careful consideration of the evidence presented by psychical research and the reports of mystical and religious experiences. James's speculations on the finite God arouse as well in response to a type of experience, that is, our sense of ourselves as free moral agents who are assisted, but not overwhelmed, by a loving and powerful spiritual personality. Unfortunately, however, James's primary arguments for the finite God depend less on empirical validation than on an inappropriate dependence upon a logic that is rooted in a literalistic and dualistic understanding of the nature of divinity. If James had been willing to grant the unseen world the same metaphysical indeterminacy that he was willing to grant to our concrete level of experience, then he could have avoided the awkward juxtaposition of his finite God and his pluralistic pantheism. If the language which is used to talk about nonordinary levels of experience could have been understood as inherently metaphorical, as inherently unable to fully or adequately encapsulate "that" to which it refers, then James could easily and legitimately have rooted his theological and ethical claims in a theoretical analysis of experience, rather than a strained ethically derived logic.[161] A nondual, metaphorically understood pluralistic pantheism could, with little difficulty, posit a rich, pluralistic, multidimensional spiritual world full of higher selves, angels, gods, and earth-souls who are assisting us in our salvific efforts, while not precluding a recognition of an underlying Oneness and perfection.

An Experience of the Problem of Evil

Because a neo-Jamesian, nondual pluralistic pantheism incorporates the understanding that every theological construction is nothing more than a fallible human attempt to express "that" which is beyond the reach of logic, and stresses the priority of experiential data as a basis for philosophical reflection, a new angle of vision is created that permits the emergence of novel answers to several seemingly irresolvable ethical questions.

For instance, it is possible from the perspective of a nondual pluralistic pantheism to posit not only that an underlying "perfection"[162] might well coexist with our day-to-day experience of suffering, but also that these two levels of experience ("perfection" and suffering) are both equally valid, *within their own sphere*. That is, from the perspective of the person who is primarily aware of his or her finitude and of his or her separation from "perfection," life will be experienced as filled with real losses, real suffering, and real evil. However, from the perspective of the advanced mystic who has an ongoing, powerful experience of the underlying "perfection" of the universe (rather than merely having a theoretical understanding *about* "perfection"), suffering and evil can be said to disappear, since for this mystic, suffering and evil are directly experienced as being rooted in a deeper, more basic, "perfection."

From an experiential standpoint, both of these seemingly contradictory understandings are perfectly sound. Philosophical problems occur only when either one or the other of these experiential perspectives attempts to claim the exclusive right to be recognized as legitimate. For instance, if we are so immersed in our day-to-day experience of suffering that depictions of mystical experiences of "perfection" appear to be, at best, nebulous abstractions, then we will, quite naturally, believe that only our perspective on evil is correct. Conversely, if our moment-to-moment reality is one in which we experience a powerful mystical apprehension of the underlying "perfection" of the world—an experience in which suffering as such is no longer seen to exist—then we too will naturally tend to believe that only *our* understanding of evil is valid.

A nondual pluralistic pantheism however, can affirm that *both* of these understandings are completely legitimate, since both are simply reasonable attempts to make sense of different fields of awareness. People who experience the stark grinding reality of suffering, and who are completely cut off from any mystical apprehension of "perfection," are simply being faithful to their level of experience, and therefore, are justified in affirming that this world is imperfect. Conversely, those (albeit rare) individuals who genuinely perceive, from moment-to-moment, an ineffable "perfection" shining in and through all the apparent experiences of suffering and imperfection, are also faithful to their field of awareness when they claim, with equal validity, that their perception of "perfection" is correct.

However, for those individuals who have had occasional mystical experiences of the world's underlying "perfection," and yet who also experience the day-to-day reality of evil and suffering (since they

262

are not, at least yet, constantly immersed in a direct, nondual mystical apprehension of reality), the situation is not quite so straightforward. Such individuals, in order to be authentic, need to attempt to hold *both* of these genuine experiences in tension with each other, even though these experiences might logically seem to be contradictory. In order to reflect adequately this multilevel experience of life, the philosophical perspective adopted by such individuals would have to claim, simultaneously, that the world is in need of healing and salvation, *and* that the world is, at this moment, fully whole and "perfect" as it is.

Within the context of a lived spirituality, this paradoxical metaphysics could support claim that if we are living within a field of awareness characterized by pain, loss, and confusion, we can and should attempt to overcome our existential suffering and move towards enlightenment or salvation. However, this paradoxical metaphysics could also argue that from the point of view of our mystical experiences of "perfection" (or perhaps more accurately, from the point of view of our potent and transformative *memories* of our mystical experiences of "perfection"), the only genuine spiritual work that needs to be done is to remind ourselves that we are *already* saved or enlightened, to remind ourselves of the irony that no work actually needs to be done at all and that all of this talk of different levels of experience is just part of the illusion that is dissolved when one is "enlightened."[163]

An important repercussion of embracing this type of paradoxical metaphysical stance is that the resolution of the problem of evil would be primarily experiential, and not intellectual. Those individuals who sought to maintain the dual awareness of the simultaneous reality of "perfection" and suffering would be unable, with any integrity, to explain away the problem of the existence of evil with any rationalistic theodicy. Needing to honor the experiential evidence of both "perfection" and imperfection, such individuals would instead be forced to confront the problem of evil as a gnawing enigma, as a type of ethical koan that could be resolved only through a personal and prolonged existential struggle.[164] For those individuals, the problem of evil would be less an intellectual dilemma to be solved, as it would be an opportunity to transform their awareness through a variety of spiritual practices (including the paradoxical practice of resting in the awareness that there is no need to practice). Spiritual life, seen in this way, would be an ongoing attempt to surmount the internal tension created by the juxtaposition of the felt reality of suffering and limitation with the transformative memory of "perfection." Propelled by this theoretically irreconcilable tension, the practice of spiritual disciplines would then become, in part at least, an attempt to find a solution to the problem

263

of evil by catapulting the issue to an entirely different level of resolution, in which evil is fully overcome if and only if an individual becomes stabilized in a mystical awareness in which "perfection" ceases to be merely an abstract concept, or even a potent memory, and becomes, instead, a constant, vibrant, felt reality.

A Spectrum Model of Ethical Life

The notion that ethical understandings differ depending upon the level of awareness that is operative in an individual's life opens up the possibility that day-to-day ethical decisions could also be depicted as functioning in a similar fashion.[165] Unfortunately, because the vast majority of Western ethical reflection is rooted in the taken-for-granted metaphysical assumption of autonomous individuals interacting with other autonomous individuals, little work has been done to reflect on what changes, if any, would occur in our ethical understandings if we operate out of a model that is open to a much wider and more fluid range of self-understandings. While it is impossible, within the constraints of this current project, to offer anything more than a skeletal outline of such an ethical model, it is nonetheless perhaps worthwhile to consider some of the ethical implications that emerge out of a neo-Jamesian, nondual, field model of the self and reality.

For instance, a neo-Jamesian, nondual pluralistic pantheism, which pictures the self, reality, and the divine as a network of interpenetrating fields of awareness, not only provides a framework from which to support an experiential, praxis-oriented solution to the problem of evil, it also creates a philosophical context that can make sense of a wide range of ethical strategies.[166] Because a nondual pluralistic pantheism recognizes that individuals have the possibility to identify themselves with different fields of awareness (anywhere from a highly constricted egoistic identification to a full scale, ongoing mystical consciousness of one's unity with all of life), it can consequently posit ethical strategies that are congruent with each of these dynamic fields of awareness. A nondual pluralistic pantheism will recognize that individuals who primarily identify themselves with a field of awareness that is characterized by a sense of separation from others and from the world might well need to articulate an ethical strategy that is quite different than the ethical stance of those individuals who primarily identify themselves with a field of awareness that is characterized by a sense of unity with broader and deeper levels of reality.

Beyond Words, Beyond Morals

If we posit a neo-Jamesian, nondual pluralistic pantheism, in which the self is not understood to be restricted to a narrow egoistic awareness, but instead, is also understood to include within its parameters broader and deeper fields of consciousness, then it becomes necessary to envision a spectrum model of ethical life that would encompass within itself several alternative possibilities of ethical decision-making, each of which would correlate to a different stage of self-identification. While only the most rudimentary sketch of such a model can be presented at this point in the discussion, what follows will serve as a basic outline of a fourfold, multitiered spectrum model of ethical decision-making.[167]

The first or foundational "level"[168] would consist of those half-automatic, barely conscious, moral decisions which are rooted in a person's early and often tacit internalization of a familial and cultural moral code. Here the individual's level of self-identification is embedded in his or her familial and social roles, and he or she possesses little sense of self-reflexivity. An example of this moral decision-making process might be a young woman who refuses to have pre-marital sexual intercourse, not because of explicit, clearly articulated ethical reasons, but rather, because such a decision just "seems right" to her, based on her cultural background and familial upbringing.[169]

The second level of ethical decision-making within this spectrum model would be those conscious, rationally based ethical choices which are dependent upon one's awareness of oneself as a self-reflexive individual who is separate from others and consequently possesses potentially conflicting goals and desires. An example of moral decision-making from within this level might be a young woman who, based on clear-cut, rationally based ethical criteria, chooses not to terminate her unexpected pregnancy.

The third level of ethical decision-making within this spectrum model would be those moral choices which spring out of a developing openness to intuitive guidance from deeper levels of one's own being, choices which originate from a growing experiential sense of oneself as extending beyond the confines of ordinary ego-awareness. An example of this "style" of moral decision-making might be a young Laotian man training to become a Buddhist monk, who, after years of austere living and countless hours of meditation, decides to follow deeply felt intuitive guidance and chooses to return to a more "worldly" lifestyle, even though this decision goes against both familial expectations and his own prior rational justifications for having chosen to follow a monastic lifestyle.

265

The fourth level of ethical decision-making would be the hypothetical limit of the spectrum model, in that it acknowledges the theoretical possibility of a mode of ethical life that, paradoxically, transcends ethics itself. (An amplification of this notion of transethical behavior will be given below.) This fourth level of ethical life emerges out the self-identification of those who are permanently and completely rooted in a mystical nondual awareness of the simultaneous unity and diversity of life. An example of this level of transmoral action might be a Sufi saint who repeatedly insults and/or ignores a disciple in order to assist that disciple in the process of his or her ego-reduction and concurrent spiritual growth.[170]

These different modes of ethical choice would, by no means, be understood as hermetically sealed from each other. Instead, this spectrum model of ethical choice could endorse a full range of alternate ways of decision-making, each congruent with a different stabilization of awareness within the moment-to-moment flux of consciousness. A spectrum model of ethical choice could recognize that those individuals who, on the whole, have no direct sense of intuitive guidance and who primarily experience themselves as autonomous egos, would very naturally make ethical choices based upon their prior character development as well as through a conscious process of rational decision-making. However, a spectrum model of ethical choice could also acknowledge an alternate possibility. These same individuals, at a later point in time, might begin to drop their prior ego-identification (perhaps as a result of spiritual practices) and consequently might begin to experience their connection to deeper and wider levels of reality. These individuals could then, little by little, learn to trust the intuitive guidance that arises out of this experiential connection, without being forced to renounce the value of either their prior moral development or their powers of rational choice, if and when this experiential connection becomes tenuous or unclear.

It should be noted that it is difficult to defend an ethical strategy which is based on following intuitive guidance if one operates out of many of the more traditional theo-metaphysical perspectives. For instance, if a person has internalized a commonsense naturalistic worldview that assumes that the self is limited to a gestalt of bodily, mental, and emotional processes, then it would be challenging, if not impossible, to justify following one's intuition, since such an understanding of the self excludes any level of reality beyond bodily, mental, and emotional processes; in such a model, there would be no source out of which intuitive guidance could emerge. Alternately, if an individual operates out of a worldview that, at least tacitly, as-

266

sumes that the universe is populated by completely autonomous selves who have been created by a God who is ontologically separate from creation, he or she would also have difficulty justifying an ethical life that is based on following intuitive guidance. While such a theistic perspective might theoretically be able to posit a source out of which inner guidance emerges (God), a theism which understands God to be an ontologically separate being has difficulty articulating how following such guidance has much to do with following one's own intuition.

However, unlike either the secular or the theistic worldview described above, both of which tacitly assume a multitude of autonomous ego-selves interacting and competing with other autonomous ego-selves (even if these atomistic selves are understood as creations of an ontologically separate divine reality), a nondual pluralistic pantheistic field model of the self and reality offers a different, if seemingly paradoxical, alternative. Because nondual pluralistic pantheism postulates a self that is simultaneously united with, yet distinct from, an underlying divine presence, it is possible to say, with equal validity, that following intuitive guidance is *both* a way to become attuned to one's own inner promptings *and* a way to align oneself with a distinct, although not ontologically separate, divinity. Therefore, from the perspective of a nondual pluralistic pantheism, choosing to follow intuitive guidance would neither be a subtle brand of ethical egoism nor blind obedience to divine commands because a nondual pluralistic pantheism allows one to claim that the source of intuitive guidance one is following is *both* a deeper aspect of one's self *and* a level of reality that is objectively distinct from one's everyday egoistic identity.

"Enlightened" Ethics

Not only would a spectrum model of ethical choice be able to make sense of a life based on following intuitive guidance, it would also be able to recognize and honor the claim frequently encountered in numerous mystical traditions: the claim that an individual has the potential to become stabilized in a nondual mystical awareness, and can, consequently, perform actions that are totally free from the distortions and taints of egoistic identification.

Traditionally, the conscious will of such "enlightened" individuals is understood to be completely harmonized with the nondual source of the universe, thus allowing their actions to emerge effortlessly, without agonized decision-making. In addition, the further assertion is usually made that the spontaneous actions of these enlightened beings are always, moment-to-moment, utterly appropriate to the needs and complexities of each situation. A spectrum model of ethical choice would, however, have to acknowledge that historically there has been, at best, an uneasy relationship between philosophical models of ethical life and the behavior of those who are considered by their culture to be enlightened. While hagiographic narratives of the lives of enlightened beings in Asian traditions are full of stories of compassionate self-sacrifice, loving attentiveness, and other exemplary behavior, they are also replete with stories of actions that appear, on the surface at least, to be amoral or at least highly unsaintly. Whether participating in ritual sexual practices, or hurling stones to keep people at a distance, or crouching naked in heaps of garbage, enlightened beings frequently display behavior that is profoundly disturbing, even to those who hold them in high esteem. Such behavior is difficult to reconcile within standard ethical models, even within the ethical models which have been constructed by the traditions themselves.

However, because these traditions typically endorse the supreme value of some form of enlightenment, it becomes imperative to offer a philosophical justification for the occasional antinomian behavior of those it regards as enlightened. Several alternative explanations are commonly found. For instance, such behavior might be seen as the result of a divinely inspired madness (a frequent Hindu and Sufi strategy), or it could be understood as an instantiation of the fecund power of chaos challenging the complacency and pious moralizing of rigid communal structures (a typical Taoist understanding), or it might be defended as the hauntingly appropriate expression of a joyous wisdom and compassion that wishes to shatter the delusive and distorted understanding of those trapped in ignorance and suffering (a common Buddhist explanation).

For those of us standing outside of these Eastern traditions, a completely satisfying explanation may not be possible; from a Western philosophical perspective, there is little, if any, theoretical space for the possibility that a person, while living, could become fully established in a nondual mystical awareness. Nonetheless, even standing within a Western philosophical tradition, it may be possible to gain some theoretical insight into how these traditions can ethically justify the antinomian behavior of those who are understood to be enlightened if we look more closely into the metaphysical and experiential roots of such behavior.

In alignment with the understanding of many Eastern traditions, if we postulate that any and all sense of ego has been eradicated within these enlightened beings and that egoistic identification has

268

been replaced by a complete and permanent awareness of a nondual fusion of perceiver and perceived, then it is theoretically legitimate to posit that the spontaneous behavior of these enlightened beings is a natural extension of this nondual awareness, and that all of his or her actions are nothing more than an organic extension of the seemingly transmoral rhythms of the natural and "supernatural" worlds. If it is true that the boundaries between an enlightened being and the entire seen and unseen universe have experientially collapsed, then, from the point of view of the enlightened being, there really is no separate individual who performs actions, and there is no separate individual who receives these actions. From *our* experiential perspective, there is, on one hand, the "saint," while, on the other hand, there is the "recipient" of the saint's seemingly wildly unacceptable behavior. However, from the nondual perspective of the saint, there is no "other" who is the recipient of these actions, just as there is no egoistic self who performs these actions. There is simply a nondual immersion in "what is going on." If this nondual awareness actually is permanent and completely untainted by the slightest lingering sense of egoistic iden-tification, if there truly is no awareness of a separate self who per-forms actions, then it is difficult to say how, from our hypothetically less illumined perspective, it would be ethically possible to assign either praise or blame to the enlightened being, since the very notion of ethical responsibility itself rests on the dualistic metaphysical as-sumption of separate selves interacting within a shared, but external world. As such, it is understandable why many traditions often regard enlightened beings as living beyond any moral restrictions. Ethical determinations need autonomous individuals, and theoretically at least, there are none to be found in the nondual experiential universe of the enlightened being.

Similarly, if the enlightened being truly is permanently stabi-lized in a mystical nondual awareness, it would be inappropriate to say that he or she makes conscious ethical decisions, since there is no one (i.e., no autonomous individual) who is there making decisions. It could not even be said that the activity of these enlightened beings is "aligned with" some deeper intuitive awareness, since this level of moral choice is based upon a dualistic separation between the indi-vidual and what he or she is "aligned" with. For the truly enlightened being, as he or she is understood in those traditions that acknowledge enlightenment as a viable possibility, there would be no consciousness of any separation between an inner intuitive prompting and conse-quent actions attuned with this prompting—there would be simply activity, activity untouched by humanly created and communally accepted ethical standards or by rational deliberation, activity that effortlessly and ceaselessly expresses the enlightened being's fusion with a nondual mystical awareness.

Of course, matters become much more ambiguous and murky in the actual cultural and historical matrices in which enlightened beings appear. As will become clear in chapter 5, during our discussion of James's understanding of saintliness, communal assessments of who actually is a saint are rarely matters of conscious, deliberate decisions based on clear-cut, universally accepted criteria. More often, the judgement that someone is a saint or an enlightened being emerges gradually, as the result of a slowly building, organic process in which different, and frequently opposing, understandings of the status and stature of the saintly individual collide, until, bit by bit, a consensus begins to emerge that this individual does, indeed, deserve this accolade. While, from the perspective of the saint or enlightened being, this new found communal recognition may have little or no effects on what actions he or she performs (the "real" acknowledgment being the stabilization of the mystical state of awareness itself), the community that forms the environment in which the saint operates may be less open-minded.[171] While typically the saint's culture will have encoded within it certain assumptions that saints should not be held to ordinary ethical criteria, if the actions of the alleged saint extend too far beyond the boundaries of what the community accepts as behavior that is expected of an enlightened being, then a substantial, and influential, percentage of that community can and will revoke the previous tacit understanding that this individual actually is a saint. Then, once again, the intracommunal dispute begins, the struggle between that faction which is convinced that the evident peace, love, spiritual power, and inner radiance of the saint demonstrates that his or her unorthodox behavior is "divinely" inspired, and that faction which claims that the alleged saint is actually a fraud or a madman, since his or her actions are so outrageous and repugnant that any seemingly compassionate and wise behavior is simply a deceptive facade.

Communities that accept the value of saintliness are far from unified, and they are far from naive. There is a vivid recognition within these communities that occasionally there will be those who will seek to justify their antinomian activity with nothing more than adroitly phrased and intellectually polished rhetoric, and that these saintly pretenders deserve a rigorous ethical examination and critique, since a merely intellectual belief in an underlying "oneness" or "perfection" should not be an acceptable excuse for the performance of hurtful actions or the absence of loving behavior. Unfortunately, it is tortuously difficult to develop workable criteria that can enable anyone, whether inside or outside the culture, to determine who deserves to be called a saint and who does not. Selfless spontaneity can look distressingly similar to egoistic impulsiveness; saintly antinomian behavior that challenges social ethical standards can be the mirror image of psychopathological indifference to communal norms.

To further complicate matters, evidence that the saint or enlightened being possesses a vivid, distinct personality does not automatically discredit the claim to enlightenment (a claim which is rarely, if ever, made by the alleged saints themselves, but rather, is almost always made by the followers or disciples of these saints), even though saints or enlightened beings are theoretically understood to be free from egoistic identification. Few will dispute the fact that every saint still retains a highly functional and very distinctive personality. Different saints act differently; they each have their own preferences, their own likes and dislikes. While, on the surface, this apparently strong evidence of selfhood might seem to contradict the frequent claims that saints are completely selfless, philosophically it is possible to reconcile a strong and developed personality with claims of utter selflessness, since complete immersion in nondual awareness does not necessarily destroy a working awareness of body and mind. Nondual awareness may simply free the saint from exclusive identification with that limited field of consciousness.

A spectrum model of ethical choice would be forced to recognize the fact that it is extremely difficult, if not impossible, to draw a clear line between those who are established in a continuous awareness of their nondual fusion with the universe and those for whom this awareness is, to one degree or another, largely intellectual and/or superficial. There is rarely, if ever, a complete separation between a merely intellectual understanding of "oneness" or "perfection" and the more directly experiential mystical apprehension of this "oneness" and "perfection." As was pointed out in chapter 2, "knowledge-by-acquaintance" and "knowledge-about" are inevitably interwoven, except in perhaps the most rarefied mystical states of awareness. Consequently, moments of genuinely selfless saintly behavior that emerge out of a direct apprehension of nondual awareness may alternate with actions that, while less selfish than most, may still be subtly driven by an egoistic identification. In fact, as a field-model of self and reality will emphasize, most spiritually active individuals will fluctuate in and out of different degrees of mystical awareness, and will therefore need to utilize a wide range of ethical decision-making strategies. There may be moments in which the mystical awareness of these individuals is so powerful that their

271

responses to particular situations are completely spontaneous and effortlessly attuned to the needs of the present moment. At other times, these individuals may primarily experience themselves as alienated from any deeper sense of themselves, and consequently, must rely either upon their prior moral training or upon their powers of reason in order to make ethical decisions.

A spectrum model of ethical choice would thereby recognize the fact that for most individuals with an active spiritual life, ambiguity and uncertainty can and do coexist with clarity and certainty; it can affirm the fact that, in most cases, the need for ethical choice is very real, and moreover, it can acknowledge that the risk is very real that mistakes in judgement can and will be made. Even those seemingly effortless and spontaneous actions which emerge out of a deep sense of mystical union would not be exempt from the ever-present possibility of a lingering egoistic distortion. A crucial component of the spiritual life of such individuals, therefore, would be the cultivation of the ability to distinguish those moments when authentic intuitive guidance is being offered and those moments when that guidance is clouded or obscured by the miasma of egoistic desires that form the basis of these individuals' experiential sense of alienation and separation.

Nonetheless, from the perspective of a nondual pluralistic pantheism, this acknowledgment of the ever-present need for discrimination and discernment is only half of the picture, since even the most abject moral failure could also be understood as springing out of a deeper underlying "perfection." This underlying "perfection" would not have to be understood literally; it would not need to imply some simplistic notion of a locked, stagnant, preordained universe in which free choice is illusory and real mistakes are impossible. The universe can be pictured as open-ended and dynamic without sacrificing a concurrent notion of an underlying "perfection." In an infinite universe, there are an infinite number of possibilities for the expression of "perfection"; there is infinite room for an ultimate good to emerge out of each freely chosen act. In such a universe, each person could act, knowing that his or her actions produce real consequences, real suffering, and yet also, simultaneously, rest secure in the mystically generated trust that, somehow, from a deeper perspective, everything is as it should be within both the seen and unseen worlds.

｡･5･｡

Telling Truths, Touching Realities:
Spiritual Judgments, Saints, and Pragmatism

Tell me of those who live established in wisdom, ever aware
of the Self, O Krishna. How do they talk? How sit? How move
about?
　　　　　　　　　　　　　　　　　　　　—*Bhagavad Gita*

Rabbi Dov Baer, the maggid of Mezritch, once begged Heaven
to show him a man whose every limb and every fibre was
holy. Then they showed him the form of the Baal Shem Tov,
and it was all of fire. There was no shred of substance in it. It
was nothing but flame.
　　　　　　　　　　　—Martin Buber, *Tales of the Hasidim*

They are the strength of the world, because they are the tab-
ernacles of God in the world. They are the ones who keep the
universe from being destroyed. They are the little ones. They
do not know themselves. The whole earth depends on them.
Nobody seems to realize it. These are the ones for whom it
was all created in the first place. . . . They are the only ones
capable of understanding joy. Everybody else is too weak for
joy. Joy would kill anybody but these meek. They are the clean
of heart. They see God. He does their will, because His will is
their own. . . . Their freedom is without limit.
　　　　　　　—Thomas Merton, *New Seeds of Contemplation*

James's visions of reality are provocative. Whether depicting overlapping, interpenetrating fields of awareness or co-conscious earth souls
or powerful and beneficent unseen spiritual worlds, James's intricate
and far-reaching psychological, theological, and metaphysical speculations present us with intriguing possibilities. However, at some point,
the question naturally arises: are these psychological, theological, and
metaphysical speculations forever relegated to the limbo-land of mere
possibility, or do they, on any level, reflect anything that is real? That
is, are these speculations true? If so, how do we go about determining

their truth-status? Furthermore, what exactly do we mean when we use such terms as "real" and "true," especially when these terms are applied to mystico-religious experiences?

James himself, realizing that it was necessary at some point to wrestle with the question of truth, worked hard to articulate clear and convincing answers to these questions. Profoundly dissatisfied with the ability of prior models of truth to cope effectively with the truth-status of nonmaterial levels of existence, James struggled to articulate alternate notions of truth and slowly began to formulate the ideas that evolved into his pragmatic understanding of the nature of the verification process.

James's pragmatism by no means revolves exclusively around religious issues; but in many ways, it is clear that the seeds of James's pragmatism are to be found in his most explicitly religious work, *The Varieties of Religious Experience*. In the *Varieties*, via an investigation of the *effects* of religious experiences, James begins, somewhat haltingly, to move away from the notion that truth can be determined by an analysis of the degree to which a belief corresponds to a preexisting external reality; he begins, instead, to move towards the notion that truth is a fallible, ongoing, communally based assessment of the ability of an idea or experience to give rise to worthwhile consequences in the world at large.

In the *Varieties*, James gathers together a wide-ranging mass of data on religious life. He discusses religious conversion experiences, the mind-cure movement, prayer, and most importantly, saintliness—not simply to examine these phenomena for their own sake, but, rather, to use this wealth of phenomenological descriptions as cumulative evidence that belief in an unseen spiritual world can catalyze positive changes in the lives of individuals, especially when that belief is accompanied by dramatic religious experiences. However, as James suggests, to say that strong religious beliefs and intense mystical experiences frequently initiate positive changes in the lives of men and women is not the same as saying that those beliefs and experiences are true. Therefore, in the *Varieties*, James also seeks to formulate criteria that can be used to assess the *truth* of religious beliefs and experiences—a truth that James already suspects cannot be determined in complete isolation from some demonstration of its personal and communal repercussions. The *Varieties* offers James a chance to rough out a group of tentative criteria for determining the truth-status of religious beliefs and experiences; these criteria, in tandem with numerous examples of the positive effects of a dynamic spiritual life, come together to create something that was, and is, philosophically unique: an

274

inspired, if unpolished, attempt to justify a belief in the reality, power, and goodness of the unseen world based solely on pragmatic, this-worldly grounds. The *Varieties*, in many ways, is simply James's sustained, if often uneven, argument with himself and with others that there are strong intellectual, moral, and experiential reasons to believe in the existence of an unseen, dynamic, and beneficent spiritual world.

Ambivalent Standards: James's Three Criteria

In order for James to succeed in his task of convincing himself (and his readers) that a vital religious life is both valuable and valid, he first had to clarify how he intended to examine and assess religious phenomena, and second, he had to demonstrate how his own methodology differed from previous scholarly attempts to study religious life. Therefore, in the first pages of the *Varieties*, as a methodological prelude to his rich descriptions of religious experiences, James makes a clear distinction between two types of scholarly inquiry: the *existential judgment* and the *spiritual judgment*.[1]

The "existential judgment" is James's term for a mode of investigation that is both descriptive and explanatory; an existential judgment takes place when an investigator assembles a complete and detailed description of a phenomenon and then goes on to analyze the various historical, economic, psychological, sociological, and cultural factors that come together to bring this phenomenon into being. Thus, a person attempting to make an existential judgment would ask, "What is the nature of [a phenomenon]? how did it come about? what is its constitution, origin, and history?"[2]

James stresses that the existential judgment, that is, the descriptive and explanatory phase of an investigation, is logically distinct from the process of making a "spiritual judgment." Unlike the existential judgment, the spiritual judgment is normative; it is concerned with assessing the *value* of a phenomenon; it seeks to determine the philosophical, ethical, or practical "importance, meaning, or significance" of what is being investigated.[3]

James emphasizes that it is crucially important to separate these two modes of inquiry, since numerous methodological problems arise if and when they are conflated. According to James, this erroneous conflation occurs especially frequently in investigations of religious phenomena. James thinks that many scholars of religion seem to believe that if they can demonstrate that religious phenomena have physiological origins, then they have somehow also proved that the spiritual value of these religious phenomena is diminished as well; that is, these scholars believe that the results of their existential judgment (i.e., their claim that religious phenomena have biological origins) has negative repercussions on the spiritual judgment of these religious phenomena (i.e., the value or worth of these phenomena).

James characterizes those scholars who seek to reduce all religious phenomena to nothing but expressions of different bodily disorders as "medical materialists." Medical materialism claims, for instance, that a nun's longing for the love of Christ is nothing but an expression of her repressed sexual drives; it "finishes up Saint Paul by calling his vision on the road to Damascus" an epileptic seizure; it "snuffs out Saint Theresa as an hysteric"; it portrays Saint Francis as suffering from a hereditary disorder, and so on.[4] As James points out, however, these medical materialists do not simply claim that these religious states of consciousness have physiological roots; instead, they go on to make the *normative* claim that the biological origins of the religious experiences undergone by various mystics somehow proves "that the spiritual authority of all such personages is successfully undermined."[5]

James readily concedes that it may well be true that all religious phenomena have organic underpinnings. But, as he cleverly points out, if we accept the theory that all states of mind have "some organic process as its condition,"[6] then we must also acknowledge that atheistic conclusions and scientific insights are connected with different physiological states as well. Why then, James wants to know, do medical materialists refuse to conclude that these nonreligious states of mind are equally discredited by their connection with physiological processes?[7] Do we ever conclude that a scientific breakthrough is invalid or useless simply because the scientist had a fever when the insight surged up from within? If not, James asks, why then do we think that religious states of mind are automatically discredited, if they are found to have physiological origins?

If we cannot legitimately assess the relative worth of different "states of mind" based on their physiological origins, then are there any criteria by which we *can* determine that "certain states of mind" are better than others? James, for one, is convinced that there are. The three criteria that James claims must come together to form a normative assessment (i.e., a "spiritual judgment") of different states of mind are *immediate luminousness, philosophical reasonableness,* and *moral helpfulness.*

Once again, it quickly becomes clear that these three criteria are simply another permutation of James's "holy trinity": experience, belief, and action. "Immediate luminousness" is that aspect of the spiritual judgment which prompts an investigator to take seriously the experiential, knowledge-by-acquaintance component of a religious state of mind—that is, its immediate force, its raw voltage, its direct, tangible feeling. "Philosophical reasonableness" is the criterion which assesses whether a religious state of mind can be shown to be reasonable and logical by virtue of its place within an articulate and defensible philosophical system of beliefs. Finally, "moral helpfulness," the overtly pragmatic aspect of the spiritual judgment, is demonstrated when and if a religious state of mind can be shown to initiate, on the whole and over the long run, positive consequences for the individual and the community.

Perhaps an example will clarify how these three criteria might be used to form a spiritual judgment of a religious state of consciousness. Let us say that we read an account of the mystical experiences of a Taoist recluse. She writes that, after years of study under a Taoist master, she went to a secluded retreat site and began to practice a visualization designed to facilitate the flow of the *chi*, or life force, through various energy centers in the body. One day, immersed in this visualization, she vividly perceived each breath moving through her body in the form of a golden thread of light. She writes that this golden light illuminated and enlivened each of her energy centers in turn, creating strong surges of joy within her and opening her to profound levels of spiritual insight. She also notes that, for days afterwards, she was filled with tremendous physical vitality and mental clarity and that subsequent visualizations prolonged and deepened this transformative shift in awareness. She then goes on to claim that, as a result of the insights and spiritual power that she received through these spiritual experiences (as well as other mystical experiences that she narrates), she was eventually able to function as a Taoist master herself to a small group of disciples.

In this relatively unambiguous example, the spiritual judgment is fairly straightforward: the "states of mind" experienced by the Taoist recluse were extremely positive. The criterion of immediate luminousness is fulfilled by the vividness, power, and immediacy of her experience: her direct and forceful perceptions of the golden light and its movement within her, as well as the sensations of joy that she felt and the insights that flooded her awareness. The criterion of philosophical reasonableness is also satisfied, in that the recluse can easily fit this experience into a complex and sophisticated philosophical system of understanding: the gestalt of beliefs and assumptions that come together to create the worldview of esoteric Taoism. Finally, the criterion

277

of moral helpfulness is fulfilled by the fact that, as a result of her spiritual experiences, the recluse became more physically energetic, mentally clear, and was able to play an important social role as a teacher to a new generation of Taoist students.

Of course, few illustrations of how the three criteria can be used to form a spiritual judgment are so straightforward. Later in this chapter the problems and complications that can often arise when these three criteria become the basis for making a spiritual judgment will be explored. First, however, it is important to note how James's own description of the three criteria contains within it several significant areas of unclarity.

For example, James is often unclear as to exactly what it is that the spiritual judgment seeks to accomplish. Does the spiritual judgment assess the worth, value, and goodness of these states of mind, or does it assess their truth? In contrast to James's later clear and impassioned defense in *Pragmatism* of a notion of truth in which truth is understood to be identical, in many respects at least, to goodness and value, James's notion of the truth in the *Varieties* is difficult to pin down. At some points in the *Varieties*, James seems to suggest that assessing value and assessing truth are essentially the same process (without any theoretical justification for this conflation); at other points, he seems to imply that determining goodness and truth are *not* the same process.

Furthermore, it is often difficult to determine what it is that a spiritual judgment actually assesses. James frequently claims that the spiritual judgment seeks to determine the worth of different "states of mind," but just what does James mean when he uses this term? Does he think that states of mind are opinions, thoughts, and beliefs (i.e., are they primarily "knowledge-about" states of consciousness) or does James think that these states of mind are experiences and feelings (i.e., are they primarily "knowledge-by-acquaintance" states of awareness)? Or are they both? Throughout his discussion of the process by which one makes a spiritual judgment, James is simply not consistent. Sometimes he claims that the spiritual judgment assesses the value of opinions or beliefs, while at other times, he claims that the spiritual judgment focuses on experiences or feelings, while at still other times, he seems to conflate these two analytically separate types of knowing.[8]

These two areas of confusion (that is, first, whether the spiritual judgment assesses value or truth and, second, whether the term "states of mind" represents opinions or experiences) permeate most, if not all, of James's discussion of the spiritual judgment. The first area of confusion is particularly glaring. A brief look at the text will suffice to illustrate James's different understandings of the relationship between "truth" and "value." For instance, at one point, James notes that "what immediately feels most 'good' is not always most 'true,' when measured by the verdict of the rest of experience. The difference between Philip drunk and Philip sober is the classic" example.[9] Here, James appears to be stating that the attempt to determine the "goodness" of a state of mind (in this case, "feelings" instead of "opinions") is distinct from the attempt to determine the "truth" of that state of mind. But compare this apparent separation of truth and value with another passage, in which James discusses how we should attempt to determine the "value" of religious "opinions":

> Their value can only be ascertained by spiritual judgments directly passed on them; judgments based on our own immediate feeling primarily; and secondarily on what we can ascertain of their experiential relations to our moral needs and to the rest of what we hold as true. *Immediate luminousness*, in short, *philosophical reasonableness*, and *moral helpfulness* are the only available criteria.[10]

In this passage, it appears that James does *not* clearly separate truth and value, in that he claims that the goal of spiritual judgments is to ascertain value, but this value is, in part at least, determined by the relationship between our immediate experience and the rest of what we believe to be *true*. Furthermore, almost immediately after this passage, this conflation of truth and value continues, when James claims that the purpose of the spiritual judgment is to ascertain "truth" (no longer "value," as in the previous passage), arguing that the "empirical" criteria that are used in the spiritual judgment are part of a "search for truth."[11]

It is clear that James thinks that at least one of the most important tasks of the spiritual judgment is this "search for truth," since he immediately contrasts his own empirically based "search for truth" with other, more dogmatic, attempts to find truth. According to James, certain philosophers want to discover "some direct mark," something by which their philosophy "can be protected immediately and absolutely, now and forever, against all mistake."[12] In their attempt to provide a metaphysical grounding for their religious beliefs, these philosophers try different strategies. For instance, they claim that their religious beliefs are true because they come from a trustworthy and authoritative source: for example, from "immediate intuition," or "pontifical authority," or "supernatural revelation," or "direct possession by a higher spirit."[13] Unfortunately, as James is all too willing to point out, this claim that one's religious beliefs are true because they come from some unimpeachable source is simply the mirror image of the strategy used by the medical materialists. James notes that the only difference between the strategies used by these philosophers and those used by the medical materialists is that the medical materialists attempt to *discredit* religion by pointing out its allegedly disreputable physiological origins, whereas these philosophers seek to *protect* religion by positing seemingly more lofty origins. As James points out, both of these strategies are simply a variation of the existential judgment in that they both seek to determine the *origin* of religious states of mind, and therefore neither can tell us anything about the truth (value?) of these religious phenomena. That task, according to James, is reserved for the spiritual judgment and its three criteria of immediate luminousness, philosophical reasonableness, and moral helpfulness.

However, as was noted above, it is difficult to determine exactly what these three criteria seek to assess. Do they attempt to ascertain the value/truth of thoughts, beliefs, and opinions or do they attempt to determine the value/truth of experiences and feelings? In the context of religious phenomena in particular, does the spiritual judgment attempt to determine the value/truth of religious *beliefs* (i.e., knowledge-about states of mind) or does the spiritual judgment attempt to ascertain the value/truth of religious *experiences* (i.e., knowledge-by-acquaintance states of mind)? While James insists that these two different modes of knowledge are always interrelated, he also stresses that they can and should, for analytical purposes, be distinguished from one another. Unfortunately, however, James does not maintain this distinction in his examination of the three criteria that make up the spiritual judgment.

For instance, if these criteria are designed to assess beliefs, why is it that many, if not most, of James's examples do not refer to *beliefs*, but rather to *experiences*, especially mystico-religious experiences? For instance, immediately after James's discussion of the difference between "Philip drunk and Philip sober," where he points out the contrast between the value of a person's drunken perceptions and the value of his or her sober insights, James goes on to note that mystical experiences often reflect a similar internal dichotomy. As James emphasizes:

> There are moments of sentimental and mystical experience . . . that carry an enormous sense of inner authority and illumination with them when they come. But they come seldom and they do not come to every one; and

the rest of life makes either no connection with them, or tends to contra-dict them more than it confirms them."[14]

Bracketing for the moment James's somewhat hasty assessment of the inability of mystical experiences to connect with the rest of life, it is evident that, in this passage, James does not claim that spiritual judgments assess opinions, thoughts, or beliefs; instead, he argues that spiritual judgments assess (as well?) states of awareness that are pri-marily rooted in knowledge-by-acquaintance, that is, mystical *experi-ences*. Therefore, it is simply not clear whether James intends that these criteria should be used to assess mystico-religious *experiences*, or the *beliefs* that the mystic holds, or both.

In the *Varieties*, James's fusion of "beliefs" and "experiences," as well as his conflation of "truth" and "value," appear to be primarily a matter of a careless use of terminology; but this conceptual unclarity sets the stage for James's later explicit discussion in *Pragmatism* of how the concepts of "truth" and "value" are interrelated, as well as his detailed exposition of the necessity to separate "beliefs" (which can be either true or false) from "reality" (which, for James, as the experiential grounding of every truth, is in itself neither true nor false, but instead, is that basic "givenness" to which truths refer).[15] Unfor-tunately, when James was writing the *Varieties*, these important dis-tinctions (value/truth, experience/belief) were not yet clarified; as a result, much of the brilliance that shines through James's discussion of the three criteria is obscured. Nevertheless, if we can, for the moment, set aside James's conceptual unclarity, we might well discover the value (truth?) of James's insights into how these three criteria can be used to assess religious phenomena.

"By Their Fruits Ye Shall Know Them"

In any discussion of James's use of the three criteria, it is crucial to remember, as was pointed out earlier, that we are seeing yet an-other permutation of James's ever-present triad: experience (i.e., "im-mediate luminousness"), thoughts (i.e., "philosophical reasonableness"), and action (i.e., "moral helpfulness"). These three criteria are not mutually exclusive, but rather interact with, and depend upon, each other. James can and does analytically distinguish between them, but when he actually attempts the concrete process of making a spiritual judgment, it is clear that these three criteria work together as a unit. The spiritual judgment, therefore, is not a matter of precisely weighing the percentage of each criteria's importance, but instead, is a holistic, cumulative process. As James emphasizes, the final test for assessing a state of mind is not the individual "score" of each of these criterion, but rather it is their cumulative weight, the way that they work as a whole, and on the whole.[16]

Nonetheless, it is crucial to emphasize that James *does* strongly underscore the importance of criterion number one: immediate luminousness—the direct evidence of an experience, the forcefulness of the way an experience feels within us, the convincing power of an experience's sheer "is-ness." Again and again, James returns to the centrality of the immediate "feeling" of an experience, especially in the context of assessing religious phenomena. In fact, James explicitly, if somewhat off-handedly, comments that our spiritual judgments are "based on our own immediate feeling primarily" and only "secondarily" on philosophical reasonableness and moral helpfulness.[17] This bequeathal of primacy to immediate luminousness need not necessarily invalidate the previous commentary on the equal significance of each of these three criteria; James is most likely simply emphasizing that, for a phenomenon to merit further evaluation, it must first manifest itself, and manifest itself convincingly. Nonetheless, regardless of whether James does or does not assign *more* weight to immediate luminousness, it is clear that he does not think that it is *less* important than philosophical reasonableness or moral helpfulness.

James realizes that it is rare that a mystic who has been "lit up" by the immediate luminousness of a powerful mystical experience will recognize the need for a subsequent philosophical examination of the validity and value of that experience; however, James does manages to find an illustration of this ideal attitude in an excerpt from the spiritual autobiography of J. Trevor, a mystically inclined individual of James's own time. Trevor writes:

> The spiritual life justifies itself to those who live it; but what can we say to those who do not understand? . . . It is a life whose experiences are proved real to their possessor, because they remain with him when brought closest into contact with the objective realities of life. Dreams cannot stand this test. . . . I have severely questioned the worth of these moments. . . . but I find that, after every questioning and test, they stand out to-day as the most real experiences of my life, and experiences which have explained and justified and unified all past experiences and all past growth. Indeed, their reality and their far-reaching significance are ever becoming more clear and evident. When they came, I was living the fullest, strongest, sanest, deepest life. I was not seeking them.[18]

Telling Truths, Touching Realities

While historically, as James is aware, many, if not most, mystics have not demonstrated this admirably post-Enlightenment critical approach to their own mystical experiences, it is nonetheless a fact that many mystics did not accept, on face value, everything that was revealed to them in their mystical states of consciousness; they often agonized over how to interpret their vivid and powerful experiences. As James points out, because some of "the visions and messages" received by these mystics were "too patently silly [i.e., philosophically unreasonable]" to be taken seriously, and because some of "the trances and convulsive seizures" were thought to be "too fruitless for conduct and character [i.e., morally unhelpful], to pass themselves off as significant, still less as divine," it was often crucially important that these mystics possessed a set of criteria by which they could determine which of these various experiences were authentic (i.e., were from God) and which were not (i.e., were from "the tempter" or the mystic's imagination).[19] James stresses, therefore, that because the origins of different mystico-religious experiences are rarely, if ever, self-evident, even to the mystic, the only clear way to determine the validity and value of a mystico-religious experience is to assess how well it works on the whole; that is, given the experience's immediate luminousness, does it also seem reasonable? Does it seem to make us better people?

Repeatedly, when examining the complex process of making a holistic assessment of the validity and value of mystico-religious experiences, James returns to the centrality of "moral helpfulness." But what, exactly, does James mean by the term "moral helpfulness"? In addition, what are some of the signs, in James's opinion, that a mystico-religious experience is actually morally helpful?

To begin with, it is clear that James intends the criteria of moral helpfulness to signify much more than an increased ability to live ethically. Moral helpfulness, broadly understood, is an acknowledgment that what is being assessed (in this case, a mystico-religious experience) has produced some sort of meaningful and long-lasting positive change, either within the individual or the community or both. Therefore, if we want to determine if a mystico-religious experience has been morally helpful to us, we might ask ourselves whether it has increased our vitality and enthusiasm, or whether it has made us better citizens, or whether it has expanded our joy and our capacity to love—in short, whether it has produced some sort of significant, observable, and positive transformation in our personal lives or within our community.

James argues that this attempt to determine the value of a religious experience by focusing on its empirically observable results is

283

simply a philosophical amplification of a perspective which has been known and practiced for many hundreds of years, a perspective which he believes is encapsulated in the biblically inspired phrase, "By their fruits ye shall know them, not by their roots."[20] James uses the theological work of Jonathan Edwards to illustrate this style of inductive methodology. James points out that Edwards, who believed that "our practice is the only sure evidence, even to ourselves, that we are genuinely Christians,"[21] was a clear example of someone who used empirical criteria to assess the validity and value of religious experiences. James goes on to argue that Catholic mystics also used similar criteria to determine the validity and value of mystico-religious experiences, saying, in essence, that "the good dispositions which a vision, or voice, or other apparent heavenly favor leave behind them are the only marks by which we may be sure they are not possible deceptions of the tempter."[22]

James is not satisfied, however, in merely establishing that the criterion of moral helpfulness has theological antecedents. He also wants to demonstrate that mystics, having used this criterion, have typically ascertained that their mystico-religious experiences were indeed morally helpful. James excerpts numerous quotes from the writings of several Spanish mystics to underscore the fact that they, at least, were convinced that mystical experiences catalyze positive, transformative effects. For example, James notes that St. Teresa of Avila writes that a "'genuine heavenly vision'" gives "'ineffable spiritual riches and an admirable renewal of bodily strength','" and leaves the mystic filled "'with masculine courage and other virtues'"; whereas the "'mere operations of the imagination'" do nothing "'but weaken the soul'," giving it "'lassitude and disgust'."[23] He also quotes St. John of the Cross, who, equally impressed with the positive psychological effects of mystical experiences, claims that mystical states of awareness "may be sufficient to abolish at a stroke certain imperfections of which the soul during its whole life had vainly tried to rid itself, and to leave it adorned with virtues and loaded with supernatural gifts."[24]

Almost as if he were hearing the mutterings of his skeptical colleagues in the background, James acknowledges that someone who is medically trained might have difficulty understanding how someone could possibly take these mystical ecstasies seriously, when it would seem obvious that they were nothing but "suggested and imitated hypnoid states."[25] James, however, holds his ground, reminding his audience that while "pathological conditions have existed in many and possibly in all" mystics, nevertheless, "that fact tells us nothing about the value" of these mystical states of awareness.[26] That task, according to James, is performed by the spiritual judgment, and in order to "pass a spiritual judgment upon these states, we must not content ourselves with superficial medical talk, but [rather, must] inquire into their fruits for life."[27]

At this point in the discussion, James appears to be attempting to convince his audience that they (or any well-educated, thoughtful person) can and should "pass a spiritual judgment" on the mystico-religious experiences of others. However, James's earlier illustrations of this evaluative process implied something quite different, in that earlier James primarily focused on the ways in which saints and mystics have attempted to ascertain the validity and value of their *own* experiences. Therefore, it is not immediately clear just who it is that James believes should engage in the process of making a spiritual judgment. On the one hand, James sometimes claims that the process of making a spiritual judgment is a philosophical endeavor that can and should be undertaken by an outside observer. On the other hand, many of James's examples of how the spiritual judgment takes place often seem to imply that this evaluative process is ideally meant for those who have themselves experienced these mystical states of consciousness.

James never comments on this methodological ambiguity, even though it would appear that the process itself would vary dramatically depending upon whether the individual attempting to make the spiritual judgment was someone who had personally experienced these states of awareness or whether the assessor was simply someone interested in evaluating mystical experiences, while never having experienced them firsthand. One immediate difference between first-hand and second-hand spiritual judgments revolves around the second criterion: philosophical reasonableness. A mystic will almost certainly differ from a nonmystic as to what beliefs are philosophically reasonable and what beliefs are not. The mystic will typically structure his or her life around a theological and philosophical system that can easily integrate and make sense of a wide range of mystico-religious experiences, whereas the philosophical and theological assumptions of someone who is not spiritually inclined might well have no place for such experiences.

Similarly, the third criterion, moral helpfulness, runs into difficulties as well. The mystic will, almost certainly, decide whether a mystical experience has been "morally helpful" based on specific religious assumptions about the purpose of human existence and the possibilities of personal fulfillment. These normative assumptions will clearly differ dramatically from those who are not spiritually inclined, leading, once again, to different assessments of whether the experience was positive or negative.[28]

Most significantly, however, it is difficult to imagine just how the criterion of "immediate luminousness" functions for an outside observer of mystical states of awareness. For the mystic, "immediate luminousness" is a critically important element of any attempt to determine the validity and value of a particular mystical experience. The vivid, direct, almost sensory impact of an experience provides the mystic, in essence, with the raw material that is the basis for any further assessment. Without immediate luminousness, there is nothing further to discuss, since if there is no "thatness" of the experience, the mystic has nothing to talk *about*. For the nonmystic, however, immediate luminousness as a criterion is, at best, a lukewarm imitation of the original. Since the nonmystic cannot personally feel the power and vividness of the mystical experience itself, all that he or she can do is to accept at face value the testimonies and narratives of those who have undergone this level of experience—an acceptance that, at best, can only be a pale counterpart to having directly experienced mystical states of awareness.

This crucial difference between first-hand knowledge of a mystical experience's immediate luminousness and a dependence upon second-hand reports is perhaps the single most important deciding factor in whether an individual will determine that a mystical experience is worthwhile or not. Unfortunately, James's delineation of the process of making a spiritual judgment does not acknowledge this crucial distinction. While it is true that mystics, throughout history and in numerous different traditions, are alert to the very real possibility that some mystical experiences may be worthless or even harmful, it is much more common to find mystics rapturously praising the joyous expansion, the deep peace, and the radiant wisdom contained within mystical states of awareness. It is a rare mystic who doubts the validity and value of their mystical experiences. The same cannot be said of the nonmystic.

If mystical experiences have any hope of being judged as valuable or valid by those who can only vicariously guess at the immediate luminousness of a mystical experience, something else has to take the place of the unshakable certainty that typically accompanies the immediate luminousness of a mystical experience. If a nonmystic is going to be convinced that mystical experiences are worthwhile and nonillusory, he or she must be persuaded that these phenomena, which are so alien to his or her everyday experience, are at least intelligible and/or that they have made a positive difference in the personal and

286

communal life of the mystic. It would seem, therefore, that the criteria of philosophical reasonableness and moral helpfulness, while perhaps useful to the mystic in the process of spiritual discernment, are in actuality more directly useful to those who are not themselves mystics, whereas the criterion of immediate luminousness is more directly applicable to the mystics themselves.

James recognized, however, that if, as he comments in a letter to Francis R. Morse, he was to succeed in his attempt to demonstrate in the *Varieties* that religious life "as a whole" is "mankind's most important function," then he had to draw upon all three of these criteria. In many ways, in fact, the criteria of immediate luminousness, philosophical reasonableness, and moral helpfulness can be said to act as the pillars upon which the argumentative structure of the *Varieties* itself is based. In order to prove his thesis, James recognized that he not only had to gather empirical data that showed that powerful mystico-religious experiences are the basis for a genuine religious life, but he also had to show clearly that these experiences make sense and that they are personally and communally transformative.[29] Therefore, after having given his non-mystically-inclined readers a repeated and detailed exposure to the most vivid accounts of mystical experiences that he could find (James's own "second-hand" version of immediate luminousness), he concentrated, in section by section of the *Varieties*, on the task of convincing his readers that these mystico-religious experiences were both philosophically reasonable and morally helpful.

The *Varieties*, seen in this way, can be understood as split into three distinct, if interrelated, argumentative components, each of which mirror James's three criteria: first, the collection of mystical narratives is a vicarious nod to immediate luminousness; second, the vigorous defense of the importance and centrality of personal experience is James's attempt to make mystical experiences seem philosophically reasonable to his audience; and, third, the depiction of the physical healings performed by the mind-cure movement, as well as the descriptions of the mystically inspired character transformations undergone by saintly converts can be seen as a way for James to persuade those who are not mystics themselves that mystico-religious experiences are indeed worthwhile—that is, morally helpful.

Therefore, throughout the *Varieties*, James's underlying intention during his discussion of the fruits of mystical experience is to show that mystical experiences, on the whole, generate worthwhile consequences. Admittedly, however, there are moments in the text where this basic intention is not so readily visible, since James often dwells, at length, on the apparently negative fruits of mystical experiences. As James makes abundantly clear in his discussion on saintliness, the lives of many saints and mystics, in his opinion, did not improve as a result of their mystical ecstasies, but instead, worsened.[30] For example, as James points out, especially if the mystic's or saint's "character [was] naturally passive and the intellect feeble," mystical states of awareness could at times bring on "stupefaction," "helplessness," and an "over-abstraction from practical life."[31]

However, after this list of the potentially negative consequences of mysticism, James quickly reverses course, and goes on to point out that "in natively strong minds and characters we find quite opposite results" from what is found in saints and mystics with less developed personal traits.[32] "The great Spanish mystics," such as St. Teresa of Avila and St. Ignatius of Loyola, for example, demonstrated, in James's eyes, "indomitable spirit and energy, and all the more so for the trances in which they indulged."[33] St. Ignatius, in particular, appears to impress James, since James makes it clear that, in his opinion, Ignatius's "mysticism made him assuredly one of the most powerfully practical engines that ever lived."[34]

It seems, therefore, that James's discussion of the negative effects of mystical experience must not be taken at face value. Although James does wish to emphasize to his audience that he is aware that mystical life is not uniformly positive, he rarely, if ever, concludes his discussion of the "fruits" of mysticism on a sour note. Over and over again in the text, James's initial presentation of the negative consequences of mystical experience is followed by a rhetorical reversal, in which James comments glowingly on the shining character traits possessed by the saints and mystics. James is convinced that mystical states of awareness are, on the whole, beneficial. He is, however, rhetorically sophisticated enough to know that he is unlikely to bring his audience around to his side if he does not first appear to sympathize with their own reluctance to see the value of mystical life.

The Mind-Cure Movement

James's attempt to convince his audience that mystical states of awareness are basically positive is not just limited to a few passing comments on saints and mystics from other times and other cultures. He also seeks to bolster his argument by presenting evidence of turn-of-the-century American transformations of mind and body that were catalyzed by mystical states of awareness.

James comments on these mental and physical transformations in his prolonged discussion in the *Varieties* of the mind-cure move-

288

ment, a system of spiritual healing that was extremely popular during James's time, especially in Boston and other major cities throughout America.[35] The mind-cure movement, a turn-of-the-century precursor of many "New Age" ideas, drew its inspiration, according to James, from a wide variety of sources: the "Gospels," "New England transcendentalism," "Berkeleyan idealism," "spiritism," Spencerian "evolutionism," and "Hinduism."[36] The primary contention of this system of spiritual healing was that noticeable physical, psychological, and spiritual benefits could be gained from cultivating an experiential and philosophical conviction of one's unity with the spiritual substratum of the universe. The mind-cure movement, as James saw it, claimed that each of us "has a dual nature"; it contended that we are "connected with two spheres of thought, a shallower and a profounder sphere, in either of which [we] may learn to live more habitually."[37] From the perspective of adherents of the mind-cure movement, a person who lives primarily in the "shallower sphere" of experience feels separate from others and from the universe, and will thus inevitably be filled with doubt and fear. Mind-cure movement thinkers claimed, however, that it was possible to remove these "isolating barriers of mistrust and anxiety" via a pantheistic identification with the greater Self of the universe, a type of mystical merger of "the narrower private self into the wider or greater self, the spirit of the universe (which is our own 'subconscious' self)."[38]

As a result of this mystical identification with the Self of the universe, seemingly miraculous healings were said to take place, miracles that, from the perspective of the mind-cure movement, were not miracles at all, but instead, were simply the natural and inevitable result of releasing the ingrained fear and doubts that were the underlying cause of disease, in order to be healed by the influx of joy and power that comes from connection with one's own deeper source.

James sums up the theological perspective of the mind-cure movement by quoting from one of its leading proponents, R. W. Trine:

> The great central fact of the universe is that Spirit of Infinite Life and Power that is back of all, that manifests itself in and through all. . . . He is the life of our life, our very life itself . . . [and therefore,] *in essence the life of God and the life of man are identically the same, and so are one.* . . . The great central fact in human life is the coming into a conscious vital realization of our oneness with this Infinite Life and the opening of ourselves fully to this divine inflow. [With this opening] we make ourselves channels through which the Infinite Intelligence and Power can work. In just the degree in which you realize your oneness with the Infinite Spirit, you will

exchange dis-ease for ease, inharmony for harmony, suffering and pain for abounding health and strength.[39]

It is clear that, in many ways, the theological tenets of the mind-cure movement reflect James's own position. For instance, the mind-cure movement believed that the essence of a vital spiritual life consisted of an energizing, healing, and experiential connection with an underlying spiritual power, a spiritual power that was, on some level, united with the deepest dimensions of our being. This understanding is strikingly similar to James's conclusion in the *Varieties* that positive emotional and spiritual consequences can be traced to an experiential connection with the "more" that manifests itself in and through the subconscious.

Similarly, James's emphasis on the dynamic power of beliefs and thoughts to shape one's experience and behavior closely corresponds to one of the mind-cure movement's central tenets: the idea that "thoughts are 'forces'."[40] The mind-cure movement emphasized that if one focused repeatedly on thoughts of "health, youth, vigor and success," then these thoughts would soon be transformed into reality."[41] Mind-cure practitioners taught that one's mental dynamism could be amplified through the disciplined practice of a variety of meditation techniques, as well as through repeated positive affirmations. Mind-cure practitioners also attempted to transform the negative and limited understandings of their patients by means of private mesmeric healing sessions. In these sessions, the mind-cure healers claimed that they were able to transmit their own more spiritually potent and affirmative vision of life into the patient's subconscious, thereby transforming the distorted self-understandings that kept their patients from a joyous and healthy life.

It is clear from James's discussion in the *Varieties* that he is convinced that physical and psychological healings often did take place as a result of the teachings and practices advocated by the mind-cure movement. However, James is not naive. He is aware that many of the ideas and methods of the mind-cure movement capitalized on the power of suggestion. But unlike other medical practitioners of his time, James refuses to throw a "wet blanket upon investigation," merely because the mind-cure movement's practices were "suggestive," since, for James, "suggestion" is "only another name for the power of ideas, so far as they prove efficacious over belief and conduct."[42] James emphasizes that, as with any other healing modality, "innumerable failures and self-deceptions" may have occurred within the mind-cure movement; nonetheless, he is still convinced that many "striking results" could be linked to the teachings and practices of this spiritual system of healing.[43] James even goes so far as to make the rather startling assertion that "their belief has in a general way been corroborated by the practical experiences of their disciples"—that is, James is willing to claim that the tenets of the mind-cure movement were, in his eyes, confirmed, not only by the "regeneration of character" and "cheerfulness" seen in mind-cure adherents, but also by numerous examples of physical healings in which "the blind [were] made to see, the halt to walk [and] lifelong invalids . . . had their health restored."[44]

James devotes several pages in the *Varieties* to detailing specific accounts of female friends who were dramatically healed as a result of their immersion in the mind-cure movement. One woman suffering with "years of bedridden invalidism with spine and lower limbs paralyzed" was transformed into someone who worked for fourteen years as a healer without "a moment of fatigue and pain," while another woman who had been ill from her childhood until her fortieth year of life began to practice the positive affirmations and visualizations of the movement and as a result of "two years of hard work" came to the point where she "expressed health continuously throughout [her] whole body."[45]

James is aware that many, if not most, of the cures attributed to the mind-cure movement are rooted in the latent healing capacities of the client's own mind. Nonetheless, he is not convinced that the methods used by practitioners of the mind-cure movement are completely suggestive. In an appendix to his discussion of the mind-cure movement, James quotes the testimonial of a friend who was willing to go to a mind-cure healer after having been treated for years by "doctors of the highest standing" for exhaustion and problems with his eyes "with no or ill result."[46] After sitting for ten days with the mind-cure healer with no apparent consequences, James's friend reports that he became "suddenly and swiftly conscious of a tide of new energy rising within" and was thereafter able "to read and walk" as he "had not done for years," noting further that "the change was sudden, marked and unmistakable."[47] James's friend writes that the "lift" which he received remained, but he then goes on to point out that the healing effects which occurred *after* he had become convinced of the efficacy of this method were never as powerful as the effects that occurred when he had possessed little faith, leading James's friend to conclude that these initial effects were not suggestive "save in a very secondary way, brought about through the influence of an excited imagination, or a consciously received suggestion of an hypnotic sort."[48] James's friend was convinced that instead of being suggestive, "the healing action . . . springs from the plane of the normally *unconscious mind"* as a "result of receiving telepathically, and upon a mental stratum quite below the level of immediate consciousness, a healthier and more energetic attitude" from the healer.[49]

James's respect for the hidden workings of the subliminal self almost certainly made him receptive to his friend's theory that mind-cure healings were perhaps linked to activity within the subconscious. Interestingly enough, however, unlike his friend, James's own experiences with a mental healer were, at best, ambiguous.[50] Even so, James did not let his own less-than-positive healing sessions dampen his appreciation of the mind-cure movement. James was convinced that mind-cure beliefs and practices worked, and as a result, was willing to use narratives of healings by mind-cure practitioners in much the same way as he frequently used accounts of powerful mystical experiences: as important ammunition in his ongoing fight against the narrow-mindedness, materialism, and dogmatism of an overly restrictive scientistic understanding of reality.

For instance, in the *Varieties*, James emphasizes that the practical successes of the mind-cure movement clearly demonstrate that its nonnaturalistic understanding of the universe is on equal philosophical footing with the naturalistic understandings of most scientists. Scientists, according to James, often believe that the numerous technological and scientific breakthroughs of the modern world are proof that their own impersonal worldview has superseded the earlier, religious way of understanding the universe, in which the universe was believed to be personally responsive to the thoughts and wishes of each individual. However, as James gleefully points out, the successes of the mind-cure movement seem to contradict the impersonal worldview of the scientists, and instead, appear to ratify the more personal outlook of the mind-cure movement. This outlook claims our "own personal thoughts are forces" and it argues "that the powers of the universe will directly respond to [our] individual appeals and needs"; in James's opinion, this personalized perspective has received just as much verification as the impersonalized perspective adopted by science.[51]

Using a proto-pragmatic understanding of truth, James concedes that it is legitimate to assert that the scientific, impersonal understanding of reality is at least partially true, in that aligning ourselves with this perspective "gives to all of us telegraphy, electric lighting, and diagnosis, and succeeds in curing a certain amount of disease."[52] But, as James hastens to add, we can just as easily claim that the religious and personal understanding of reality that underlies the mind-cure movement is also partially true, because alignment with this perspective produces results as well: it not only "prevents certain forms of disease as well as science does, or even better in a certain class of persons," but it can also catalyze moral transformations, bringing in its wake "serenity, moral poise, and happiness."[53]

For James, therefore, both the impersonal and the personal understandings of the universe seem to be verified, in that both science and the mind-cure movement generate "experiences that agree with more or less isolated systems of ideas . . . that our minds have framed."[54] This apparent contradiction, however, is not problematic to James, since, as he notes, "why in the name of common sense need we assume that only one such system of ideas can be true?"[55] For James, reality is much more intricate and superabundant than any possible conceptual system. From James's point of view, it is a very real possibility that the world may be "so complex as to consist of many interpenetrating spheres of reality, which we can thus approach in alternation by using different conceptions and assuming different attitudes."[56] For James, therefore, while both schools of thought (science and mind-cure) are "genuine keys for unlocking the world's treasure-house," neither of them can claim to be "exhaustive or exclusive of the other's simultaneous use."[57]

A "Bad Speculative Omission": The Mind-Cure Movement and the Problem of Evil

Keeping in mind that the mind-cure movement mirrors many of James's own conceptions and that this system of spiritual healing demonstrates (at least to James's apparent satisfaction) a dramatic ability to generate long-lasting and medically unexplainable mental and physical cures, it would seem, at first glance, that James would have enthusiastically endorsed this movement.[58] However, James's endorsement of the mind-cure movement is, at best, ambivalent. There is one major stumbling block that prevents him from a complete acceptance of the tenets of the mind-cure movement: James's belief that it does not give any "speculative explanation" for the existence of evil.[59] For James, the apparent inability or unwillingness of the mind-cure movement to account philosophically for evil is a "bad speculative omission," since, in James's view, an acknowledgment of the reality of evil "may after all be the best key to life's significance, and possibly the only openers of our eyes to the deepest levels of truth."[60]

The mind-cure movement's seeming inability or unwillingness to deal philosophically with evil is the reason why James groups this

293

system of mental healing with a cluster of other philosophical perspectives that he gives the generic name of "healthy-mindedness." Healthy-mindedness, according to James, is that optimistic outlook on life, most clearly seen in nonreligious moralists, that "looks on all things and sees that they are good."[61] This tendency to see the positive aspects of life is in vivid contrast with "morbid-mindedness," that philosophical outlook which, unlike healthy-mindedness, is willing to "accord to sorrow, pain, and death . . . positive and active attention."[62]

Morbid-mindedness is the outlook adopted by "sick souls," such as Leo Tolstoy and John Bunyan (as well as James himself), individuals who have to struggle against an ingrained sense of pessimism and despair. Morbid-mindedness is frequently fused (or perhaps *confused*) by James with the outlook adopted by the "twice-born," those individuals who attain lasting peace within themselves only through a process of conversion, in which they "die" to this natural world and are "reborn" into an awareness of the unseen world of spirit.[63] Healthy-mindedness, meanwhile, is also frequently connected by James to the worldview held by the "once-born," those individuals for whom purely "natural" happiness is quite sufficient.[64]

Unfortunately, this fusion of separate categories (morbid-mindedness with both sick souls and the twice-born, and healthy-mindedness with the once-born) is highly problematic. For instance, James often acts as if healthy-minded individuals who philosophically deny the ultimate reality of evil and look upon life with joy and gladness are inevitably "once-born," but this simply does not seem to be supported by the facts. Indeed, it often seems that James's descriptions of those individuals who are perpetually radiant and joyous could just as easily fit "twice-born" converts as they could apply to "healthy-minded" individuals, in that, as will be shown later in this chapter, James explicitly claims that one of the primary fruits of conversion is a deep and abiding sense of joy and peace. In addition, it is difficult to see why James would contend that mind-cure adherents should be grouped together with once-born and/or healthy-minded individuals, since, as James himself points out, many mind-cure adherents actually are twice-born, at least in the sense that some mind-cure practitioners go through a process of salvific self-surrender that, as James notes, is almost identical to the "Lutheran salvation by faith" and "methodistic conversions."[65] Furthermore, James's assumption that all "twice-born" converts accept the ultimate reality of evil seems untenable as well, in that many "twice-born" followers of the mind-cure movement, as James is well aware, could and often did philosophically deny the ultimate reality of evil.

Finally, even James's basic decision to label the followers of the mind-cure movement as "healthy-minded" appears to be questionable. To begin with, James's contention that those who follow the mind-cure movement belong in the same category as "sky-blue healthy-minded" moralists seems strained, at best, since the mind-cure adherents, unlike the moralists, are clearly firm believers in the existence and power of an unseen spiritual world.[66] In addition, it is quite possible that James oversimplifies or misunderstands the mind-cure movement's attitude towards evil. (This seeming oversimplification is significant because the desire to ignore evil and the tendency towards perpetual optimism are the two qualities that are integral to James's definition of healthy-mindedness.) A careful examination of the statements made by the followers of the mind-cure movement reveals that the mind-cure adherents, on the whole, neither ignored evil nor asserted that evil was philosophically unreal—at least in terms of everyday experience. Instead, evil and suffering were more commonly understood by adherents of the mind-cure movement as something which comes about as the result of each individual's ignorance of her or his innate connection to an indwelling divinity or as something which arises as a consequence of each individual's egoistic sense of limitation and contraction. This understanding of evil may not be acceptable to James, but his contention that the mind-cure movement ignores evil hardly appears to be warranted.

Even James, at one point, appears to acknowledge that the mind-cure movement's attitude towards evil is worthy of philosophical respect. In a surprising about-face, James claims to admire the "dignity and importance" of the mind-cure "gospel," specifically because of its understanding of evil.[67] James notes that, unlike the Hegelian monistic system, the mind-cure movement does not believe that evil is "dialectically required" and "consecrated," but instead, believes that evil is "an alien reality, a waste element" that should be overcome as quickly as possible—an understanding of evil that is, in fact, point for point, almost identical to James's own conception.[68]

It appears, in the end, that the mind-cure movement's understanding of evil is not as problematic to James as its monistic theological perspective, especially since, in James's view, many of the mind-cure movement's "monistic utterances" are "inconsistent with their attitude toward disease."[69] James points out that if disease and suffering are indeed alien realities, then it is unreasonable to expect to dispel them through "experiences of a Higher Presence" who is "the absolute whole of things," since, understood monistically, disease and suffering are only another aspect of that all-pervasive Higher Presence.[70]

295

James argues that the mind-cure adherents would be more philosophically consistent if they would, instead, seek to dispel disease via the
assistance of a "Higher Presence," who, like James's finite God, "is
[only a] part, if . . . the most ideal part" of the universe.[71]

Saintliness: "Ripe Fruits of Religion in a Character"

Regardless of whether James's philosophical dissatisfaction with
the mind-cure movement's understanding of evil was correct or not,
that dissatisfaction never disappeared, and as such, made it difficult
for him to utilize the mind-cure movement wholeheartedly as a demonstration of the beneficial consequences of an experiential connection
to the unseen spiritual world. Therefore, even though James maintained a strong respect for the often miraculous healing abilities affiliated with this movement, he had to look elsewhere to find evidence
to support what is arguably the central thesis of the *Varieties:* James's
contention that a vital religious life is "on the whole . . . the most important of all human functions," as long as the more extreme examples
of that life are "corrected and sobered down and pruned away."[72] If
the data provided by the mind-cure movement was not sufficient to
support this contention, then where else could James turn in order to
obtain concrete evidence that a genuine religious life yields beneficial
fruits and is thus valuable and worth pursuing? In the end, James
decided to investigate saintliness in hopes that it would offer him
what the mind-cure movement could not.

Saintliness, for James, is a vivid illustration of "the practical fruits
for life" that are often the result of conversion experiences.[73] According to James, saints are those individuals who have undergone one or
more mystically charged conversion experiences—experiences which
have taken them to "an altogether new level of spiritual vitality, a
relatively heroic level, in which impossible things have become possible, and new energies and endurances are shown."[74] In James's opinion, the mystical conversions experienced by the saintly individual are
so profound that "the personality is changed, the man *is* born anew."[75]

However, it is important to stress that, according to James, every
convert is by no means a saint. James takes great pains to emphasize
that he finds no special supernatural radiance which separates the
ordinary convert from nonreligious individuals whose virtues can at
times "even excel" the newfound virtues possessed by this class of
converts; but he *also* stresses (and this emphasis is often forgotten in
most commentaries on this section of James's work) that when he

examines the fruits of conversion, he consciously chooses not to consider that "class of preeminent saints of whom the names illumine history," but rather, looks only at "the usual run of 'saints'" who were the "recipients of instantaneous conversion."[76] Therefore, when James comes to the conclusion that "there is no flagrant difference in worth" between converts and those who have not had this sort of experiential connection with the spiritual world, he is explicitly *not* including those converts who have gone on to become genuine saints.[77]

According to James, *saintly* converts embody the "ripe fruits of religion in a character"; they no longer "backslide"; they are solidly transformed individuals whose "exalted affections . . . have 'come to stay' "; they are people for whom "spiritual emotions are the habitual centre of the personal energy."[78] James eventually concludes that these converts *are* better than most human beings, for it is these individuals who are able to demonstrate concretely that "the best fruits of religious experience are the best things that history has to show."[79] Not only have these saints, throughout history and from culture to culture, repeatedly been acknowledged as embodying the normative ideal of humanness, but, as James himself tries hard to demonstrate philosophically, the nearly universal admiration for saintliness is warranted, since "here if anywhere is the genuinely strenuous life."[80]

The "strenuous life" is James's own normative ideal, his vision of how every person can and should live life. For James, the individual living the "strenuous life" is not the moralist who grits his or her teeth and fights to do good, constantly struggling against unwanted personality traits. Instead, as Don Browning, a noted Jamesian scholar, perceptively points out, "the person living in the strenuous mood [is] for James an individual who [is] simultaneously mystical, ethical, and heroic."[81] The person living the strenuous life is someone who is willing to struggle, who is willing to suffer in the present as long as that suffering leads to something greater in the future. According to James, he or she is also someone who lives life to its fullest, "getting out of the game of existence its keenest possibilities of zest"; nonetheless, this sacrificial and energetic approach to life is harmonized with a receptive openness to, and trust in, the healing resources that come from an experiential connection to the unseen world.[82]

For James, saints exemplify that it is possible to live the strenuous life to a degree that would seem unimaginable to most people. In James's view, saints are highly moral individuals, but they are also much more. As James points out, a primarily moral person may be "less swayed by paltry personal considerations" than most; he or she may be someone who practices "patience, resignation, trust";

nevertheless, this ethically impeccable individual still "lacks something which the Christian *par excellence*, the mystic and ascetic saint, for example, has in abundant measure, and which makes of him [or her] a human being of an altogether different denomination."[83] Whereas the moral life requires an effort of will, not so for the saints and mystics, for whom "the service of the highest is never felt as a yoke"; the saints are prompted by a "higher kind of emotion, in the presence of which no exertion of volition is required."[84] James argues that these saints and mystics are infused with an "added dimension of emotion" that is specifically religious; they are swept away by "a state of mind, known to religious men, but to no others, in which the will to assert [them]selves and hold [their] own has been displaced by a willingness to close [their] mouths and be as nothing in the floods and waterspouts of God."[85]

For James, this mystical receptivity to God, this ability to leave behind one's restricting sense of egoism, is the hallmark of the saint. As such, according to James, the saint is not merely someone whose actions are exemplary, but the saint, in addition, is someone whose very being has been transformed; the saint is someone who has surrendered the confining boundaries of selfhood in an ecstatic openness to divine power; the saint is someone whose "moral death has turned into [a] spiritual birthday."[86]

For James, saintliness is not completely equated with mysticism; instead, saintliness is the lasting character transformation that is wrought by profound mystical experiences. The saint is a religious "genius," a religious "hero," someone with an "inborn passion," someone who does not need "deliberately to overcome his [or her] inhibitions," someone who innately possesses an intensely powerful build-up of psychic "steam pressure chronically driving [him or her] in the ideal direction."[87] This saintly individual, who "lives in his [or her] religious centre of personal energy," burns with a "new ardor," which "consumes in its glow" previous limitations and weaknesses; because the "stone wall inside" this saintly individual has disappeared and the "hardness in his [or her] heart has broken down," therefore, a new freedom to act virtuously has emerged, so that "magnanimities once impossible are now easy; paltry conventionalities and mean incentives once tyrannical hold no sway."[88] In much the same way as "maternal love annuls fear" and "respect checks sensuality," the saint, relying on the "expulsive power" of this religiously charged "higher emotion," no longer has to repress or negate his or her negative emotional qualities, but instead, effortlessly performs loving and virtuous actions.[89]

James argues that this revolutionary transformation of character does not typically occur as the result of prolonged efforts of the will. Instead, James hypothesizes that in much the same way as when stubbornly ingrained character traits can disappear as the result of hypnosis, due to the power of "subliminal influences," saintliness may also emerge as a result of the grace of God operating "through the subliminal door."[90] James, picturing the personality of a saintly convert as similar to a "many-sided solid with different surfaces on which it could lie flat," hypothesizes that, under the internal pressure of a subliminal "mental and emotional revolution," the personality of the saintly individual might be pried off of one previously stable surface and then come to rest on another stable surface (i.e., on another habitual center of personal energy), thus enabling the saintly convert to become, for all practical purposes, a "new" person.[91]

James's strong emphasis on the character transformations of the saintly individual make it difficult to detect his more fundamental emphasis on the saint's mystico-religious connection to the divine. Contemporary discussions of saintliness also frequently echo this bipolar depiction of saintliness, in that some scholars argue that exemplary ethical behavior is the defining characteristic of saintliness, while other scholars contend that mystical awareness is sainthood's primary feature.

Edith Wyschogrod, for instance, in *Saints and Postmodernism*, defines the saint as someone "whose adult life in its entirety is devoted to the alleviation of sorrow (the psychological suffering) and pain (the physical suffering) that afflicts other persons without distinction of rank or group or, alternatively, that afflicts sentient beings, whatever the cost to the saint in pain or sorrow"—a definition that is sufficiently open and sufficiently secular to permit her to assert that "not all saints are mystics nor are all mystics saints."[92] Wyschogrod argues that "even if saints have traditionally emerged within specifiable theological and institutional frameworks," one does not have to be a mystic in order to devote oneself completely to relieving the suffering of others.[93] Wyschogrod recognizes that hagiographic accounts are almost inevitably interwoven with mystical doctrines, but she asserts that "the mystical aspect of experience is functionally distinct from the radical altruism that is *constitutive* of saintly praxis"; this said, she then goes on to add that "the contemplative and often mystical strain in saints' lives on the one hand and active tendencies on the other . . . must be distinguished if we are to see what is distinctive to saintliness."[94] Wyschogrod claims that if we make this analytical distinction between the mystic and the saint, then "the saint's experience

299

can be considered in terms of her/his actual or envisioned acts," not in the depth of her/his mystical experiences.[95]

John Coleman, in the concluding essay of *Saints and Virtues*, presents a striking contrast to Wyschogrod's attempt to ground saintliness primarily in moral praxis. Coleman claims that "as a comparative category in the study of religion, sainthood is not primarily about ethics. Religion always deals with a tension between the mystical and the ethical, and with sainthood the mystical dimension is the controlling one. Mystical experience shapes the way we must think about ethics, not the other way around."[96]

Coleman's assessment that mystical awareness is the fundamental attribute of saintliness is based, unlike Wyschogrod's primarily philosophical and literary methodology, on an examination of the category of saintliness in the context of different religious traditions. In his phenomenological examination of saintliness, Coleman attempts to "discover universal traits that accompany sainthood wherever it is found."[97] In light of the fact that "saintliness" is a notion that emerged out of a Christian context, Coleman acknowledges the difficulty of using the concept of saintliness as a vehicle for cross-cultural comparison; but he argues that it is possible to articulate an "intermediary position" between a theoretical perspective that ignores the crucial differences in the ways in which various religious traditions understand saintliness and a theoretical perspective that so strongly emphasizes cross-cultural differences that it denies even the possibility of constructing any worthwhile comparative categories.[98] Coleman's alternative to these two competing theoretical perspectives is to suggest that it would be more productive to "search for overlapping 'family resemblances' " that might enable a researcher "to guide the task of translating the stories of saints from one tradition or era to another without doing violence to their inherent differences."[99]

Coleman argues that a cross-cultural analysis of saintliness reveals a cluster of five functions that frequently, but not inevitably, appear in different traditional understandings of sainthood: the saint often plays the role of "(1) exemplary model, (2) extraordinary teacher, (3) wonder worker or source of benevolent power, (4) intercessor, and (5) possessor of a special and revelatory relation to the holy."[100] After an explication of the first four of these roles typically played by saints in different cultures, Coleman goes on to emphasize that these functions of saintliness "link up with a 5th, the saint's connection with the holy. In fact, only a special relation to the holy operates as a constant in the preceding set of traits. As such, it is the most important of the features defining 'family resemblances' among saints of different traditions."[101]

This mystical and experiential relationship to the holy, according to Coleman, may well engender ethical behavior in the saint; but, as he notes, saints are frequently liminal figures in a culture, individuals who live in the interstices of civilization, and as such, they often "function to break down and transform ordinary notions of virtue."[102] Coleman stresses that saints are different than us: they are not prudent, they are not moderate, and as such, they intrigue us; they show us alternative possibilities of wholeness, possibilities that, paradoxically, often shatter "our ordinary notions of what makes a human life whole."[103] Coleman even goes so far as to argue that the saints do not "really follow an ethical logic at all"; instead, they demonstrate that wholeness ultimately "depends on allowing oneself to be transformed by the encompassing logic of a life lived in and through God"; their charismatic, and often inimitable, example does not show us how we should ethically structure our lives, but instead, serves to "lure us beyond virtue to virtue's source," to "the center of the universe, the holy *coincidentia oppositorum* that alone gives adequate grounds to integrity and makes possible a total 'fit' between the disparate virtues needed in a particular life."[104]

James's own understanding of the relationship between mysticism and saintliness is, in the end, much closer to Coleman's perspective than to Wyschogrod's. Although many of James's descriptions of saints revolve around the positive virtues that saints, at their best, appear to possess, he also contends that these virtues only emerge as the result of the transforming effects of a profound mystico-religious surrender to an ego-transcending power. James argues that even though isolated aspects of saintliness can be present in a nonreligious person, saintly attributes more typically seem "to flow from the sense of the divine," an experiential connection to the unseen world which allows the saints to be happier and more at peace than other, less religious individuals.[105] It is this experiential connection with the unseen world (and with the deeper selves of other human beings) that enables the saints to awaken "unsuspected" abilities in those they come in contact with; furthermore, it is this "sense of the divine" which empowers saints with a "higher kind of inner excitement" that prompts them to dedicate their life to serving others, both physically and spiritually.[106]

James's methodological approach to saintliness also mirrors Coleman's approach in that, many decades earlier, James had attempted to distill from an analysis of different religious traditions several characteristic features of saintliness that seem nearly universal, qualities that highly religious individuals of every religion almost inevitably appear to possess.[107]

In his exuberant, if incautious, rhetorical style, James notes that the first characteristic of this "composite photograph of universal saintliness, the same in all religions" is the saint's possession of "a feeling of being in a wider life than that of this world's selfish little interests; and a conviction, not merely intellectual, but as it were sensible, of the existence of an Ideal Power."[108] This "Ideal Power" is defined very broadly by James. Whereas for Christians, this power would be understood to be God, James acknowledges that other understandings of this power are equally possible: it could be someone's moral ideals, or someone's dream of an ideal society, or someone's sense of holiness—whatever serves to give someone a vivid, mystically tinged experience of a palpable spiritual presence, a presence that can work powerfully, and often invisibly, within a person, empowering him or her to let go of a constricting sense of egoism and embrace a larger sense of self.

The second quality of saintliness that James mentions is "a sense of the friendly continuity of the ideal power with our own life, and a willing self-surrender to its control."[109] The ideal power which is sensed so strongly by the saint feels intimately united with the saint's own being; there is no feeling of foreignness, no feeling of alienation for the saint. Furthermore, as James points out, because this ideal power is sensed in the depths of the saint's own consciousness, the saint is willing to believe that its purposes mirror the deepest and truest purposes of the saint as well. This deep intuitive feeling of trust is, in turn, what enables the saint to release whatever lingering egoistic concerns might be blocking an ongoing and joyous mystical connection with that ideal power.

The third characteristic of saintliness that James notes is "an immense elation and freedom as the outlines of the confining selfhood melt down."[110] Here, the saint's willingness to let go of any limited sense of self in order to unite with the ideal power that is strongly sensed in the depths of his or her own being is rewarded by an almost overwhelming feeling of ecstasy and liberation, or by a joy and peace that, most traditions insist, is tangibly perceptible in the company of saintly individuals.[111]

The fourth and final characteristic of saintliness listed by James is that saints typically manifest "a shifting of the emotional centre towards loving and harmonious affections, towards 'yes, yes,' and away from 'no,' where the claims of the non-ego are concerned."[112] In other words, the saints, having been freed from their sense of selfhood, and having been buoyed up and enlivened by their connection with the spiritual world, no longer need to protect their own petty interests, no longer need to put up walls to keep others away, but instead, are able to reach out with love and compassion to those who were previously kept at a distance.

As with Coleman, James believes that "the fundamental feature in the spiritual life" of these saintly individuals is a deep and abiding mystical awareness, an awareness that James terms "the sense of a higher and friendly Power."[113] This mystico-religious quality of experience manifests in various forms of "unifying states of mind," such as "religious rapture, moral enthusiasm, ontological wonder, [and] cosmic emotion"; further, these differing types of mystical experiences are themselves simply part of a "natural complex" that James terms "the faith-state"—that mystically generated transformation of being in which the "sand and grit of the selfhood" of the saint disappears, enabling the saint to make the "transition from tenseness, self-responsibility, and worry to equanimity, receptivity and peace."[114]

This "abandonment of self-responsibility," this renunciation of egoistic identification and concerns, which James posits as "the fundamental act in specifically religious, as distinguished from moral practice," is in turn connected with the four "practical consequences of saintliness":

1. Asceticism (self-denying activities, ranging from a willingness to live the strenuous life to a perverse self-mutilation);

2. Strength of soul (a complex quality of being, in which personal desires are dissolved, "patience and fortitude" is increased, "fears and anxieties" are destroyed, and "blissful equanimity" is attained);

3. Purity (a sensitivity to the discordant effects upon one's spiritual life of the "brutal and sensual elements" of worldly existence);

4. Charity ("tenderness for fellow-creatures" and love for everyone, even one's enemies).[115]

James investigates each of these four qualities in turn, illustrating with numerous specific examples the range of different types of saintly behavior. But finally, after pages of elaborate and colorful descriptions of how these phenomenological characteristics of saintliness are embodied in the lives of specific saints, James turns his attention to a task that would likely intimidate most contemporary scholars of religion: a normative assessment of the value of saintliness, a process that James playfully, in a nod to Kant, refers to as a "Critique of Pure Saintliness."[116] After having gathered and described the prominent characteristics of saintliness (i.e., after having performed the existential judgment), true to his methodological model, James must now go on to evaluate the worth of what he has been studying (i.e., he must undertake the process of making the spiritual judgment).

The Ever-Changing Value of Saintliness

James begins his foray into normative territory with an initial disclaimer. He stresses that because his empirically based assessment of religion, unlike the procedure adopted by "Catholic theologians," cannot rely on "fixed definitions of man and man's perfection" or on "positive dogmas about God," his conclusions will be neither completely objective nor irrevocable.[117] James frankly admits the historically situated, fallible nature of this normative attempt to assess the value of religion and clearly acknowledges that his intention is simply to make several "piecemeal judgments," using only his "general philosophic prejudices," "instincts," and "common sense."[118] James is conscious of the fact that he brings his own angle of vision, his own theological preferences, to the task of assessing saintliness. However, as he points out, this theological perspective has at least one distinct advantage over many, if not most, other theological points of view: a reflective awareness of its own mutable, humanly created, and fallible nature.

James acknowledges that there are bound to be criticisms of the "vagueness and subjectivity and 'on the whole'-ness," of his attempt to "test saintliness by common sense"; that is, some scholars are bound to find fault with his attempt "to use human standards to help us decide how far the religious life commends itself as an ideal kind of human activity."[119] However, James is convinced that all understandings of God, not just his own, are changeable and are rooted in human needs, even if different religious traditions have difficulty acknowledging that this is the case. James reminds his readers that various cultures throughout the course of history have frequently changed the type of God that they were willing to believe in, radically altering their understanding of this God's nature to suit the needs of that particular period of time. As James notes, as soon as the fruits that came from worshipping a specific deity "conflicted with indispensable human ideals, or thwarted too extensively other values," or as soon as this God "appeared childish, contemptible, or immoral when reflected on," that culture would end up first discrediting, then forgetting, its initial understanding of God.[120]

In the light of the fact that humanity's religious conceptions have constantly changed throughout history, how then, James asks, can any theological or philosophical perspective claim that its conclusions are absolutely certain? As James goes on to argue, it is more likely that we will actually be able to grasp a larger percentage of the truth, if we admit our imperfections rather than if we claim to be infallible. As James points out, "the wisest of critics is an altering being, subject to the better insight of the morrow, and right at any moment, only 'up to date' and 'on the whole.' When larger ranges of truth open, it is surely best to be able to open ourselves to their reception, unfettered by our previous pretensions."[121]

After having argued that his "empirical method" of assessing saintliness is fallible, while maintaining nonetheless that it is still worth pursuing, James's next step is to apply this methodology to the information that he has gathered on saintliness. James begins his assessment of the value of saintliness by asking: is it really necessary "to be quite so fantastically good as that?"[122] James's answer to this question comes quickly: he, for one, does not think so. James believes that, although we should thank the saints for living so passionately, we should be "glad there are also other ways of seeing and taking life."[123] James argues that the ethical guidelines that most individuals set for themselves are "nearer to the middle line of human effort," and thankfully so, since the path "of the golden mean," for the most part, is a much safer course to follow, for as James points out, the "fruits of religion," that is, saintliness, are often "liable to corruption by excess."[124]

It is clear that James believes that there most certainly *can* be too much of a good thing, especially in the lives of the saints; in particular, in the lives of those saints who, according to James, demonstrate a "relative deficiency of intellect."[125] As Don Browning aptly notes, James claims that "if certain qualities of the saint such as charity, purity, devoutness, and asceticism are rigid ends in themselves and largely isolated from other values, then the saint may actually be destructive to the human community."[126] For example, while some might argue that there should be no limit to one's devotion towards God, James thinks otherwise, claiming that saintly devotion, "when unbalanced," can easily become either "fanaticism" in those saints whose personalities are forceful or can turn into a "theopathic condition" in those saints who are less domineering.[127]

To illustrate the devotional pathology of this "theopathic condition," James draws upon excerpts from accounts of the life of Margaret Mary Alacoque. James argues that while Margaret Mary might well have been blessed with the vision of the Sacred Heart, the fruits of her lofty visions are difficult to discern. James contends that, while it does seem that Margaret Mary was indeed "amiable and good," the

305

overwhelming force of her devotional ecstasies caused her to become "increasingly useless around the convent," a deficiency so intolerable to James that he is willing to conclude, somewhat caustically, that Margaret Mary's visions appear to have yielded "little else but sufferings and prayers and absences of mind and swoons and ecstasies."[128] In James's opinion, Margaret Mary Alacoque was "so feeble of intellectual outlook that it would be too much to ask of us, with our Protestant and modern education, to feel anything but indulgent pity for the kind of saintship which she embodies."[129]

James then moves on to assess the life of St. Teresa of Avila. At the beginning of James's discussion, it seems that his assessment will be extremely positive. He first stresses that St. Teresa was "one of the ablest women, in many respects, of whose life we have the record"; he then compiles the following highly appreciative depiction of her talents: "She had a powerful intellect of the practical order. She wrote admirable descriptive psychology, possessed a will equal to any emergency, great talent for politics and business, a buoyant disposition, and a first-rate literary style. She was tenaciously aspiring, and put her whole life at the service of her religious ideals."[130] Here, it seems, is a saint with eminent pragmatic qualifications, someone whose devotional life yielded fruits that James, even at his most tough-minded, could appreciate.

Unfortunately, one aspect of Teresa's life does not meet with James's approval: her theology. In James's opinion, Teresa's "religious ideals," when measured against the theological understandings of the late nineteenth century, were "so paltry" that he confesses that his "only feeling in reading her has been pity that so much vitality of soul should have found such poor employment."[131] James sees Teresa's religious life as revolving around "an endless amatory flirtation . . . between the devotee and the deity"; he has difficulty seeing the value in this passionately loving relationship between God and Teresa, since, from his perspective, "science, idealism, and democracy" had altered the theological climate to such an extent that individuals of the late nineteenth century had "grown to need a God of an entirely different temperament from that Being interested exclusively in dealing out personal favors."[132] James is aware that the "spirit of her age, far from rebuking her, exalted her as superhuman"; but so strong is James's distaste for Teresa's theology, that in his final assessment of her saintliness he asserts that, "apart from helping younger nuns" to follow in her devotional footsteps "by the inspiration of her example and instruction, there is absolutely no human use in her."[133]

James's heavy-handed and one-sided assessment of St. Teresa's life, emerging out of his own, perhaps inevitable, failure to transcend the theological prejudices of his era, clearly illustrates the difficulties inherent in any attempt to assess the value of the religious understandings and practices of another historical period or culture. In the same way that James realizes "the gap" that exists between his time period and the time period of Margaret Mary and Teresa, it is quite likely that, for many contemporary readers of the *Varieties*, a similar chasm yawns between our own late twentieth-century sensibilities and James's own brisk, no-nonsense, turn-of-the-century manner. For instance, in today's world, James's impatience with such intangibles as devotion, ecstasy, and absorption in God, might well seem somewhat stiff and straightlaced, and his Protestant distaste for the mysticoerotic passion of Catholic women saints could easily appear a bit narrow-minded, sexist, and overly moralistic.

James's attempt to use solely pragmatic and empirical criteria to assess the value of Teresa's life underscores another difficulty inherent in James's methodological approach. As will become clear further on in this chapter, James's avowed task is to determine whether Teresa's religious beliefs are given credence by the evidence of positive, transformative effects in her life. If James actually intended to assess the value and validity of Teresa's beliefs by examining the degree to which her life was a success, it would seem that James would take note of Teresa's increased vitality, her literary gifts, and her political and administrative skills, and he would quickly give an enthusiastic endorsement of the religious understandings and experiences that, from a pragmatic perspective, had been the catalysts of her highly effective life. But it appears that James simply could not bring himself to commend Teresa's religious understandings. In fact, there is every indication that Teresa's theology was so innately repugnant to James that, perhaps hidden even to himself, he completely reverses his empirical methodology in mid-stream and, ironically, uses the alleged "small minded" nature of her theology as the basis for his negative assessment of her life accomplishments.[134]

Nevertheless, James at least makes no pretense that his evaluation of saintliness transcends his own theological predilections, his own cultural assumptions, or his own historical situation. He willingly acknowledges that he is a child of his times and realizes that cultural sensibilities can and will change. He therefore does not attempt to conceal his own culturally and historically molded theological preferences.

James's open acknowledgment of the fact that his critique of saintliness is affected by his own theological preferences is vividly demonstrated during his discussion of St. Louis of Gonzaga.[135] In order

307

to illustrate the possibilities of saintly overpurification, James presents excerpts from a biography of Louis of Gonzaga that clearly demonstrates St. Louis's deep and abiding, and perhaps even pathological, fear of women and sexuality. James freely admits that "our final judgment of the worth of such a life as this will depend largely on our conception of God, and of the sort of conduct he is best pleased with in his creatures."[136] For James, our evaluation of the fruits of St. Louis's life (or the life of any saint) cannot and should not take place in a vacuum. Instead, he argues that such an assessment will always be rooted in the ever-shifting, socially formed standards of "our empirical common sense and ordinary practical prejudices," standards that include our ingrained, rarely explicit sense of the contours of the divine world as well as our understandings of how to live a life that is best aligned with that divine world.[137] Acknowledging his own theological prejudices, James is willing to state quite candidly that, in his opinion, St. Louis's God is excessively narrow, exceedingly demanding, and a God who pays "little heed to social righteousness."[138] Based on this theological appraisal, James's assessment of St. Louis's sexual restraint, humility, penances, and ascetic practices is, consequently, somewhat less than positive: they are deemed by James to be "on the whole repulsive."[139]

Here, James once again rebels against his own methodological insistence that saintliness should be assessed using solely empirical criteria. His reasons for rejecting St. Louis's saintliness are clearly more theological than empirical. Furthermore, James's use of the life of St. Louis to illustrate saintly tendencies towards excessive purification demonstrates another difficulty that arises in any pragmatic evaluation of the lives of saints: before we evaluate saints, we should clearly state the criteria by which we are determining that someone is indeed a saint and then stick by this criteria. It is questionable, at least based on the information that James presents, whether St. Louis actually fulfills James's own criteria for saintliness, since St. Louis's alleged "saintliness" seems to have very little to do with possession of any mystical awareness, abiding joy, or genuine love for others. St. Louis might well have been acknowledged as a saint within his own tradition, but based solely on James's own criteria, St. Louis's claim to "saintliness" seems fragile, at best.[140] More than likely, James simply uses St. Louis because he was given this honorific by the Catholic tradition. If this is the case, and if St. Louis actually is not a saint (using James's criteria), then James's attempt to illustrate the excesses of saintly purification by drawing upon the life of St. Louis seems highly questionable.

Fortunately, James's assessment of saintly charity is much more nuanced and persuasive than his commentary on the excesses of saintly purity as exemplified by St. Louis. James begins his assessment of the value of the saintly "virtues of sympathy, charity, and non-resistance" by arguing that these virtues, similar to the virtues of devotion, purity, and asceticism, can become excessive in saints, at least if these virtues are evaluated using the neo-Darwinian understanding that one's actions are positive only if they allow one to thrive in one's present environment and are "ill-adapted" if they do not.[141] James points out that in a world in which most people still believe that it is important to fight back against injustice and desire to protect themselves against harm from others, the saint's love and forgiveness can seem out-of-place and inappropriate. And yet, as James goes on to emphasize, if this world were "confined to these hard-headed, hard-hearted, and hard-fisted methods exclusively," it would most certainly "be an infinitely worse place than it is now to live in."[142]

On the whole, James seems unwilling to criticize saintly charity with the same vigor that he bestows upon the saintly virtues of devotion, purity, and asceticism. Although he attempts to assemble a hard-edged critique of the excesses of saintly love, his heart is just not in it. It seems that, for James, the quality of saintly love, even when excessive, is exceedingly valuable. In fact, some of James's most stirring and eloquent writing can be found in his descriptions of the transforming effects of saintly love.[143] James insists that while the saints may well be "ill-adapted" to this world, they still point in the direction that we all should aspire to: "with their extravagance of human tenderness," the saints are "like the single drops which sparkle in the sun as they are flung far ahead of the advancing edge of a wave-crest or of a flood, they show the way and are forerunners"; they are "the great torch-bearers" of the claim that every individual is sacred; they are "the tip of the wedge, the cleavers of the darkness . . ; they are impregnators of the world, vivifiers and animators of potentialities of goodness which but for them would lie forever dormant."[144] James argues that although the behavior of the saints might seem "preposterous" to a world that has not yet risen to the level of love and forgiveness that is manifested in the lives of the saints, nonetheless, the saint's charity, even if it exceeds the boundaries of common sense, can be "a genuinely creative social force."[145] In James's opinion, these saints, who by the power of "their radiant example and by the challenge of their expectation," have "miraculously transformed" even people seemingly beyond hope, can and should be seen as "authors, *auctores*, increasers of goodness"; they in essence act as "creative energies" that prompt social evolution; their charity and forgiveness is nothing less than "an effective ferment of goodness, a slow transmuter of the earthly into a more heavenly order."[146]

James, by no means, believes that the saints are "infallible"; in fact, he emphasizes that if their "intellectual outlook is narrow," they may become worse than the average person, in that they can "fall into all sorts of holy excesses, fanaticism or theopathic absorption, self-torment, prudery, scrupulosity, gullibility, and morbid inability to meet the world."[147] But as James goes on to stress, because saints inevitably inherit much of the intellectual narrowness of their particular culture and historical period, it is important that the "essentials of saintliness" (i.e., their experiential connection to an ideal power, their abandonment of egoistic identification and concerns, their elation and freedom, and their increased ability to love) be distinguished from the way in which these qualities are inevitably shaped by each culture and historical period.[148] James argues that, while the form in which saintliness manifests may change from one historical period to the next, the substance will not. James illustrates this contention by pointing out that, just as "taking refuge in monasteries" during the Middle Ages was a cultural prerequisite for aspiring saints, in the same way, anyone who wished to become a saint in the late nineteenth century would surely dedicate themselves actively to solving the world's problems.[149] As James points out, if St. Francis or St. Bernard were alive in the late nineteenth century, they would "undoubtedly be leading consecrated lives of some sort, but quite as undoubtedly they would not lead them in retirement."[150]

James also emphasizes that different periods of time and different cultures have frequently endorsed normative ideals that contrast dramatically with saintliness. For instance, during certain historical periods, the Nietzchean "strongman" has been seen by various cultures as embodying the qualities that a human being should ideally possess: aggressiveness, dominance, courage, decisiveness, ruthlessness, and leadership. In contrast, for other cultures, the meek, gentle, and loving saint (and here James especially emphasizes the Christian mode of saintliness in which nonresistance to evil is accentuated) is seen to be ideal. For James, because the strongman and the saint are exemplars of diametrically opposed but equally valuable virtues, the question arises: by what criteria do we determine which of these normative visions of humanity is preferable?

James initially provides a pluralistic response to this question: there is no single "intrinsically ideal type of human character."[151] As James points out, our determination of what is ideal is inextricably connected to the task that needs to be performed. For example, in the same way that a race horse is ideal for the task of winning races, but is not ideal for hauling heavy loads, the "strongman" is ideal for winning wars, but not for transforming others through the power of love. Our assessment of what is ideal, therefore, is inseparable from the context in which such a judgment takes place. As James emphasizes, in an ideal society, where no one is aggressive and justice inevitably prevails, the saint would most certainly be considered the ideal type of human being, whereas the "strongman" would not, since this type of aggressive personality would immediately cause the ethical level of such a society to deteriorate. We can legitimately conclude, therefore, according to James, that the saint is "abstractly a higher type of man than the 'strong man,'" because he or she "is adapted to the highest society conceivable"; however, from the perspective of our concrete, less-than-ideal society, such an unequivocal judgment is not possible.[152]

Success in life, from James's pluralistic point of view, is dependent upon one's ability to act appropriately in each situation. James also argues that the determination of whether someone has been successful or not will differ "according to the point of view adopted."[153] Coming from this relativistic perspective, James is willing to claim that "there is . . . no absoluteness in the excellence of sainthood."[154] In fact, as James points out, "as far as this world goes, any one who makes an out-and-out saint of himself does so at his peril. If he is not a large enough man, he may appear more insignificant and contemptible, for all his saintship, than if he had remained a worldling."[155]

James, at this point, appears to be heading to the purely relativistic conclusion that there is no way we can determine, outside of the boundaries of each context, the overall merit of saintliness. But James's designs are not so straightforward. Reversing his rhetorical direction, James goes on to claim that we can, after all, make certain tentative overall assessments of the value of saintliness, if we do not restrict ourselves simply to the immediacies of each situation, and instead, adopt a long-term and overarching perspective. From this more encompassing point of view, James, rather surprisingly, is willing to conclude that saintliness, even if judged using purely worldly standards, *is* worthwhile:

> So far as any saint's example is a leaven of righteousness in the world, and draws it in the direction of more prevalent habits of saintliness, he is a success, no matter what his immediate bad fortune may be. The greatest saints, the spiritual heroes whom every one acknowledges, the Francises,

311

Bernards, Luthers, Loyolas, Wesleys . . . are successes from the outset. They show themselves, and there is no question; every one perceives their strength and stature. Their sense of mystery in things, their passion, their goodness, irradiate about them.[156]

In James's opinion, therefore, since few deny that the "great saints are immediate successes," while "the smaller ones are at least heralds and harbingers . . . of a better mundane order," it is philosophically legitimate to conclude, that in the long run, "the saintly group of qualities is indispensable to the world's welfare."[157]

This positive spiritual judgment of saintliness permits James, after all of his equivocations, to offer a muted endorsement of saintliness as an ideal to which human beings can and should aspire. Even though he underscores the fact that there are different types of saintliness, and that each person "must discover for himself the kind of religion and the amount of saintship which best comports with what he believes to be his powers and feels to be his truest mission and vocation," James does, at last, offer the following subdued conclusion: "Let us be saints, then, if we can, whether or not we succeed visibly and temporally."[158]

Saintliness, having proved its worth, provides potent ammunition in James's rhetorical battle to convince his readers that religion is not an antiquated relic with no relevance for contemporary life, but rather, is "mankind's most important function."[159] For James, establishing the value of saintliness also establishes the value of religion. The thrust of James's argument is as follows: the saints, as embodiments of the fruits of religion, are the exemplars of the religious life; therefore, if these religious geniuses are successes, then so is religion. James can thus confidently state that it is safe to conclude, even after having given up "theological criteria" and after having tested religion simply "by practical common sense and the empirical method," that religious life, "in a general way . . . and 'on the whole,' " is left with a "towering place in history."[160]

A Critique of the Critique: An Examination of James's Assessment of Saintliness

What are we to make of these provocative conclusions? To begin with, while saintliness might well deserve an overall positive spiritual judgment, it is doubtful that James can support his claim that he has been able to make this normative assessment without utilizing theological criteria. To begin with, as was pointed out above, James openly admits to applying his own theological standards to the assessment of different saints. Furthermore, if we are true to James's own epistemological perspective, which emphasizes that we always experience and understand whatever we are investigating through the lens of our own, typically hidden, and invariably circumscribed, presuppositions and interests, then we have to concede that all of our attempts to determine whether saintliness is worthwhile will inevitably be affected by whatever theological or philosophical categories we use to make this determination. The seemingly empirical examination of the fruits of saintly living (i.e., its moral helpfulness) will, therefore, always be based upon a cluster of less tangible, but unavoidable, ethical, philosophical, and religious assumptions as to what exactly constitutes the "good life" (i.e., upon our notions of philosophical reasonableness).[161]

Our theological and philosophical presuppositions matter, especially when attempting to assess the worthiness of sainthood. For instance, James's own assessment of saintliness appears to have been crippled by an extremely narrow range of underlying presuppositions as to what qualifies as genuine saintly behavior and what does not. James's depiction of sainthood often tacitly and without question assumes Christian categories of saintliness and relies heavily on a rather sketchy, and often simplistic, portrayal of Catholic saints. James's Christian notions of saintliness are what underlie his claim that saints are meek and nonassertive, that they are like gentle "herbivorous animals, tame and harmless barn-yard poultry" in comparison to the Nietzchean "beaked and taloned graspers of the world"; and James's lingering Protestant mistrust of Catholic saintliness is conceivably what drives James to portray saints (especially female saints) as addled by the extremes of their devotion, or as isolated and cut off from the world, or (especially in the case of male saints) as pathologically masochistic.[162] If James had possessed a broader and more detailed knowledge of saintliness as it is understood in religious traditions other than Christianity, it is possible that his characterization of saintliness would have been more nuanced and appreciative. Given the Eurocentric nature of his time, James was unable to draw readily upon the knowledge of, for instance, the warrior saints of the Sikh tradition, or the highly skilled artisans who frequent the ranks of Sufi saints, or the sturdy, practical, and "this-worldly" masters of Zen. Because of the narrowness of his sampling, James's depictions of saintliness are, inevitably, rather two-dimensional and imbalanced. Even if many non-Christian saints might well have appeared to be equally, if not even more, bizarre to James than the Catholic saints which populate the pages of the *Varieties*, it would be fascinating to see in what ways James would have altered his assessment of saintliness, if his tacit notions of saintliness had incorporated a wider range of cultural models.

James's evaluation of saintliness is also affected by another, perhaps less obvious, cluster of philosophical and theological presuppositions. James believes in the reality of an unseen spiritual world, and in light of this belief, he is willing to take saintliness seriously. For James (as well as the majority of the world's religious traditions), saintliness is a character transformation which takes place as the result of a deep, sustained mystical connection to a powerful, deeply beneficial, transnatural level of reality. Operating out of an interpretative framework that accepts the reality, power, and beneficence of an unseen spiritual level of existence, it makes sense to posit that saintliness might well be the fulfillment of human existence. For others, however, who operate out of a purely naturalistic perspective, the claim that human beings can be transformed by contact with a transnatural level of reality seems, at best, childish or nonsensical, and at worst, highly deluded. From this point of view, any claims of sainthood or enlightenment are automatically suspect, and the saint, if not understood as socially aberrant or insane, will be forced to demonstrate his or her worthiness based on purely socially determined criteria.

However, as James himself reluctantly acknowledges, the attempt to evaluate saintliness based purely on social norms inevitably leads to theoretical problems. If sainthood is assessed using only the criteria by which different cultures attempt to measure worldly success, we might well be able to gather enough stories of saintly successes to argue convincingly that saintliness is worth pursuing, but it would be impossible to claim that saints are *more* valuable than, for instance, Nietzchean "strongmen," since these "strongmen" can often easily point to an equal, if not superior, degree of worldly success. As James is well aware, the question of whether the "strongman" or the saint is the most ideal model for human emulation is relative to whether those doing the assessing believe solely in this world of everyday experience or also take into account the existence of an unseen spiritual world as well. As James aptly notes, in order to conclude that saints are ultimately *more* ideal than "strongmen," then "in some sense and to some degree both worlds must be acknowledged and taken account of."[163]

Nonetheless, as James also realizes, evaluations of saintliness cannot and should not be based on purely "otherworldly" criteria. In order to retain its position as a normative ideal, saintliness *must* provide evidence of positive, this-worldly effects. I would add that, from

314

culture to culture and throughout history, saints are only understood to be saints by their community if they produce "miracles"—that is, if the community believes that contact with a particular saint, for example, heals the sick, gives jobs to the poor, creates pregnancies in previously barren women, or more subtly, generates a feeling of renewed energy and purpose, an upsurge of devotion and love, or a deep and tangible experience of stillness and peace within those people who spend time in the saint's presence. A saint, therefore, can be understood to be "morally helpful" only if the saint's community believes that association with the saint produces publicly observable, communally valued, tangible results.[164]

However, as was pointed out earlier, the judgment that something is "morally helpful" itself only takes place within a specific philosophical and theological context. For instance, from an atheistic or skeptical perspective, the "miracles" attributed to different saints would likely be understood as simply the result of delusions, mass hysteria, wish fulfillment, or suggestibility, whereas the conquests and political acumen of the "strongman" might well be deemed highly valuable. However, individuals coming from a theistic, monistic, or "Buddhistic" perspective would likely reverse this assessment, looking upon the activities of the "strongman" with abhorrence, while giving the saintly "miracles" much more respect (even if that respect is leavened with an underlying alertness to the possibility of saintly fraud and delusion). Those judged to be saints rarely, if ever, will be given the respect and admiration of the community, if they do not offer that community a corpus of tangible and valued demonstrations of their intimate connection with a transnatural reality (i.e., they will not be respected or valued if they do not perform "miracles"); but these "miracles" will typically only be interpreted to be signs of the saint's connection with this spiritual level of existence, if this spiritual reality is already a theo-philosophical given. Therefore, in order for someone to be considered a saint, the unseen world has to be a reality, not only in the form of a mystically felt unitive experience within the individual, but also as a philosophically reasonable notion within the intellectual framework of those attempting to assess the would-be saint's overall worth.

A Philosophical Sleight-of-Hand: Valuable Mystical Experiences or Verified Mystical Truths?

As long as James's three criteria (i.e., immediate luminousness, philosophical reasonableness, and moral helpfulness) are not kept artificially separated, then they would appear to offer a potentially useful framework from which to begin any normative assessment of different religious phenomena. However, the question remains: what would be the underlying purpose for making such an assessment? For James, the answer is fairly straightforward: the spiritual judgment of religious phenomena is intended to produce compelling evidence that living a rich and deep religious life is positive and worthwhile. Throughout the *Varieties*, James's overt intention is clear. Whether he is providing vivid accounts of the immediate luminousness of highly charged mystical experiences, or is defending the philosophical reasonableness of his contention that direct experiences are the foundation of a genuine religious life, or is describing the character transformations catalyzed by mystically charged conversion experiences, all three modes of analysis are simply different ways in which James seeks to demonstrate that mystico-religious experiences are vindicated by his three criteria, and consequently, that living a full and deep religious life is a worthwhile pursuit.

However, examined more carefully, it becomes apparent that James is not simply attempting to justify his overt contention that religion is one of the most valuable components of human existence. Instead, James is also covertly attempting to prove the *truth* of his own religious belief in the reality of the unseen world, via a pragmatic evaluation of the transformative effects of powerful religious experiences.[165] This hidden attempt to provide empirical grounds for the truth of religious beliefs in the reality of the unseen world is particularly evident during James's lectures on the "Value of Saintliness." In this section of the *Varieties*, James performs a philosophical sleight of hand, and shifts his focus from the relatively innocuous attempt "to use human standards to help us decide how far the religious life commends itself as an ideal kind of human activity," to the much more controversial and difficult task of demonstrating that, if the religious life *is* demonstrated to be valuable, "then any theological beliefs that may inspire it" will thereby "stand accredited."[166]

James argues that we only come to believe in something's reality if we can observe that our interaction with this level of experience generates tangible results. Operating out of this pragmatic perspective, James is willing to contend that an examination of the personal and social effects of a saint's mystical experiences not only demonstrates that religion has value, but also serves to warrant the truth of religious beliefs in the unseen world. The assessment of saintliness, therefore, is not only intended to establish whether religion is worth pursuing (a normative task), but it is also intended to establish, via

James's nascent pragmatism, whether religious beliefs in the reality of the unseen world are *true*.

This covert attempt to justify his belief in the reality of the unseen world using pragmatic criteria is difficult to perceive, because in the *Varieties*, James is in transition between one understanding of truth and another. On the one hand, James at times aligns himself with an understanding of truth in which truth is seen as that knowledge which correctly mirrors an objective reality. On the other hand, James at times also supports a rough-edged, still developing, proto-pragmatic understanding of truth. From the point of James's nascent pragmatism, truth is seen not as something that is eternal, objective, and aloof from the nitty-gritty intersubjective process of verification, but rather is understood to be something that emerges out of an examination of the way a belief works, on the whole, and in the long run. Therefore, there are frequently moments in the *Varieties* when James, aligning himself with the older understanding of truth, makes a clear-cut separation between truth and utility; but there are other, equally compelling, instances when James reverses himself and argues for a pragmatic understanding of truth. As a developing pragmatist, James is clearly biting at the bit in his eagerness to prove that mind-cure healings and saintliness warrant a belief in the unseen world, but as a careful philosopher, James appears to be equally reluctant to articulate such an audacious claim, either because he believes that he does not yet possess the philosophical tools necessary to convince his audience (tools which he will subsequently develop in *Pragmatism*), or more likely, because he has not yet completely convinced *himself* that a pragmatic understanding of truth is defensible.

James *is* convinced, however, that he has sufficient empirical data to prove his contention that powerful mystico-religious experiences have "enormous biological worth"; for James, it is evident that "spiritual strength really increases in the subject when he has [these experiences], a new life opens for him, and they seem to him a place of conflux where the forces of two universes meet."[167] However, James is reluctant at first to make any claims that the fruits of these mystico-religious experiences establish the *truth* of the unseen world, since, as he hastens to add, all of this spiritual abundance may simply "be nothing but [the mystic's] subjective way of feeling things."[168] In order to come to some conclusions as to the "objective 'truth'" of the "content" of these experiences, especially the truth of the "more" which is in harmonious relation with a person's own "higher self," James claims that we need to go beyond the level of personal conviction that is established by the immediate luminousness of these experiences and ask ourselves whether this "more" is, as he puts it, "merely our own notion" or whether it "really" exists.[169] According to James (at least the James who still assumes the existence of an "objective" truth), mystico-religious experiences may well make "the soul more energetic," but this increased vitality, in James's opinion, is positive only if the mystic's or saint's inspiration is "true."[170] If the mystic's inspiration is false, according to James, then the "energy" gained by the mystic is "all the more mistaken and misbegotten."[171]

This notion that it is possible, indeed necessary, to use some sort of objective "truth" to evaluate the worth of the increased vitality that comes to saints or mystics by virtue of their mystical experiences is, in many ways, the exact opposite of the validation process that James later develops in *Pragmatism*. At this point in the *Varieties*, James seems to accept the notion of some stable, self-existent truth, a truth that is "true" in and of itself. However, from the perspective of truth that James articulates in *Pragmatism*, a self-existent, stable, objective "truth" does not exist, and therefore, cannot act as a criterion by which we can assess the effects of mystical experiences. Instead, in *Pragmatism*, James argues that truth is itself determined by a nuanced assessment of the results that follow in the wake of acting upon a certain set of beliefs or undergoing a particular range of experiences. From this point of view, truth can never be separated from an assessment of the long-range value of that "truth" to an individual or community. Therefore, from this pragmatic perspective, if mystics receive increased vitality by virtue of their contact with the unseen world, if their mystical inspirations produce positive effects on the whole and over the long run, then we have every right to maintain that the mystic's inspiration is true—true at least for that mystic, in that context, and during that period of time.

However, even in his most pragmatic moments, James never clearly discusses the specifics of how we can determine, with any degree of certainty, that the positive transformations observed in the lives of mystics or saints actually *are* the result of their mystical inspirations. James's pragmatic justification of the truth of religious beliefs is based on the argument that positive effects point to true beliefs. But this argument itself depends upon what appears to be an unexamined assumption: that a certain belief is the cause of a corresponding observable effect (e.g., a mystic's belief in the reality of the unseen world causes the mystic to feel increased vitality). But is there ever really such a clear-cut, one-to-one correspondence between a distinct belief and an equally distinct outcome of that belief? Can we really map the repercussions of each of our beliefs in the same way that we can observe the effects of one billiard ball striking another? Cannot odious beliefs at times lead to beneficial results and worthy beliefs to horrific effects? Few would dispute James's contention that our structures of belief have clearly observable ramifications. But James never explicitly addresses the ways in which the complexity, ambiguity, and internal inconsistencies of every person's belief system make it difficult, if not impossible, to contend that we can trace a certain personally or socially valuable transformation back to the impetus received from one clearly defined belief.

Furthermore, from a mystical perspective, James's contention that truth is inescapably tied to the complexities and ambiguities of culturally based normative assessments is problematic. Mystical truths are often depicted as self-evident, luminous, above and beyond our mundane and inevitably distorted half-truths and self-deceptions. Many, if not most, mystical traditions would claim that our everyday truths and understandings of reality are themselves fundamentally illusory; they would insist that our everyday beliefs are less clear, less accurate, than the insights that are available in mystical states of consciousness. From this perspective, the pragmatic attempt to base our evaluation of the truth or falsehood of our religious beliefs on systematically distorted opinions and values is nothing but another demonstration of our deeply rooted ignorance of the true nature of reality.

Furthermore, there are some mystically based traditions (for instance, Mahāyāna Buddhism) which would contend that even the desire to establish that our religious beliefs are true is nothing more than a reflection of a profound psychological and philosophical insecurity; it is indicative of a deep-seated anxiety, a fear of that unknowable, unthinkable abyss which looms outside the safe and secure borders of language and rational thought. According to these traditions, the desire to have "correct" beliefs or "true" opinions does nothing more than to help reify the deluded notion that a self-sufficient ego exists who has true knowledge of an equally autonomous universe.

Ch'an Buddhism, for example, is especially radical in its denunciation of the value of any attempt to formulate true statements about a self-sufficient reality. Proponents of Ch'an, therefore, must practice alternative modes of discourse which are not intended to express true beliefs, but instead, are meant to disrupt egoistic clinging to comfortable, taken-for-granted modes of cognition.[172] Ch'an's frontal assault upon all systems of belief (including those of Ch'an itself) is designed to catalyze a radical openness that, in turn, engenders a direct seeing, an immediate contact with a mode of experience that transcends limitations and boundaries. It is claimed that immersion in the praxis of

Ch'an ideally gives birth to a "truth" that is capable of being known only by a knower so radically transfigured that the sense of being a subject separate from what is being known has entirely disappeared, a "truth" that is revealed in electrifying glimpses, transfixing insights, alluring flashes, but which, jealous of "its" freedom, refuses to be bound in the constricting nets of overly literal systems of belief.

Interestingly, James himself recognizes that the ultimate limit of truth would be a "total conflux of the mind with . . . reality"; it would be an experience of "an actual merging of ourselves with the object, to an utter mutual confluence and identification."[173] As James puts it, "if an idea should ever lead us not only *towards*, or *up to*, or *against*, a reality, but so close that we and the reality should melt together, it would be absolutely true, according to me, by that performance."[174] However, because James is reluctant to admit that this union of the knower and what is known is anything more than a hypothetical possibility (as this would undercut his emphasis on pragmatic verification), James quickly goes on to assert that "in point of fact philosophers doubt that this ever occurs."[175]

When James makes this rather hasty assertion, he is focusing primarily on rather prosaic modes of knowledge; but if pressed, he almost certainly would also have questioned whether mystical experiences might, in fact, be an empirical example of a complete union of the knower and the known (even though it would seem quite reasonable that it is this union, itself, which generates such conviction in many mystics). In the *Varieties*, James points out that mystics, almost inevitably, claim that their experiences *feel* true, but as was shown in chapter 4's discussion of the authority of mystical consciousness, James does not believe that this sense of conviction has any right to extend beyond the sphere of the mystic's own personal religious life.[176] In fact, while the "immediate luminousness" of mystical experiences may well generate complete conviction within the mystic, James argues that this powerful sense of conviction is not utterly dependable even for the mystic (as James's discussion of the practice of spiritual discernment attempts to demonstrate). According to James, in order for any mystical experience to be genuinely trustworthy, something else must occur: the mystic must decide whether the mystical experience makes sense and must determine whether its effects have been basically positive.[177]

Nonetheless, James is impressed by the self-authenticating power of a mystical experience's "immediate luminousness"; he is fascinated by the fact that, from a phenomenological perspective, almost every mystical experience comes with a very strong sense that what has

320

been experienced is beyond doubt. Repeatedly, James underscores this "noetic" aspect of mystical experiences, and in several sections of the *Varieties* he attempts to demonstrate just "how strong an impression [mystical experiences] leave of being revelations of new depths of truth."[178] In fact, James believes that this noetic dimension of mysticism is so central to the phenomena that, in certain respects, mysticism to James is nothing more, and nothing less, than a special manner in which religious individuals profess to see the truth.

During James's investigation of mystical truth, he attempts to illustrate the different types of truths that mystics have claimed to have received via their immersion in mystical states of consciousness. He points out that some of the truths that are revealed to the mystic "relate to this world—visions of the future, the reading of hearts, the sudden understanding of texts, the knowledge of distant events," or even, as in the case of George Fox and Jacob Boehme, medical knowledge or information on the properties of herbs; but he goes on to stress that "the most important revelations" that a mystic receives "are theological or metaphysical," as, for example, when a mystic has insights into the nature of the Trinity, or is given knowledge about his or her mystical union with God.[179]

All of these truths, according to James, are trustworthy only if they are tested further to assess the degree of their reasonableness and effectiveness. For James, these mystical insights are not to be considered authoritative solely on the basis of their "immediate luminousness." In the end, James gives a negative answer to his rhetorical question: do "mystical states establish the truth of those theological affections in which the saintly life has its root?"[180] James argues that mystical experiences in-and-of-themselves can legitimately provide individuals with a basis for religious beliefs and can offer intriguing possibilities to those who have not directly experienced these mystical insights; but if assessed solely on the basis of their immediate luminousness, mystical experiences cannot "claim universal authority," since they are simply "too private" and the beliefs that they seek to validate are too contradictory to warrant any claims of truth that extend into the public sphere.[181]

However, as James then goes on to contend, all *philosophical* attempts to warrant our religious beliefs fail as well, both because philosophy needs mystical experiences to provide it with its "subject matter" and because philosophy is itself inevitably influenced by our personal predilections; thus, philosophy as well can make no claims to objectivity or "universal authority." According to James, therefore, any and all of our attempts to root our claims to religious truth in

321

some infallible, unimpeachable foundation, whether mystical or logical, cannot, and should not, succeed. James's chapters on mysticism and philosophy in the *Varieties* are, in many ways, nothing more than concerted attempts to show that these supposed avenues to direct, undeniable truth fail to provide any public, verifiable, noncontroversial truths.

However, James does not want to leave us wallowing in a morass of skeptical doubt and debilitating nihilism. While infallible, unimpeachable truth may well be beyond our grasp, a more modest version of truth might indeed be possible, especially if we do not claim more certainty and authority for our conclusions than they deserve. James clearly states that, although it might seem as if he has a "perverse delight in intellectual instability," he simply is not able to agree with the idea that any human being "can attain on a given day to absolutely incorrigible and unimprovable truth about such matters of fact as those with which religions deal."[182] James goes on, however, to claim that he does believe that we can "gain more and more [truth] by moving always in the right direction."[183] James emphasizes that, in his opinion, truth does exist, even if the only truths that we can actually come to know are always changing and humanly created. In fact, in many ways, James's three criteria, if examined closely, are nothing less than his attempt to provide us with the tools we would need in order to possess just this sort of truth—a truth that is grounded, reasonable, and useful, while not rooted in some unchanging essential foundation.

In our attempts to discover the truth or falsehood of religious beliefs about the existence of an unseen spiritual world, the "immediate luminousness" of mystical experiences is an important and necessary first step in that it provides the concrete "raw material" to which our theological claims must, to some degree at least, correspond. Next, these mystical experiences must be "philosophically reasonable"; that is, any claims that one has directly experienced the reality of an unseen spiritual world must fit intelligibly within a rationally articulated worldview. Finally, an experientially based belief in the reality of the unseen world must be morally helpful; that is, it must produce tangible results that are deemed valuable by an individual and/or by an individual's wider cultural matrix.[184]

In a very real sense, James's task in the *Varieties* is to reverse the standard religiously based verification process. James does not attempt to use "mystical states" to "establish the truth" of the theology of saints and mystics; instead, he attempts to demonstrate that mystically based beliefs in the reality of an unseen spiritual world are justified

322

via a philosophical assessment of the long-term psychological and cultural ramifications of the saintly life (taken broadly).[185] Therefore, after rejecting mystical and philosophical attempts to authorize religious truth claims, James with little or no warning, abandons his original claim that truth is objective and nonutilitarian, and instead, embraces a newfound pragmatic understanding of truth. From this pragmatic perspective, it is "the uses of religion, its uses to the individual who has it, and the uses of the individual himself to the world" that present "the best arguments for the truth" of religious beliefs, even if, as James hurriedly adds, "the qualification 'on the whole' may always have to be added."[186] After James's half-hearted attempt to discover whether mysticism or philosophy might provide us with an objective, authoritative truth, James offers the solution that was always waiting in the wings: his "empirical philosophy"—that is, his nascent pragmatism. Here, at last, in James's opinion, is a philosophical perspective which *can* warrant the truth of religious beliefs in the reality of the unseen world.[187]

James's utilization of this pragmatic justification of the truth of religious beliefs in the reality of the unseen world is vividly demonstrated in the final pages of the *Varieties:*

> The unseen region . . . is not merely ideal, for it produces effects in this world. When we commune with it, work is actually done upon our finite personality, for we are turned into new men, and consequences in the way of conduct follow in the natural world upon our regenerative change. But that which produces effects within another reality must be termed a reality itself, so I feel as if we had no philosophic excuse for calling the unseen or mystical world unreal.[188]

At this point in the *Varieties*, James is no longer waffling. Instead, he has fully embraced a pragmatic justification of the truth of religious beliefs in the reality of the unseen spiritual world, a perspective that allows him to claim, in his characteristically blunt fashion, that "God is real since he produces real effects."[189] Nonetheless, James still appears to be of two minds as to exactly which "effects" should qualify as "real." At certain times, James argues that only when we can demonstrate the "remote objective consequences" of a unitive experience of God can we rightfully claim that God has any existence that extends beyond the sphere of each individual's personal religious experience.[190] From this point of view, if God is only experienced within, if mystical experiences do not create observable effects in the wider, shared world of experience, then we cannot legitimately argue that

323

God is real, except on a purely subjective level. As James forcefully observes:

> Religion in her fullest exercise of function, is not a mere illumination of facts already elsewhere given, not a mere passion, like love, which views things in a rosier light. It is indeed that, as we have seen abundantly. But it is something more, namely, a postulator of new facts as well. The world interpreted religiously is not the materialistic world over again, with an altered expression; it must have, over and above the altered expression, a natural constitution different at some point from that which a materialistic world would have. It must be such that different events can be expected in it, different conduct must be required.[191]

James in this passage is seeking to differentiate his position from the philosophical perspective of the neo-Hegelians, philosophers who argue that the entire universe, as it stands, is divine. For James, this "refined" variety of supernaturalism is not appealing, since it is not amenable to pragmatic verification. James points out that, from the perspective of neo-Hegelian philosophical idealism, the natural world need not, and in fact cannot, demonstrate any tangible effects of God's activity, because every natural event is *de facto* interpreted to be a manifestation of the divine. From this perspective, it makes no sense to talk about "miracles," since the Absolute is already fully present in every activity—making some sort of special divine intervention unnecessary. James suggests that his own "crasser" form of supernaturalism is a superior philosophical alternative. This "piecemeal supernaturalism" believes in "miracles and providential leadings"; it is a supernaturalism that insists that one can have a personal and intimate relationship with God and that assistance from the unseen divine world actually does come "in response to prayer."[192] In James's opinion, this is a "pragmatic" understanding of religion; this is an empirically-based theological perspective which insists that God or the spiritual world can only be considered real if it is somehow possible to point to specific "differences in fact" that arise as a result of contact with that divine realm of existence.[193]

Prayerful "Differences in Fact"

Following James's argument up to this point, we might expect him to point to a variety of "objective" effects of God's activity in this world (i.e., publicly observable healings, miracles, and so on) as examples of the nonsubjective "differences in fact" that serve to indicate the reality of the unseen divine world. Surprisingly, however, the examples that James offers of the observable effects of God's activity in this world are, at first blush, not "objective" at all. Rather, he focuses almost exclusively on the seemingly "subjective" effects brought about due to the "inflow of energy in the faith-state and the prayer-state"; he claims that he has "no hypothesis to offer beyond what the phenomenon of 'prayerful communion,' . . . immediately suggests."[194]

It might seem odd that James would bring in prayer at this point in the discussion, but "prayer," for James, is not simply an internal conversation with God. In fact, for James, deep moments of prayer are, in themselves, muted forms of mystico-religious experience. Prayer, which James defines very broadly as "every kind of inward communion or conversation with the power recognized as divine," is not necessarily petitional; it does not have to take the form of an inner conversation in which a person asks the divine for assistance.[195] Conversational forms of prayer, as James realizes, frequently have little to do with mystical awareness. But, as James points out, prayer might also take the form of a "guided sort of life," in which an individual, by becoming inwardly and experientially aligned with the divine, is able to live his or her life in such a way that events in the external world unfold easily and naturally, "as if all doors were opened, and all paths freshly smoothed."[196] Furthermore, very deep forms of prayer, according to James, are overtly mystical, in that they can catalyze a transfiguration of the external world in which all of nature seems to come alive, a transformation of perception that strikes James as being analogous to the mystical transfigurations that frequently occur during powerful conversion experiences.

For James, genuine prayer, or inner communion with the "higher universe," is not utterly private or completely cut off from the world in which we live, since prayer is "a process wherein work is really done, and spiritual energy flows in and produces effects, psychological or material, within the material world."[197] James argues that "at all stages of the prayerful life we find the persuasion that in the process of communion energy from on high flows in to meet demand, and becomes operative within the phenomenal world. . . . In prayer, spiritual energy, which otherwise would slumber, does become active, and spiritual work of some kind" actually occurs.[198]

James's understanding of prayer appears to be in complete agreement with the theological perspective adopted by his friend and fellow psychical researcher Fredrick W. H. Meyers. Myers's perspective is encapsulated in a quote that James includes in the *Varieties*:

Exploring Unseen Worlds

There exists around us a spiritual universe, and that universe is in actual relation with the material. From the spiritual universe comes the energy which maintains the material; the energy which makes the life of each individual spirit. Our spirits are supported by a perpetual indrawal of this energy, and the vigor of that indrawal is perpetually changing. . . . How, then, should we *act* on these facts? Plainly we must endeavor to draw in as much spiritual life as possible, and we must place our minds in any attitude which experience shows to be favorable to such indrawal. *Prayer* is the general name for that attitude of open and earnest expectancy. If we then ask to *whom* to pray, the answer (strangely enough) must be that *that* does not much matter. The prayer is not indeed a purely subjective thing;—it means a real increase in intensity of absorption of spiritual power or grace;—but we do not know enough of what takes place in the spiritual world to know how the prayer operates;—*who* is cognizant of it, or through what channel the grace is given.[199]

Prayer, therefore, for both Myers and James, is a dynamic process by which one is connected with, and affected by, the unseen world. James agrees with Myers that the specific details of the configuration of that unseen spiritual world can easily remain somewhat vague, as long as through prayer a person becomes energized and enlivened. In fact, at one point, James even approvingly quotes from fellow psychologist James Henry Leuba, who claims that "so long as men can use their God, they care very little who he is, or even whether he is at all. . . . Not God, but life, more life, a larger, richer, more satisfying life, is, in the last analysis, the end of religion."[200] For James, the fine points of theological doctrine are not nearly as important in the long run as the question of whether something significant occurs, either internally or externally, when a person feels aligned with the spiritual universe, however that universe might be conceived. According to James, a prayer that is lacking in some sort of repercussions, whether subjective or objective, is not genuine prayer. He argues that, if nothing is felt to have happened as a result of prayer, "if the world is in no whit different for its having taken place; then prayer, taken in this wide meaning of a sense that something is transacting, is of course a feeling of what is illusory"; and if prayer is illusory, then religion itself is an illusion as well, since in James's eyes, prayer, as an experiential communion with the divine, is nothing less than "the very soul and essence of religion."[201]

However, James's argument, as he is well aware, can also be reversed: if it can be determined that prayer is *not* illusory, then the truth of religion itself will also be affirmed. It is this very reversal that

James's discussion of "prayerful communion" attempts to accomplish. James's investigation of prayer is, in this way, nothing more than a further attempt to use pragmatic criteria to justify the truth of religious beliefs in the reality of the unseen world. Based on his study of the dynamics of "prayerful communion," James is willing to conclude that during deep moments of prayer "something ideal, which in one sense is part of ourselves and in another sense is not ourselves, actually exerts and influences, raises our centre of personal energy and produces regenerative effects unattainable in other ways."[202] These energizing and rejuvenating effects of prayer demonstrate to James that when individuals, especially those who are receptive to the subconscious dimensions of their being, open themselves up through the process of prayer, they are creating a situation in which "transmundane energies, God, if you will," can flow into them and thereby produce "immediate effects within the natural world to which the rest of our experience belongs."[203]

At this point in the *Varieties*, James is no longer claiming that the pragmatic effects of prayer, in order to be legitimate, must transcend personal experience. Instead, James is extending the boundaries of "experience" to such a degree that experience is now understood to be an integral aspect of the natural world rather than a "subjective," utterly private occurrence within an encapsulated individual cut off from the world of nature. From this point of view, if our experience shifts during prayer, and we emerge energized, healed, or transformed, then something in the "objective" world has altered as well. Therefore, in James's view, if personal religious experiences generate psychological and spiritual transformations, then these transformations are not merely "subjective," but instead, can count as valid, "objective" evidence of the reality of the spiritual world.[204]

It seems, by the end of the *Varieties*, that James is beginning to realize that an overly stringent insistence on maintaining a strict dichotomy between the categories of "subjective" and "objective" is problematic in the area of religious experience. Recognizing that religious experiences are often simultaneously "subjective" and "objective" allows James to drop his initial claim that powerful inner psychological or spiritual transformations are too "subjective" to provide us with reliable evidence of the "objective" existence of the unseen spiritual world; this enables him to accept that these personal experiences of increased energy and improved psychological resiliency actually do offer, at least to some degree, pragmatic verification of the objective existence of a transmundane reality.

As James wrote in a letter to James Henry Leuba, several years after the publication of the *Varieties*:

Exploring Unseen Worlds

I find it preposterous to suppose that if there be a feeling of unseen reality shared by large numbers of the best men in their best moments, responded to by other men in their "deep" moments, good to live by, strength-giving,—I find it preposterous, I say, to suppose that the goodness of that feeling for living purposes should be held to carry no objective significance, and especially preposterous if it combines harmoniously with our otherwise grounded philosophy of objective truth. *You* say we must consider it a purely subjective affection. But this opens the whole subject of what the word "truth" means, and I cannot enter that except to say that if inferences from "good for life" to "true" were on principle forbidden, not religion but the whole notion of truth would probably have to be the thing overhauled and revised.[205]

A Pragmatic Theory of Truth

In the *Varieties*, James began the process of overhauling and revising standard philosophical understandings of the nature of truth, but evidently, James, for one, was not completely satisfied with his newly developed pragmatism. Even though the *Varieties* presents, and defends, a pragmatic justification for the truth of religious beliefs in the reality of an unseen world, the pragmatic thrust of the *Varieties* is neither forcefully announced nor carefully delineated. If one reads the *Varieties* with a knowledge of James's later arguments supporting a pragmatic understanding of truth, then it is possible to detect James's pragmatic arguments; but the reader of the *Varieties* has to read the text with a great deal of care in order to uncover James's almost invisible, and yet audacious, attempt to demonstrate pragmatically that an authentic religious life is not only valuable, but is also based on truth.

Clearly, much more work needed to be done in order to clarify and to refine the theoretical foundations that undergirded this bold attempt to warrant religious beliefs in nonmaterial levels of existence using solely pragmatic criteria. James must have realized that he would have to attempt to answer, in explicit detail, several fundamental questions that remained unresolved in the *Varieties*. For instance: What exactly is truth? What is the relationship between value and truth? How do we go about determining the truth? By what marks do we come to know that our beliefs are true and not false? What distinction, if any, is there between reality and truth? In many ways, the final decade of James's life would be devoted, in large part, to an attempt to hammer out reasonable and persuasive answers to these questions and to defend those answers within different academic and public settings.

Unfortunately, after the *Varieties*, James never made a deliberate, focused, and sustained attempt to apply his more refined and polished pragmatism to the question of the truth of religious beliefs. Although, as Gerald Myers points out, James's "pragmatic writings are not entirely distinct from those on religion"; it is also undeniable that pragmatism, as a whole, is by no means exclusively interested in religious issues.[206] Therefore, if we want to know in what ways, if any, James's mature pragmatism might be relevant to contemporary discussions on the nature and extent of religious truth claims, then it is crucial that we first come to an understanding of James's pragmatism as a whole.

Exactly what then does James's pragmatism entail? To begin with, pragmatism, as James understands it, is "primarily a method of settling metaphysical disputes that otherwise might be interminable."[207] According to James, "the whole function of philosophy ought to be to find out what definite difference it will make to you and me, at definite instants of our life, if this world-formula or that world-formula be the true one."[208] Pragmatism's basic postulate is that "beliefs ... are rules for action"; working from this assumption, the pragmatist asserts that "if there were any part of a thought that made no difference in the thought's practical consequences, then that part would be no proper element of the thought's significance."[209] In James's view, if it is not possible to discern any differences in the practical consequences that flow from one conceptual system or another, then, as James puts it, "the alternatives mean practically the same thing, and all dispute is idle."[210]

Pragmatism, however, is not only a certain methodological stance; it is also a theoretical perspective that attempts to alter radically our understandings of the nature of truth and the process by which we go about determining truth. In *Pragmatism*, James refuses to support the idea that truth is "an absolute correspondence of our thoughts with an equally absolute reality."[211] Truth, for James, is not "something non-utilitarian, haughty, refined, remote, august, exalted"; it is not some undefinable quality that is pristinely present, isolated and completely separate from the public, social process of verification.[212] Instead, true ideas are "invaluable instruments of action,"[213] which permit us to "increase and elevate, rather than simply to imitate and reduplicate, existence."[214] According to James, true ideas are defined by their ability to prompt a variety of valuable consequences; true ideas are those ideas which "work"; they are not simply static essences existing in some platonic realm. As James puts it, true ideas "lead us into useful verbal and conceptual quarters as well as directly up to useful sensible termini. They lead to consistency, stability and flowing human intercourse. They lead away from eccentricity and isolation, from foiled and barren thinking."[215]

For James, true ideas, therefore, are useful ideas; they are concepts that "carry us prosperously from any one part of our experience to any other part, linking things satisfactorily, working securely, simplifying, saving labor."[216] From a pragmatic perspective, an idea is true when it leads us, in a harmonious, connected, and satisfactory way, to other aspects of experience that "agree" with that idea. As James puts it, "any idea that helps us to *deal*, whether practically or intellectually, with . . . reality, . . . that doesn't entangle our progress in frustrations, that *fits*, in fact, and adapts our life to the reality's whole setting, . . . will hold true of that reality."[217] Thus, for James, truth and value are basically indistinguishable qualities. According to James, the phrases "it is useful because it is true" and "it is true because it is useful" have essentially the same meaning, since truth is nothing more than "the name of whatever proves itself to be good in the way of belief, and good, too, for definite, assignable reasons."[218]

This emphasis on the utilitarian nature of truth does not imply that, for James, true ideas need always demonstrate tangible repercussions in the physical world. Instead, as James stresses, a true idea can just as easily generate theoretical consequences, as long as these consequences are distinctive, concrete, "individual, particular and effective."[219] Furthermore, James is not attempting to defend, as some critics have charged, the proposition that truth is whatever is good for each individual (no matter how bad it might be for someone else), nor is he trying to claim that truth is whatever feels good to a person at the moment. James is quite aware that "it is notorious that the temporarily satisfactory is often false"; he recognizes the complexity of attempting to determine exactly what is "good to believe" (i.e., what is "true"), since as individuals and as a culture, we inevitably possess incompatible, and often warring, needs and priorities.[220] Therefore, because the satisfactoriness of an idea can, and often does, clash with the satisfactoriness of other ideas, James argues that satisfactions have to be determined over the long term and within the broader context of the individual's social and cultural milieu. According to James, for something to be true, it has to work "in the long run and on the whole . . . for what meets expediently all the experience in sight won't necessarily meet all farther experiences equally satisfactorily."[221]

Telling Truths, Touching Realities

For James, truth is never separable from the dynamic, fallible, ongoing struggle to determine what is most true in a given situation. This apparent conflation of truth with the process of verification is preferable, in James's opinion, to the opposing philosophical position that seeks to demonstrate that truth is "a stagnant property" that is inherent in an idea, or that attempts to argue that truth is a self-apparent "inert static relation."[222] While James is theoretically open to the proposition that truth, as an ideal, is that perfect "set of formulations towards which all opinions may in the long run of experience be expected to converge,"[223] he nonetheless insists that in the concrete give-and-take of the dynamics of verification, "no point of view can ever be the last one."[224] For James, truth is always "on the whole," always in process—"truth *happens* to an idea. It *becomes* true, is *made* true by events."[225]

James supports this dynamic vision of truth by offering a detailed account of the complex, multitextured process by which a new truth replaces an older truth. According to James, the substitution of one truth for another occurs for numerous reasons: perhaps an individual might undergo experiences that contradict her or his previous "stock of old opinions"; or perhaps an internal contradiction in this opinion stockpile might be uncovered; or then again, perhaps desires might arise that the older truths fail to satisfy.[226] Attempting to relieve the psychological tension that arises due to this theoretical or emotional conflict, a person seeking the truth will feel impelled to formulate a new idea that can resolve these contradictions, however, without permitting this new idea to lose complete continuity with "the ancient stock."[227] James argues that "this new idea is then adopted as the true one ... [since it is able to act as] a go-between, a smoother-over-of-transitions [and since it] ... marries old opinion to new fact so as ever to show a minimum of jolt, a maximum of continuity."[228]

According to James, this new and "true" opinion has a twofold task: it "must both lean on old truth and grasp new fact"; understood in this way, a new truth "makes itself true, gets itself classed as true, by the way it works"; it becomes true by its ability to graft itself "upon the ancient body of truth" as well as by virtue of its capacity to account effectively for any new facts of experience.[229] James emphasizes that once this new truth is accepted (either personally or communally), it then becomes endowed with tremendous power, since by following its lead, we are propelled in directions that we might previously have ignored or overlooked. On the basis of these new truths, we act in new ways, and thereby catalyze new experiences, which in turn help to define further new truths. As James points out, "truths

331

emerge from facts; but they dip forward into facts again and add to them; which facts again create or reveal new truth . . . and so on indefinitely."[230]

The interaction between mystical "facts" and religious beliefs is a clear demonstration of the snowballing momentum that can be generated by this ongoing, seemingly never-ending process. For instance, picture the following sequence of events: A mystical "fact" (i.e., the knowledge-by-acquaintance aspect of any powerful mystical experience) emerges within the consciousness of a mystic. Even though this experience can only appear in-and-through the consciousness of the mystic, it feels objective, not only because it shapes the mystic's consciousness in ways that are unexpected, but also because it seemingly manifests itself without the mystic's conscious instigation. To the degree that this experience is in tension with the mystic's previous preconscious psychological and cultural expectations, it will catalyze a corresponding sense of anxiety. This sense of psychological discomfort in turn impels the mystic to search for an interpretative grid that, while maximizing continuity with his or her previous set of beliefs, can also adequately address the unexpected differences inherent in this uniquely structured mystical experience. Little by little, as the mystic comes to interpret this experience in light of his or her new interpretative framework, he or she will feel prompted to live in a way that is more congruent with this newly acquired set of beliefs (perhaps praying more often, meditating in a different manner, associating with previously excluded social classes, and so on). These changes in the mystic's contemplative, ritual, and mundane activities, in conjunction with his or her new set of beliefs, in turn sets the stage for further mystical experiences, which will either confirm and deepen the mystic's new set of beliefs, or will again subtly alter the mystic's worldview and behavior.

It is important to point out that this Jamesian emphasis on the historically and culturally conditioned nature of the process by which we come to accept that certain beliefs are true does not automatically imply a completely relativistic position. Truth, according to James, does contain an "objective" component. While James emphasizes that "human motives sharpen all our questions," that "human satisfactions lurk in all our answers," and that "all our formulas have a human twist," he also argues that "all our truths are beliefs about 'Reality'; and in any particular belief that reality acts as something independent, as a thing *found*, not manufactured."[231] Although James emphasizes that "the trail of the human serpent is . . . over everything," and that, therefore, we should not revere truth as some sort of radiant, immutable, eternal

essence, he never goes so far as to claim that truth is a rhetorical chimera or that truth is nothing more than a relatively incidental precipi-
tate of the power-plays of various competing factions; instead, he argues
that our truths "must agree with realities, be such realities concrete or
abstract, be they facts or be they principles" unless we want to suffer
the "penalty of endless inconsistency and frustration."[232]

Furthermore, according to James, not any and every competitor
for the title of "truth" will succeed, since before any new truth can be
accepted, it must "mediate between all previous truths" and whatever
new experiences emerge to challenge these older formulations.[233] Because "the squeeze is so tight," between our prior "truths" and our
new experiences, James argues that those formulations that are able to
deal successfully with both our traditional understandings and our
present experiences are by no means arbitrary or groundless; in fact,
in James's view, these new formulations are "wedged and controlled
as nothing else."[234] James's perspective is supportive of the argument
that truth is linguistic and social in nature, as long as truth is not
understood to be *completely* linguistic or social. According to James,
truth will always emerge within a particular cultural matrix, but in
addition, truth can also reflect a level of reality that exists independently of human needs and interactions; truth can refer, at least in
theory, to a reality which has the capacity to resist inappropriate interpretations; truth can be guided by a level of experience that, as he
puts it , has the ability to "boil over" and make us "correct our present
formulas."[235]

Worlds of Belief

In order to sort out the complexities inherent in James's depiction of the interaction that takes place between "truth" and "reality,"
it is important to realize that, from the beginning of his career, James
was dissatisfied with commonsense understandings of the nature of
reality and refused to endorse the idea that reality is self-evident,
autonomous, and completely objective. For James, reality, in itself, is
only a limited concept, since "reality" *per se* never comes to us separate from our *understandings of* reality; we always come to know
what reality is through the filters of our personal prejudices, hopes,
fears, and assumptions. It is difficult, if not impossible, therefore, to
make any definitive claims about what is real and what is not, especially since our concepts about reality themselves are extremely fluid.
As James points out in an early essay, all of our ideas about reality are

333

"relative and provisional"; our only warrant for calling something "real," according to James, is "the faith of the present critic or inquirer."[236] Even years later, after the development of his mature pragmatism, James continued to emphasize the inextricable link between our ideas about reality and reality itself, arguing that "since the only realities we can talk about are ... objects-believed-in, the pragmatist whenever he says 'reality,' means in the first instance what may count for the man himself as a reality, what he believes at the moment to be such."[237]

James's most developed exposition of the connection between our ideas about reality and reality in and of itself occurs in the *Principles*, during James's detailed analysis of the psychology of belief. James argues that, as a psychological phenomena, belief is closely linked to our understandings of reality in that belief is nothing more than the conviction that an object or event is real and not imaginary. Belief, according to James, is our ingrained, taken-for-granted "sense of reality"; it is our certainty that what we are experiencing is not illusory; it is that feeling of psychological stability that arises when we have no doubts or theoretical uncertainty about whether or not something is actually real.[238]

James claims that we *want* to believe, and adds, furthermore, that our tendency is to "believe as much as we can. We would believe everything if we only could."[239] James argues that we will almost automatically believe in the reality of whatever we experience, so long as that experience is not contradicted by any other beliefs. As he puts it, "any relation to our mind at all, in the absence of a stronger contradicting relation, suffices to make an object real. The barest appeal to our attention is enough for that."[240] According to James, our inclination to believe in the reality of everything that enters into our mind is so powerful that we will only begin to disbelieve when forced to do so by the evidence provided by other contradictory experiences; that is, we only start to doubt the reality of something that we have seen, heard, felt, or even thought about, when this object of our experience is forced to "run the gauntlet" of the "rivalry" of the "various candidates for attention."[241]

To support this rather startling claim, James proposes a thought experiment. Suppose, he says, that a new mind suddenly comes into existence and sees in front of it an image of a lighted candle against a dark background. This mind would, of course, believe in the reality of that candle, even if the image of the candle was, from the point of view of other, more seasoned and knowledgeable observers, simply imaginary. As James points out, why should that mind disbelieve what it so clearly experiences as a self-evident reality? Its single reality is the image of the candle; it is not aware of any other world which might supply it with any information which would contradict that initial impression. Doubts about the reality of the candle could only come if and when that mind could compare the impression of the candle with other experiences that it believes to be more real (for instance, to use an anachronistic example, if that mind could be shown that the image of the candle was, in actuality, a holographic projection, and not a physical candle that could be touched or smelled.)

James goes on to argue that there are, in essence, different "worlds" of belief: the world perceived by our senses, the world posited by science, the world of mathematics and logic, the worlds created by each culture's tacit prejudices and presuppositions, the worlds assumed by each religious tradition's mythology and theology, the worlds that arise out of the imaginative vision of great literary artists, the worlds of madness and delusion, and the almost infinite worlds that underlie each individual's psychological point of view. According to James, every object we could possibly think of belongs at least to one of these many "sub-universes"; every event inhabits at least one of these different levels of reality. As James points out, if, for instance, a boy daydreams about a horse with wings, then that winged horse is real—in the boy's world of imagination. As long as that horse stays within the boy's fantasy-world, we can conclude that, as a daydream, it is real. However, if that boy should come to believe that this day-dreamed horse is identical to his "old mare Maggie, having grown a pair of wings," then the situation would become much more problematic, since that daydreamed image would then contradict what the boy (and others) would see in the physical world if he (or they) went to the barn to see this wondrous horse.[242] According to James, as a mental object, the winged horse is real, but as a physical object, it is unreal. As long as the boy's attention is directed to the daydream horse, it is real, relative to that particular world. But when his attention shifts, for instance to the necessity of plowing, then the reality of the daydreamed horse quickly fades.

James points out that most people do not give much credence to many, if not most, of these alternate worlds of belief, since out of all of the various possible "worlds" of belief, people will tend to choose one world that they consider to be the most fully real. For most people, according to James, this absolutely real world revolves around sense-data. Even if other worlds (e.g., the world of science, or the world of moral life, or the world of Christian theology) are also believed to be real, they are "usually real with a less real reality than that of the

335

things of sense. They are taken less seriously; and the very utmost that can be said for anyone's belief in them is that it is as strong as his 'belief in his own senses.' "[243] James suggests that any experience that fulfills the taken-for-granted criteria of what counts as "real" within the world of the senses is believed, whereas any other experience is tacitly judged to be a type of lesser reality, and is promptly shuttled off to one of the less important, less real, sub-universes of belief.

In the *Principles*, James argues that the bedrock test of whether an event or object is real is whether that object or event creates observable effects upon the world that is perceived by our senses. As he puts it, "sensible objects are . . . either our realities or the tests of our realities. Conceived objects must show sensible effects or else be disbelieved."[244] Even as early as his essay "The Function of Cognition," James argues for the importance of using the criterion of "sensible effects" to determine the reality of an object or event. In order to highlight the centrality of this criterion, James constructs the following hypothetical scenario: Someone has a dream in which a rich man dies, and during the same night, in the waking world, this rich man actually does die. James asks, how would we go about ascertaining whether this dream was just a coincidence or whether it was a case of accurate, if somewhat atypically acquired, knowledge of reality? James argues that if, on the one hand, the dreamer had never had dreams like this before and the details of the dream did not match the details of the rich man's actual death, then we would probably call the dream a coincidence. If, on the other hand, this dream was point for point aligned with the details of the rich man's death in "real life," and if the dreamer often had similar dreams, and in fact frequently used that information in his or her waking life to get a jump on everyone else, then we would be quite justified in saying that this dream was real, since it gave useful and verifiable information about a publicly shared waking reality. Finally, as James goes on to note, all of our doubts would completely vanish if this dreamer could, in the middle of his or her dreams, regularly and predictably affect events in the waking world.[245]

Although it might appear that James presents this hypothetical situation in order to highlight the possibility that alternate modes of experience might be just as real as our more everyday levels of experience, James actually uses the example of dream-knowledge to illustrate the centrality of sensory effects for any determination of the reality of one's experiences. At this point in James's philosophical development, he is fairly traditional in his belief that the world revealed by our senses is our bedrock reality. Therefore, it is difficult to predict how he would assess contemporary anthropological accounts of experiences whose structure has strong, if more overtly mystical, parallels to James's own hypothetical musings about the ability of dreams to act as alternate sources of knowledge about our sensory level of reality.

One such ethnographic description concerns the healing ceremonies of the Canelos Quichua, a tribe in South America. In this community, the tribal shaman (typically a male) will initiate a group healing ritual, if he believes that someone is suffering from the malevolent effects of spirit darts sent by a sorcerer's magical power. During this communal enterprise, the shaman, along with all the males who are present, drinks *ayahuasca*, a potent psychotropic substance, while the women who are participating in the ceremony ingest a similarly potent tobacco-water concoction. After ingesting these sacred substances, it is said that all those present share a common series of perceptions: for instance, they might hear the sound of a mythic waterfall cascading around the house and feel the earth tremble; they might "watch souls emerge from within their bodies, and spirits come from faraway spaces or times to glow before the spectators"; they might perceive the leaves in the shaman's curing-leaf bundle as "a flickering of snakes' tongues with three tips"; they might watch as an boa- or anaconda person examines "the shaman's torso-innards for any evil substances"; or they might "behold the spirit darts in the body of the patient," shining from within with a brilliant blue color.[246]

If this healing ceremony proves to be effective (and there is much evidence to indicate that shamanic rituals frequently are), and if the participants are sincere in their claims to have experienced identical visions of nonordinary realities, then this ethnographic account (along with many others of a similar nature) should, ideally, call into question the criteria by which we commonly ascertain that our everyday level of experience has a privileged degree of reality. Unlike the majority of mystical visionary episodes, which typically are confined to the consciousness of a solitary mystic, these perceptions appear to be shared by all of those participating in the ceremony. In addition, these shared perceptions, like most mystical visions, are vivid, culturally affirmed, and emotionally charged. Furthermore, if a cure actually does take place, then it could be argued that these ayahuasca-generated visions do not remain limited to an entirely separate, if fascinating, nonordinary realm of experience, but rather, are directly linked to observable, verifiable effects within this ordinary realm of reality. It would seem that, unless we dogmatically deny the validity of any other perceptions than those commonly affirmed by our cultural matrix, then following James's own criteria, we would have to claim that it is quite possible that what the participants experience during this ceremony is indeed real—at least real to them, real in that context, and during that time.

Even early in his philosophical career, James was willing to acknowledge that occasionally there are times when other contenders for reality momentarily manage to capture our attention; at least during those moments of time, the alternate realities we are immersed in will seem just as real as sense experiences. For instance, James points out that our assumption that the world of our physical senses is more real than the world of dreams is itself dependent upon the fact that we are immersed in the world of our senses when we make this determination. According to James, our belief in the bedrock reality of sense experiences disappears while we were dreaming, in that at least for that period of time, our dreams capture our attention and thus feel extremely real, whereas during this same time period, the waking world is forgotten, and is thus, by default, unreal. The waking world only assumes its preeminent position once again when we awake and shift our attention to the world revealed by our senses. However, as James points out, if a certain dream is particularly vivid and compelling, and if we continue to think about it after waking, then by virtue of the fact that it has managed to continue to capture our attention, this dream will retain a relatively high degree of reality.[247]

Dreams are not the only examples of non-sensory experiences that can so powerfully capture our attention that they, in a sense, compel our belief. As James stresses in the *Varieties*, mystical states of consciousness also have the power to shape our belief-structures, in that, for the mystic, they appear to offer direct, unimpeachable insights into reality—insights that appear to be even more dependable than those given by sense experience. A mystical experience feels real, even long after the experience itself has disappeared.

To illustrate the factors that work to solidify the powerful sense of reality engendered by mystical experiences, imagine a medieval Islamic mystic who, when immersed in prayer, suddenly and unexpectedly sees a radiant figure that he identifies as an angel of Allah. While engrossed in contemplating the beauty and glory of this radiant figure, the external world fades from the awareness of the Islamic visionary and he feels a surge of joy and thankfulness, feelings that only intensify when this angelic being speaks to the mystic, offering loving words that compassionately and wisely speak to the heart of his present situation. After a time, the radiant angelic being disappears from the mystic's visionary awareness and he gradually returns to a consciousness of everyday reality. However, in the days that follow, the mystic frequently relives this awe-inspiring and extremely vivid experience in his memory and continues to feel strongly a spiritual presence whenever the memory of the miraculous visit resurfaces. In addition, the Islamic visionary nurtures this lingering spiritual presence through the process of writing down an account of his experience, and then further concretizes the experience by narrating the encounter to a circle of fellow spiritual aspirants—mystics who, by virtue of their own spiritual experiences and scriptural training, are able to affirm the validity and value of this powerful religious encounter.

Would this mystic have any reason to doubt the reality of this visitation? There would be nothing within his cultural background (unlike our more secular context) to raise doubts about the reality of this experience. Medieval Islamic culture assumed that mystical visions of Allah's messengers can and do occur, especially to those individuals who have dedicated themselves to a path of purification and contemplation.

From a Jamesian perspective as well, this experience could be said to possess all of the qualities that would prompt an individual to believe that his or her experience was indeed real and not illusory. The visitation was "interesting and important," and it excited and stimulated the interest of the mystic.[248] The visionary experience also possessed "coerciveness over attention" (that is, it was impossible to ignore), "sensible pungency" (that is, it was just as vivid and clear as sensory experiences, if not more so), "independence of other causes" (that is, it seemed to come into the mystic's awareness of its own accord), and "congruency with certain favorite forms of contemplation—unity, simplicity, permanence and the like" (that is, it was aesthetically and philosophically harmonious).[249] What possible reason would this Islamic visionary have for doubting the reality of what he experienced, especially since this experience was also able to fulfill another Jamesian criteria for reality-testing: the experience intimately and continuously connected, in numerous ways, with the mystic's overall sense of his own life, his moment-to-moment concrete experience of being alive. When any experience manages to fulfill all of these varied criteria, then that experience, according to James, will be (and most likely should be) believed.

James goes on to point out that there are additional factors that can prompt us to believe in the reality of an object, event, or idea. One of the most important, and potentially problematic, stimulants of belief is our emotional life. According to James, most individuals are strongly inclined to believe in the reality of an object, event, or idea, if that object, event or idea arouses their emotions, or incites them to

339

action. James stresses that there is a natural tendency to believe any emotionally exciting idea, perhaps because these ideas catalyze a "bodily commotion," leading a person to think: "nothing which I can feel like *that* can be false."[250] James argues that while this receptivity to emotionally exciting beliefs is a frequent catalyst of even our most beneficial religious assumptions, it is necessary, if difficult, to train ourselves (typically via a thorough education) to suspend our belief in the presence of emotionally exciting ideas, since to believe automatically in something simply because it arouses a passion within us is a frequent source of wrong judgments, judgments which can often lead, in turn, to disastrous consequences.

James stresses that regardless of whether emotionally-impelled beliefs arise out of the "revelations of mysticism " or the "delusions of insanity," these impassioned beliefs are embraced for basically the same reason as that cluster of "sudden beliefs which animate mobs of men . . . the stoning of a prophet, the hailing of a conqueror, the burning of a witch, the baiting of a heretic or Jew."[251] These emotionally prompted beliefs may indeed be quite persuasive. But, according to James, it is crucially important to resist the seductive, and frequently delusive, temptation of automatically accepting these emotionally impelled beliefs. In fact, for James, one of the most important functions of a philosophical examination of the nature of reality is to critique and undermine just these sorts of irrational, intolerant, and taken-for-granted belief systems. We need to do this so that we can come to understand that reality is not a simple given and so that we will ideally be less eager to persecute those among us who do not share our particular circumscribed understanding of reality.

James himself, over the course of his career, slowly became more open-minded as to what types of experiences are real and what types are not. For instance, although James, during the time in which he wrote the *Principles*, was not willing to accept the claim that nonsensory mystical experiences can bring with them a "sense" of reality that is just as vivid and convincing as sense experiences, he changed his mind several years later. By the time that James wrote the *Varieties*, he had become persuaded that religious and mystical experiences were excellent examples of how a person can come to possess a strong "sense" of reality, even without any overt stimulation of the physical senses. In fact, even during the time period of the *Principles*, James's initial exposure to information gathered by the Society for Psychical Research had already begun to arouse his speculative curiosity, although James frankly admitted that he still had difficulty comprehending how a person could come to possess an extremely vivid sense that an object or event was real without any overt use of his or her sense organs.

James confessed, for example, that he was especially bewildered by some of the information that he had collected for the "Census of Hallucinations." In this census, James came upon several narratives that seemed to illustrate that a person could have an experience that instills all of the conviction associated with sense experiences, without any apparent sensory imput. In one of these experiences that particularly struck James, a Mr. P. narrated that, while practicing the piano in Boston, he frequently experienced a sudden cold draft of air upon his face, conjoined with a prickling sensation at the roots of his hair. Mr. P. would then turn from the piano and would see a distinct figure of a man sliding under the crack of the door, flattening itself to squeeze through, and then rounding out again to take the shape of a man. Mr. P. recognized this man, and knew that the man, in "real" life, had died. This ghostly figure would never make a sound and never came close to Mr. P., but Mr. P. invariably could distinctly see this figure; Mr. P. could vividly see that this figure had a full beard that was partially grey, and that this ghostly visitor wore a certain style of suit. What made this narrative so striking to James, was the fact that Mr. P. had been completely blind since the age of two, and yet, during this experience, it was as if Mr. P. actually physically saw this deceased acquaintance. James frankly admitted his puzzlement, noting that Mr. P. had all of the conviction associated with physically seeing an object, but with none of the corresponding sense abilities.[252]

Although while James was writing the *Principles*, he still struggled with how to reconcile theoretically the strong sense of reality generated by nonsensory psychical and mystical experiences, in many ways, his work in the *Principles* did set the stage for his later willingness, in the *Varieties*, to extend this sense of reality to nonsensory experiences. For instance, James argues in the *Principles* that although most individuals tacitly tend to believe whatever their culture claims is "really real," as a matter of psychological fact, the culturally imposed assumptive world of an individual can be overturned if an event, object, or conception that is considered to be illusory or unreal by the culture is, nevertheless, forcefully and directly experienced by that individual.

In order to illustrate the power that our culture typically possesses to dictate what should be accepted as "real," James points to the battle between scientific conceptions of reality and the conception of reality supported by psychical experiences. James states that, if an individual has merely heard about a manifestation of psychic ability (such as, for instance, the ability to move heavy furniture without any physical contact), then the chances are high that the culture's scientific perspective on reality will prevail. As James notes, in such circumstances, the tendency is to brand these reports of "spiritualistic phenomena" as lies or to call such phenomena " 'illusions' of sense, produced by fraud or due to hallucination."[253] However, as James goes on to point out, if an individual, in a rigorous and controlled setting, has personally observed a table floating in the air with no visible means of support, then he or she will be strongly, and James argues, correctly, impelled to cling to that "sensible experience through thick and thin, even though the whole fabric of 'science' should be rent in twain."[254] James recognizes that in cases such as this, individuals could easily err in their stubborn insistence on the reality of what they have personally experienced. Nevertheless, in James's opinion, even if this obstinate refusal to deny one's personal experience can at times lead to mistakes in judgment, this willingness to trust the evidence of what one has directly perceived is itself the bedrock of worthwhile scientific investigation. According to James, science itself is based on trusting the evidence that one receives, regardless if that evidence goes against current scientific assumptions.

"The Fight is Still Under Way": Different Understandings of Reality

From a Jamesian perspective, reality is clearly not self-evident. Because our notions of what is real and what is illusory are intimately linked to a complex gestalt of individual prejudices, desires, hopes, and tacit cultural assumptions, there are no objective standards by which we can easily determine whether any object or event is real or illusory. As James succinctly puts it, "no general offhand answer can be given as to which objects mankind shall choose as its realities. The fight is still under way."[255]

However, even though much of James's work appears to be designed to challenge our taken-for-granted assumption that reality is something which is self-evident and easily agreed upon by any rational individual, James at times (especially in *Pragmatism* and *The Meaning of Truth*) appears to forget his own insistence that there can be many different, and equally acceptable, understandings of reality. There are moments when James seems to want a touchstone, something that is reliably solid, something by which he can refute the frequent, and mistaken, assumption that pragmatism is a purely subjective theory of truth. During these moments, James appears to abandon his previous fluid understandings of reality, and instead, seems to align himself with the understanding that reality is something that is self-apparent, indisputable, and purely objective. For instance, at one point, lashing out at those "absurd" understandings of pragmatism that claim that pragmatists think that truth is something that "could fall altogether inside of the thinker's private experience and be something purely psychological," James stresses that the "truth-relation" involves both an "idea" and an "object," an object that provides the "mirrored matter" that keeps our ideas from being "so much flat psychological surface," an "object" that serves as the "givenness" to which our true ideas can refer.[256] James sees himself, in this sense, as "an epistemological realist" because, in his opinion, "there can be no truth if there if nothing to be true about."[257]

James in this context appears to be claiming that reality is an "object," an "object" that is not amorphous, that is not in dispute, an "object" that is simply there and self-evident. Unfortunately, this willingness to depict reality as an "object" or as "mirrored matter" can make it appear that James is simply acceding to the commonsense understanding that reality is something which is completely external to the perceiver, and completely independent of the perceiver's psychological framework. James, at times, seems strangely unaware that this stubborn insistence that he is an "epistemological realist" is highly problematic, especially since James himself, in other, arguably more sophisticated moments, emphasizes that everything that we believe in (i.e., our realities) comes to us filtered through a highly complex, and typically tacit, cultural system of assumptions. As such, the notion of some "reality" that is completely separate from these preconscious assumptions is, in effect, quite un-Jamesian.

Oddly, James also often seems to forget that the realities which are the reference points for true ideas are quite frequently less pristine and obvious than the sense objects that he typically prefers to use in his examples.[258] For instance, to which "reality" would we be referring if we were to ask, "Is James's pragmatism true?"? Similarly, if we were to ask, "Is it true that Emily loves Paul?" or "Is it true that Picasso was a more skilled painter than Miro?," are the realities referred to by these questions self-evident, autonomous "objects" that can be accurately "mirrored"?

Fortunately, James, for the most part, is aware that truth is not a matter of "copying" an objective reality. James typically goes out of his way to emphasize that any attempt to describe accurately the process of making true statements is bedeviled with unexpected

343

complexities. Unfortunately, however, these complexities become even more exasperating when we attempt to examine the assumptions that underlie any attempt to justify pragmatically the truth of religious beliefs in a nonmaterial reality.

At first glance, it would seem that there would be no major difficulties standing in the way of a pragmatic assessment of the validity of religious beliefs. Although many of James's examples of pragmatism in action draw upon relatively mundane examples (i.e., the location of a building, whether a beer is in the next room, and so on), at other times, James specifically applies pragmatic principles to theological and metaphysical questions (monism versus pluralism is a particular favorite). James goes out of his way to stress that pragmatism, as a methodology, "has no *a priori* prejudices against theology."[259] In many ways, in fact, James believes that pragmatism is an ideal methodology for wrestling with questions of religious truth. James points out that pragmatism, unlike other methodological perspectives, actually "widens the field of search for God," since pragmatism, unlike rationalism, is not restricted to logic and unlike classical empiricism, pragmatism is not limited to the data provided by the senses.[260] James describes pragmatism's theological openness in this way:

> Pragmatism is willing to take anything . . . to count the humblest and most personal experiences. She will count mystical experiences if they have practical consequences. . . . Her only test of probable truth is what works best in the way of leading us, what fits every part of life best and combines with the collectivity of experience's demands, nothing being omitted. If theological ideas should do this, if the notion of God, in particular, should prove to do it, how could pragmatism possibly deny God's existence? She could see no meaning in treating as "not true" a notion that was pragmatically so successful. What other kind of truth could there be, for her, than all this agreement with concrete reality?[261]

James is personally convinced that pragmatism can adequately establish the truth of religious beliefs in God, since, as he puts it, even if there are "residual difficulties . . . experience shows" that a belief in God can produce valuable effects in our life, and if this is the case (which James believes that he has adequately established in the *Varieties*), then "on pragmatistic principles, if the hypothesis of God works satisfactorily in the widest sense of the word, it is true."[262] All that is left to do at this point then is to specify exactly what is meant by the term "God," and to insure that this theological understanding can "combine satisfactorily with all the other working truths."[263]

In some respects, it might seem that pragmatism, as a methodological process designed to adjudicate differing metaphysical positions, could not, and should not, align itself with any specific theological understanding. James himself says as much early on in *Pragmatism* when he contends that pragmatism, at least in the beginnings of an investigation, "stands for no particular results. It has no dogmas, and no doctrines save its method. . It lies in the midst of our theories, like a corridor in a hotel. Innumerable chambers open out of it."[264] However, in the final pages of *Pragmatism*, James admits that *his* pragmatism most certainly does have specific theological preferences. After having applied pragmatic principles to an investigation of monism versus pluralism, and optimism versus meliorism, James is confident that the theological perspective that is the most fully aligned with pragmatism is, not surprisingly, "pluralistic and moralistic" or "melioristic in type."[265]

In *Pragmatism*, James is still a staunch theist—the pluralistic pantheism of *A Pluralistic Universe* is yet to come. And in many ways, it makes sense that James would maintain a theistic perspective, not only because pragmatic justifications of religious realities are much simpler if religious realities are understood to be distinct, localized "objects" known by separate subjects, but also because theism dovetails nicely with James's "epistemological realism," which also assumes that independent "objects" exist separately from equally autonomous "subjects."

However, if pragmatism is based on this type of "epistemological realism," then it clearly would have great difficulty in verifying the truth of any monistic or nondualistic understandings of reality. In order to understand why this is so, it is important to realize that "truth," for pragmatism, is always determined in relation to the effects that theological beliefs or religious experiences have on relatively autonomous persons or communities. Pragmatism depends upon the logic of cause and effect: this belief/experience can be shown to produce a corresponding effect. But the logic of cause and effect, in turn, depends upon a basic duality between that which causes and that which is effected, and it is this very duality that most monistic or nondualistic metaphysical positions will deny.

Therefore, even if, in other situations, a pragmatic investigator could succeed in establishing a clear causal connection between a certain belief or experience and a certain corresponding effect (which is, as has been shown, a very big "if"), in the case of nondualistic beliefs or experiences, this causal connection can never be established, since if "that" which one is attempting to verify does exist, then "it" exists in

345

such a way as to be nondifferent from the effects that are allegedly caused by these nondualistic or monistic beliefs or experiences, and "it" is also nondifferent than the person doing the assessment. (For instance, if Fechner's conception of the all-pervasive earth-soul is true, then how could one possibly hope to verify that truth pragmatically, since that consciousness itself would be the assessor, the assessed, and any and all possible effects.)

Furthermore, James never discusses the ways in which the "epistemological realism" he at times claims to align himself with, is in tension with the nondualism of his radical empiricism, in which "subjects" and "objects" are simply functional distinctions emerging out of a more basic ontological unity.[266] Indeed, it appears that James is simply not consistent about which epistemological perspective he prefers, since as Craig Eisendrath lucidly points out, many of James's pragmatic writings actually do operate out of the nondual perspective assumed by his radical empiricism.[267]

In order to underscore the distinction between the understandings of truth which are based on epistemological realism and those which are rooted in epistemological nondualism, it is important to look carefully into the differing ways in which each epistemology breaks down the process of knowing. Unfortunately, this analysis, which is already rather complex and abstract, is even further complicated by the fact that both of the understandings of truth posited by pragmatism (i.e., the realistic and the nondual understandings of truth) also differ radically from other, nonpragmatic, theories of truth. For instance, realistic versions of nonpragmatic theories of truth posit three separate components, that is, "reality," "knowledge," and "truth." However, the pragmatic perspective based on James's epistemological realism reduces these three terms to two, that is, "truth" and "reality," with "truth" understood as a type of knowledge-relation to "reality." But when James operates out of the nondual perspective of his theory of "pure experience," the two terms of his "realistic" version of pragmatism finally coalesce into only one term, that is, "experience"; from this nondual point of view, "verification is then simply the relations of one part of our experience to another."[268] When James is working out of this nondual perspective, therefore, "truth" is simply a "relation, not of our ideas to nonhuman realities, but of conceptual parts of our experience to sensational parts."[269]

The contrast is clear: from the perspective of James's epistemological realism, truth is separate from a reality which gives that truth its "cognitive luster."[270] From the perspective of James's radical empiricism, however, truth is nothing more than a relationship between two functionally distinct, but ontologically united, aspects of experience. Unfortunately, James never makes any overt effort to distinguish between these two understandings of truth, and certainly never clearly indicates which "version" of truth he prefers. But the choice between these two notions of truth is critical, especially for the philosophy of mysticism, in that the very attempt to establish (or deny) the cognitivity of religious experiences is itself based on an implicit epistemological realism.

Philosophers of religion who assume an epistemological realism typically claim that mystico-religious experiences are cognitive if and only if the mystic (understood as a self-existent, autonomous subject) has correct knowledge of God (understood, likewise, as an ontologically independent reality that is separate from the subject). However, what if the mystic has an experience in which the subject/object distinction itself disappears? Are these nondual mystical experiences cognitive or are they not? From a dualistic point of view, this interweaving of the experiencer and the experienced will make the experience itself appear suspiciously "subjective," that is, noncognitive, in that the experience happens entirely "within" the psyche of the mystic, with no "objective" referent for the experience. However, from a nondual point of view, this type of experience makes complete sense, because within a nondual framework of understanding, the categories of "subject" and "object" are understood to be nothing more than functional distinctions emerging out of a more basic, nondual "suchness." From a nondual perspective, all experiences, mystical or otherwise, are an inextricable fusion of "subjectivity" and "objectivity" (or to make the same point in a different way—all experiences are neither completely "subjective" nor "objective," because these categories of "subjective" and "objective" are themselves later impositions upon a more primal nonduality).

However, it is crucially important to underscore the fact that a nondual perspective does not turn the world into an amorphous mush—it does not eliminate the ability to make worthwhile and meaningful functional distinctions between "subject" and "object." Valuable and significant distinctions between different levels of nondual experience can be made, and indeed, must be made, especially if one hopes to undertake a pragmatic justification of the truth of mystical experiences. Pragmatism, as was mentioned above, needs to demonstrate that the beliefs or experiences of "subjects" create "objective" effects in the world at large (i.e., dramatic healings, long-lasting transformations of character, and so on). Fortunately, these "objective" effects *can* be demonstrated within a nondual perspective, as long as the categories of "subjective" and "objective" are recognized as simply functional, context-specific distinctions taking place within a more "encompassing" nondual matrix.

The "Cash-Basis" of Truth

For the most part, James's pragmatism remains alert to the complexities inherent in any discussion of the nature of reality; he refuses to codify a narrow band of acceptable understandings of what counts as "really real." For James, reality, as experienced, is never uni-vocal; reality is always interwoven with what a person is willing and able to believe. When James uses the term "reality," it typically refers either to some sort of "concrete sensible presence," such as the "sight and taste of the beer" which is believed to be in the next room, or less often, to mathematical or logical insights, such as the geometric relation "between the sides and hypotenuse of a triangle"; however, he will, at times, defend the viability of alternate, less commonplace understandings of the forms that reality might take.[271] For James, realities such as an earth-soul or ghostly presences are also viable ontological possibilities, even if they are less tangible or logically irrefutable than beer or mathematical equations. The question then becomes, are our *beliefs in* these realities true or false? According to James, it is this epistemological question that pragmatism seeks to unravel, not the ontological question of whether earth-souls, ghostly presences, or any other putative realities are *really* true.[272]

It is important to underline the fact that "truth" and "reality" are not synonymous for James. Quite often, in our everyday usage of these words, we act as if these terms were virtually interchangeable (for instance, it does not matter syntactically whether we say, "Are you *truly* going to move next month?" or "Are you *really* going to move next month?"). For James, however, there is a clear distinction between "reality" and "truth." According to James, "realities are not *true*, they *are*; and beliefs are true *of* them."[273] Truth has to do with our ideas and opinions *about* reality, while reality is that which simply exists, quasi-independently of these opinions.

What complicates matters is that, as was pointed out above, James does *not* think that truth is a simple matter of an automatic "duplication by the mind of a ready-made and given reality."[274] While this "copying" of reality by the mind may occur in relation to concrete objects (i.e., our true ideas of a clock on the wall will give us an accurate picture of its dial), matters become much more complex when what must be copied is something that is not readily apparent to the

348

senses (i.e., it is difficult to see in what way a true idea of time "copies" this abstract principle). James is willing to concede that truth has to do with the "agreement" of our ideas with "reality." However, for James, this "agreement" is not a matter of simply copying or mirroring reality. Instead, an idea or belief "agrees" with our experience of reality (and is thus "true") when it helps us to interact with this reality in an effective way; to "agree" with a reality means "to be guided either straight up to it or into its surroundings, or to be put into such working touch with it as to handle either it or something connected with it better than if we disagreed. Better either intellectually or practically!"[275]

James is aware of the paradox: truth is both something which comes into existence as the result of human effort *and* it is something which is found, that is, something which seemingly existed prior to its discovery. James points out, for instance, that our knowledge of the Big Dipper constellation has, in one sense, always been true, in that the reality which our knowledge "agrees with" has existed long before the birth of any human beings. Yet, in another sense, because it is human beings who decide that those seven stars, out of all of the mass of stars in the sky, form the shape of the dipper, "something comes by the counting that was not there before. . . . In one sense [we] create it, and in another sense [we] find it."[276]

James's double-edged, interactive understanding of the nature of truth owes much to James's earlier contrast between knowledge-by-acquaintance and knowledge-about. In one sense, according to James, the majority of our truths are almost entirely knowledge-about, in that they are, for the most part, based on ideas, theories, and opinions about objects or events that we have never directly experienced. As James emphasizes, the vast majority of our truths need never be personally verified, since "indirect as well as direct verifications pass muster. Where circumstantial evidence is sufficient, we can go without eye-witnessing. . . . [We] assume Japan to exist without ever having been there, because it works to do so."[277] In this way, in most cases, the *verifiability* of an idea is basically equivalent to direct verification. However, at some point in time, our truths have to be grounded in some form of direct experience, some form of knowledge-by-acquaintance. As James stresses, while "truth lives, in fact, for the most part on a credit system," allowing "our thoughts and beliefs [to] 'pass,' so long as nothing challenges them," eventually, some sort of face-to-face verification has to occur, for "beliefs verified concretely by somebody are the posts of the whole superstructure"; without this direct verification, "the fabric of truth collapses like a financial system with no cash-basis whatever."[278]

349

In order to illustrate the interaction between these two types of knowledge, James pictures himself sitting at home thinking about Memorial Hall at Harvard. James's knowledge-about Memorial Hall is verifiable: his memories of the campus can lead him, if he wishes, step by step from his home to Memorial Hall. In this sense, James's knowledge-about the building is true, if it leads him, at least potentially, to a knowledge-by-acquaintance of that building. For James, therefore, knowledge-by-acquaintance is what verifies our knowledge-about truths (and, more subtly, is what creates these truths in the first place); in this sense, our knowledge-by-acquaintance of something is the reality to which pragmatic truths refer.

However, in James's discussions of his pragmatic theory of truth, he rarely acknowledges his previous psychological insights that this knowledge-by-acquaintance of something, during a concrete moment of perception, is itself not pristine or purely objective, since it is inevitably interwoven with our knowledge-about. We do not just simply see the building—we see the building filtered through our complex nexus of previous understandings, expectations, interests, and so on. That seemingly concrete, external reality, as experienced, is always interwoven with our internalized knowledge-about that building. In this way, the clear-cut distinction that James seeks to make between reality (which simply *is*) and truth (which is *about* reality) begins to be much more nebulous and problematic than James may have wished. Instead of reality and truth as two theoretically distinct principles, we have an interactive, mutable relationship between primarily knowledge-about truths, which are verified by realities which are themselves shifting combinations of knowledge-about and knowledge-by-acquaintance.[279]

This recognition that even the realities supposedly contacted by our senses are not as purely objective as we might assume allows us to posit the existence of religious, nonsensory realities that are *also* a combination of "subjective" and "objective" components. The realities posited by different religious traditions (whether fox spirits, thunder beings, ancestral ghosts, the Holy Spirit, and so on) must inevitably manifest in and through the psyche of the one experiencing these realities, and as such, are always shaped and colored by differing degrees of internalized, tacit knowledge-about (culturally encoded expectations, beliefs, etc.); however, these religious realities, as *experienced*, can also be theoretically understood to contain a relatively high percentage of knowledge-by-acquaintance. The knowledge-about "portion" of each mystico-religious experience will be constituted from the "materials" given by the mystic's cultural and psychological background, but the knowledge-by-acquaintance "portion" of this mystico-religious experience is that which has a stubborn independence, that which has the ability to resist inappropriate post-facto interpretations, that which has the power to generate and compel new cultural and psychological worldviews.[280] In this sense, it is not the religious experiences in-and-of-themselves that could be termed the "cash-basis" of the individual's religious truths (since these experiences are always a complex, dynamic gestalt of knowledge-about and knowledge-by-acquaintance); instead, it is the knowledge-by-acquaintance "portion" of religious experiences which fulfills this role in the verification process.

Of course, this directly felt, intuitively sensed aspect of various mystico-religious experiences differs from the sensory data that is the knowledge-by-acquaintance component of our perceptions of external objects, in that the knowledge-by-acquaintance aspect of mystico-religious experiences is not publicly shared information that is directly and easily accessible to any mature and sane member of the culture.[281] The relatively private nature of this knowledge-by-acquaintance aspect of a mystico-religious experience means that verification of a mystico-religious experience is much more problematic than verification of sense experiences (hence, almost everyone believes that it is true that Japan exists, whereas there is much less consensus about the truth of God's existence).

However, the difference in difficulty between verifying external objects and verifying religious "objects" may not be quite as extreme as it might first appear. In the same way that Japan may be relatively difficult, if not impossible, for some people to verify concretely, due to financial and other practical difficulties, it may well be that verifying the existence of spiritual realities is also an individual matter—easy for some, but for a variety of reasons (time restraints, lack of personal interest, psychological barriers, and so on) difficult for others. The verification of both material and spiritual realities, therefore, can be said to depend, to a vast degree, on the reliability of a network of expert witnesses—those individuals who *do* have the time, willingness, money, desire, and aptitude necessary to experience directly the existence of these realities.

In this sense, for many, if not most individuals within different cultures, the existence of a non-material reality is based primarily on *verifiability*, on the premise that either you can experience its reality for yourself if you are willing and able to practice the necessary spiritual disciplines (bracketing for the moment the idea of grace) or that you can trust in its reality based on the testimony of reliable witnesses—that is, the testimony of the saints, shamans, and mystics of various traditions throughout history. From a pragmatic standpoint,

351

therefore, testimonials should not dismissed out of hand, but rather, should be recognized as forming an integral part of the process by which a religious idea comes to be accepted as true, in that it is the testimonies of these "professional" mystics, acting as spiritual proxies or envoys for those of us who are less gifted or inclined, that enable us to indirectly verify these realities for ourselves.

In this way, just as most Americans believe that Japan exists because that belief both "works" for us and is ultimately verifiable, either by us or by our trusted experts, it could also be argued that it is legitimate to believe in different nonmaterial religious realties, if our beliefs in these realities "work" for us and are reliably verifiable. For instance, let us posit a culture in which the reality of unseen spiritual phenomena is taken for granted. If, in the context of this culture, a sizable percentage of the population could be led, through appropriate rituals and spiritual disciplines, to a vividly felt, "sensory-like" experience of what their conceptual "map" predicts, and if similar experiences were to keep reoccurring on a regular basis, both to them and to others willing to follow a similar pattern of behavior, and if these experiences, over the long term, and on the whole, could consistently produce effects that were interpreted within the context of that culture as psychologically, socially, and physically healing, then by what possible criteria could the culture's beliefs in these spiritual phenomena be termed "false"?

This hypothetical situation may appear to be riddled with so many qualifiers that its conclusion becomes, at best, suspect, but perhaps a concrete example will give rhetorical flesh to these rickety speculative bones. In an ethnographic study of the Kalahari !Kung that took place during the late nineteen sixties, Richard Katz provides a vivid account of the healing dances that are a central focus of the religious and social life of this hunting-gathering people.[282] The goal of these all-night dances is to activate the *num*, a spiritual energy that "resides in the pit of the stomach and the base of the spine."[283] During these dances, men circle for hours around an inner ring of women who surround a fire, clapping and singing spiritually potent songs.[284] While dancing, these men experience the *num* beginning to "heat up" within them, and then finally, as it begins to "boil," sense the *num* rising up their spines to the back of their heads.[285] As one healer comments: "You dance, dance, dance, dance. The num lifts you up in your belly and lifts you in your back, and you start to shiver. Num makes you tremble; it's hot."[286] Another healer adds: "In your backbone you feel a pointed something and it works its way up. The base of your spine is tingling, tingling, tingling, tingling. Then num makes your thoughts nothing in your head."[287]

With the boiling of the *num*, the healers begin to *kia*, that is, they enter into a state of heightened or altered awareness. The *kia* state is painful, and greatly feared, because it is experienced as a type of death, in which the healer's soul leaves the body and ascends into the sky in order to confront the gods and spirits who are attempting to lure the souls of the living into their realm of death. As one healer says, "As we enter kia, we fear death. We fear we may die and not come back!"[288]

However, even if they are afraid, the !Kung healers also consciously attempt to bring about this state of *kia*, since this heightened awareness is essential if the healer is going to *twe*, that is, to "pull out sickness."[289] *Kia* gives the healers, those who are "masters" or "owners" of the *num*, the powers needed to diagnosis and to heal. During *kia*, the healers gain clairvoyant powers. This amplified perception enables them to see into the bodies of those who need healing, it allows them to perceive the "death things" that have been put inside those who are ill, and it gives them the ability to see the spirits attempting to lure their living relatives to the realm of death.[290] *Kia* also grants the healers the ability to transfer some of their own *num* into the bodies of those they are attempting to heal, as well as the ability to pull out the sicknesses that lie hidden within the members of the community. Katz vividly describes this interaction between *kia* and the ability to heal:

> They may shudder or shake violently, their whole body convulsing in apparent pain and anguish. The experience of kia has begun. And then, either on their own or under the guidance of those who are more steady, the healers who are in kia go to each person at the dance and begin to heal. They lay their fluttering hands on a person, one hand usually on the chest, the other on the back, pulling out the sickness, while shrieking earth-shattering screams and howls known as *kowhedili*, an expression for the pain and difficulty of this healing work. Then they shake their hands vigorously toward the empty space beyond the dance, casting the sickness they have taken from the person out into the darkness.[291]

Within the community, the ability of the healers is taken for granted. Stories of cures range from the occasionally dramatic (such as when "someone who has been clawed by a leopard and 'given up for dead' is healed and recovers miraculously")[292] to the more frequent, and less dramatic examples, such as when a mother who cannot nurse her infant regains her milk or when a person notices that the swelling caused by infection has subsided. In addition, the healing is not simply

353

physical, in that the dance itself is an occasion for community bonding. The dance provides a context in which the spiritual power of the community can successfully challenge and overcome the threatening forces of the spirits and the gods. Further, the dance also offers an opportunity for lighthearted and playful interactions (the dance is punctuated with raucous joking and laughter).

For the !Kung, the reality of the gods, the spirits, and the *num*, is simply assumed, and for good reason. Within their culture, why would anyone question the truth-status of these beliefs? Since a large percentage of the culture vividly and regularly experiences the reality of these spiritual phenomena during a heightened state of awareness that is dependably catalyzed by the performance of a certain set of spiritual practices, and furthermore, since the whole community frequently witnesses the positive healing effects that follow in the wake of the performance of the dance, then the culture's belief in these spiritual phenomena that are so vividly experienced seems imminently sound and reasonable. By what possible criteria could an observer outside of that culture argue with their truth-claims? Their truths may not easily conform with the scientific understanding of reality that is taken for granted by many, if not most, individuals in contemporary Western culture, but from what Archimedean standpoint do we claim that this Western understanding of reality is innately superior? Is it anything more than simply cultural arrogance that denies truth to anything outside of one's own culturally defined parameters?

It is important to point out that an argument is not being made at this point for the incommensurability of truth. I am not arguing here that truths are hermetically-sealed within the parameters of each culture's language-games and life-world. While, from a Jamesian perspective, truths will always be assessed within a particular cultural, historical, and linguistic matrix, each matrix will be understood, not as a self-contained monad, but rather, as a dynamic field that overlaps and interpenetrates other energetic, permeable matrices. This "fields within fields within fields" perspective is highly versatile, in that it can offer a theoretical perspective that can recognize both intracultural uniqueness and cross-cultural communication. While a Jamesian understanding of truth would emphasize that the religious experiences indigenous to one culture will be more easily verified within that cultural context (since those truths must answer to the needs and assumptions of that culture), a Jamesian perspective would also stress that, to the degree that these needs and assumptions overlap with the needs and assumptions of another culture, the possibility is created for a genuine exchange of cultural truths.

354

Telling Truths, Touching Realities

For instance, Richard Katz's culturally prepared and historically situated need to understand holistic healing practices might well intersect with the needs of the !Kung to be healed, and Katz's assumptions about the efficacy of altered states of awareness could also connect with the !Kung assumptions about the power of *kia* to catalyze spiritual healing. To the degree that this cultural overlap takes place, the condition is created in which !Kung truths could become a viable possibility for Katz as well, perhaps prompting a willingness within Katz to participate in the dances himself. Indubitably, Katz, as a Western observer, would still lack the depth of cultural insight available to the most novice healer in the !Kung religious tradition, even if he were to participate in the !Kung healing dances on a regular basis. However, if Katz, during several consecutive dances, were to experience an energy beginning to boil within himself and consequently felt himself propelled into a powerful altered state of awareness, and if he were to see continued connections between the dances and occurrences of healing that could not be easily explained using the models available to Western medical practice, then the likelihood is excellent that some of the !Kung's truths would become some of Katz's truths, and legitimately so.[293]

Transforming Visions

A pragmatically oriented "fields within fields within fields" perspective offers a provocative, and potentially valuable, philosophical orientation to such cross-cultural, experientially grounded exchanges of truths, in that it posits the existence of fields of experience that are wider or deeper than the conceptual fields generated by each particular culture. Transcending the particularities of each culture, and yet capable of manifesting within them all, these wider or deeper fields of experience could be understood to provide the "raw material" that underlies the religious truth-claims of each culture. These wider or deeper fields of experience could be said to provide the knowledge-by-acquaintance component of each religious experience, that quality of the experience that is directly and powerfully felt, and is immediately convincing. Dynamic, multiformed, open to numerous interpretations and yet capable of initiating startling and often revolutionary shifts in personal and cultural understandings, these fields of experience could be seen as a fecund "suchness" that underlies and informs the rich variety of mystico-religious experiences. A Jamesian "fields within fields within fields" perspective on the self and reality would contend that it is these fields of experience that manifest as the immediacy and power of, for example, the satori experience that convinces a Western novice Zen practitioner of the validity of her new beliefs; it would be these fields of experience that would provide the depth and ecstasy of the experience of God's love that persuades a Liberian tribesman to convert to the Christian beliefs he has been exposed to by the local Lutheran missionary; it would be these fields of experience that would take the form of the shimmering sparks, flying rattles, and laughing voices that convinces a skeptical American nurse participating in an Oglala Sioux *yuwipi* healing ceremony that spiritual levels of reality do indeed exist.

From a pragmatic point of view, the concept of transcultural, spiritually potent fields of experience that provide the "immediate luminousness" or "voltage" of mystico-religious experiences would not be understood as literally true, but instead, would be seen as a philosophically reasonable attempt to honor both the diversity and the potential unity of mystico-religious experiences. The exact configurations taken by these fields of experience would inevitably remain elusive, not only because of the inherent inability of language to represent this level of awareness adequately and fully, but also because the aim of a pragmatic methodology, as Eugene Fontinell aptly notes, is "participation in, rather than abstract representation of, reality."[294]

Because pragmatism, as James emphasizes, is "against dogma, artificiality and the pretence of finality in truth," and instead, looks upon philosophical theories as ways "in which existing realities may be changed," a pragmatically oriented "fields within fields within fields" perspective would make no claims that its philosophical outlook is final, that its arguments are conclusive, that its definitions are rigorous.[295] As James notes, in order to truly appreciate the pragmatic point of view, it is necessary to "renounce rectilinear arguments and ancient ideals of rigor and finality"; one must, instead, recognize that the "satisfactoriness" of one's philosophical conclusions have "to be measured by a multitude of standards, of which some, for aught we know, may fail in any given case"; one must be prepared that "what is more satisfactory than any alternative in sight, may to the end be a sum of *pluses* and *minuses*."[296] As Fontinell observes, all pragmatic conclusions are "open to modification and correction"; there can be no attempt to claim that pragmatic arguments are logically coercive, since for pragmatism, logic itself is only one of several equally valid criteria by which it is possible to determine the overall reasonableness of a philosophical proposal.[297]

James does not deny the importance of intellectual exactitude, when possible, but he also recognizes that other factors, such as aes-

356

thetic appeal, practical usefulness, and transformative potential, can also, legitimately, act as criteria by which we are able to decide between opposing philosophical or religious points of view. James admits that "the superiority of one of our formulas to another may not consist so much in its literal 'objectivity,' as in subjective qualities like its usefulness, its 'elegance' or its congruity with our residual beliefs," but James goes on to argue that, although this holistic, multidimensional process of philosophical decision-making may appear to be "full of vagueness and ambiguity," in the end, a plurality of at least potentially complementary touchstones for sound philosophical argumentation is more likely to do justice to the rich fecundity of our experiential world than an exclusive reliance upon logical rigor.[298]

It may never be possible theoretically to reconcile the visions of reality assumed by the Kalahari !Kung, Zen Buddhism, Lutheran Christianity, and the Oglala Sioux, without a certain amount of vagueness and ambiguity, but the process of making such an attempt, if taken seriously, can itself perhaps begin to challenge our own limited, distorted, and embedded notions of who we are and why we are here. A pragmatically based "fields within fields within fields" understanding of mystico-religious experience would not be measured by its consistency with scripture, by its impeccable logic, or by its correspondence to some allegedly eternal, static Truth, but rather, by its capacity to offer a vision of the self and reality that is vivid and enlivening enough to act as an antidote to nihilism and skepticism, while it simultaneously remains open and flexible enough to combat fanaticism, dogmatism, and intolerance. Such a vision of the self and reality would prove its worth, not by its ability to demonstrate the logical necessity of its argumentation, but instead, by its ability to catalyze transformations in our personal and communal experience and practice; by its ability to prompt us to reexamine our taken-for-granted premises; by its ability to reunite, to renew, to reenvision; and by its ability to empower and endorse our ongoing attempts to explore the unseen worlds that lie within and around us.

Notes

Introduction

1. Charlene Haddock Seigfried, *William James's Radical Reconstruction of Philosophy* (Albany: SUNY Press, 1990), 159.
2. Ibid., 210.
3. Gerald E. Myers, *William James: His Life and Thought* (New Haven: Yale University Press, 1986), 464.
4. William James, *A Pluralistic Universe* (Cambridge, MA: Harvard University Press, 1977), 131.
5. William James, *The Varieties of Religious Experience* (Cambridge, MA: Harvard University Press, 1985), 377.

1. Establishing Foundations

1. For an insightful, if rather terse, analysis of several criticisms of James's perspective on religious experience and mysticism in the *Varieties*, see David M. Wulff, *Psychology of Religion* (New York: John Wiley and Sons, 1991), 494–501. Nicholas Lash also challenges many of the most fundamental ideas proposed by James in the *Varieties*. Unfortunately, Lash's work came to my attention too late for me to offer the sort of detailed response that his work deserves. See Nicholas Lash, *Easter in Ordinary* (Charlottesville: University Press of Virginia, 1988).
2. William James, *The Varieties of Religious Experience* (Cambridge, MA: Harvard University Press, 1985), 301.
3. Ibid.
4. For a discussion of mysticism that draws heavily on James's perspective see Walter Clark, *The Psychology of Religion* (New York: Macmillan, 1958), 261–290.
5. *Varieties*, 302.
6. Ibid.
7. In a fascinating article, Eugene I. Taylor notes that James was "often invited to attend the monthly meetings of the History of Religions Club at Harvard," and goes on to list some of the works in comparative religion that James had in his personal library. But, as Taylor points out, "James's knowledge was unsystematic." To be fair to James, present day scholars studying non-Western religious traditions have the benefit of almost one hundred years of focused academic research that was not available in James's time. See Eugene Taylor, "Psychology of Religion and Asian Studies: The

William James Legacy," *The Journal of Transpersonal Psychology* 10.1 (1978): 69–71.

    8. *Varieties* , 322.

    9. Ibid., 317.

    10. Ibid., 302–3.

    11. Ibid., 303.

    12. Ibid.

    13. Ralph Barton Perry, *The Thought and Character of William James*, 2 vols. (Boston: Little, Brown and Co., 1935), 2: 350–51.

    14. Henry James, ed., *The Letters of William James*, 2 vols. (Boston: Atlantic Monthly Press, 1920), 2:76–77.

    15. *Varieties*, 301.

    16. Ibid., 303.

    17. Ibid.

    18. Ibid.

    19. John E. Smith also suggests that the ordering of the experiences is perhaps determined by how commonplace each experience is—the most commonplace type of experience lowest on the ladder and so on. See his article, "William James's Account of Mysticism" in Steven T. Katz, ed., *Mysticism and Religious Traditions* (New York: Oxford University Press, 1983), 252.

    20. *Varieties*, 304.

    21. Ibid.

    22. Ibid., 305.

    23. Ibid.

    24. Ibid.

    25. Ibid., 306.

    26. Ibid.

    27. Ibid.

    28. Ibid.

    29. Ibid.

    30. Ibid., 306-7.

    31. Ibid., 307.

    32. Ibid.

    33. Ibid., 307–8.

    34. William James, *The Will to Believe and Other Essays in Popular Philosophy* (Cambridge, MA: Harvard University Press, 1979), 218.

    35. Ibid.

    36. Ibid.

    37. Ibid.

    38. Ibid., 219.

    39. Ibid., 220.

    40. Ibid.

    41. *Varieties*, 308.

    42. This phrase is taken from the title of an obscure pamphlet published by James's friend Benjamin Paul Blood, "The Anaesthetic Revelation and the Gist of Philosophy."

43. William James, *Essays in Philosophy* (Cambridge, MA: Harvard University Press, 1978), 173.
44. Perry, 2:227.
45. Ibid., 555.
46. *Essays in Philosophy,* 173.
47. Ibid.
48. Ibid., 174.
49. Ibid., 181.
50. Ibid., 184–85.
51. Ibid., 189.
52. Ibid., 186–87.
53. Ibid., 187.
54. Ibid., 188.
55. Ibid., 189.
56. Ibid.
57. Ibid.
58. Ibid., 189–90.
59. Perry, 2:658.
60. Ibid.
61. *Varieties,* 22.
62. Ibid., 310.
63. Ibid., 310–11.
64. Ibid., 311.
65. Ibid., 312.
66. Ibid., 313.
67. R. C. Zaehner, *Mysticism Sacred and Profane* (Oxford: Clarendon Press, 1957).
68. Conceivably, however, James's later discussion of the methodical cultivation of mystical experiences might also be included as part of the ladder of mysticism.
69. *Varieties,* 316.
70. Ibid., 317.
71. Ibid.
72. *Essays in Philosophy,* 133.
73. *Varieties,* 33.
74. Ibid., 15.
75. James is vulnerable to the charge that he is excessively anti-institutional and anti-theological in his religious analysis, but he is not as vulnerable as it appears at first blush. Chapters 2 and 5 will investigate these issues in more detail.
76. *Varieties,* 61–62.
77. Ibid., 62–63.
78. Ibid., 59.
79. Ibid., 55.
80. Ibid., 55.
81. William James, *The Principles of Psychology,* 3 vols. (Cambridge, MA: Harvard University Press, 1981), 2:759.

82. Ibid., 762.
83. Robert A. McDermott, Introduction to *Essays in Psychical Research*, by William James (Cambridge, MA: Harvard University Press, 1986), xiv.
84. Ibid., xix.
85. Ibid., xxxi.
86. Perry, vol. 2:168.
87. McDermott, Introduction, xix.
88. Notice here the almost complete merging of "mystical" and "psychical" phenomena. James, *Will to Believe*, 223.
89. *Will to Believe*, 239.
90. Ibid.
91. Ibid., 240.
92. Ibid., 241.
93. *Varieties*, 395.
94. Ibid.
95. Ibid.
96. *Will to Believe*, 239.
97. Ibid., 224.
98. Ibid.
99. Ibid.
100. James met the founding members of the Society in England in the winter of 1882, and helped to found the American branch of the organization in 1885.
101. *Will to Believe*, 266.
102. Ibid., 234.
103. *Essays Psychical*, 362.
104. Ibid., 140.
105. Ibid., 371.
106. It is hopefully clear at this point that mystical and psychical phenomena were not always clearly distinguished by James.
107. *Essays Psychical*, 371.
108. An earlier term that James rarely used—the "semi-supernatural order"— is perhaps more precise than "supernatural," since the term "semi-supernatural" implies that this spiritual "locale" is "super"-natural (i.e., beyond the world revealed by the senses), and yet not *completely* supernatural (since it is not completely different from the natural world, but rather, is the unseen component of a broader understanding of the universe as a whole). See *Essays Psychical*, 117.
109. *Will to Believe*, 234.
110. Ibid., 236.
111. Ibid.
112. *Essays Psychical*, 88.
113. Ibid., 88.
114. Ibid., 81.
115. Ibid.

116. Ibid., 188.
117. Ibid., 397.
118. Ibid., 84.
119. Ibid.
120. Ibid., 83.
121. Ibid., 83-84.
122. Ibid., 190.
123. Ibid., 254.
124. Ibid., 255.
125. Ibid., 86.
126. Ibid., 191.
127. Ibid., 253.
128. Ibid., 255.
129. Ibid.
130. Ibid., 354.
131. Ibid., 355.
132. Ibid.
133. Ibid., 357.
134. Eugene Taylor, *William James on Exceptional Mental States: The 1896 Lowell Lectures* (Amherst: The University of Massachusetts Press, 1984), 92.
135. *Essays Psychical*, 357.
136. Ibid., 359.
137. Ibid., 374.
138. Ibid.
139. *Essays in Philosophy*, 157.
140. Ibid., 157-58.
141. Ibid., 158.
142. Ibid., 158-59.
143. Ibid., 159.
144. I first encountered the term "pure consciousness event" in an article by Robert K. C. Forman, in the book he edited, *The Problem of Pure Consciousness: Mysticism and Philosophy* (New York: Oxford University Press, 1990), 8.
145. My use of the term "transpersonal" is not meant to be a statement of unqualified support for the positions held by the different theorists in what has come to be called "transpersonal psychology," but rather is used as a neutral word to designate something which is beyond the boundaries we normally associate with the realm of the personal (and yet which may also manifest in and through the personal realm).
146. *Essays in Philosophy*, 160.
147. Ibid.
148. Ibid., 161.
149. Ibid.
150. Ibid., 163.

363

151. Ibid., 164

152. Ibid. For a fascinating exploration of the issue of the philosophical status of the reality of dreams and other altered states of consciousness in the Hindu tradition, see Wendy Doniger O'Flaherty, *Dreams, Illusion and Other Realities* (Chicago: University of Chicago Press, 1984).

153. William James, *Talks to Teachers on Psychology and to Students on Some of Life's Ideals* (Cambridge, MA: Harvard University Press, 1983), 4.

154. Ibid.

155. Ibid., 244.

156. Ibid., 4.

157. Ibid., 137.

158. Ibid., 138.

159. There are interesting correspondences to this theme in the work of the Jewish philosopher Martin Buber. See Martin Buber, *I and Thou* (New York: Charles Scribner's Sons, 1958).

160. *Talks*, 138–39.

161. Ibid., 139.

162. Ibid.

163. Ibid.

164. Ibid.

165. Ibid.

166. Ibid., 140.

167. Ibid., 140–41.

168. As a matter of fact, however, if we look more closely, I would argue that many crucially important phenomena, such as beautiful works of art, literary masterpieces, and miraculous cures, can frequently be traced to the insights and power of mystics.

169. *Talks*, 144.

170. Ibid.

171. Ibid., 146.

172. Ibid.

173. Ibid., 147.

174. Ibid., 149.

175. Ibid.

176. Ibid., 149.

177. *Varieties*, 337.

178. Ibid.

179. Ibid.

180. Ibid., 13.

181. Ibid., 20.

182. Ibid., 338.

183. Ibid., 26.

184. Ibid., 29, 28.

185. It is admittedly difficult to distinguish between hagiographical idealization and reality, but even so, it is clear that moderate and balanced

saintly personalities were far less interesting to James than other, less temperate examples.

186. William James, *Essays in Religion and Morality* (Cambridge, MA: Harvard University Press, 1982), 37.

187. Here I am in disagreement with Julius Bixler, who in a classic study of James's philosophy of religion, notes that "the records we have of the religious belief of [James's] father, who considered himself a follower of Swedenborg, show only a very superficial resemblance to James's personal views." Oddly however, Bixler goes on to say immediately afterwards that "James's sympathy with his father, intellectually, became greater rather than less as he grew older." See Julius Seelye Bixler, *Religion in the Philosophy of William James* (Boston: Marshall Jones Co., 1926), 2.

188. *Essays in Religion*, 37.

189. R. W. B. Lewis, *The Jameses: A Family Narrative* (New York: Farrar, Straus & Giroux, 1991), 51.

190. Ibid., 52.

191. Ibid., 53.

192. Ibid., 54.

193. Ibid., 53.

194. Perry, 1:20.

195. *Essays in Religion*, 39.

196. Ibid., 38.

197. Henry James Sr. died in December 1882, when William was forty years old. At the time, William was living in London and was dissuaded from returning to America by his family, since it had become apparent that his father would die before his return.

198. Lewis, 350–51.

199. Perry, 1:165.

200. Ibid., 152.

201. *Varieties*, 134–35.

202. Ibid., 135.

203. Ibid.

204. I am heavily indebted here to Lewis's extremely perceptive commentary, 203–4.

205. Lewis, 204–5.

206. Perry, 1:324.

207. Ibid., 339.

2. Experiencing Unseen Worlds

1. While it is always problematic to group together scholars, as this tends to imply that they are in fundamental agreement on every issue, I would argue that investigators of mysticism such as Baron von Hügel, Evelyn Underhill, Joseph Maréchal, W. T. Stace, and Rudolph Otto are, on the whole, representatives of this understanding of mysticism. See for instance Baron

Friedrich von Hügel, *The Mystical Element of Religion* (New York: Dutton, 1923); Evelyn Underhill, *Mysticism* (New York: Dutton, 1911); Joseph Maréchal, S. J., *Studies in the Psychology of the Mystics,* trans. Algar Thorold (Albany: Magi Books, 1964); W. T. Stace, *Mysticism and Philosophy* (Los Angeles: Jeremy P. Tarcher, Inc., 1960); and Rudolph Otto, *The Idea of the Holy* (New York: Oxford University Press, 1958).

2. Once again, groupings such as this are perilous, but I would argue that, for the most part, scholars such as Steven Katz, Wayne Proudfoot, Hans Penner, and Robert Gimello, and are representatives of this perspective on mystical experience. See for instance Wayne Proudfoot, *Religious Experience* (Berkeley: University of California Press, 1985), and the volumes edited by Steven Katz (in which the work of Gimello and Penner appear): *Mysticism and Philosophical Analysis* (New York: Oxford University Press, 1978) and *Mysticism and Religious Traditions* (New York: Oxford University Press, 1983).

3. Nancy Frankenberry, *Religion and Radical Empiricism* (Albany: SUNY Press, 1987), 31.

4. William James, *The Varieties of Religious Experience* (Cambridge, MA: Harvard University Press, 1985), 341.

5. Ibid., 358.

6. Ibid., 358–59.

7. Ibid., 359.

8. For James's discussion on these terms, see William James, *The Principles of Psychology,* 3 vols. (Cambridge, MA: Harvard University Press, 1981), 1:185–86.

9. John Wild, *The Radical Empiricism of William James* (Garden City, NY: Doubleday, 1969), 253.

10. *Principles,* 1066.

11. Ibid., 1067–68.

12. Ibid., 1072.

13. Gerald E. Myers, *William James: His Life and Thought* (New Haven: Yale University Press, 1986), 222.

14. Ibid., 222.

15. *Principles,* 1059.

16. *Varieties,* 31.

17. John Wild is especially perceptive in his analysis of James's utilization of this model.

18. *Varieties,* 352.

19. Ibid., 344.

20. Ibid., 341.

21. Ibid., 67.

22. Wayne Proudfoot is one of the most forceful proponents of the argument that religious feelings, according to James, are completely noncognitive. For instance, he makes this argument in *Religious Experience* (Berkeley: University of California Press, 1985), 7.

23. We will be investigating these two types of knowing in more detail at a later point in this chapter.

24. Chapter 4 will investigate in more detail James's understanding of the role philosophy and science can and should play when studying religious experiences.

25. Proudfoot, 63.

26. Ibid., 90.

27. Ibid., 91.

28. Ibid., 92.

29. Ibid.

30. Ibid., 96.

31. Ibid., 95.

32. Ibid., 107.

33. For a further analysis and critique of Proudfoot's theories of emotion and religious experience, see G. William Barnard, "Explaining the Unexplainable: Wayne Proudfoot's *Religious Experience*," *Journal of the American Academy of Religion* 60 (Summer 1992): 231–56.

34. The work of Steven Katz has been especially important in this discussion. See Steven T. Katz, ed., *Mysticism and Philosophical Analysis* (New York: Oxford University Press, 1978) and Steven T. Katz, ed., *Mysticism and Religious Traditions* (New York: Oxford University Press, 1983).

35. Robert K. C. Forman, ed., *The Problem of Pure Consciousness* (New York: Oxford University Press, 1990), 3.

36. Ken Wilber, a contemporary transpersonal theorist, has written some pointed and powerful critiques of this position. See Ken Wilber, *Sex, Ecology, Spirituality* (Boston: Shambhala Publications, 1995), 599–605, 620–23, 678–81.

37. Forman, 13.

38. Proudfoot, 121.

39. Ibid., 125.

40. Ibid., 132.

41. Ibid., 182.

42. Ibid., 231.

43. James's methodology is based on an insistence that an investigator of religious phenomena should let the experiences speak for themselves in as rich and detailed manner as possible before the investigator makes his or her analytic contribution.

44. *Varieties*, 183.

45. Ibid., 184–85.

46. Proudfoot, 154.

47. Ibid., 161.

48. Ibid.

49. Ibid., 163; cf. *Varieties*, 56.

50. Ibid.

51. *Varieties*, 55–56.

52. Ibid., 335.

53. In the *Varieties* (p. 335), James also defends the mystic's invulnerability to our criticism by using a style of moral argumentation that is rooted in his nascent theory of pragmatism, saying that "if the mystical truth that comes to a man proves to be a force that he can live by, what mandate have we of the majority to order him to live in another way?" This style of argumentation will be explored in more detail in chapter 5.

54. *Varieties*, 335–36.

55. Ibid., 327.

56. Proudfoot, 169.

57. In a footnote to page 164 of this book, Proudfoot acknowledges that James possesses rich and nuanced theories of sense perception in the *Principles* and in *Pragmatism*. It is not clear why Proudfoot thinks that James would abandon this sophisticated understanding of the nature of sense experience during the time period of the *Varieties* (approximately a decade after the *Principles*), only to take it up again several years later when writing *Pragmatism*.

58. Ironically, as James was fully aware, it is only possible to verify the "immediacy" of sense experiences via a highly mediated, abstract, post-facto intellectual analysis.

59. Bernard McGinn, *The Foundations of Mysticism: Origins to the Fifth Century* (New York: Crossroad, 1991), 292.

60. *Principles*, 216. James points out that many languages recognize this distinction (e.g., *kennen* and *wissen*, *connaitre* and *savoir*, etc.)

61. Ibid., 653–54.

62. Ibid., 656.

63. James does not explicitly connect the ineffability of knowledge-by-acquaintance and the ineffability of mystical experiences, but the similarities are striking.

64. *Principles*, 217.

65. Myers, 275.

66. William James, *Pragmatism* (Cambridge, MA: Harvard University Press, 1975), 119.

67. Frankenberry, 91.

68. *Principles*, 249–50.

69. Ibid., 189.

70. Ibid., 195.

71. This metaphor of two elements combining into one is dubious from a Jamesian perspective, but it will have to suffice until the time that this issue is explored in more detail at a later point in this chapter.

72. Steven Katz, ed., *Mysticism and Philosophical Analysis* (New York, Oxford University Press, 1978), 57.

73. Anthony N. Perovich, Jr. argues, quite persuasively, that the positions taken by "complete constructivists" like Katz and Proudfoot are based on a mis-reading of Kant. See his chapter, "Does the Philosophy of Mysticism Rest on a Mistake," pp. 237–53, in *The Problem of Pure Consciousness*.

74. In this example, the woman might still, for instance, retain the underlying sense that she has a body that is separate from the other forms that are sharing space with her, or still possess the terrifying feeling that she should know more than she does, and so on. James, for one, doubts whether it is ever possible to experience moments of sheer knowledge-by-acquaintance, completely devoid of knowledge-about, but he nonetheless argues that a retrospective analysis of our experience (especially out-of-the-ordinary experiences such as the example above) reveals a qualitative difference between knowledge-about and knowledge-by-acquaintance.

75. John Wild, *The Radical Empiricism of William James* (Garden City, NY: Doubleday, 1969), 52.

76. Admittedly, it is relatively easy to claim that meaningful patterns are already present in our knowledge-by-acquaintance. It is much more difficult to account for the *origin* of these patterns.

77. Frankenberry, 67.

78. The term "something" is placed in quotes to emphasize that the "otherness" that appears to the mystic is not necessarily an object separate from the mystic's consciousness.

79. Robert Forman, in a recent article in the *Journal of the American Academy of Religion*, discusses another mode of knowledge which he terms "knowledge by identity." Forman defines knowledge by identity as a nonintentional awareness of one's own consciousness. In the article, Forman points out the philosophical difficulties surrounding any attempts to theorize about this type of knowing, and makes a concerted attempt to point out the mystical implications of knowledge by identity. While I am in basic agreement with much, if not most, of what Forman says, I would argue that Forman's observations would be strengthened if he incorporated the Jamesian distinction between knowledge-by-acquaintance and knowledge-about into his theoretical model, especially since knowledge by identity has difficulty accounting for the internal "otherness" that characterizes the phenomenology of many mystical experiences. For further details on Forman's perspective, see Robert K. C. Forman, "Mystical Knowledge: Knowledge by Identity," *Journal of the American Academy of Religion* 61.4 (Winter 1993): 705–39.

80. For a stimulating, if somewhat technical discussion of the issues surrounding consciousness and intentionality, see Mark B. Woodhouse's chapter, "On the Possibility of Pure Consciousness," pp. 254–268, in *The Problem of Pure Consciousness*.

81. James was willing to make philosophical conclusions based on less-ordinary experiences as well (whether psychical, pathological, or mystical). Admittedly however, the vast majority of these experiences still appear to be intentional, i.e., they refer to "someone" experiencing "something" instead of illustrating moments in which the subject and object merge.

82. There are intriguing correspondences between "pure" moments of knowledge-by-acquaintance and this contentless consciousness. Both can

369

be understood as ineffable, directly experienced, and free from cognitive content. Nonetheless, as was mentioned above, knowledge-by-acquaintance is based on an implicit duality between the knower and what is known, whereas most Eastern traditions typically depict this contentless consciousness in nondual terms.

83. Myers, 275.

84. Ibid., 277.

85. Chapter 5 will offer a detailed investigation of James's approach to the issues of verification, factuality, and truth.

86. McGinn, 293.

87. Interestingly however, the theory of mysticism that James develops in "A Suggestion about Mysticism" (see chapter 1 for further details) is actually strongly connected to knowledge-about, since mystical experiences are seen as sudden and vast expansions of an individual's awareness of beliefs, memories and impulses that where previously hidden in his or her marginal (or transmarginal) awareness.

88. *Principles*, 269. The italics are James's.

89. Ibid.

90. Ibid., 271.

91. Ibid., 266.

92. Ibid., 246.

93. Ibid., 747.

94. Ibid., 724.

95. Ironically, Proudfoot makes almost identical points in his attempt to refute James's supposedly simplistic understanding of sense perception. See for instance his discussion on page 170 of *Religious Experience*.

96. William James, *Essays in Philosophy* (Cambridge, MA: Harvard University Press, 1978), 21.

97. *Principles*, 274.

98. Ibid., 380–81.

99. *Pragmatism*, 123.

100. Ibid., 122.

101. William James, *The Meaning of Truth* (Cambridge, MA: Harvard University Press, 1975), 45.

102. *Pragmatism*, 99.

103. *Meaning*, 115.

104. I make no claims here that anecdotal evidence is binding on others, but I would claim that it can become part of a cumulative argument in favor of specific metaphysical/theological truth claims. For a further discussion of the concept of the cumulative argument, see Caroline Frank Davis, *The Evidential Force of Religious Experience* (New York: Oxford University Press, 1989).

105. James did not limit social change to the effects of just famous or powerful individuals. He also recognized the more subtle, yet significant influences of countless, historically invisible persons. However, James did

believe that the more dramatic social changes could be traced back to the efforts and ideas of the world's "great men."

106. William James, *The Will to Believe and Other Essays in Popular Philosophy* (Cambridge, MA: Harvard University Press, 1979), 174.

107. Ibid., 188.

108. Ibid., 170.

109. Ibid.

110. Ralph Barton Perry, *The Thought and Character of William James*, 2 vols. (Boston: Little, Brown and Co., 1935), 2:349–50. The end of this same letter is where James discusses his "mystical germ".

111. The quote marks around the word "it" indicate that "it" is not necessarily an object separate from the perceiver.

112. The metaphor breaks down at this point because while the metaphor implies that the spiritual experiences of the individuals are seen directly by the outside observers (in the form of different colors), in our world, an individual's spiritual experiences would always have to be communicated to another person indirectly through the medium of language.

113. These last "panes" are the least Jamesian aspect of this metaphor, since he spends so little time examining mystical experiences in the context of different meditative and contemplative traditions.

114. Richard J. Bernstein, *Beyond Objectivism and Relativism* (Philadelphia: University of Pennsylvania Press, 1985), 8.

115. *Varieties*, 324.

116. *Principles*, 228.

117. I am thinking here specifically of the philosophers represented in *The Problem of Pure Consciousness*.

118. Forman, 8.

119. *Principles*, 243–44.

120. Ibid., 243.

121. Ibid., 238–39.

122. Ibid., 214.

123. *Meaning*, 6.

124. Ibid., 7.

125. Some Jamesian scholars present a rather more truncated version of what James was willing to discuss in his radical empiricism. William Dean, for instance, in his *American Religious Empiricism* (Albany: SUNY Press, 1986), 27, says that "James's empiricism was, however, newly explicit in grounding truth only on what is physically experienced and in affirming that relations are experienced just as surely as atomic things are." It is not clear how Dean justifies limiting the parameters of James's radical empiricism to only "what is physically experienced" when James is so evidently willing to use mystical experiences as empirical data.

126. William James, *Essays in Radical Empiricism* (Cambridge, MA: Harvard University Press, 1976), 123.

127. Ibid., 24.

371

128. Ibid., 42.
129. Ibid.
130. Ibid., 7.
131. Marcus Peter Ford, *William James's Philosophy: A New Perspective* (Amherst: The University of Massachusetts Press, 1982), 75–88.
132. Ford, 81.
133. *Essays in Radical Empiricism*, 46.
134. Ibid.
135. As Ford points out, is seems that James never recognized that he had, in fact, developed two alternate conceptions of pure experience.
136. *Meaning*, 36.
137. *Essays in Radical Empiricism*, 13.
138. Ibid., 4.
139. Ibid., 14–15.
140. Ibid., 36–37.
141. Ibid., 8.
142. Ibid.
143. Ibid., 8–9.
144. Ibid., 9.
145. Ibid., 17.
146. We will be discussing the pragmatic evaluation of the truth status of mystical experiences in much greater detail in chapter 5.
147. *Essays in Radical Empiricism*, 73.
148. Ibid., 18.
149. Ibid., 73.
150. John G. Neihardt, *Black Elk Speaks* (Lincoln: The University of Nebraska Press, 1988), 186–97.
151. Richard Katz, *Boiling Energy: Community Healing Among the Kalahari Kung* (Cambridge, MA: Harvard University Press, 1982).
152. Frankenberry, 103.
153. Frankenberry, 88.

3. "Fields within Fields within Fields"

1. William James, *The Principles of Psychology*, 3 vols. (Cambridge, MA: Harvard University Press, 1981), 1:321.
2. Ibid., 279.
3. Don Browning, *Pluralism and Personality* (Cranbury, NJ: Associated University Press, 1980), 91.
4. Quote marks are placed around the word "external" since the metaphysical status of the world as something separate from the self was not resolved at this point in James's career, even though he was willing to operate temporarily with a methodological assumption of a duality between the self and the world. See *Principles*, 214.

5. *Principles*, 281.
6. Browning, 89.
7. *Principles*, 300.
8. Ibid., 300–301.
9. Ibid., 301. James is, unknowingly, setting the stage here for his later attempts to justify pragmatically the existence of God through God's this-worldly effects.
10. No effort is made here to claim that all mystical experiences possess these features. Certain mystical experiences are characterized by extreme feelings of isolation from the world and disconnection from the world.
11. For an explication of these ideas from a neo-Freudian perspective, see Ana-Maria Rizzuto, *The Birth of a Living God* (Chicago: The University of Chicago Press, 1979).
12. *Principles*, 283.
13. Ibid., 285–87.
14. Ibid., 287.
15. Ibid., 288.
16. Ibid.
17. John Wild and Eugene Fontinell are especially persuasive. See John Wild, *The Radical Empiricism of William James* (Garden City, NY: Doubleday, 1969) and Eugene Fontinell, *Self, God, and Immortality* (Philadelphia: Temple University Press, 1986).
18. For James, this understanding of the interrelationship between the body and the mind has important practical implications. For instance, he stresses that changes in the body's posture and health will create corresponding changes in our self-esteem, volitional ability, and mental sharpness, while changes in our attitudes, emotions, and ideas will in turn create corresponding changes in our physical vitality and well-being. James's respect for the mind-cure movement that was active during his time needs to be seen, from this point of view, as an extension of James's belief that the mind and body are practically distinguishable, yet integrally linked, aspects of a single complex activity. James's evaluation of the mind-cure movement will be investigated in more detail in chapter 5.
19. Wild, 89. If Wild's interpretation is correct, then James's understanding of the body/mind connection could be a potentially important philosophical perspective from which to explore the body/mind unity expressed within different spiritual disciplines such as *tai chi, hatha yoga,* and *zazen.* It would also be interesting to investigate the correspondences between James's understanding of the mind/body with the Chinese and Indian doctrines of *chi* and *prāṇa* as semi-physical, semi-mental substances.
20. James maintains his emphasis on the centrality of the physical body, even after his shift to a consistent radical empiricism. For instance, in his essay, "The Experience of Activity," James claims that "the world experienced (otherwise called the 'field of consciousness') comes at all times with our body as its centre, center of vision, centre of action, centre of interest. . . . The body is the storm centre, the origin of co-ordinates, the constant place

of stress in all that experience-train." William James, *Essays in Radical Empiricism* (Cambridge, MA: Harvard University Press, 1976), 86.

    21. It is important to remember that in the *Principles*, James accepts an epistemological dualism between the knower and the known as a stopgap measure. See *Principles*, 214.

    22. *Principles*, 290.

    23. Ibid., 314.

    24. For James's discussion of the "mind-stuff" theory, see ibid., 148–82.

    25. Ibid., 327.

    26. Ibid.

    27. James's antipathy towards the concept of the soul is thematically similar to his father's philosophical and theological distrust of the individual self.

    28. *Principles*, 345.

    29. Ibid., 316.

    30. Ibid.

    31. Ibid., 318.

    32. Ibid.

    33. Ibid., 352.

    34. Ibid.

    35. Ibid., 321.

    36. Ibid.

    37. Ibid., 321–22.

    38. The epistemological status of the Thought is extremely unclear. At one point it appears that James claims that the Thought is the knower of the stream, and yet at other times, it seems that James claims that the Thought is itself a "section" of the stream of consciousness, and therefore, an object of knowledge.

    39. *Principles*, 323.

    40. Ibid. The italics are James's.

    41. Some scholars argue that the Buddha's anātman (no-self) doctrine was meant to apply only to the phenomenal ego, not to the Ātman understood in the Upanishadic sense as the Self of all existence. While it is difficult, if not impossible, to conclusively prove the historical Buddha's intentions on this issue, I would argue that there is philosophical "room," at least within certain Mahāyāna Buddhist perspectives, to defend the "existence" of an underlying knower, as long as all analytical accounts of this "knower" are considered to be merely metaphorical, "finger-pointings" at "that" which is, in actuality, "empty" of all concrete designations (including emptiness itself). For an alternative perspective, as well as a fascinating (if at times strained) comparison of James's psychology with that of Buddhism, see David J. Kalupahana, *The Principles of Buddhist Psychology* (Albany: SUNY Press, 1987).

    42. I am aware that most philosophers at the present are highly suspicious of our ability to coherently talk about a "*true* apprehension of the

nature of the self and reality," but this claim is at the heart of every mystical tradition. A detailed discussion on the relationship between truth and mysticism will take place in chapter 5.

43. I was first exposed to the term "systemic distortion" in David Tracy's book, *Plurality and Ambiguity* (San Francisco: Harper & Row, 1987). His use of the term takes place within the context of a discussion on postmodernism, but I believe that my appropriation and application of this term is congruent with Tracy's basic premise.

44. Charlene Haddock Seigfried, in her work *William James's Radical Reconstruction of Philosophy* (Albany: SUNY Press, 1990) discusses this tension in James's thought in great detail.

45. James also draws upon experimental work and comparisons with data from other academic disciplines to form his psychological conclusions, but introspection has pride of place in James's psychology.

46. *Principles*, 221.

47. Ibid., 331.

48. Gerald Myers, *William James: His Life and Thought* (New Haven: Yale University Press, 1986), 350.

49. *Principles*, 328.

50. William James, *Essays in Religion and Morality* (Cambridge, MA: Harvard University Press, 1982), 81. James emphasizes that during this essay he is only provisionally using dualistic terminology to describe the realm of "mental facts" and the realm of "physical facts."

51. *Essays in Religion*, 84.

52. Ibid., 83.

53. Ibid., 86. In an earlier lecture, "The Knowing of Things Together," James points out that transcendentalism could use physiology to support their own thesis of the "oversoul," using a similar example: "As the pipes of an organ let the pressing mass of air escape only in single notes, so do our brains, the organ pipes of the infinite, keep back everything but the slender threads of truth to which they may be pervious. As they obstruct more, the insulation increases, as they obstruct less it disappears." William James, *Essays in Philosophy* (Cambridge, MA: Harvard University Press, 1978), 86.

54. *Essays in Religion*, 89.

55. Ibid.

56. Ibid.

57. Ibid., 92.

58. Ibid., 93.

59. Ibid.

60. Ibid.

61. Ibid., 86.

62. Ibid., 87.

63. Ibid.

64. Ibid., 95.

65. Ibid., 95–96.

66. See chapter 1 for a further discussion of this essay.
67. *Essays in Religion,* 90.
68. Ibid., 92.
69. Ibid., 94.
70. Ibid., 89.
71. Ibid., 75–76.
72. Ibid., 76.
73. R. W. B. Lewis, *The Jameses* (New York: Farrar, Straus & Giroux, 1991), 461–62. From Alice's reply to William, it appears that she was very appreciative of William's willingness to speak so candidly about her approaching death.
74. Eugene Taylor, in a remarkable feat of scholarly thoroughness, has, in essence, recreated these unpublished lectures, drawing upon James's lecture notes, references in the margins of books from James's personal library (books that were scattered throughout the Harvard library system), and previous comments on similar themes in other texts. See Eugene Taylor, *William James on Exceptional Mental States: The 1896 Lowell Lectures* (Amherst: The University of Massachusetts Press, 1984).
75. *Principles,* 166.
76. This conception is often referred to in the literature as the *esse est sentiri* doctrine.
77. *Principles,* 174.
78. According to Jacques Barzun, Janet coined the term "subconscious." See Jacques Barzun, *A Stroll With William James* (New York: Harper & Row, 1983), 229.
79. Myers, 60. See Sigmund Freud, *An Autobiographical Study* (New York: Norton, 1963), 59. See also Freud's *Five Lectures on Psycho-Analysis* (New York: Norton, 1977), 21–22, 25–26. In 1909, the year before his death, James met both Freud and Jung for the first time at an international congress at Clark University where Freud and Jung were keynote speakers. In a letter to his Swiss friend and fellow psychologist Theodore Flournoy, James described his response to these new standard-bearers of psychology: "I went there [Clark University] for one day in order to see what Freud was like, and met also Yung [sic] of Zurich, who professed great esteem for you, and made a very pleasant impression. I hope that Freud and his pupils will push their ideas to their utmost limits, so that we may learn what they are. They can't fail to throw light on human nature; but I confess that he made on me personally the impression of a man obsessed with fixed ideas. I can make nothing in my own case with his dream theories, and obviously 'symbolism' is a most dangerous method. A newspaper report of the congress said that Freud had condemned the American religious therapy (which has such extensive results) as very 'dangerous' because so 'unscientific.' Bah!" Henry James, ed., *The Letters of William James,* 2 vols. (Boston: The Atlantic Monthly Press, 1920), 2:327–28. Freud, in an account written in his autobiography, mentions that James made a "lasting

impression" upon him when they met at Clark, and adds this anecdote: "I shall never forget one little scene that occurred as we were on a walk together. He stopped suddenly, handed me a bag he was carrying and asked me to walk on, saying he would catch up as soon as he had got through an attack of angina pectoris which was just coming on. He died of that disease a year later; and I have always wished that I might be as fearless as he was in the face of approaching death." Quoted in Barzun, 232.

    80. William James, *The Varieties of Religious Experience* (Cambridge, MA: Harvard University Press, 1985), 189.

    81. Ibid., 190.

    82. Ibid.

    83. See Barzun, 230.

    84. William James, *Essays in Psychical Research* (Cambridge, MA: Harvard University Press, 1986), 195.

    85. William James, *The Will To Believe* (Cambridge, MA: Harvard University Press, 1979), 234.

    86. Ibid.

    87. In much the same manner, James in the *Varieties* would later posit a spectrum of experiences ranging from insanity at the lower end of the spectrum, to profound religious mystical experiences at the spectrum's upper end.

    88. *Essays Psychical*, 164–65.

    89. Ibid., 196.

    90. Ibid.

    91. *Varieties*, 403.

    92. *Essays Psychical*, 207.

    93. Ibid., 213.

    94. Ibid., 204.

    95. Ibid., 195.

    96. Ibid., 193.

    97. Ibid.

    98. Ibid.

    99. Ibid., 194.

    100. Ibid., 201.

    101. Ibid.

    102. Ibid., 199.

    103. *Varieties*, 381.

    104. Ibid.

    105. Ibid., 191.

    106. Ibid.

    107. Ibid., 377.

    108. Ibid.

    109. Ibid., 381.

    110. This issue will be discussed at length in chapter 5 during an investigation of the connections between saintliness and mystical experiences.

111. Ralph Barton Perry, *The Thought and Character of William James*, 2 vols. (Boston: Little, Brown and Co., 1935), 2:273. Particularly vivid examples of James's interest in the beneficial effects of tapping into latent reserves of inner energy occur in James's essays "The Powers of Men" and "The Energies of Men." For instance, in these essays, James mentions his fascination with his friend Wincenty Lutoslawski's improvement in physical and mental health as a result of his immersion in the spiritual disciplines of *hatha yoga*. James does not explicitly link the practices of *hatha yoga* with the moral strenuousness he describes in the *Varieties*, but it is clear that James considered conscious spiritual disciplines as exercises designed to cultivate the will. However, it is questionable whether spiritual disciplines are indeed solely volitional exercises. James appears to have difficulty conceiving of the possibility that spiritual exercises might integrate self-effort and grace. See *Essays Religion*, 129–61.

112. *Varieties*, 95.

113. Ibid.

114. Ibid., 95–96. The mind-cure movement (as well as the end-results of conversion) will be discussed in more detail in chapter 5.

115. Ibid., 96.

116. *Essays Religion*, 60–61.

117. *Varieties*, 146–47.

118. Ibid., 141.

119. Ibid., 124.

120. Ibid., 142.

121. Ibid., 170.

122. Ibid.

123. Ibid., 157.

124. Ibid., 162.

125. Ibid., 187.

126. Ibid., 200.

127. Ibid.

128. Ibid., 336.

129. Ibid., 225.

130. In chapter 5, I will argue that James's understanding of saintliness is intrinsically related to his interest in the results of mystical experience.

131. *Varieties*, 208.

132. Ibid., 173.

133. Ibid.

134. Ibid., 197.

135. Ibid., 400.

136. Ibid.

137. Ibid.

138. Ibid., 401.

139. Ibid. Chapter 5 will attempt to demonstrate that in the *Varieties*, James has not yet fully embraced his later pragmatic understanding of truth,

although he is, almost unknowingly, already moving strongly in that direction. From a pragmatic perspective, truth is not an objective quality of something (for instance, the "more"), but rather, truth is contingent on that thing's ability to produce observable effects that can be communally assessed. From the point of view of James's later pragmatism, his apparent opposition in sections of the *Varieties* between the psychological value and the objective truth of the "more" becomes a false dichotomy, since value itself becomes the index of truth.

    140. *Varieties*, 174.
    141. Ibid.
    142. Ibid., 198.
    143. Ibid., 403.
    144. The experience of this paradoxical union of self and other is perhaps most accented during unitive mystical experiences, a fact that James is quick to underscore, noting the comment by a French author that "when mystical activity is at its height, we find consciousness possessed by the sense of a being at once *excessive* and *identical* with the self: great enough to be God; interior enough to be *me*. The 'objectivity' of it ought in that case to be called *excessivity*, rather, or exceedingness." Quoted in *Varieties*, 401. (Récéjac, *Essai sur les fondements de la connaissance mystique*, 1897, 46.)
    145. *Varieties*, 403. James also recognizes, however, that he does not discuss the "practical difficulties" connected with how someone can come to a direct realization of his or her "higher part," or how that person can manage to maintain an exclusive identification with that "higher" aspect of the self, or finally, what that person can do to experience this higher aspect of the self as identical with the "more" that exists outside, or beyond, the individual's personality structure. See *Varieties*, 400.
    146. *Varieties*, 405.
    147. Ibid., 404.
    148. Ibid.
    149. Ibid., 406.
    150. Ibid., 408.
    151. Ibid., 413.
    152. Ibid.
    153. Chapter 4 will offer a detailed critique of James's notion of the "finite God."
    154. William James, *A Pluralistic Universe* (Cambridge, MA: Harvard University Press, 1977), 64.
    155. Ibid., 70.
    156. Ibid., 71.
    157. Ibid., 81.
    158. Ibid., 72.
    159. See, for instance, Matthew Fox, *Creation Spirituality* (San Francisco: Harper San Francisco, 1991) and Thomas Berry, *The Dream of the Earth* (San Francisco: Sierra Books, 1988). Henry Corbin also discusses in

    379

intricate detail various Persian and Islamic ideas of an earth-angel. See Henry Corbin, *Spiritual Body and Celestial Earth* (Princeton: Princeton University Press, 1977).

160. *Pluralistic,* 74.

161. Ibid., 76.

162. Ibid., 76–77.

163. In fact, James explicitly notes the correspondence between his thought and Fechner's in *Essays on Radical Empiricism,* where he says that since "a pure experience can be postulated with any amount whatever of span or field . . . speculations like Fechner's of an Earth-soul, of wider spans of consciousness enveloping narrower ones throughout the cosmos, are, therefore, philosophically quite in order, provided they distinguish the functional from the entitative point of view, and do not treat the minor consciousness under discussion as a kind of standing material of which the wider ones *consist.*" *Essays Radical,* 66–67. As we will see further in this chapter, James appears to have changed his mind on these reservations about Fechner's work.

164. *Pluralistic,* 130.

165. Ibid.

166. Ibid.

167. Ibid.

168. Ibid., 138.

169. Ibid., 139.

170. Ibid.

171. Ibid.

172. Ibid., 140.

173. *Essays Philosophy,* 71–72.

174. Myers, 357.

175. *Pluralistic,* 120.

176. Ibid., 94. This quote probably refers to what have come to be known as the "Miller-Bode notebooks," after the scholars who pointed out to James certain difficulties in his philosophy. See Perry, 2:750–65 for a selection from these notebooks.

177. *Pluralistic,* 96.

178. Ibid., 94.

179. Ibid., 113.

180. Ibid., 105.

181. Ibid., 109.

182. Ibid., 113.

183. Ibid., 121.

184. Ibid., 117.

185. Ibid., 129.

186. Ibid.

187. Ibid., 72.

188. Ibid., 91.

189. Ibid., 78.
190. Ibid.
191. Ibid., 90.
192. Ibid., 132.
193. Ibid., 132–33.
194. Ibid., 140.
195. The term "theo-metaphysical" is used to refer to formulations that are simultaneously theological and metaphysical in nature.
196. Fontinell, 27. This field model of the self and reality is "Jamesian" in its approach, rather than a literal reiteration of every aspect of James's philosophical perspective.
197. Ibid., 154. Fontinell stresses that although it might appear that any sense of personhood would be lost in this onrushing flux, personhood and individuality *is* possible within this model. Since these fields shift and change at different rates, enough stability and cohesiveness remains in the flux to legitimately speak of individuals, even if we can no longer speak of individuals as self-contained atomistic egos.
198. Much further philosophical work needs to be done to justify how these different physical, emotional, and mental levels of experience can all be legitimately considered interactive fields. A good start in this direction would be an attempt to reconcile James's radical empiricism with this field notion of the self and reality.
199. Fontinell, 27.
200. Although Myers claims that James fails to establish the validity of his analogy between the compounding of consciousness in our individual states of consciousness and the conflux of consciousnesses within the cosmic self since "there is no experience that indicates that we can literally experience ourselves being at once both ourselves and others," he is either unaware of the numerous accounts of mystical experience that make just this very claim, or he discounts their validity. See Myers, 360.
201. As will become clear in chapter 4, "nondual" does not mean "monistic." Nonduality is more apophatic than monism; that is, a nondual understanding of the self and reality claims that all metaphysical proposals, including its own, are invariably metaphorical, unlike monism, which typically argues that its claims about the oneness of existence are literally true.
202. This nondual Jamesian field model of the self and reality has much in common with Ken Wilber's notion of holons. For more details on Wilber's controversial yet intriguing perspective, see Ken Wilber, *Sex, Ecology, Spirituality* (Boston: Shambhala Publications, 1995).
203. Fontinell brings up many thoughtful comments on the tensions between a Jamesian field model of the self and reality and James's doctrine of pure experience. While appreciative of the subtlety of many of Fontinell's observations, I am more optimistic about the possibility of a philosophical reconciliation between James's notion of pure experience and a Jamesian

field model (a reconciliation that James himself never explicitly attempted). See Fontinell, 32–43.

204. The ethical implications of this field model of the self and reality will be further explicated in chapter 4.

205. I recognize that the categories of "theism," "monism," and "polytheism," are overly simplistic, but these remarks are meant to be suggestive, not comprehensive. Furthermore, I take the coward's way out, and simply refuse to discuss several other viable philosophical alternatives such as numerous Buddhist options, as well as the contributions of numerous psychoanalytic, sociological and economic theories. I would suggest however that a field conception of the self and reality could be harmonized with important aspects of each of these philosophical alternatives, but such an endeavor, even in its broadest outlines, would take us far "afield" from our present discussion.

206. For an illuminating discussion of the role of *māyā* in Advaita Vedānta, as well as a thoughtful discussion of the philosophical implications of different Eastern nondual systems of thought, see David Loy, *Nonduality* (New Haven: Yale University Press, 1988).

207. Fontinell, 137.

4. Beyond Words, Beyond Morals

1. After Kant (to say nothing of Heidegger), the term "metaphysical" (as opposed to "ontological") comes loaded with numerous negative connotations. Nonetheless, I will continue to utilize this term, not only because it is frequently found in James's writings, but also because I want to defend the validity and value of picturing levels of reality that may be beyond our day-to-day experience, but which might, nonetheless, be accessible to mystical levels of awareness.

2. William James, *The Varieties of Religious Experience* (Cambridge, MA: Harvard University Press, 1985), 51.

3. The term "mystico-religious experiences" refers to those experiences that are simultaneously mystical and religious in nature. Because, as was argued in chapter 1, James does not clearly distinguish between mystical and religious experiences, this neologism is necessary.

4. *Varieties*, 335.

5. Ibid., 336.

6. Ibid., 66. James would argue that mystical experiences, while innately persuasive, are especially convincing if such perceptions can be made to fit into a viable philosophical framework and can, as well, enable the individual to live a richer and more effective life. This tripartite assessment of the truth-claims of mystical and religious experiences forms the theoretical basis for James's investigation of saintliness, as well as, to a lesser de-

gree, his discussion of mental healing and conversion. See chapter 5 for a more complete discussion of James's work in this area.

7. See, for instance, James's discussion of the problem of fanaticism in Christian saints in *Varieties*, 274.

8. *Varieties*, 332.

9. Ibid. , 337.

10. Ibid.

11. Ibid.

12. In chapter 2 I argue that we must admit the possibility that there might be highly rarefied states of mystical awareness in which there were no elements of "knowledge-about" present, but since James himself makes no such claim, it seems only fair to hold him accountable for his previous claim that all states of awareness are mixtures of these two types of knowledge.

13. *Varieties*, 404.

14. William James, *Pragmatism* (Cambridge, MA: Harvard University Press, 1975), 15.

15. *Varieties*, 338.

16. William James, *The Will To Believe* (Cambridge, MA: Harvard University Press, 1979), 50.

17. Ibid., 51.

18. *Varieties*, 339.

19. Ibid., 338–39.

20. *Will To Believe*, 48.

21. Ibid., 52.

22. Ibid.

23. Ibid.

24. Ibid., 53. Interestingly, James's use of the term "unseen" in this instance implies that the "unseen world" is not so much physically invisible, as it is unseen to us because we are unable to "see" the deeper significance and perfection of this world.

25. William James, *Essays in Religion and Morality* (Cambridge, MA: Harvard University Press, 1982), 142.

26. *Will To Believe*, 29.

27. Ibid., 26.

28. Ibid., 55.

29. I am aware that numerous philosophical minefields surround any overly easy assumption that all mystical experiences come from the same source, to say nothing of any attempts to claim that this source has certain generic characteristics (e.g., love, wisdom, compassion, oneness, and so on). I intend, however, to address these issues at a later point in this chapter.

30. *Varieties*, 339.

31. William James, *A Pluralistic Universe* (Cambridge, MA: Harvard University Press, 1977), 142.

32. *Varieties*, 360.

33. *Essays in Religion*, 127.

34. *Pluralistic,* 141.

35. Ibid., 142–43.

36. Henry Samuel Levinson argues that James's advocacy of a science of religions in the *Varieties* signals an abandonment of his previous will-to-believe doctrine (in which a person chooses to believe in an unseen order in lieu of firm proof). According to Levinson, James believed that the science of religions, via a pragmatic assessment of religious experiences, could decide, once and for all, whether materialism or theism was correct, thereby rendering decisions based on faith unnecessary. However, this dichotomy between James's will-to-believe doctrine and his science of religions appears to be incorrect, since even late in his career, James still stressed the vital role of faith in religious life. For a further discussion of these issues, see Henry Samuel Levinson, *The Religious Investigations of William James* (Chapel Hill: The University of North Carolina Press, 1981), 58, 67.

37. Like all of us, James was a creature of his time and place, and his own cultural biases often prevented an empathetic and open-minded appreciation of non-Western religious traditions.

38. *Varieties,* 359.

39. Ibid.

40. *Pluralistic,* 143.

41. *Varieties,* 359. James was so optimistic about the possibilities of a science of religions that he rather naively believed that it might gain the same respect as that given by the public to the physical sciences. He hoped that "the personally non-religious might accept its conclusions on trust, much as blind persons now accept the facts of optics." *Varieties,* 360.

42. Ibid., 384.

43. Ibid., 385.

44. Ibid., 360.

45. Ibid.

46. Ibid.

47. Ibid., 342.

48. William James, *Essays in Philosophy* (Cambridge, MA: Harvard University Press, 1978), 4.

49. William James, *Some Problems of Philosophy* (Cambridge, MA: Harvard University Press, 1979), 11.

50. *Essays in Philosophy,* 18.

51. Ibid., 142.

52. I borrow this term from Eugene Fontinell, an insightful Jamesian scholar. See, for instance, Eugene Fontinell, *Self, God, and Immortality* (Philadelphia: Temple University Press, 1986), 10.

53. For a persuasive discussion of the ways in which psychological models become available as cultural resources, see Don Browning, *Religious Thought and the Modern Psychologies* (Philadelphia: Fortress Press, 1987).

54. *Varieties,* 413.

55. The relatively arbitrary decision of whether to focus primarily on oneness or on manyness is especially relevant to contemporary arguments

between philosophers who emphasize the cultural relativity of every mystical experience and those within the *philosophia perennis* tradition who stress the underlying similarities inherent within every mystical tradition. For representatives of the former position, see Steven Katz, ed., *Mysticism and Philosophical Analysis.* (New York: Oxford Press, 1978) and Steven Katz, ed., *Mysticism and Religious Traditions* (New York: Oxford Press, 1983). For representatives of the *philosophia perennis* tradition, see Ananda Coomaraswamy, *What is Civilization?* (Great Barrington, MA: Lindisfarne Press, 1989); Frithjof Schuon, *The Transcendent Unity of Religions* (Wheaton, IL: The Theosophical Publishing House, 1984); Seyyed Hossein Nasr, *Knowledge and the Sacred* (New York: Crossroad, 1981); Houston Smith, *Beyond the Postmodern Mind* (Wheaton, IL: The Theosophical Publishing House, 1989).

56. Here I differ from the analysis of Julius Bixler, who claims that James, especially by the time of *A Pluralistic Universe,* had overcome any lingering attraction for monism and had definitely decided in favor of pluralism. As my analysis will show below, James's philosophical ambiguity never was so clearly resolved. For Bixler's argument, see Julius Seelye Bixler, *Religion in the Philosophy of William James* (Boston: Marshall Jones Co., 1926), 25.

57. Marcus Ford, *William James's Philosophy* (Amherst: The University of Massachusetts Press, 1982), 39.

58. *Pragmatism,* 74.

59. Ibid., 76.

60. Ibid., 75.

61. Ibid.

62. Ibid., 76.

63. Ibid., 66.

64. Ibid., 67.

65. Ibid., 67–68.

66. *Pluralistic,* 147.

67. *Pragmatism,* 68.

68. Ibid., 72.

69. *Will To Believe,* 201.

70. *Pragmatism,* 78.

71. Ibid.

72. *Pluralistic,* 31.

73. Ibid.

74. Ibid., 32.

75. William James, *The Meaning of Truth* (Cambridge, MA: Harvard University Press, 1975), 72.

76. *Pluralistic,* 62.

77. *Pragmatism,* 78.

78. Ibid., 73.

79. *Pluralistic,* 41.

80. *Pragmatism,* 76. Nonetheless, because of monism's purported dogmatism, it is clear that at this point in career, James's own metaphysical

preference is for a muted pluralism. Despite an early claim in *Pragmatism* that pragmatism as a method is metaphysically neutral, James ultimately reverses himself and willingly admits that pragmatism more easily aligns itself with a pluralistic vision of the universe. See *Pragmatism*, 79.

81. *Will To Believe*, 201.

82. For a nuanced and insightful examination of the similarities and differences between these traditions, see David Loy, *Nonduality* (New Haven: Yale University Press, 1988).

83. A case could also be made to include those Western traditions which are generally neo-Platonic in structure, but this work is not the place to attempt such an ambitious project. As it is, even if the discussion is limited to Eastern representatives of nondualism, the extensive and crucial differences between one Eastern tradition and the next (even though they do share numerous equally important similarities in outlook and praxis) make it exceedingly difficult (although not impossible) to speak of them as representatives of a single philosophical perspective.

84. *Pragmatism*, 14.

85. Ibid.

86. Ibid., 141.

87. *Will To Believe*, 204.

88. Ibid.

89. *Varieties*, 333.

90. Ibid., 331.

91. *Pragmatism*, 135.

92. *Pluralistic*, 40.

93. *Essays in Religion*, 60–61.

94. Ibid., 61.

95. Ibid.

96. Ibid., 62.

97. Ibid.

98. Ibid.

99. Ibid., 61.

100. Ibid., 63.

101. *Pragmatism*, 128.

102. Ibid., 41.

103. Ibid.

104. Ibid., 126.

105. *Meaning of Truth*, 125.

106. *Pragmatism*, 140.

107. *Will To Believe*, 132.

108. In the *Varieties*, James does point out that antinomian tendencies are also present in Christianity. See *Varieties*, 336.

109. *Pragmatism*, 56.

110. Even having the luxury to choose a certain set of beliefs is, in and of itself, rather rare. Most individuals, in most cultures, during most peri-

ods of history, typically never question the philosophical and religious beliefs that are passed down to them within their cultural context.
111. *Meaning of Truth*, 124.
112. Ibid., 123.
113. *Pluralistic*, 28.
114. *Meaning of Truth*, 124.
115. *Pragmatism*, 137.
116. Ibid., 139.
117. Ibid., 142.
118. *Pluralistic*, 63.
119. *Pragmatism*, 143.
120. *Meaning of Truth*, 72.
121. *Pluralistic*, 141.
122. *Will To Believe*, 55.
123. Ibid.
124. Ibid.
125. *Pragmatism*, 135.
126. *Pluralistic*, 92.
127. *Varieties*, 112.
128. *Essays in Religion*, 60.
129. *Pragmatism*, 142. James often implies that simply picturing God as a principle that is distinct from evil solves the problems inherent in any discussion of the relationship between evil and the unseen world. But even if God is understand theistically rather than monistically, a host of philosophical problems still remain, especially with James's own almost Manichaean separation of God and evil into two distinct principles.
130. *Pluralistic*, 60.
131. Ibid.
132. Ibid., 61.
133. Ibid., 141.
134. Ibid., 54.
135. Ibid., 16.
136. Ibid., 17.
137. Ibid., 19.
138. Ibid., 143.
139. Ibid., 26, 27.
140. Ibid., 27. James's monistic opponents, of course, objected to James's portrayal of their understanding of the Absolute, pointing out that a principle that is incarnate in every aspect of creation can hardly be considered cut off from our daily experience.
141. Ibid., 144.
142. *Will To Believe*, 97–98.
143. Ibid., 106.
144. Ibid.
145. Ibid.

146. Ibid., 107.
147. Ibid.
148. Ibid.
149. Ibid.
150. Ibid., 108.
151. Ibid.
152. Ibid., 111.
153. Ibid.
154. *Essays in Religion*, 100.
155. Wayne Proudfoot, "Mysticism, the Numinous, and the Moral," *The Journal of Religious Ethics* 4 (Spring 1976): 3–28. The following discussion will focus exclusively on Proudfoot's examination of the link between mystical experience, monism and ethics, and will overlook Proudfoot's equally provocative discussion of numinous experience and the social dimensions of the self.
156. Proudfoot, 7.
157. Ibid.
158. Ibid., 8–9. For a further discussion of the relationship between mysticism and ethics, see also Arthur C. Danto, *Mysticism and Morality* (New York: Basic Books, 1972) and William J. Wainright, "Morality and Mysticism," *The Journal of Religious Ethics* 4 (Spring 1976): 29–36.
159. James emphasizes that the ineffability is one of the primary phenomenological characteristics of mystical experiences, but he fails to draw out many of the most important theological implications of this ineffability. For a detailed, if controversial, discussion of mystical ineffability, see W. T. Stace, *Mysticism and Philosophy* (Los Angeles: Jeremy P. Tarcher, 1960), 277–306.
160. For a detailed discussion of the link between ineffability and mystical states of consciousness, see David Loy, *Nonduality* (New Haven: Yale University Press, 1988).
161. I would also argue, however, that experience is not the only legitimate material from which to create theological, metaphysical and ethical frameworks. The myths and theo-metaphysical speculations of other cultures also present us with an abundance of valuable conceptual maps which we can and should draw upon. As an empiricist fighting against the prior hegemony of hundreds of years of Christian authority, James often dramatically underestimated the value of utilizing alternative metaphysical speculations as resources for the creation of new metaphysical models, but it seems clear that a close examination of these traditional metaphysical and mythic accounts can be tremendously helpful as long as these accounts are understood to be fallible, if useful, maps instead of as unimpeachable revelations.
162. The quote marks do *not* imply that the level of reality referred to by the term "perfection" is somehow not quite perfect. Instead, the use of quote marks indicates that this term is metaphorical. In addition, the term

"perfection" does not refer to that which lives up to certain cultural standards of excellence, but rather, refers to the mystical apprehension that everything, as it is (warts and all) has a purpose, place and meaning in the whole scheme of things.

163. For an illuminating discussion of the ways in which the Chinese Ch'an tradition attempted to resolve the problems associated with the need to recognize, simultaneously, the inherently enlightened nature of the universe and the self-apparent fact that most human beings are not aware of this enlightenment, see Peter N. Gregory, ed., *Sudden and Gradual: Approaches to Enlightenment in Chinese Thought* (Honolulu: The University of Hawaii Press, 1988). Furthermore, this paradoxical call to honor both the need for self-development and the need to embrace the perfection of the present moment is not limited to those individuals who alternate between a dual and nondual experience of reality, but is also mirrored by the process of in-depth psychotherapeutic self-exploration. Within a psychotherapeutic context, clients must, ideally, not only recognize the personal blocks and limitations that they need to overcome and work through, but they must also, almost as a precursor to further growth, learn to love themselves unconditionally, even *with* all of their blocks and limitations.

164. At certain points in James's own career, he also claimed that the existence of evil should be treated less as a speculative issue than as a practical problem to be concretely resolved, contending at one point, for instance, that evil is best understood as "an ultimated [sic] inscrutable fact" that resists any and all intellectual solutions. See Ralph Barton Perry, *The Thought and Character of William James*, 2 vols. (Boston: Little, Brown, and Co., 1935), 2:161.

165. "Ethical decisions" in this context are not limited to the rather narrow parameters of situations in which an individual is presented with a clear-cut need to determine what action is morally "right" versus which action is morally "wrong." Instead, "ethical decisions" embrace any situation in which an individual is unclear as to what he or she "should" do. In this sense, "ethical decisions" encompass those numerous moments when an individual is unsure which action or response is called for in a particularly ambiguous situation. For instance, I would claim that a person asking "should I go to this party to which my boss has invited me or should I stay home and spend time with my children?" is struggling with an ethical decision just as much as a doctor trying to decide whether to end the physical existence of a brain-dead patient.

166. See chapter 3 for a more in-depth discussion of a neo-Jamesian, nondual, pantheistic field model of reality and the self.

167. A more detailed articulation of this model would certainly need to take into account the foundational work done on stage theory in moral and faith development by theorists such as Lawrence Kohlberg, Carol Gilligan and James Fowler. See for instance Lawrence Kohlberg, *The Philosophy of Moral Development* (San Francisco: Harper & Row, 1981); Carol

Gilligan, *In a Different Voice* (Cambridge, MA: Harvard University Press, 1982); James W. Fowler, *Stages of Faith* (San Francisco: Harper & Row, 1981).

168. The term "level" is put in quote marks to underscore the understanding that these modes of self-identification are not reified and unchanging, but rather, are moments in a dynamic process that have been "freeze-framed" for analytical purposes.

169. I make no attempt, in this highly abbreviated discussion, to defend the "rightness" or "wrongness" of any of the choices made by the hypothetical individuals in these examples.

170. I am aware of two autobiographical texts in which apparently cruel behavior by Sufi saints is ultimately seen as highly beneficial to the disciple. See Reshad Feild, *The Last Barrier* (New York: Harper & Row, 1976) and Irina Tweedie, *Daughter of Fire* (Nevada City, CA: Blue Dolphin Publishing, 1989). *The Chasm of Fire*, also written by Tweedie, is an abridged version of *Daughter of Fire*. See Irina Tweedie, *The Chasm of Fire* (Rockport, MA: Element, 1993).

171. Often, however, saints will have a highly sophisticated rationale for their antinomian behavior.

5. Telling Truths, Touching Realities

1. James's references to the "existential judgment" and the "spiritual judgment" are rather sparse in the *Varieties*. I would argue, however, that this methodological division permeates the text, even if it is not always clearly announced.

2. William James, *The Varieties of Religious Experience* (Cambridge, MA: Harvard University Press, 1985), 13.

3. Ibid., 13

4. Ibid., 20

5. Ibid.

6. Ibid.

7. Ibid.

8. While in the *Principles of Psychology* James does make an analytical distinction between knowledge-about and knowledge-by-acquaintance, it is also true that in another section of the *Principles* James discusses the need to have a neutral generic term that would serve as a catch-all designation for any-and-all states of consciousness. Perhaps the root cause of James's willingness to incorporate both thoughts and feelings as subject matter for the spiritual judgment can be traced to his willingness to let the terms "thought" and "feeling" serve equally as neutral, generic designations of states of consciousness in general.

9. *Varieties*, 22.

10. Ibid., 23. Notice that at this point James is assessing "opinions," and no longer "feelings" or "experiences."

11. Ibid., 24.

12. Ibid.

13. Ibid.

14. Ibid., 22.

15. From the standpoint of James's later work in *Pragmatism*, whenever James in the *Varieties* focuses on how the three criteria can be utilized to assess mystical *experiences*, he ideally should have used these criteria to determine the *reality* of these experiences, instead of attempting to assess their *truth* (since, from the perspective of James's pragmatism, truth applies only to beliefs).

16. *Varieties*, 24.

17. Ibid., 23.

18. Ibid., 315. James is quoting from J. Trevor, *My Quest for God*, (London: n.p. 1897), 256–57.

19. Ibid., 25. In contemporary spiritual settings, the questioning might take a different slant, but be no less agonized, i.e., "Is this experience from the divine (or the archetypal realm, my Buddha Nature, etc.) or is it an indication of impending psychosis?"

20. Ibid.

21. Ibid.

22. Ibid.

23. Ibid., 25-26.

24. Ibid., 328.

25. Ibid., 327.

26. Ibid.

27. Ibid.

28. Later in the chapter we will see where James's spiritual judgment of the mystical experiences of certain saints differs from the assessment made by the saints themselves, a clear demonstration that philosophical, theological, and ethical differences between mystics and nonmystics can often determine whether a spiritual judgment is, in the end, positive or negative.

29. Ralph Barton Perry, *The Thought and Character of William James*, 2 vols. (Boston: Little, Brown, 1935), 2:326–27.

30. Significantly, (at least for our future discussion of the interaction between mysticism and saintliness) James rarely makes a distinction between mystics and saints.

31. *Varieties*, 327–28.

32. Ibid., 328.

33. Ibid. "Teresa" is the correct spelling of the name of this saint, even though in the *Varieties*, James calls her "Theresa."

34. Ibid.

35. Robert C. Fuller notes that the mind-cure movement was a predecessor of Christian Science as well as of many contemporary New Age systems of belief and practice. See Robert C. Fuller, *Mesmerism and the American Cure of Souls* (Philadelphia: University of Pennsylvania Press, 1982).

36. *Varieties,* 83–84. James omits the mind-cure movement's most influential theological and philosophical influence: mesmerism. Fuller's work (see the note above) gives a detailed and insightful exploration of the process by which mesmerism evolved into the mind-cure movement.

37. Ibid., 86.

38. Ibid., 96.

39. Ibid., 88–89.

40. Ibid., 93.

41. Ibid.

42. Ibid., 97.

43. Ibid., 84.

44. Ibid. James quotes, quite extensively, from the work of a Dr. H. H. Goddard, who concludes that the power of the mind can indeed heal, even when more mainstream doctors have failed. *Varieties,* 85.

45. Ibid., 89, 92.

46. Ibid., 106.

47. Ibid.

48. Ibid., 107.

49. Ibid. This account by James's friend vividly demonstrates the effect that confessional narratives had on the development of James's own thought (or, at the very least, his willingness to use these accounts as a rhetorical mask for his own ideas). James's friend shares three important beliefs with James's: an acceptance of the existence of a subconscious level of awareness, an openness to telepathy, and an emphasis on the ability of one's thoughts to have power to help create one's world.

50. In a letter to F. W. H. Myers in 1893, James describes the results of his own experiments with mind-cure healing techniques: "My state of mind is also revolutionized since that time. I had a pretty bad spell, and know now a new kind of melancholy. It is barely possible that the recovery may be due to a mind-curer with whom I tried eighteen sittings. " Unfortunately, however, as Ralph Barton Perry underscores in his commentary on this letter, "the ultimate results of James's treatments [by mind-curers] were almost invariably negative." Quoted in Perry, 2:159.

51. *Varieties,* 102.

52. Ibid., 105.

53. Ibid.

54. Ibid., 104.

55. Ibid.

56. Ibid., 105.

57. Ibid.

58. It seems clear that Ralph Barton Perry, like many of James's commentators, dramatically overemphasizes James's ambivalence towards the mind-cure movement, when he claims that "the theories by which mental healers supported their practices were entirely repugnant to his mind." Perry, 2:159.

59. *Varieties*, 93.

60. Ibid., 93, 136. James reluctantly acknowledges that this seeming unwillingness to give credence to evil and suffering is "intimately linked with the practical merits of the system," in that, according to the mind-cure movement, since "thoughts are 'forces' . . . if your thoughts are of health, youth, vigor and success" then these thoughts will have effects on the external world, while if your thoughts are fearful or "contracted and egoistic" then you will attract these types of corresponding experiences to you as well. *Varieties*, 93.

61. Ibid., 78.

62. Ibid., 138.

63. Brian Mahan, in his excellent dissertation on James's understanding of the spiritual judgement, claims that "twice-born" is James's term for the "saintly character type" (as opposed to converts). For Mahan, the "twice-born" individual synthesizes the "sick-soul's" willingness to confront evil and the "healthy-minded" individual's possession of a unified consciousness. While it is possible that James does equate the "twice-born" with saintliness, I tend to think that James's use of the term "twice-born" includes less saintly converts as well. I agree with Mahan that James does not equate saints with converts, but I argue that James distinguishes saints and converts based on different criteria than Mahan proposes. See: Brian Mahan, "The Ethics of Belief" (Ph.D. dissertation, University of Chicago, 1989), 79.

64. Notice, for instance, the fusion of these categories when James claims that the "healthy-minded . . . need to be born only once," while the "sick souls" . . . must be twice-born in order to be happy." *Varieties*, 139.

65. *Varieties*, 95. James himself acknowledges that "in many instances it is quite arbitrary whether we class the individual as a once-born or a twice-born subject". *Varieties*, 385.

66. Ibid., 140.

67. Ibid., 113.

68. Ibid.

69. Ibid.

70. Ibid.

71. Ibid.

72. Ibid., 48–49.

73. Ibid., 210.

74. Ibid., 196.

75. Ibid.

76. Ibid., 194, 193.

77. Ibid., 383.

78. Ibid., 210

79. Ibid., 219, 216.

80. Ibid., 210.

81. Don Browning, *Pluralism and Personality* (Lewisburg, PA: Bucknell University Press, 1980), 28.

393

82. William James, *The Will to Believe* (Cambridge, MA: Harvard University Press, 1979), 159, 161.
83. *Varieties*, 45.
84. Ibid., 41, 45.
85. Ibid., 46.
86. Ibid.
87. *Varieties*, 214.
88. Ibid., 216.
89. William James, *Talks to Teachers on Psychology* (Cambridge, MA: Harvard University Press, 1983), 103.
90. *Varieties*, 218.
91. Ibid., 219.
92. Edith Wyschogrod, *Saints and Postmodernism* (Chicago: The University of Chicago Press, 1990), 34. Oddly, Wyschogrod defends her claim that not all saints have to be mystics by noting that "nonbelievers or Buddhists who alleviated suffering in epidemics and wars meet the criteria" which she proposes for sainthood, a comment which seems to imply that one has to be a "believer" (in her terms, a theist) in order to be a mystic, and that Buddhists (as nonbelievers?) are not mystics. Wyschogrod, 34-35.
93. Wyschogrod, 35.
94. Wyschogrod, 39, 36.
95. Wyschogrod, 35.
96. John Coleman, in *Saints and Virtues*, ed. John Stratton Hawley (Berkeley: University of California Press, 1987), 207.
97. Ibid., 213
98. Ibid. In their preface to *Sainthood: Its Manifestations in World Religions*, Richard Kieckhefer and George D. Bond also mention the difficulties that surround the attempt to use "sainthood" as a cross-cultural comparative category. They ask the reader: "if one speaks of Muslim saints, Hindu saints, Buddhist saints, and so forth, is one stretching a Christian concept beyond its acceptable limits and risking the hazard of viewing these other traditions through Christian lens?" See: Richard Kieckhefer and George D. Bond, eds. *Sainthood: Its Manifestations in World Religions* (Berkeley: University of California Press, 1988), vii.
99. Coleman, 213.
100. Ibid., 214.
101. Ibid., 216.
102. Ibid., 217. Coleman's perspective is mirrored by John Stratton Hawley, who writes in the introduction to *Saints and Virtues* that "often saints do not just heighten ordinary morality. They implicitly question it by seeming to embody a strange, higher standard that does not quite fit with the moral system that governs ordinary propriety and often cannot be articulated in normal discourse. . . . One might wonder at the saints, one might try to imitate the virtues they teach, but one should not necessarily imitate what they themselves do, for their actions are sometimes unpredictable, even outlandish." Hawley, xvi.

103. Coleman, 211.

104. Ibid., 212, 220.

105. *Varieties*, 294.

106. Ibid. James's notion of saintliness differs from Coleman's primarily by virtue of the fact that Coleman, operating out of a broader and deeper knowledge of non-Christian traditions than was available in James's time, is more sensitive to the wide variety of ways in which saintliness is understood in different religious traditions. James's saints are recognizably Christian, and as such, inevitably reflect many of James's own unexamined presuppositions and prejudices about saintliness.

107. Ibid., 219. For a detailed examination of the role of saints in the Catholic Christian tradition, as well as the complex process by which saints are chosen within that tradition, see Lawrence S. Cunningham, *The Meaning of Saints* (San Francisco: Harper & Row, 1980) and Kenneth L. Woodward, *Making Saints* (New York: Simon & Schuster, 1990).

108. *Varieties*, 219–20.

109. Ibid., 220.

110. Ibid.

111. John Hick, a contemporary philosopher of religion, comments that saints manifest a further "by-product of freedom from self-concern," a quality that "in its more passive form is an inner peace or serenity and in its more active form is a positive and radiant joy"; Hick further notes that this quality is "one of the most attractive features of saintliness and one that draws people towards religious faith in response to a quality which they find in the saints rather than in themselves." John Hick, *An Interpretation of Religion* (New Haven: Yale University Press, 1989), 302.

112. *Varieties*, 220.

113. Ibid., 221.

114. Ibid., 225, 233. See above, chapter 3, for a detailed discussion of the "faith-state," and its relationship to the process of conversion.

115. Ibid., 233, 221. John Hick's understanding of saintliness also assumes that the fundamental characteristic of saintliness is the loss of egoistic identification. Hick, who "for the sake of simplicity" uses the term "saint" to "generically cover" all "those who have already been recognized within their own traditions as individuals in whom the signs of salvation or liberation are strikingly visible," defines the saint as "one in whom the transformation of human existence from self-centeredness to Reality-centeredness is so much more advanced than in the generality of us that it is readily noticed and acknowledged." Hick realizes that this "soteriological transformation normally occurs within the context of a particular tradition," and that, consequently, there are "Buddhist saints, Muslim saints, Christian saints and so on, rather than simply saints." But he goes on to claim that there is a crucial common feature to every account of saintliness: "a transcendence of the ego point of view and its replacement by devotion to or centered concentration upon some manifestation of the Real, response to which produces compassion/love towards other human beings or towards all of life." Hick, 301.

116. *Varieties*, 262.
117. Ibid.
118. Ibid., 263.
119. Ibid., 266.
120. Ibid., 264.
121. Ibid., 267.
122. Ibid., 272.
123. Ibid.
124. Ibid.
125. Ibid., 273.
126. Browning, 255.
127. *Varieties*, 273, 275.
128. Ibid., 276.
129. Ibid.
130. Ibid., 277.
131. Ibid.
132. Ibid., 278, 276.
133. Ibid., 278.
134. Ibid.
135. See *Varieties*, 280-82, for James's account of St. Louis's life.
136. *Varieties*, 283.
137. Ibid., 284.
138. Ibid., 283.
139. Ibid.
140. Based solely on James's depiction of St. Louis, one has to wonder why he *was* canonized within the Catholic tradition.
141. *Varieties*, 284.
142. Ibid.
143. As Brian Mahan points out, "nowhere else within [the] *Varieties*, and perhaps nowhere else in all his writings, can passages of equal power and beauty be found." Mahan, 100.
144. *Varieties*, 285.
145. Ibid.
146. Ibid., 285, 286, 287.
147. Ibid., 294.
148. Ibid., 295.
149. Ibid.
150. Ibid.
151. Ibid., 297.
152. Ibid., 298.
153. Ibid., 299.
154. Ibid., 298.
155. Ibid. James does, however, go on to assert that if an "under-witted strong man " is compared to an "under-witted saint," the saint is superior to the strong-man. *Varieties*, 298.

156. Ibid., 299.

157. Ibid.

158. Ibid. Interestingly enough, sainthood is accepted as a normative ideal by James based on his willingness to assess the value of saintliness using solely the common sense values of his own contemporary society. However, once sainthood has gained this newfound stature, it is thus in the position to reflect critically on the same commonsense social values that were the criteria by which it became a normative ideal in the first place. In this dialectical interaction, saintliness is assessed using the common sense norms of society, but saintliness, in turn, in its role as the newly accepted normative ideal, sets standards that society itself can rarely embody. See Mahan, 83, for a discussion of this issue. Coleman also recognizes this dialectical aspect to James's understanding of saintliness. He notes that saints, according to James, are " 'the best things that history has to show' " and as such, in James eyes, they "represent a critical negativity, challenging the mediocre to a higher life . . . in much the same way that utopian dreams criticize the mediocrity of ordinary schemes of justice." Coleman, 221. However, Coleman also argues that "despite William James's best efforts, saints do not quite pass any utilitarian test. Holiness is never really justified by its results. " Coleman, 212. As was underscored in chapter 4, the relationship between ethics and saintliness raises a host of philosophically complex questions. It is extremely difficult to decide whether James or Coleman is more correct. Does ethics have priority or does holiness? By what criteria do we make such a decision? Is there behavior that is beyond moral judgment? Is it the saint's job to critique society, or society's job to critique the saint?

159. Perry, 2 :326–27. Excerpted from a letter to Francis R. Morse.

160. Varieties, 299.

161. If it is true that we cannot avoid bringing our often unexamined philosophical and theological perspectives into our normative assessment of the fruits of saintliness, then it becomes critically important that we do not attempt to mask our hermeneutic pre-understandings with any pretense at complete objectivity. It is crucial that we allow the blind-spots of our philosophical vision to be exposed through the (hopefully well-meaning) give-and-take of scholarly discourse, and it is equally important that we take full responsibility for publicly defending why we believe that our philosophical and theological position is best capable of interpreting and assessing the phenomena that we are studying.

162. Varieties, 296.

163. Ibid.

164. Because these tangible effects of contact with an unseen world are such a critical component of any pragmatic assessment of saintliness, the "magical," or "miraculous" aspects of sainthood and mysticism assume a theoretical importance that they are often denied. From a pragmatic perspective, it is crucially important to pay close philosophical attention to the healing and psychic abilities of the saint and mystic, abilities which are so

frequently ignored, or even despised, not only by Western philosophers, but also by philosophers within the various traditions themselves.

165. Brian Mahan is reluctant to connect the "empirical" approach to religious phenomena that James demonstrates in the *Varieties*, with his later fully developed pragmatism. I would argue, however, that James's approach in the *Varieties* is at least proto-pragmatic, and is actually, perhaps more pragmatic than even James himself realized. Mahan, 29.

166. *Varieties*, 266.

167. Ibid., 401.

168. Ibid.

169. Ibid. It is interesting that James puts the term 'truth' in quotes during this discussion. Perhaps this use of quote makes indicates that James, even at this point, is reluctant to align himself completely with the notion of the objective truth of religious experiences. Or perhaps, in the context of this discussion, James is simply attempting to argue that that we must establish that the spiritual world is not solely a mental, imaginary creation.

170. Ibid., 329.

171. Ibid.

172. For an insightful and thought provoking discussion of the rhetorical practices of Ch'an Buddhism, see Dale S. Wright, "The Discourse of Awakening," *Journal of the American Academy of Religion* 61 (Spring 1993): 23–40.

173. William James, *The Meaning of Truth* (Cambridge, MA: Harvard University Press, 1975), 87.

174. *Meaning*, 88.

175. Ibid.

176. See chapter 4 for a further discussion of this issue.

177. Henry Samuel Levinson has James suggesting that "in the face of the doubts of others, the mystic might systematically suppress reasons that could persuade him to change his mind," and he further claims that, for James, the mystic's "proclamations" of his or her inability to believe anything else than what he or she has experienced during mystical states of awareness were, "in fact, at least rhetorical deflectors of any reasonable debate." I would argue that Levinson's contention that James believes that mystics consciously suppress doubts and debate comes more from Levinson's philosophical prejudices than it does from an accurate reading of James. See: Henry Samuel Levinson, *The Religious Investigations of William James* (Chapel Hill: The University of North Carolina Press, 1981), 142.

178. *Varieties*, 324.

179. Ibid., 325, 326, 324.

180. Ibid., 329.

181. Ibid., 300, 340.

182. Ibid., 268.

183. Ibid.

184. Interestingly, if it was asked: "By what criteria does one claim that these three criteria themselves are valid and workable?" it would be

difficult to answer without once more using these three criteria. Either these three criteria feel intuitively correct (immediate luminousness) or they, overall and for the most part, makes sense (intellectual reasonableness) or we personally and communally believe that the use of these three criteria is more helpful than any other contenders (moral helpfulness). Whether this loop is an unavoidable and beneficial hermeneutic "circle of understanding" or whether it is indicative of a tautological process of reasoning, will depend upon one's philosophical preferences.

185. *Varieties*, 329. Admittedly, it is difficult at times to see whether James's pragmatic assessment, especially in the rudimentary form it takes in the *Varieties*, is attempting to justify the *reality* of the unseen world, or the truth of religious *beliefs* in the unseen world.

186. Ibid., 361.

187. Gerald Myers argues that James's "philosophy of religion is indeed intriguing, but it is certainly not pragmatic," a claim that Myers is willing to make because he contends that James's arguments run "not from phenomenon to consequences but from phenomenon to inferred origins, such that there [is] no way for such an interpretation to be tested." Gerald Myers, *William James: His Life and Thought* (New Haven: Yale University Press, 1986), 466. I would argue, however, that Myers is misrepresenting James at this point. James's actual process is to move from phenomenon to consequences and then to inferred origins. While James does claim that the pragmatist "turns away from . . . bad *a priori* reasons, from fixed principles, closed systems and pretended absolutes and origins," this rejection of origins does not thereby imply that the pragmatist's focus on "last things, fruits, consequences, facts" cannot be utilized to determine the legitimacy of religious speculations about the origins of religious phenomena. William James, *Pragmatism* (Cambridge, MA: Harvard University Press, 1975), 31, 32.

188. *Varieties*, 406.

189. Ibid., 407 As will be made clear in our discussion of James's more mature pragmatism, in which there is a clear distinction between reality and truth, James perhaps should have said, "our belief in the reality of God is true since he produces real effects."

190. Ibid.

191. Ibid., 407–8.

192. Ibid., 409–10.

193. Ibid., 411.

194. Ibid., 408, 411–12.

195. Ibid., 365.

196. Ibid., 372, 373.

197. Ibid., 382.

198. Ibid., 376.

199. Ibid., 367–368.

200. Ibid., 399. Perry comments that while James approved of Leuba's pragmatic sense of religion as based on a richer satisfying life, he also did not want to give up the sense that God is an "objective" reality. Perry, 2:348.

201. *Varieties*, 366–67, 365.
202. Ibid., 412.
203. Ibid.
204. I am much less sanguine than James that these sorts of psychological shifts can, in any straightforward way, be used as evidence of the existence of a spiritual level of reality. James, at least at this point in his argument, does not address the fact that these various transformations could simply be the results of various natural causes. The psychological phenomena may well be visible, but the alleged spiritual cause of these phenomena is much less so.
205. Perry, 2:349–51.
206. Myers, 291.
207. *Pragmatism*, 28.
208. Ibid., 30.
209. *Varieties*, 351. James states that Charles Sanders Pierce initiated the formal beginnings of this method of adjudicating between differing philosophical perspectives, but James also notes that the roots of pragmatism can be traced back to the English empiricists.
210. *Pragmatism*, 28.
211. Ibid., 38.
212. Ibid., 38.
213. Ibid., 97.
214. *Meaning*, 50.
215. *Pragmatism*, 103.
216. Ibid., 34.
217. Ibid., 102.
218. Ibid., 42.
219. *Meaning*, 113.
220. Ibid., 54. James, however, does not give an adequate analysis of the specific issues that would have to be addressed in any attempt to determine exactly *why* something is "good to believe." Furthermore, there are times when James appears to back down altogether from his attempts to link truth with what is "good to believe." For instance, at one point, James claims that he does not mean to say that "anyone who believes a proposition to be true must first have made out clearly that its consequences *are* good." Instead, according to James, he is simply attempting to demonstrate that the search for good consequences is "the lurking *motive* inside of every truth claim." *Meaning*, 146. This apparent softening of James's theoretical position occurred in response to Bertrand Russell's insightful observation that it is much simpler to determine the factual question of whether popes have always been infallible, than it is to determine whether believing the popes to be infallible is, on the whole, good.
221. *Pragmatism*, 106.
222. Ibid., 97, 96.
223. *Meaning*, 143.
224. Ibid., 55.

Notes to Pages 331–342

225. *Pragmatism*, 97.
226. Ibid., 34.
227. Ibid., 35.
228. Ibid.
229. Ibid., 36. These new facts, meanwhile, as James repeatedly stresses, are themselves "not true, they simply come and are. Truth is what we say about them." *Pragmatism*, 36.
230. Ibid., 108.
231. Ibid., 117.
232. Ibid., 37, 101.
233. Ibid., 104.
234. Ibid.
235. Ibid., 106.
236. *Meaning*, 16.
237. Ibid., 129.
238. *Principles*, 913.
239. Ibid., 928.
240. Ibid.
241. Ibid.
242. Ibid., 919.
243. Ibid., 923.
244. Ibid., 930.
245. For a brilliant analysis of issues related to the reality status of dreams, see Wendy Doniger O'Flaherty, *Dreams, Illusion and Other Realities* (Chicago: The University of Chicago Press, 1984).
246. Lawrence Sullivan, *Icanchu's Drum* (New York: Macmillan, 1988), 455–56.
247. *Principles*, 923.
248. Ibid., 924.
249. Ibid., 928–29.
250. Ibid., 936.
251. Ibid., 937.
252. Ibid., 950.
253. Ibid., 930.
254. Ibid.
255. Ibid., 944. Even though, by the time of the *Varieties*, James begins to take seriously the possibility that alternate levels of reality might actually exist that are as significant as the world of the senses, he never seems to give much theoretical and philosophical attention to the value and truth of *symbolic* realities, realities such as those experienced (and created) by individuals pursuing intensive visualization practices (e.g., Tibetan Buddhists, or members of Wiccan covens, or those engaged in Jungian therapeutic practices). James never explores in great detail the philosophical implications of these "imaginal" experiences—experiences that are not simply imaginary fantasies and yet which are also not straightforward encounters with something that is "objectively" different than the experiencer.

256. *Meaning,* 92, 106.
257. Ibid.
258. In the context of James's discussions of the nature of truth, "reality" typically implies "things of common sense, sensibly present," or common sense abstractions "such as dates, places, distances" and so on. *Meaning,* 129.
259. *Pragmatism,* 40.
260. Ibid., 44.
261. Ibid.
262. Ibid., 143.
263. Ibid.
264. Ibid., 32.
265. Ibid., 144.
266. Ellen Kappy Suckiel, in a clearly written analysis of the contrasts between James's pragmatism and his radical empiricism, argues that these two perspectives can theoretically be reconciled, if the "subjects" and "objects" needed by pragmatism are understood as simply functional distinctions within the wider flux of pure experience. I agree with Suckiel, but there is little, if any, evidence that James himself ever clearly reconciled these two perspectives, or for that matter, that he ever even noticed that there was any tension between the epistemological realism assumed by much of his pragmatism and his radical empiricism. See Ellen Kappy Suckiel, *The Pragmatic Philosophy of William James* (Notre Dame: University of Notre Dame Press, 1982), 135–42.
267. Craig R. Eisendrath, *The Unifying Moment* (Cambridge, MA: Harvard University Press, 1948), 168.
268. Ibid., 168.
269. *Meaning,* 51.
270. Ibid., 106.
271. Ibid., 129. As long as pragmatism is willing to relax its stress on the priority of sensory evidence, which I have argued that James, at his best, is willing to do, then pragmatism is, in some ways, an ideal framework from which a meaningful discussion of the truth of nonphysical events can take place. Pragmatism can help us to assess the "truth" not only of our beliefs about God, but also the "truth" of our beliefs in other intangible phenomena as well: beliefs arising out of aesthetic experiences of dance, music, art, and theatrical performances; beliefs about the unconscious/subconscious; beliefs about intuitions; beliefs about psychical phenomena, and so on.
272. Ibid., 97.
273. Ibid., 106.
274. *Pragmatism,* 93.
275. Ibid., 102.
276. *Meaning,* 56.
277. *Pragmatism,* 99.
278. Ibid., 100.

279. To illustrate the different "percentages" of knowledge-by-acquaintance and knowledge-about in different realities, compare the reality implied by the statement "Meg is pregnant" with the reality implied by the statement "Meg is angry at Betsy." While Meg's pregnancy is, arguably, rooted primarily in knowledge-by-acquaintance, her anger is, again, arguably, not so readily observable, and contains within it a higher degree of knowledge-about (our socially constructed ideas about what should anger a person, the power relationships between Meg and Becky, and so on).

280. The term "portion" is put in quotes to underscore that it is not possible to give mathematically precise boundaries to these analytical distinct, but existentially inseparable, aspects of each mystico-religious experience.

281. The judgment that someone is mature or sane, is of course, itself highly complex, and interwoven with a shifting, historically situated network of economic, social, cultural and psychological forces.

282. Although this study took place several decades ago, and many changes have taken place in this culture since then, I nonetheless prefer, as is traditional in recounting ethnographic details, to use the present tense. Richard Katz, *Boiling Energy* (Cambridge, MA: Harvard University Press, 1982).

283. Ibid., 41.

284. Women also participate in these dances, but much less frequently than men.

285. Katz, 41.

286. Ibid., 42.

287. Ibid.

288. Ibid., 45.

289. Ibid., 42.

290. Ibid.

291. Ibid., 40.

292. Ibid., 54.

293. Richard Katz's latest book, *The Straight Path*, gives intriguing details of how, several years later, in the Fiji Islands, this type of cross-cultural appropriation of truths actually did take place, as Katz himself became a practitioner of a spiritual mode of Fiji healing. See Richard Katz, *The Straight Path* (New York: Addison-Wesley, 1993).

294. Eugene Fontinell, *Self, God, and Immortality* (Philadelphia: Temple University Press, 1986), 29.

295. *Pragmatism*, 31, 32.

296. *Meaning*, 39, 40.

297. Fontinell, 16.

298. *Meaning*, 41.

Bibliography

Barnard, G. William. "Explaining the Unexplainable: Wayne Proudfoot's *Religious Experience*." *Journal of the American Academy of Religion* 60.2 (Summer 1992): 231–56.

Barzun, Jacques. *A Stroll with William James*. New York: Harper & Row, 1983.

Bernstein, Richard J. *Beyond Objectivism and Relativism*. Philadelphia: University of Pennsylvania Press, 1985.

Berry, Thomas. *The Dream of the Earth*. San Francisco: Sierra Books, 1988.

Bixler, Julius Seelye. *Religion in the Philosophy of William James*. Boston: Marshall Jones Co., 1926.

Browning, Don. *Pluralism and Personality*. Cranbury, NJ: Associated University Press, 1980.

———. *Religious Thought and the Modern Psychologies*. Philadelphia: Fortress Press, 1987.

Buber, Martin. *I and Thou*. New York: Charles Scribner's Sons, 1958.

———. *Tales of the Hasidim: Early Masters*. New York: Schocken Books, 1978.

Clark, Walter Houston. *The Psychology of Religion*. New York: Macmillan, 1958.

Coleman, John. "Conclusion: After Sainthood?" In *Saints and Virtues*, ed. John Stratton Hawley. Berkeley: University of California Press, 1987.

Coomaraswamy, Ananda. *What is Civilization?* Great Barrington, MA: Lindisfarne Press, 1989.

Corbin, Henry. *Spiritual Body and Celestial Earth*. Princeton: Princeton University Press, 1977.

Cunningham, Lawrence S. *The Meaning of Saints*. San Francisco: Harper & Row, 1980.

Danto, Arthur C. *Mysticism and Morality*. New York: Basic Books, 1972.

Davis, Caroline Frank. *The Evidential Force of Religious Experience*. New York: Oxford University Press, 1989.

Dean, William. *American Religious Empiricism*. Albany: SUNY Press, 1986.

Bibliography

Eisendrath, Craig R. *The Unifying Moment.* Cambridge, MA: Harvard University Press, 1971.

Easwaran, Eknath, trans. *The Bhagavad Gita.* Tomales, CA: Nilgiri Press, 1985.

Feild, Reshad. *The Last Barrier.* New York: Harper & Row, 1976.

Fontinell, Eugene. *Self, God, and Immortality.* Philadelphia: Temple University Press, 1986.

Ford, Marcus Peter. *William James's Philosophy: A New Perspective.* Amherst: The University of Massachusetts Press, 1982.

Forman, Robert K. C. "Mystical Knowledge: Knowledge by Identity." *Journal of the American Academy of Religion* 61.4 (Winter 1993): 705–38.

———, ed. *The Problem of Pure Consciousness.* New York: Oxford University Press, 1990.

Fowler, James W. *Stages of Faith.* San Francisco: Harper & Row, 1981.

Fox, Matthew. *Creation Spirituality.* San Francisco: Harper San Francisco, 1991.

Freud, Sigmund. *An Autobiographical Study.* New York: Norton, 1963.

———. *Five Lectures on Psycho-Analysis.* New York: Norton, 1977.

Frankenberry, Nancy. *Religion and Radical Empiricism.* Albany: SUNY Press, 1987.

Fuller, Robert C. *Mesmerism and the American Cure of Souls.* Philadelphia: University of Pennsylvania Press, 1982.

Gilligan, Carol. *In a Different Voice.* Cambridge, MA: Harvard University Press, 1982.

Gregory, Peter N., ed. *Sudden and Gradual: Approaches to Enlightenment in Chinese Thought.* Honolulu: The University of Hawaii Press, 1988.

Harvey, Andrew. *Hidden Journey.* New York: Viking Penguin, 1991.

Hawley, John Stratton, ed. *Saints and Virtues.* Berkeley: University of California Press, 1987.

Hick, John. *An Interpretation of Religion.* New Haven: Yale University Press, 1989.

Hügel, Baron Friedrich von. *The Mystical Element of Religion.* New York: Dutton, 1923.

James, William. *A Pluralistic Universe.* Cambridge: Harvard University Press, 1977.

———. *Essays in Philosophy.* Cambridge, MA: Harvard University Press, 1978.

Bibliography

———. *Essays in Psychical Research.* Cambridge, MA: Harvard University Press, 1986.

———. *Essays in Radical Empiricism.* Cambridge, MA: Harvard University Press, 1976.

———. *Essays in Religion and Morality.* Cambridge, MA: Harvard University Press, 1982.

———. James, Henry Jr., ed. *The Letters of William James.* 2 vols. Boston: Atlantic Monthly Press, 1920.

———. *The Meaning of Truth.* Cambridge, MA: Harvard University Press, 1975.

———. *Pragmatism.* Cambridge, MA: Harvard University Press, 1975.

———.*The Principles of Psychology.* 3 vols. Cambridge, MA: Harvard University Press, 1981.

———. *Some Problems of Philosophy.* Cambridge, MA: Harvard University Press, 1979.

———. *Talks to Teachers on Psychology and to Students on Some of Life's Ideals.* Cambridge, MA: Harvard University Press, 1983.

———. *The Varieties of Religious Experience.* Cambridge, MA: Harvard University Press, 1985.

———.*The Will to Believe and Other Essays in Popular Philosophy.* Cambridge, MA: Harvard University Press, 1979.

Kalupahana, David J. *The Principles of Buddhist Psychology.* Albany: SUNY Press, 1987.

Katz, Richard. *Boiling Energy: Community Healing Among the Kalahari Kung.* Cambridge, MA: Harvard University Press, 1982.

———. *The Straight Path.* New York: Addison-Wesley, 1993.

Katz, Steven T., ed. *Mysticism and Philosophical Analysis.* New York: Oxford University Press, 1978.

———. *Mysticism and Religious Traditions.* New York: Oxford University Press, 1983.

Kieckhefer, Richard and George D. Bond, eds. *Sainthood: Its Manifestations in World Religions.* Berkeley: University of California Press, 1988.

Kohlberg, Lawrence. *The Philosophy of Moral Development.* San Francisco: Harper & Row, 1981.

Lash, Nicholas. *Easter in Ordinary.* Charlottesville: University Press of Virginia, 1988.

Bibliography

Levinson, Henry Samuel. *The Religious Investigations of William James.* Chapel Hill: The University of North Carolina Press, 1981.

Lewis, R. W. B. *The Jameses: A Family Narrative.* New York: Farrar, Straus & Giroux, 1991.

Loy, David. *Nonduality.* New Haven: Yale University Press, 1988.

Mahan, Brian. "The Ethics of Belief." Ph.D. dissertation, University of Chicago, 1989.

Maréchal S. J., Joseph. *Studies in the Psychology of the Mystics,* trans. Algar Thorold. Albany: Magi Books, 1964.

McDermott, Robert A. Introduction to William James. *Essays in Psychical Research.* Cambridge, MA: Harvard University Press, 1986.

McGinn, Bernard. *The Foundations of Mysticism: Origins to the Fifth Century.* New York: Crossroad, 1991.

Merton, Thomas. *New Seeds of Contemplation.* New York: New Directions, 1961.

Myers, Gerald E. *William James: His Life and Thought.* New Haven: Yale University Press, 1986.

Nasr, Seyyed Hossein. *Knowledge and the Sacred.* New York: Crossroad, 1981.

Neihardt, John G. *Black Elk Speaks.* Lincoln: The University of Nebraska Press, 1988.

O'Flaherty, Wendy Doniger. *Dreams, Illusion and Other Realities.* Chicago: University of Chicago Press, 1984.

Otto, Rudolph. *The Idea of the Holy.* New York: Oxford University Press, 1958.

Perovich, Anthony N. Jr. "Does the Philosophy of Mysticism Rest on a Mistake." In *The Problem of Pure Consciousness,* ed. Robert K. C. Forman. New York: Oxford University Press, 1990.

Perry, Ralph Barton. *The Thought and Character of William James.* 2 vols. Boston: Little, Brown and Company, 1935.

Proudfoot, Wayne. "Mysticism, the Numinous, and the Moral." *The Journal of Religious Ethics* 4 (Spring 1976): 3–28.

———. *Religious Experience.* Berkeley: University of California Press, 1985.

Rizzuto, Ana-Maria. *The Birth of a Living God.* Chicago: The University of Chicago Press, 1979.

Schleiermacher, Friedrich. *On Religion.* New York: Harper & Row, 1958.

Bibliography

Schuon, Frithjof. *The Transcendent Unity of Religions*. Wheaton, IL: The Theosophical Publishing House, 1984.

Seigfried, Charlene Haddock. *William James's Radical Reconstruction of Philosophy*. Albany: SUNY Press, 1990.

Smith, Houston. *Beyond the Postmodern Mind*. Wheaton, IL: The Theosophical Publishing House, 1989.

Smith, John E. "William James's Account of Mysticism." In *Mysticism and Religious Traditions*, ed. Steven T. Katz. New York: Oxford University Press, 1983.

Stace, W. T. *Mysticism and Philosophy*. Los Angeles: Jeremy P. Tarcher, 1960.

Suckiel, Ellen Kappy. *The Pragmatic Philosophy of William James*. Notre Dame: University of Notre Dame Press, 1982.

Sullivan, Lawrence. *Icanchu's Drum*. New York: Macmillan, 1988.

Tagore, Rabindranath, trans. *Songs of Kabir*. New York: Samuel Weiser, 1977.

Taylor, Eugene. "Psychology of Religion and Asian Studies: The William James Legacy" *The Journal of Transpersonal Psychology* 10.1 (1978): 67–79.

———. *William James on Exceptional Mental States: The 1896 Lowell Lectures*. Amherst: The University of Massachusetts Press, 1984.

Tracy, David. *Plurality and Ambiguity*. San Francisco: Harper & Row, 1987.

Tsu, Chuang. *Inner Chapters*, trans. Gia-Fu Feng and Jane English. New York: Vintage Books, 1974.

Turīyānanda, Svāmī, trans. *Vivekacūḍāmaṇi of Śrī Śaṅkarācārya*. Madras: Sri Ramakrishna Math, 1991.

Tweedie, Irina. *Chasm of Fire*. Rockport, MA: Element, 1993.

———. *Daughter of Fire*. Nevada City, CA: Blue Dolphin Publishing, 1986.

Underhill, Evelyn. *Mysticism*. New York: Dutton, 1911.

Wainwright, William J. "Morality and Mysticism." *The Journal of Religious Ethics* 4 (Spring 1976): 29–36.

Whitaker, Kay Cordell. *The Reluctant Shaman*. San Francisco: Harper San Francisco, 1991.

Wild, John. *The Radical Empiricism of William James*. Garden City, NY: Doubleday, 1969.

Wilber, Ken. *Sex, Ecology, Spirituality*. Boston: Shambhala Publications, 1995.

Woodhouse, Mark B. "On the Possibility of Pure Consciousness." In *The Problem of Pure Consciousness*, ed. Robert K. C. Forman. New York: Oxford University Press, 1990.

Bibliography

Woodward, Kenneth L. *Making Saints*. New York: Simon & Schuster, 1990.

Wright, Dale S. "The Discourse of Awakening." *Journal of the American Academy of Religion* 61 (Spring 1993): 23–40.

Wulff, David. M. *Psychology of Religion*. New York: John Wiley and Sons, 1991.

Wyschogrod, Edith. *Saints and Postmodernism*. Chicago: The University of Chicago Press, 1990.

Zaehner, R. C. *Mysticism Sacred and Profane*. (Oxford: Clarendon Press, 1957).

410

Index

I have only lightly indexed the subject "James, William." The entire book, after all, is about this individual.

Index

Ethical life
from the standpoint of
enlightenment, 267–71, 394n.
102
spectrum model, 264–67, 271–72,
389n. 165, 389–90n. 167, 390n.
168, 390n. 169
See also antinomian behavior;
intuition, as ethical factor;
perfection; saints, ethical life
Evil, philosophical problem of,
250–51, 262–64, 293–96, 387n.
129, 389n. 164, 393n. 60
See also God, finite; mind-cure
movement
Existential judgment (technical
term), 275–76, 304, 390n. 1
See also spiritual judgment
(technical term)
Experience, philosophical
centrality of, 32, 37–40, 89–90,
95–97, 102–7, 224–25, 227–28,
236, 261
See also God, relationship to
mystical experiences;
immediate luminousness
(technical term); mystical
experiences, source of
religious beliefs; theology,
secondary to religious
experience

Faith-state (technical term), 183–84,
303
See also conversion, psychology
of; mystical experiences,
transformative; saintliness,
connection to mystical
experience
Fechner, Gustave, 59, 61, 167,
170, 189–96, 201–2, 204, 380n.
163
Feelings, as emotive and cognitive,
14, 91–2, 94–5, 112–13, 366n.
22, 390n. 8
Feild, Reshad, 390n. 170

Field model of self and reality,
6–7, 186, 205–11, 264–67, 354–
57, 381n. 196, 381n. 197, 381n.
198, 381n. 202, 381–82n. 203,
382n. 205
See also pluralistic pantheism
Fontinell, Eugene, 205–6, 210,
356, 381n. 197, 381–82n. 203,
384n. 52
Ford, Marcus, 142, 372n. 135
Forman, Robert K. C., 100, 369n. 79
Fourier, Charles, 51
Fowler, James W., 389–90n. 167
Fox, George, 38, 78, 321
Fox, Matthew, 379–80n. 159
Francis, Saint, 276, 310
Frankenberry, Nancy, 90, 113–14,
117
Freud, Sigmund, 76–77, 172–73,
176, 376–77n. 79
See also unconscious awareness,
James's critique of
Fuller, Robert C., 391n. 35, 392n. 36

Geniuses, religious, 38–39, 77–78,
130–32, 364–65n. 185, 370–71n.
105
Gilligan, Carol, 389–90n. 167
Gimello, Robert, 366n. 2
God
changeable understandings of,
304
component of psychological
structure, 151–53
finite, 180, 188, 204–5, 248, 251–
57, 387n. 129
relationship to mystical
experiences, 37–40
as separate being, 203–4, 255–56
See also evil, philosophical
problem of; higher power, as
element of mystical
experiences; mystical
experiences, source of
religious beliefs
Goddard, H. H., 392n. 44

413

Index

Green, T. H., 149
Gregory, Peter N., 389n. 163

Hallucinations, 41–43
Hartmann, Heinz, 151
Hawley, John Stratton, 394n. 102
Healing
  connection to changes in beliefs,
    289–91, 397–98n. 164, 403n. 293
  connection to mystical
    experiences, 289–90
  reality of shamanic experiences,
    145, 337, 352–54
  See also mind-cure movement
Healthy-mindedness (technical
  term), 181, 294–95, 393n. 63,
  393n. 64
  See also sick souls (technical
  term); twice-born (technical
  term), relationship to once-
  born (technical term)
Hegel, Georg, 242
Heidegger, Martin, 155, 382n. 1
Hick, John, 395n. 111, 395n. 115
Higher power, as element of mystical
  experiences, 133–35, 179
  See also God, relationship to
  mystical experiences; mystical
  experiences, as dialectical
Hodgson, Richard, 52, 55–59
Hudson, W. H., 74
Hügel, Baron Friedrich von,
  365–66n. 1
Hume, David, 5, 139, 149, 155

Ignatious of Loyola, Saint, 288
Immediate luminousness (technical
  term), 276–77, 279–83, 286–88,
  320–22
  See also experience,
  philosophical centrality of;
  spiritual judgment (technical
  term)
Immortality, alternative theories,
  166–70, 192

See also consciousness, deeper
  or wider levels; earth soul
  (earth angel); self, deeper or
  wider levels
Ineffability
  of experiences of selfhood, 160–
    61, 374n. 41
  as mark of mystical experience,
    13, 101–2, 388n. 159
  of mystical experiences, 215,
    259–60, 368n. 63, 388n. 159,
    388n. 160
  See also mystical experiences,
  ineffability
Introspection, methodological
  difficulties, 153–54, 375n. 45
Intuition, as ethical factor, 265–67,
  269

James, Alice (sister), 169, 376n. 73
James, Alice (wife), 19–20
James, Henry (brother), 72, 87
James, Henry Sr. (father)
  influence on William James, 5,
    78, 82–87, 181, 243, 365n. 187,
    365n. 197
  moment of despair (vastation),
    79–80, 85–87, 182
James, Robertson (brother), 25
James, William
  ambivalence towards mysticism,
    21–2, 30, 34, 75
  ambivalence towards science,
    44–8, 50, 292–93
  experience of "panic fear," 84–
    86, 182
  interest in psychical research, 5,
    43–60
  knowledge of non-Christian
    mysticism, 14–16, 313–14,
    359n. 7, 395n. 106
  mystical germ, 5, 18–19, 21,
    371n. 110
  opposed to religious dogmatism,
    214, 216–17, 226–27

Copyrighted Material

Index

personal mystical experiences,
19–21, 26–28, 61, 65–66
pluralist or monist, 231–33, 241–
44, 249, 252–56, 385n. 56, 385–
86n. 80
Janet, Pierre, 171–72
Jefferies, Richard, 71–72
Jesus Christ, 118, 130
John of the Cross, Saint, 284
Jung, Carl, 76–77, 376–77n. 79

Kalahari !Kung, 145, 352–55, 403n.
282, 403n. 284
Kālī, 118
Kalupahana, David J., 374n. 41
Kant, Immanuel, 116, 149, 303,
368n. 73, 382n. 1
Katz, Richard, 352–55, 403n. 282,
403n. 293
Katz, Steven, 6, 115, 117, 366n. 2,
367n. 34, 384–85n. 54
Kieckhefer, Richard, 394n. 98
Knowledge by acquaintance
(technical term), relationship
to knowledge about (technical
term), 14, 111–19, 217–18, 278,
349–51, 368n. 60, 369n. 74,
369n. 76, 369n. 79, 369n. 82,
370n. 87, 383n. 12, 390n. 8,
403n. 279, 403n. 280
See also mystical experiences, as
dialectical; perception, James's
psychology of; truth,
connection to knowledge by
acquaintance and knowledge
about; world, as objective,
pre-existing
Kohlberg, Lawrence, 389–90n. 167

Lange, C. G., 92
Lash, Nicholas, 359n. 1
Laughing Gas. See nitrous oxide,
mystical effects
Leuba, James Henry, 19, 132, 183,
326–27, 399n. 200

Levinson, Henry Samuel, 384n. 36,
398n. 177
Lewis, R. W. B., 79
Logic of identity, 199–201, 380n.
176
Locke, John, 5, 139
Lotze, Rudolph, 235
Louis of Gonzaga, Saint, 307–9,
396n. 135, 396n. 140
Loy, David, 382n. 206, 386n. 82,
388n. 160
Lutoslawski, Wincenty, 378n. 111

Mādhyamika Buddhism, 238–39
Mahan, Brian, 393n. 63, 396n. 143,
397n. 158, 398n. 165
Mahāyāna Buddhism, 160, 210,
238, 240, 319, 374n. 41
Maréchal, Joseph, 90, 365–66n. 1
Mary, Virgin, 103–6
McDermott, Robert A., 43–45
McGinn, Bernard, 111, 120–21
Mead, George Herbert, 151
Medical materialism (technical
term), 76, 276, 279
See also mystical experiences,
normative assessment;
spiritual judgment (technical
term)
Meliorism, 247–49
Metaphorical language. See
mystical language,
metaphorical
Metaphysical myths, 229–30, 260,
384n. 52
See also philosophy,
constructing metaphysical
models; religious beliefs,
transformative effects
Mills, James, 139
Mind-cure movement, 179, 288–96,
373n. 18, 392n. 36, 392n. 50,
392n. 58, 393n. 60
See also evil, philosophical
problem of; healing,

415

Index

Philosophy of mysticism,
constructivist position, 6,
100–1, 125–26, 128–30, 213,
222, 367n. 36
See also Proudfoot, Wayne, as
constructivist
Pierce, Charles Sanders, 400n. 209
Piper, Lenora, 50–59, 165, 172, 174
Pluralism, supported by mystical
experiences, 30–34, 231–32
See also James, William,
pluralist or monist
Pluralistic pantheism, 8, 180, 204–
5, 242, 249, 252–56, 261–67
See also field model of self and
reality
Possession, 58–59
Pragmatism
assessment of religious beliefs,
344–47, 350–57, 399n. 187,
399n. 200, 400n. 204
implicit in *The Varieties of
Religious Experience*, 8, 274–
75, 316–18, 323–24, 328, 379–
80n. 139, 398n. 165, 399n. 185
theories about the nature of
truth, 329–33, 345–57, 399n.
187, 400n. 220, 402n. 266
See also mystical experiences,
normative assessment;
religious beliefs, truth-status
of; saintliness, normative
assessment of; spiritual
judgment (technical term);
truth, pragmatic assessments;
*Varieties of Religious
Experience, The,* as proto-
pragmatic; world, as objective,
pre-existing
Prayer, 325–27
Proudfoot, Wayne
as constructivist, 6, 22, 100–1,
125–26, 366n. 2
emotions, causal theories of, 98–
99, 336n. 22, 367n. 33

ethics and religious experience,
258–59, 388n. 155
philosophy of religious
experience, 97–110, 397n. 33,
368n. 57, 370n. 95
See also emotion, causal theories
of; philosophy of mysticism,
constructivist position
Psychical phenomena
causal hypotheses, 52–60, 165–66
catalyzing belief, 341–42, 397–
98n. 164
relationship to mystical
experiences, 16–17, 45–46, 57,
362n. 88, 362n. 106, 397–98n.
164
relationship to theories of
selfhood, 165–66, 173–76
Psychical research, relationship to
science, 44–48, 50
See also James, William, interest
in psychical research; Society
for Psychical Research;
spiritualism
Psychopathology, relationship to
theories of selfhood, 171–78,
403n. 281
Pure Consciousness Event (PCE),
136–38, 363n. 144, 369n. 80,
369n. 82, 383n. 12
See also nonduality
Pure experience (technical term),
6, 142–44, 199, 207, 372n. 135,
381–82n. 203
See also consciousness, diversity
within unity; nonduality;
radical empiricism,
metaphysical stance

Radical empiricism
metaphysical stance, 141–45,
199, 207, 371n. 125, 381n. 198,
402n. 266
methodology, 139–40, 371n. 125

See also consciousness, diversity
within unity; empiricism, as a
Jamesian methodology;
nonduality; pure experience
(technical term)
Rationalism. See neo-Hegelian
monism
Ratisbonne, Alphonse, 103–6, 108
Reality
criteria for assessing, 335–40,
401n. 255, 402n. 258
link to beliefs, 333–36, 339–40,
342–44, 348–50, 391n. 15, 399n.
185, 399n. 189
See also belief, connection to
sense of reality; dreams,
reality of; truth, relationship
to reality; world, as objective,
pre-existing
Reconciliation, as aspect of
mystical experience, 28–29
Religious beliefs
catalyzing mystico-religious
experiences, 221–24, 260,
332
different than morality, 219, 244,
294–98
transformative effects, 220–21,
260, 318–19, 373n. 9
truth-status, 274–75, 280–81,
316–18, 322–28, 344–47,
350–57, 399n. 200
See also metaphysical myths;
mind-cure movement;
mystical experiences, source
of religious beliefs;
pragmatism, assessment of
religious beliefs
Religious experiences, relationship
to mystical experiences, 12–13,
23
Religious geniuses. See Geniuses,
religious
Religious life, positive value of,
287, 296, 312, 316–17

See also saintliness, normative
assessment of; saints,
normative human ideal
Rizzuto, Ana-Maria, 373n. 11
Rogers, Carl, 151
Royce, Josiah, 31, 140, 189–90, 204,
232, 237
Russell, Bertrand, 400n. 220

Saintliness
connection to mystical
experience, 298–303, 391n. 30,
394n. 92, 397n. 158
as cross-cultural category, 300,
302, 394n. 98, 395n. 115
connection to conversion
experiences, 296–303
connection to miracles, 314–15,
397–98n. 164
normative assessment of, 303–
19, 395n. 107, 397n. 158, 397n.
161, 397–98n. 164
as pragmatic evidence of unseen
worlds, 8, 316–19, 323–24
as a primarily moral category,
299–301, 394n. 102, 397n. 158
psychology of, 298–99
See also conversion, psychology
of; faith state (technical term);
mystical experiences,
transformative; religious life,
positive value of
Saints
ethical life, 267–71, 299–301,
394n. 102
connection to communal criteria,
270–71, 314–15, 395n. 107,
397n. 158
negative qualities, 305–6
normative human ideal, 310–11,
394n. 102, 396n. 155, 397n. 158
positive qualities, 297–303, 309–
12, 395n. 111, 395n. 115
See also antinomian behavior;
ethical life, from the

420   *Copyrighted Material*

Index

normative assessment;
philosophical reasonableness
(technical term); truth,
determined by spiritual
judgment
Spiritual world. *See* unseen worlds
Spiritualism, 53–55, 58
See also psychical phenomena
Stace, W. T., 90, 365–66n. 1, 388n.
159
Stevenson, Robert Louis, 69
Strenuous life (technical term), 297
Subconscious. *See* self,
subconscious, subliminal
Suckiel, Ellen Kappy, 402n. 266
Suffering
given meaning by religious
beliefs, 220–21
rooted in experience, 262–64
Sufism (Islamic mysticism), 15, 72,
101, 160, 268, 313, 338–39,
379–80n. 159
Sullivan, Harry Stack, 151
Suso, Heinrich, 78
Swendenborg, Emanuel, 51, 80–81
Symonds, J. A., 24–25, 35

Tantra, 72, 207, 238–41
Taoism, 101, 210, 238, 240–41, 268,
277
Taylor, Eugene I., 359n. 7, 363n.
134, 376n. 74
Teresa of Avila, Saint, 276, 284,
288, 306–7, 391n. 33
Theodicy. *See* evil, philosophical
problem of
Theology, secondary to religious
experience, 95–97
See also experience,
philosophical centrality of
Theravāda Buddhism, 115
Thought (aspect of self: technical
term), 158–59, 374n. 38
See also self, transitory
Tibetan Buddhism, 401n. 255
Tolstoy, Leo, 294

Tracy, David, 375n. 43
Transcendental-ego, 139, 155–56
See also personal identity,
theories of
Transpersonal psychology, 363n.
145
Trevor, J., 282
Trine, R. W., 289
Truth
changing and fallible, 305, 321–
22, 331–33, 356
determined by spiritual
judgment, 278–81, 316–19,
321–24, 391n. 15
connection to determination of
value, 278–81, 292, 316–18,
323–24, 329–33
connection to knowledge by
acquaintance and knowledge
about, 349–51, 355–57, 403n.
279, 403n. 280
pragmatic assessments, 292–93,
316–18, 322–24, 326–33, 344–
57, 398n. 169, 400n. 204, 400n.
220, 402n. 266, 402n. 271
non-pragmatic assessments, 279–
80, 317–18, 320–22, 398n. 169,
400n. 220
relationship to reality, 332–33,
342–43, 348–57, 374–75n. 42
See also knowledge by
acquaintance (technical term),
relationship to knowledge
about (technical term);
mystical experiences, truth
status; pragmatism, theories
about the nature of truth;
religious beliefs, truth-status;
spiritual judgment (technical
term); world, as objective, preexisting
Tweedie, Irina, 390n. 170
Twice-born (technical term),
relationship to once-born
(technical term), 294, 393n. 63,
393n. 64, 393n. 65

Printed in Great Britain
by Amazon

26334496R00249